HISTORICAL ATLAS OF THE AMERICAN WEST

HISTORICAL ATLAS
OF THE AMERICAN WEST

BY WARREN A. BECK AND YNEZ D. HAASE

UNIVERSITY OF OKLAHOMA PRESS : NORMAN AND LONDON

By Warren A. Beck

New Mexico: A History of Four Centuries (Norman, 1962)
(with Ynez D. Haase) *Historical Atlas of California* (Norman, 1985)
(with Ynez D. Haase) *Historical Atlas of New Mexico* (Norman, 1985)
(with Ynez D. Haase) *Historical Atlas of the American West* (Norman, 1989)

By Ynez D. Haase

(with Warren A. Beck) *Historical Atlas of California* (Norman, 1985)
(with Warren A. Beck) *Historical Atlas of New Mexico* (Norman, 1985)
(with Warren A. Beck) *Historical Atlas of the American West* (Norman, 1989)

Library of Congress Cataloging-in-Publication Data

Beck, Warren A.
  Historical atlas of the American West.

  Includes bibliography and index.
  1. West (U.S.)—Historical geography—Maps.   2. West
(U.S.)—History.   I. Haase, Ynez D.   II. Title.
III. Title: American West.
G1381.S1B4   1989   911′.78   88-40540
ISBN 0-8061-2193-9

The paper in this book meets the guidelines for permanence and durability of the Committee on Production Guidelines for Book Longevity of the Council on Library Resources, Inc.

Dedicated to the Memory of Oscar W. Haase

Contents

Preface

1. Relief
2. Geomorphic Provinces
3. Mean Annual Rainfall
4. Daily Average Temperature—January
5. Daily Average Temperature—July
6. Barriers to the West
7. Major Forest Types
8. Native Tribal Areas
9. Dispersion of the Horse
10. The Buffalo Herds
11. Native Fauna I
12. Native Fauna II
13. Fur-Bearing Mammals
14. Extinct and Rare Birds
15. Explorations, 1500–1599
16. Explorations, 1600–1699
17. Explorations, 1700–1771
18. Northern Frontier of New Spain, 1766–1780
19. Explorations, 1772–1799
20. Spanish-Mexican Land Grants
21. Empresario Grants, 1833
22. Spanish-Mexican Land Grants, Lower Rio Grande Valley, West of the Nueces River, Texas
23. Spanish-Mexican Land Grants, Eagle Pass–Del Rio, Texas
24. Explorations, 1800–1810
25. Explorations, 1810–1820
26. Fur Trapper Rendezvous (Mountain Fairs)
27. Explorations of Peter S. Ogden
28. Expeditions of Jedediah S. Smith
29. First Commerce Trails
30. Texas Cattle Trails, 1840–1897
31. The Great Sheep Trails, 1870–1900
32. Oregon-California Trail
33. Overland Tragedies
34. Overland Mail and Connecting Lines
35. Pony Express Routes
36. Explorations of John C. Frémont
37. U.S. Military Forts, 1819–1895
38. Federal Wagon Roads, 1849–1869
39. The Mormon Empire
40. Territorial Expansion I
41. Territorial Expansion II
42. Territorial Expansion III
43. European Settlement
44. The Mexican War, 1846–1848
45. Battles of the Civil War
46. Battles Between Indian Forces and the U.S. Army
47. Cheyenne and Nez Percé Evasion Treks
48. Battle of the Little Big Horn
49. Ghost Dance Religion
50. Tragedy at Wounded Knee, December 29, 1890
51. Indian Lands
52. Indian Judicial Land Areas
53. Principal Meridians and Base Lines Governing Public Land Surveys
54. Gold and Silver Bonanzas
55. Stagecoach Routes
56. Railroads I—Union Pacific
57. Railroads II—Atchison, Topeka & Santa Fe
58. Railroads III—Southern Pacific
59. Railroads IV—Burlington Northern
60. Railroads V—Denver & Rio Grande Western and Western Pacific
61. States and Their Capitals
62. Counties
63. Agricultural Regions
64. Field Crops I
65. Field Crops II
66. Fruits and Nuts
67. Livestock and Poultry
68. Major Mineral Lodes
69. Petroleum Fuels
70. Catastrophic Natural Events
71. The Great Salt Lake, Utah
72. Mount St. Helens, Washington, May 18, 1980
73. Federal Lands
74. Major Army Installations: World War II and After
75. Major Air Force Installations: World War II and After
76. Major Naval and Marine Installations: World War II and After
77. Japanese-American Internment Camps During World War II
78. World War II POW Camps
    Appendix: Spanish-Mexican Land Grants—Lower Rio Grande Valley, West of the Nueces River, Texas
    References
    Index

PREFACE

IN PREPARING THIS ATLAS, which covers such a long period of time and so vast an area, we faced many perplexing problems. First, we had to decide just what constituted the "American West." After consulting many people, we decided that seventeen states along the hundredth meridian and westward would be our vision of the West. Second, we had to determine what maps we would include in our work. Specialists on the American West assisted us in our selection with many helpful suggestions. Among those who replied to our request for advice were Gordon M. Bakken, Jackson K. Putnam, and Imre Sutton of California State University, Fullerton; the late John Francis Bannon, S.J., of Saint Louis University; the late Ray A. Billington of the Henry E. Huntington Library; Odie B. Faulk, historian, National Cowboy Hall of Fame, Oklahoma City; William Greever of the University of Idaho; Norris Hundley of the University of California, Los Angeles; Wilbur Jacobs of the University of California, Santa Barbara; Robert W. Larson of the University of Northern Colorado; W. Michael Mathes of the University of San Francisco; Doyce Nunis of the University of Southern California; A. Ray Stephens of North Texas State University; David J. Weber of Southern Methodist University; and David A. Williams, formerly of California State University, Long Beach.

We express our deepest thanks to all these individuals. If we have neglected to fully carry out their many recommendations, it is because we had to make difficult choices and omit many maps to keep our work to a manageable size. We have not intentionally slighted any area. However, we have placed less emphasis upon subjects adequately covered in previously published atlases while stressing topics, such as the Texas land grants, that have been hitherto neglected. The herculean task of the au-

thors has been to produce an atlas of the American West for the student, the scholar, and the many people who have a general interest in the subject.

Libraries that have been especially helpful to us are the Map and Imagery Library of the University of California, Santa Barbara; the library of the California State University, Fullerton; the library of the University of California, Los Angeles; the Bancroft Library of the University of California, Berkeley; and the Henry E. Huntington Library. The Water Resources Division, U.S. Geological Survey, Salt Lake City, also provided valuable assistance.

Many individuals gave of their valuable time to the preparation of this work. The late Charles F. Outland was frequently available for consultation and was most generous in allowing use of his private library. Gordon M. Bakken and Jackson K. Putnam made many important recommendations to improve both maps and manuscript. B. Carmon Hardy of California State University, Fullerton, drew from his vast knowledge of Mormon history to assist us in this area. Imre Sutton, an expert on Indian land tenure, provided the authors with valuable insights on that subject. We were the recipients of contributions from Donald Duke, an authority on railroad history. Finally, our appreciation goes to Richard H. Dahlke and Associates for their contribution in completing many of the map plates.

The bibliography contains the works we have used in our research for this atlas. There are countless other sources we would like to have added, but space limitations dictated otherwise.

WARREN A. BECK
YNEZ D. HAASE

HISTORICAL ATLAS OF THE AMERICAN WEST

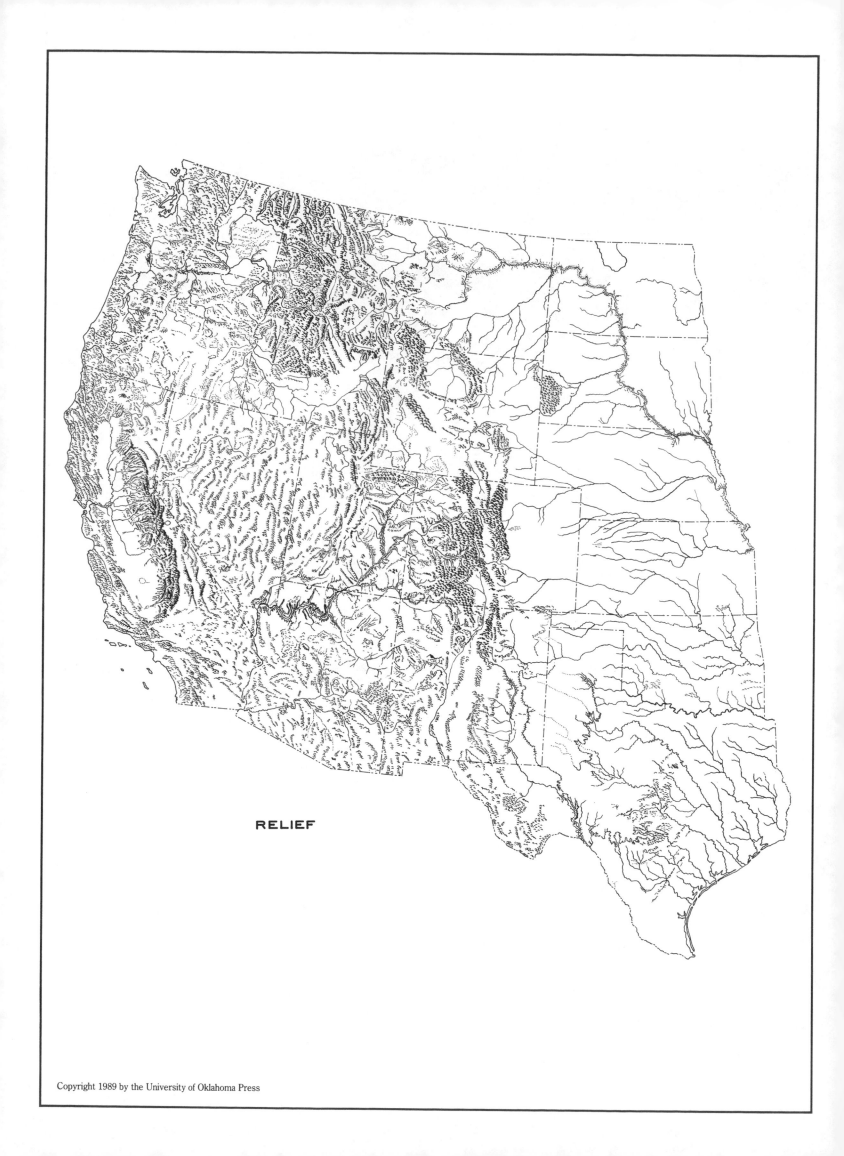

RELIEF

1. RELIEF

THE SEVENTEEN WESTERN STATES comprise more than one-half of the nation's land area and include the greatest of extremes of relief. The Gulf Plain along the Texas coast has a maximum elevation of less than five hundred feet, while peaks in the western mountains may exceed fifteen thousand feet.

The Great Plains, which average four hundred miles in width and extend from Canada through Texas, are the eastern portion of this vast area. They slope upward westward from an altitude of fifteen hundred to two thousand feet to a height, at the base of the Rocky Mountains, of five thousand to six thousand feet. The topography of the Great Plains is typified by landscapes of seemingly uniform flatness, although they do contain areas of hills and river valleys. The flattest portion of these plains is the Staked Plain (Llano Estacado) of West Texas and eastern New Mexico. As the map indicates, the Great Plains are traversed by numerous rivers, most important of which is the Missouri; some of these streams have cut deep valleys. Although trees are generally absent on the Great Plains, they are often found along the banks of the streams. In the north are isolated mountains such as the Black Hills, Judith Mountains, Bearpaw Mountains, and Sweetgrass Hills.

The Rocky Mountains lie to the west of the Great Plains. The northern section extends from Canada into Montana and Idaho as a series of parallel ranges such as the Lewis, Flathead, Selkirk, and Bitterroot ranges. Then the mountains spread into a number of irregular groups such as the Absaroka, Wasatch, Wind River, and Big Horn mountains of the Middle Rockies. In southern Wyoming the mountains fade into a high plateau region known as the Wyoming Basin, which is actually several basins. Located there are the South Pass and Bridger Pass, which provided relatively easy passage for emigrant wagons over the Continental Divide. The southern section of the Rockies is mainly in Colorado, where there are fifty-one mountain peaks in excess of fourteen thousand feet, and extends south into New Mexico. The Front, Park, Sawatch, and Sangre de Cristo groups are the main mountain ranges. The lowest crossing of the Continental Divide in Colorado is at Cochetopa Pass, with an elevation over ten thousand feet.

Farther west, the Intermontane Plateau comprises many small mountain ranges separated by desert plains. The most important regions are the Columbia Plateau, the Colorado Plateau, and the Basin and Range Province. Much of the Columbia Plateau, which includes most of the drainage area of the Columbia and Snake rivers, has been covered with relatively recent lava flows. Wind erosion has added a top layer of loess, which, when watered, produces abundant crops. The rivers have etched canyons sometimes hundreds of feet deep.

The Colorado Plateau has also been dissected by gorges like the Grand Canyon, the most impressive canyon in the nation. The Black Canyon of the Gunnison River and the canyons of the Greek and Yampa rivers are also remarkable.

The Basin and Range Province includes the Great Basin of Nevada and Utah. This vast area has no outlet to the sea. Deserts abound in this inhospitable land in the valleys between the mostly parallel ranges; the most notable is the Great Salt Desert and the nearby Great Salt Lake. With less than ten inches of rainfall the annual average, when greater moisture falls, rapid runoff and lack of drainage can lead to catastrophic flooding. The southern part of the Basin and Range Province is the elevated desert area of Arizona and New Mexico, with the main drainage provided by the Gila and Salt rivers and the Rio Grande.

The Pacific Coast area is virtually isolated from the rest of the country by the massive Cascade Range and Sierra Nevada, one of the highest and steepest mountain fronts on the continent, including several peaks over fourteen thousand feet. The Pacific Coast Ranges are usually so close to the ocean they allow little in the way of a coastal plain. The main rivers, generally running north and south, including the Willamette River of Oregon and the Sacramento and San Joaquin rivers in California. The two latter streams dissect the Great Central Valley, about 450 miles long and 50 miles wide, which is one of the nation's most productive agricultural regions, thanks to irrigation. The basin of a former inland sea, the Salton Sea, lies in southeastern California. Cut off by the delta of the Colorado River, its waters evaporated, and where it has been irrigated it has become the rich Imperial Valley. A number of California valleys are open to the ocean and hence are the recipients of cooling ocean breezes and greater rainfall than other areas.

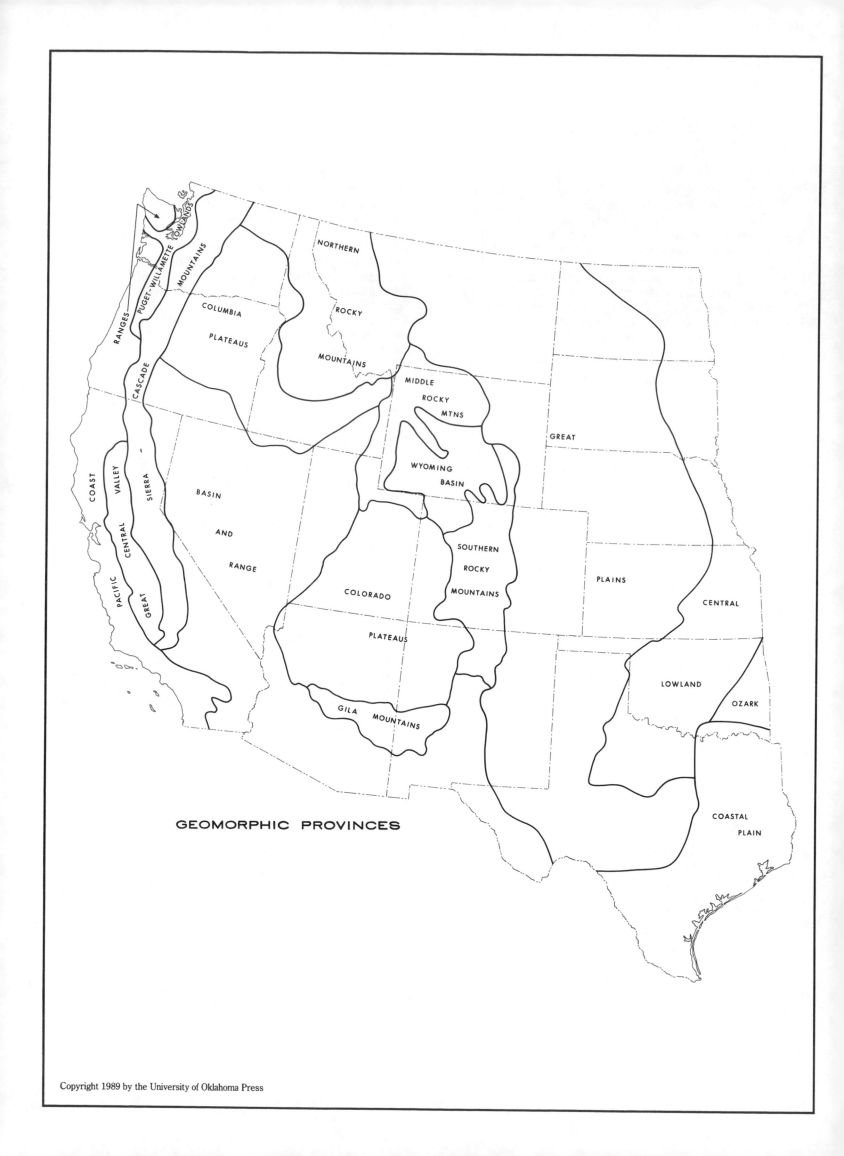

GEOMORPHIC PROVINCES

2. GEOMORPHIC PROVINCES

THE GEOMORPHIC PROVINCES of the American West are regions with a distinctive geologic history. The formation of land, topography, soils, water, minerals, and other resources were the result of great geologic forces.

The Central Lowland is a vast plain beginning west of the Appalachian Mountains. Rivers, lakes, rich soils, hardwood forests, plenty of rain, and abundant fish and game made the region attractive to early settlers. Vast grasslands marked the area of the west in this province from eastern Kansas south through Oklahoma into Texas. In truth, this region has more in common with the Midwest than with the Far West.

The Great Plains are the most characteristic region of the American West. At first they were so forbidding to early frontiersmen accustomed to more humid lands that they were called the "Great American Desert." They are distinguished by a comparatively level surface, few trees, and insufficient rainfall for the kind of agriculture common in the more humid climates to the east. Indian civilization in the plains country was made possible by sufficient grass, which supported countless buffalo—animals which furnished the native Americans with all of the necessities of life. At first the whites hurried across these inhospitable lands, but when they did substitute the raising of cattle for buffalo, they were successful. Efforts to farm the plains, however, have often met with failure.

The Wyoming Basin is really a westward extension of the Great Plains, intruding some 250 miles into the Rocky Mountains. This area, dotted with hills, played a key role in the settling of the West, as it provided a relatively level route through the mountains. Its ten inches of rainfall supports mainly sagebrush and short grass.

South of the Wyoming Basin are the Southern Rocky Mountains, which tower above the plains and constituted a major barrier to early travelers. All of the Rocky Mountain Provinces were important for beaver pelts and for streams, which relieved the parched land of the plains.

The Columbia Plateaus are upland areas of lava soil laid down by now extinct volcanoes. Relatively level, they are semiarid lands with usually little more than sagebrush as vegetation. The Basin and Range Province was an extension of the Columbia Plateau which ran southward to blend with Mexico's Sonora Desert. It is one of the harshest environments in the West, for the mountains surrounding it have kept its annual rainfall near the ten-inch mark. The region's ability to support flora and fauna is minimal; Indians who lived there practiced a hunting and gathering subsistence and had a use for virtually everything in their environment. Only by irrigation can the land be used for agriculture today.

The Sierra Nevada and Cascade Mountains were formidable barriers to the pioneers, but today they provide timber and, above all, the water so indispensable to the people of the lowlands. They also provide a fish and game preserve as well as an important recreational area. The Pacific Coast Ranges have cliffs which often reach the Pacific Ocean and have limited the number of good harbors along the coast. These ranges also are an important source of timber. There are a number of openings through these mountains into the interior valleys, where population has concentrated.

Behind the Coast Ranges are four valleys important for agriculture and for urban enclaves. The Puget-Willamette Lowlands are fertile and well watered. In California, the Sacramento River to the north and the San Joaquin River to the south form the Great Central Valley. Inadequate rainfall for agriculture has been supplanted by irrigation, making this one of the richest farm areas in the world.

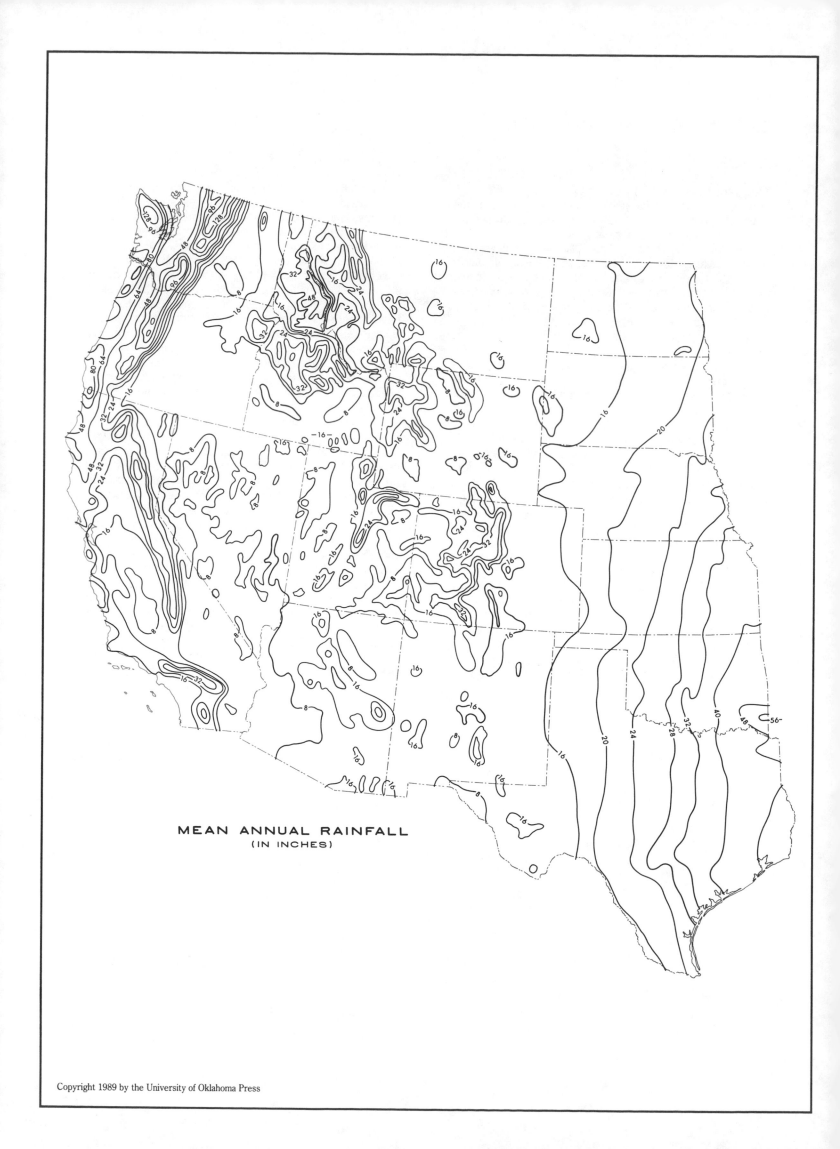

MEAN ANNUAL RAINFALL
(IN INCHES)

3. MEAN ANNUAL RAINFALL

THIS MAP UNDERSCORES the greatest natural deficiency suffered by the West. The region lacks sufficient precipitation for most of the basic needs of human beings. It has been responsible for the treeless plains and, naturally, the desert. Although herculean efforts have satisfied immediate needs for ground and surface water for irrigation and for livestock and human use, there is still the threat of future shortages which could spell disaster. Only along the Texas Gulf Coast and the North Pacific Slope can the rainfall be considered adequate.

The lack of sufficient moisture for agriculture is most evident over the Great Plains. There the isohyetal lines illustrate that rainfall decreases as one travels north and west, evidence that the amount of moisture on the plains is influenced by the Gulf of Mexico and the Atlantic Ocean. Another factor is the presence of the Sierra Nevada and Cascades to the west. These mountains drain the prevailing onshore winds of their moisture, and the drying winds do not deposit rain until they reach central Kansas or Nebraska. The twenty-inch rainfall line, to the west of which there is not enough moisture for ordinary farming, lies approximately along the one-hundredth meridian. Matters are made worse because most rain falls on the Great Plains between April and November, when the glaring sun and hot summer winds quickly evaporate the water from the soil. The southern region suffers most from a rapid rate of evaporation.

In the more elevated plateau states of Montana, Wyoming, Colorado, and New Mexico there are more topographic controls over rainfall. The isohyetal lines enclose hills or mountains, demonstrating the effect of these obstructions in wringing moisture from the winds. However, in no cases are the amounts of precipitation excessive. The usual annual amount is sixteen to twenty-four inches, and only occasionally does it reach thirty-two inches. In the northern plateau there is as much as forty-eight inches—the greatest in the Rocky Mountain area. Only a short distance away in the Snake River Valley there is only eight inches; where the annual amount is less than fifteen inches and irrigation is not possible, dry farming and grazing are the dominant agricultural activities. To the south in Nevada, Utah, and Arizona rainfall is even less, and these states, along with nearby southern California, are some of the driest in the West. The great aridity of the entire plateau area is basically caused when the winds descend the leeward side of the Sierra Nevada and Cascade Range and are heated, thereby increasing their capacity to retain moisture.

The heaviest rainfall in the United States, up to 128 inches annually, is found in the Pacific Northwest. The rainfall there is a product of the prevailing onshore winds and the mountains, which act as barriers to the moisture-laden air, especially in winter, when the mountains are much colder than the warm Pacific. South of San Francisco Bay the area is much drier because it is beyond the reach of most of the rain-bringing storms and because the mountain slopes are warmer, even in winter, so less rain is caused as the winds blow up the mountainsides.

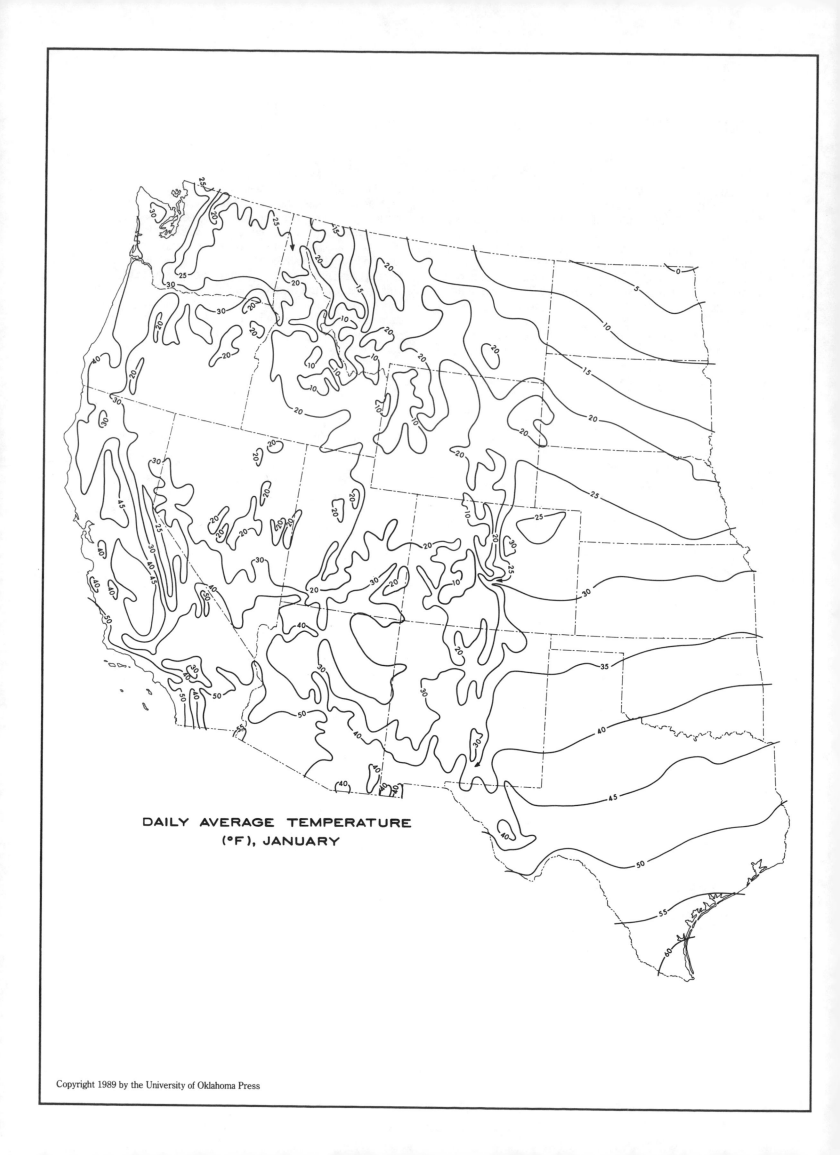

DAILY AVERAGE TEMPERATURE (°F), JANUARY

4. DAILY AVERAGE TEMPERATURE—JANUARY

THE DAILY AVERAGE TEMPERATURES in the American West during January are as diverse as other geographic features of this vast area. Except in the Pacific Coast area, the deserts of California and Arizona, and the Texas Coastal Plain, the weather is bitterly cold. In fact, the Great Plains have recorded some of North America's lowest temperatures—as low as −60°F. The dry continental zone embraces approximately the eastern half of the American West and is marked by aridity and by temperature extremes in both summer and winter.

As the isothermic lines beginning in Texas and going north to the Canadian border indicate, latitude is the prime determinant of temperature in the plains. In addition, an extreme continental cooling effect in January is the result of distance from the moderating influence of large bodies of water. High winds add to the discomfort brought by low temperatures. In fact, winds are stronger on the Great Plains than any other place in the world except the polar icecaps. Chinook winds, however, help make the long winter tolerable. These winds are created when the air is warmed as it rapidly descends the lee side of a mountain; in some instances a Chinook wind may cause a rise in temperature of forty degrees in twenty-four hours. As a result, the snow melts and cattle and sheep are able to survive the harsh winter by grazing on the exposed grass.

In the mountainous areas, as the isothermic lines demonstrate, elevation is a far greater influence on temperature than is latitude. Mountain ranges, especially the Rockies and the Cascades, shield the interior from extreme cold. In the coastal states of Washington, Oregon, and California, isotherms generally run north and south instead of the more common east and west. An exception to this rule occurs where river valleys (like the Columbia) or mountain passes permit moderating temperatures to penetrate far inland so that grass, and some crops, can flourish even in January. Temperatures along the Pacific Coast actually vary little from Washington to southern California.

Despite frequent winter low temperatures, human beings have always been able to adapt to life in the harsher climates of the American West. This has been true because cyclonic storms cause frequent periods of relief from the cold. The Indian developed a culture around the buffalo and other game animals that survived winters there, and white settlers quickly made a permanent home when they discovered that cattle and sheep could also live through the bitter cold of the winter months. The search for mineral riches and the use of fossil fuels for heating led to lasting settlement of the mountain areas, the recreational uses of which in the twentieth century have attracted thousands of people the year around. Great cities have emerged at many places in the mountains, and of course the more attractive climates along the Pacific slope and in southern Arizona have likewise drawn large populations.

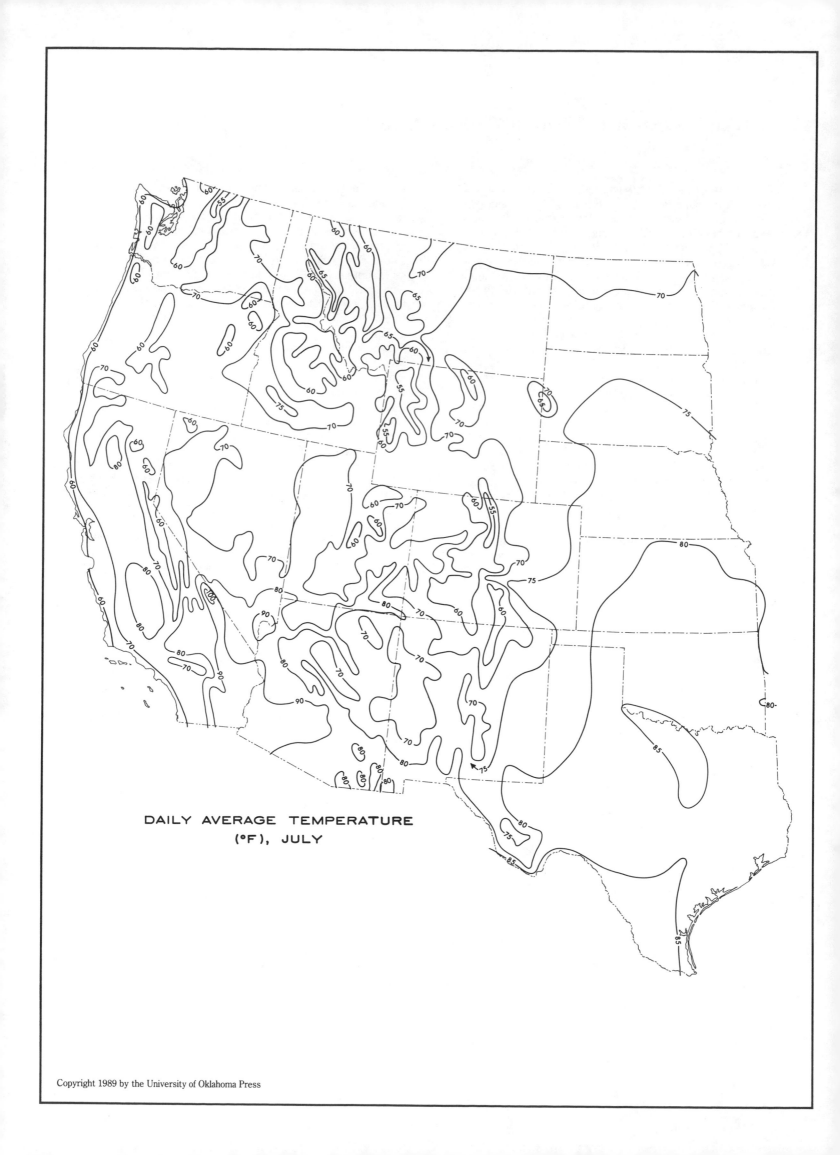

DAILY AVERAGE TEMPERATURE
(°F), JULY

5. DAILY AVERAGE TEMPERATURE—JULY

WHEN THE FIRST ANGLO-AMERICAN PIONEERS reached the American West, they were surprised at just how hot it was, but they were also amazed at how pleasant the warm July temperatures were. The low relative humidity makes them more tolerable than the same temperatures in the more humid areas to the east. Nights are cool even in the summer—the result of rapid radiation made possible by dry air and clear skies. In fact, evaporation is everywhere great, often with serious consequences in view of the limited rainfall. A procession of cyclonic storms also causes frequent weather changes, even in the summer. Many visitors to the West recommended the high, dry plains or mountains to their friends back east who suffered from respiratory problems. Today, the popularity of summer vacation resorts in the mountains of the West is partially a result of the excessive summer heat in the East.

The tempering effects of even moderate altitudes are shown by the 75°F isotherm, which starts in southern New Mexico and goes northward to South Dakota following the eastern base of the Rocky Mountains. The isothermal map is essentiality a rough contour map enclosing mountain ranges. Daily average temperatures of 55°F only a short distance from 75°F indicate a mountain range adjacent to a plateau area. In some cases one can experience that difference by a journey of only a few miles up a mountain slope.

The isotherms of 80°F and 90°F indicate desert areas which were virtually uninhabitable before the advent of air conditioning, at least in July. Temperatures of 120°F are common in these areas. The record high was 134°F in Death Valley, California.

As the 85°F isotherm shows, Texas, at least in certain areas, suffers from excessive heat. Unlike most of the American West, this heat is more debilitating because of the high humidity there. This situation results from about one-half of Texas having an elevation of less than 1,500 feet. Not until one reaches the Llano Estacado in the middle of the Texas Panhandle, at an elevation of more than 2,500 feet, does the Texas temperature become more like that of the rest of the American West. This is a case in which latitude does determine the temperature.

On the Pacific slope the map shows several interesting features. The isotherms closely parallel the coast, indicating that temperatures are virtually unchanged from Washington to the Mexican border. One may travel from Seattle to San Francisco without encountering any change in the daily average July temperature. In fact, one could even travel to the Mexican border without reaching an average temperature of 70°F. The temperature gradient between Seattle and San Diego is only 0.7°F per latitude degree. In other words, the absolute maximum change is 12° or 1° per hundred miles of latitude.

Another notable feature of the southern California Coast is the cool summer resulting from the prevailing onshore winds. Still another aspect is the marked contrast between the higher temperatures of the interior valleys and the cooler mountain slopes. The Sacramento–San Joaquin Valley has a uniformly high summer temperature. Finally, summers on the Pacific Coast are usually several degrees cooler than a corresponding location of the same latitude on the Atlantic Coast.

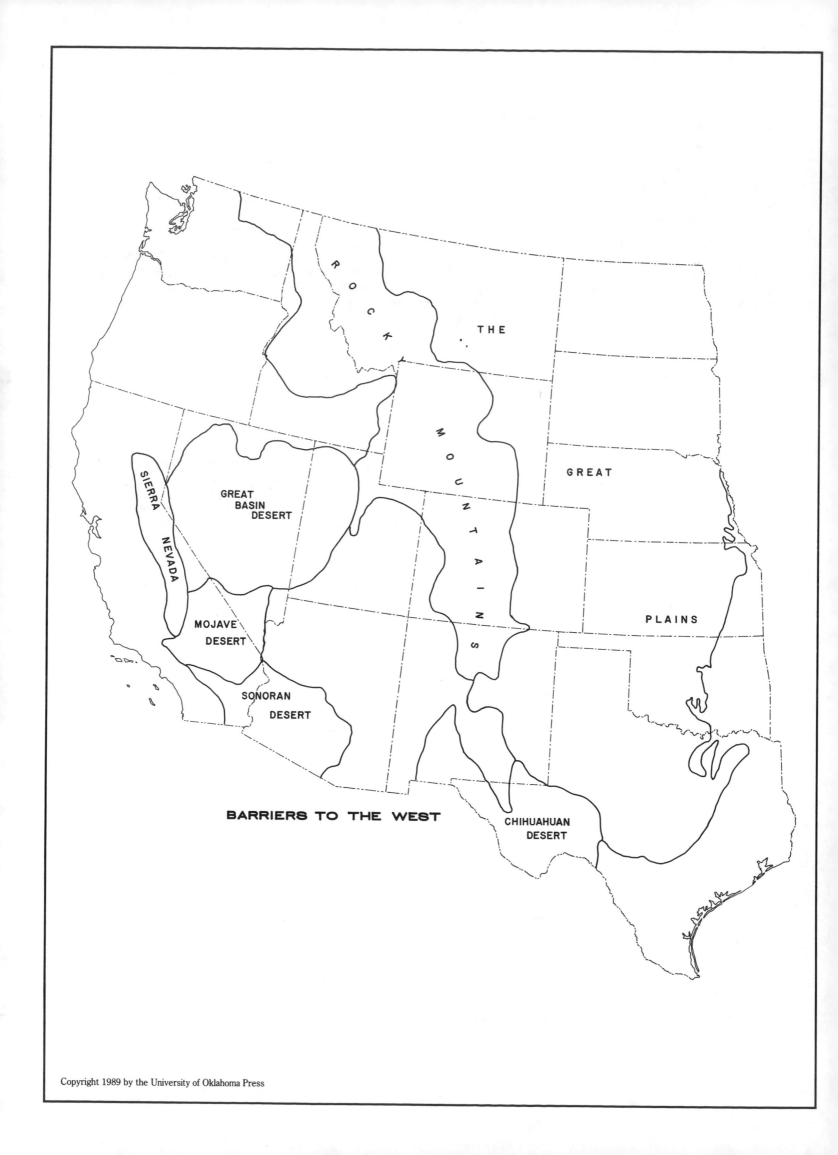

ROCK
THE
MOUNTAINS
GREAT
PLAINS

SIERRA
NEVADA

GREAT
BASIN
DESERT

MOJAVE
DESERT

SONORAN
DESERT

BARRIERS TO THE WEST

CHIHUAHUAN
DESERT

6. BARRIERS TO THE WEST

As PIONEERS MADE THEIR WAY westward, they found the first tier of states beyond the Mississippi similar to the lands immediately east of the river. The next tier, from North Dakota to Texas, was likewise comparable to the world they had known. However, as the pioneers neared the ninety-eighth meridian, conditions changed, and the treeless, short-grass country formed the first barrier to the West. This arid land, the "Great American Desert," was often short of water and grass for livestock and was made uncomfortable by hot, drying winds, sandstorms, and clouds of locusts. Wagons often sank to their hubs in sand, and streams, though shallow, were often difficult to cross because of canyons, quicksand, or their width. Yet the westward travelers, as they made their way across the limitless prairies, did not realize that this was the easiest part of the trip; more formidable barriers were ahead.

Americans moving westward may have been ill prepared for the strange conditions of the Great Plains; they were totally unprepared for their encounter with the great mountain ranges and desert terrain. In fact, some considered the Rockies to be an impassable barrier. One New Yorker even declared, "Nature has fixed limits for our nation, she has kindly introduced as our western barriers, mountains almost inaccessible, whose base she has skirted with irreclaimable deserts of sand." However, the Lewis and Clark expedition stilled such pessimism by proving that there were passes through the mountains.

The ranges of Colorado have no pass under ten thousand feet, and wagon trains found them impassable. Traders and trappers early discovered the paths through the Wyoming Basin through which the Mormon, Overland, and Oregon trails made their way. Even then, the elevation at South Pass was eight thousand feet. One traveler was so unimpressed with what he had seen that upon entering South Pass, he wrote home: "The whole western world thus far, is good for nothing except to serve as a bridge to California." The mountains through New Mexico and Arizona were easier to traverse, but once through them the Mojave and Sonoran deserts were an even greater challenge.

Arid lands with rainfall less than five inches per year, in some instances, were completely outside the experience of most Americans moving westward. A relatively small number of argonauts en route to the California gold fields dared to go across Texas or northern Mexico and thus had to cross the Chihuahuan and Sonoran deserts. As noted in Map 33, those who elected to cross the Mojave Desert often met with disaster.

Most westward travelers used the central route through the Wyoming Basin. To cross the Great Basin desert, they followed the Humboldt River, which provided adequate water for man and beast. However, the hot, dry atmosphere was uncomfortable for humans. In addition, it dried out equipment. Wagon tongues broke easily after drying over a period of time. Worst of all, spokes of wheels would shrink so rapidly that the wheels would fall apart if corrective measures were not taken. It was often necessary to unload the wagons, take the wheels off, and immerse them in a stream until they again fit the rim firmly. Randolph B. Marcy, in his advice to emigrants, recommended a specific type of wood for wheel spokes.

The final barrier to the West was the Sierra Nevada. When John Bidwell, the leader of an early overland emigrant train in 1841, saw this massive wall, he commented: "If California lies beyond those mountains we shall never be able to reach it." Most travelers experienced similar doubts on observing that rugged range. However, there are a number of passes which breach the seemingly impregnable Sierra. Even then, it was often necessary to unload the wagons and winch the empty vehicles up the steep slopes while the goods were hand-carried to the top.

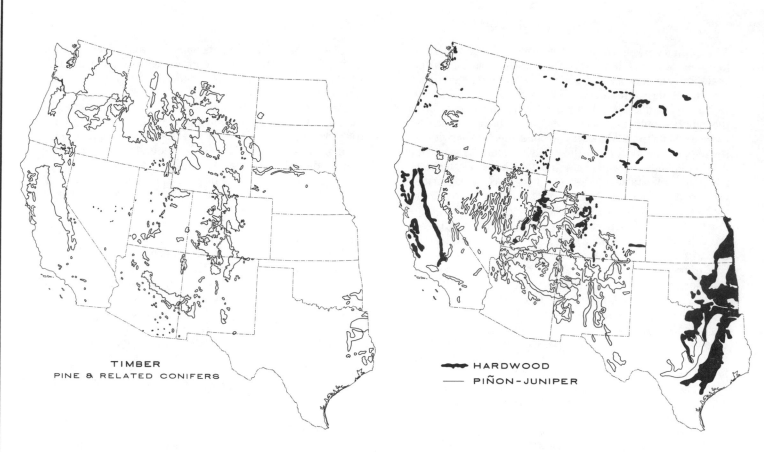

TIMBER
PINE & RELATED CONIFERS

▰▰▰ HARDWOOD
——— PIÑON-JUNIPER

MAJOR FOREST TYPES

CHAPARRAL

COTTONWOOD, ASH, ELM

7. MAJOR FOREST TYPES

THE LIFE-STYLE of the American pioneer evolved in the primeval forests that originally covered virtually all the eastern United States. Early farmers found it difficult to remove the hardwood trees in order to cultivate the land. But from these forests settlers obtained logs for their buildings, unlimited supplies of firewood, and timber for roads and bridges. When the pioneers first reached the grasslands of the Old Northwest, their initial reaction was that land which did not grow trees was worthless for crops. As they reached the treeless Great Plains, they were similarly convinced of the lack of value of the area. They were reinforced in this view by the 1820 report of the explorer Maj. Stephen H. Long, who declared of the region: "It is almost wholly unfit for cultivation, and of course, uninhabitable by a people depending upon agriculture for their subsistence."

The lack of forests in the American West arose out of the fact that of all plant life, trees need the most water. This also explains why along the eastern edge of the grasslands, mainly in North and South Dakota, Nebraska, and Kansas, groves of cottonwoods were found in the river valleys. Scattered among these, where moisture conditions were most favorable, were stands of ash and elm, along with a few other deciduous trees such as oak, maple, and beech. By eastern standards these groves did not amount to much, but the plains pioneers drove many miles to them to obtain building materials, fence posts, or firewood.

Chaparral is a shrub that has tough and thick evergreen leaves and abounds where rainfall is at least ten inches annually but no more than thirty inches. It is found on the western slopes of California's coastal mountains, on the eastern slopes of the Sierra Nevada, and in the desert woodland areas of the Rocky Mountains. The dense thickets of chaparral burn well, and fire is a constant problem in the long, hot summers of these regions.

The forest types of the western mountains are determined by elevation, latitude, and topography. An additional influence is the west-to-east movement of weather patterns, which brings greater precipitation to the western slopes of mountains. In the Southern Rockies the hardwood forests are mainly oak and mountain mahogany, most of which are under thirty-five feet in height. Up the mountain slope from the hardwoods grow the piñons and junipers. These constitute the lowest conifer forests of the mountains and are found as far north as the Canadian border.

The Douglas fir and the ponderosa pine can withstand a wide range of conditions, such as shade, wind, and cold. Therefore these trees are found from the mountains of Arizona and New Mexico northward to Montana and Idaho. The ponderosa pine forests have been described as the most beautiful in the world.

The greatest forest areas of the United States are in the Pacific Northwest, in Washington, Oregon, and northern California. A mild climate and heavy precipitation of 80 to 120 inches annually combine to promote rapid growth—as much as one thousand board feet of wood per acre. Douglas fir is the most extensive and commercially important forest type. Ponderosa pine flourishes where rainfall is lower, as on the leeward side of the mountains. There are several other types of pine in the area which have adapted to specific rainfall or weather conditions and perhaps a particular elevation. Commercial growth of timber is common to this region, which produces more than one-half of the nation's lumber needs.

The redwoods, remarkable for their great size and age, are found along the California coast in a narrow strip ten to thirty miles wide from just over the Oregon boundary southward to Bodega Bay. There are also small stands scattered as far south as Santa Cruz County. The giant sequoias grow along the west slope of the Sierra Nevada between elevations of 4,500 and 8,000 feet from California's Placer County to Tulare County.

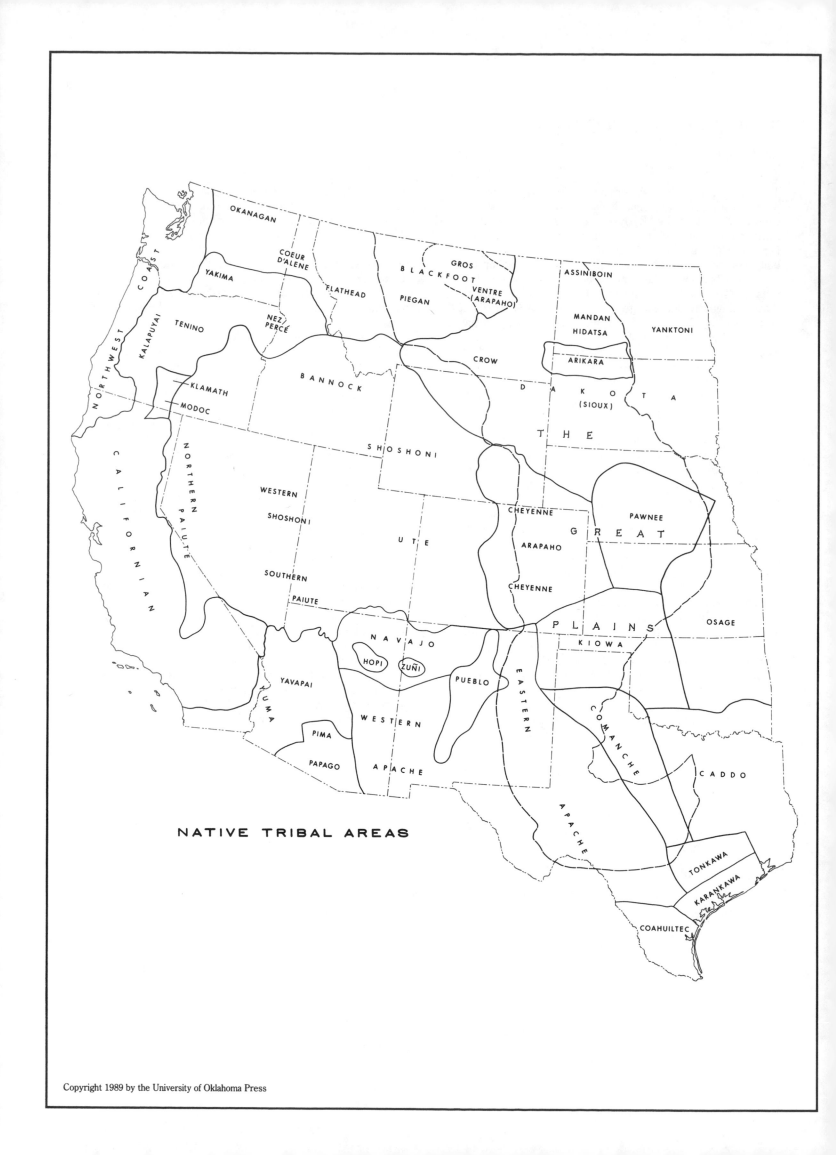

NATIVE TRIBAL AREAS

8. NATIVE TRIBAL AREAS

THE INDIANS OF THE AMERICAN WEST were as diverse as the landscapes they inhabited. The Indian civilization of the Great Plains was determined by the presence of the huge herds of buffalo that roamed from Texas to Canada. Astride the horse, which they acquired after the first whites arrived on this continent, these Indians were superb hunters and fierce warriors. They had no permanent villages and followed the buffalo herds, from which they obtained their food, clothing, homes, and even their boats. All of them used stone knives and scrapers, bone awls, bows and arrows, and a long lance tipped with stone.

On the eastern edge of the Great Plains, and possibly reflecting the greater rainfall there, were tribes such as Mandans, Arikaras, Hidatsas, Omahas, Osages, and Sioux, who planted maize, beans, pumpkins, and melons and left their permanent villages twice a year to hunt buffalo. To the west of the Great Plains lived the Nez Percés, Utes, and Shoshonis, who also lived in permanent villages gathering wild roots and berries and who also hunted buffalo once or twice a year.

In New Mexico and Arizona were Indians with among the most advanced civilizations in North America. The Pueblos, Zuñis, and Hopis developed a sedentary society built around typical Indian crops such as maize, beans, squash, and melons. They wove cotton into cloth and were superb pottery makers and basket weavers. They were not warlike but were able to defend their adobe dwellings if they had to. The Pimas, Papagos, and Yumas had a similar agricultural base but lived in thatched huts. The Navajos were originally a nomadic plains tribe, but through the years they gradually became more sedentary as they copied the Pueblo culture. The Apaches, on the other hand, remained nomadic and warlike and lived mainly by raiding whites and other tribes.

The Great Basin is perhaps the poorest area of the American West. East of the Sierra Nevada and west of the Rockies the region is dry and the flora and fauna are sparse. The result is that the Bannocks, Shoshonis, Utes, and Paiutes who lived there were materially less advantaged than other Indian civilizations. Yet they adapted to the harsh environment and in spite of it lived on a varied diet of piñon nuts, grass seeds, berries, and small game.

California Indians, on the other hand, lived in a veritable paradise. When the first Spaniards arrived in 1769, there were some three hundred thousand natives, divided into a large number of different linguistic families, in the region. Most were sedentary and had shown great resourcefulness in processing acorns as their staple food. Some groups also fished and hunted small game. The large population reflects the richness of their environment.

Stretching along the Pacific Coast from northern California into Canada was an Indian civilization unique in North America. These tribes developed a marine society with their food supply almost solely dependent upon fish, shellfish, sea mammals, and even seaweed. Above all, their basic staple was salmon, which were abundant and were gathered seasonally, resulting in permanent settlements, a surplus of food, and thus one of the largest populations in North America. In addition, an abundance of wood enabled the Pacific Coast tribes to build large homes and great dugout canoes. They also carved masks, religious objects, and totem poles from wood; their sculpture and painting rival those of the Mayas and Incas. Clothing and blankets were made from mountain goat wool or from the inner bark fiber of spruce and cypress. An extensive trade network characterized the region with major summer trade fairs, the most important of which was located at The Dalles on the Columbia River in present-day Oregon and Washington.

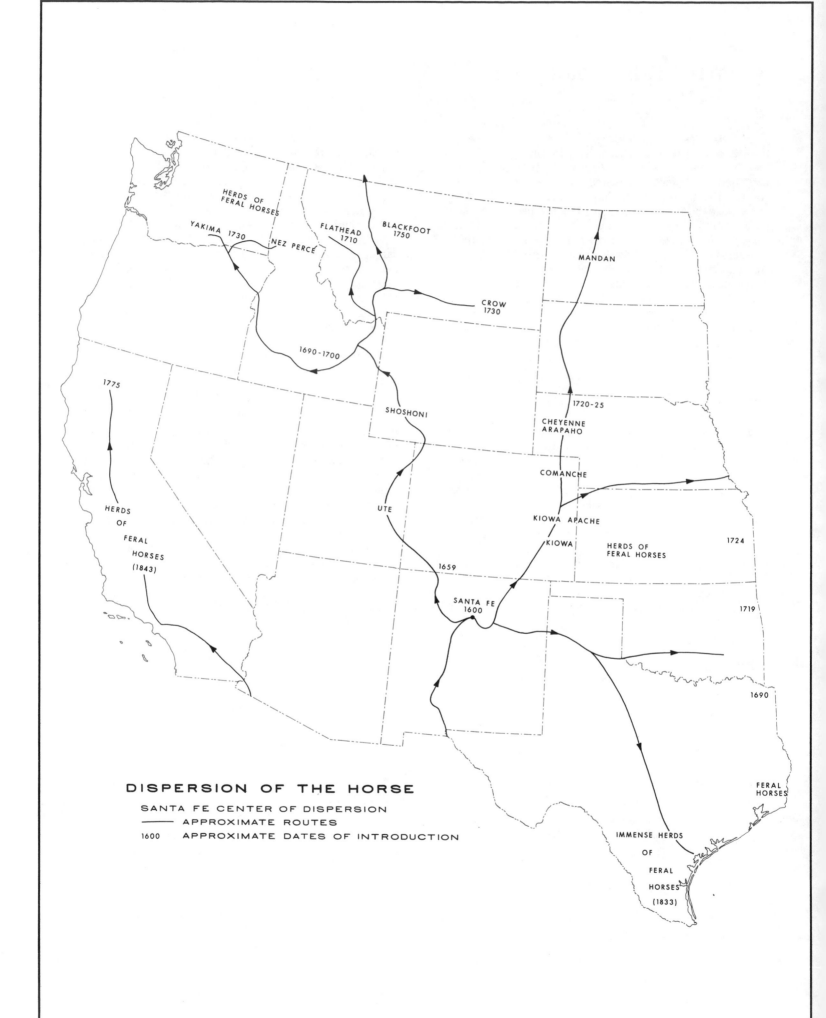

HERDS OF
FERAL HORSES

YAKIMA 1730
NEZ PERCÉ
FLATHEAD
1710
BLACKFOOT
1750

MANDAN

CROW
1730

1690-1700

SHOSHONI

1720-25

CHEYENNE
ARAPAHO

1775

COMANCHE

UTE

KIOWA APACHE

HERDS
OF
FERAL
HORSES
(1843)

KIOWA

HERDS OF
FERAL HORSES

1724

1659

1719

SANTA FE
1600

1690

FERAL
HORSES

DISPERSION OF THE HORSE

SANTA FE CENTER OF DISPERSION
——— APPROXIMATE ROUTES
1600   APPROXIMATE DATES OF INTRODUCTION

IMMENSE HERDS
OF
FERAL
HORSES
(1833)

9. DISPERSION OF THE HORSE

THE COMING OF THE HORSE was probably the most significant event in the history of the American West before the Anglo entry. This animal brought a profound revolution in the life-style of many western Indian tribes. The extent of this change was graphically summarized by one authority:

> With the horse he was transformed into the daring buffalo hunter, able to procure in a single day enough food to supply his family for a year, leaving him free to sweep the plains with his war parties along a range of a thousand miles.[1]

Before the arrival of the horse, a camp could seldom move more than six miles a day. The weight of goods that could be carried was limited, as only women and dogs were available as porters; men had to carry weapons and be on the alert for an attack. A horse-borne camp could move thirty miles in a day. With horses available, the tepee grew in size and the amount of personal property likewise increased.

Afoot, the Indian hunted deer or antelope by chasing them in relays until the animals dropped from exhaustion, and the preferred way of killing buffalo was to drive them over a cliff. In any event, such hunting was difficult and dangerous, and because the area in which game could be sought was so hunted, Indians constantly were threatened with starvation. Mounted, Indians could follow the wandering herds for hundreds of miles. Astride a horse and armed only with a lance or bow and arrow, they could kill enough game to provide a surplus of food and hides; they had enough to put aside dried meat for the winter. If game could not be found, the Indians could always butcher their horses in an emergency. The ample diet produced healthier people; more babies were born, and more were raised to maturity. In most tribes the introduction of the horse led to a rapid increase in population within a generation or two.

The Spanish grasped the advantage the horse gave them in the initial conflicts with the native Americans and sought to keep the horse out of the hands of the Indians. Laws to that effect were passed but simply could not be enforced, especially on the frontier. The first and most important center of distribution of Spanish horses for the plains was at Santa Fe. When Juan de Oñate began the settlement on the upper Rio Grande in 1598, he brought large numbers of horses with him. The Apaches were the first to raid the herds, which were poorly tended. Initially, the horses and mules were used for food by the Indians.

It is not possible to say just when or how the Apaches saw the value of the horse as a beast of burden. However, it is reasonable to assume that sedentary Pueblo Indians were trained by the Spanish to care for the herds of horses. Pueblos with such knowledge then either were captured by the Apaches or fled to join them. In a short time the mysteries of horsemanship were passed on to the Apaches, who thus became the first mounted native Americans. They, in turn, traded Spanish horses to other Plains Indians, and within a short period these animals were in great demand. Apaches stole horses, but Spaniards also traded the animals for buffalo robes or furs. In addition, the Pueblo Revolt of 1680 drove the Spanish out of New Mexico for a time, and the horses left behind were soon in the hands of the Indians.

From 1659, when the Navajos were first encountered on horseback, until 1770, when the Sioux on the Canadian border obtained horses, these animals moved out from Santa Fe north and northwest at the approximate average rate of ten miles per year along the lines indicated on the map. In addition to the horses domesticated by the Indians, great herds of feral horses developed in the areas noted on the map. The Spanish brought the horse to California when they first settled there in 1769, and in a few years the animals' numbers had multiplied so rapidly that they were a nuisance to the *rancheros*.

[1] Frank Gilbert Roe, *The Indian and the Horse* (Norman: University of Oklahoma Press, 1955), p. 175.

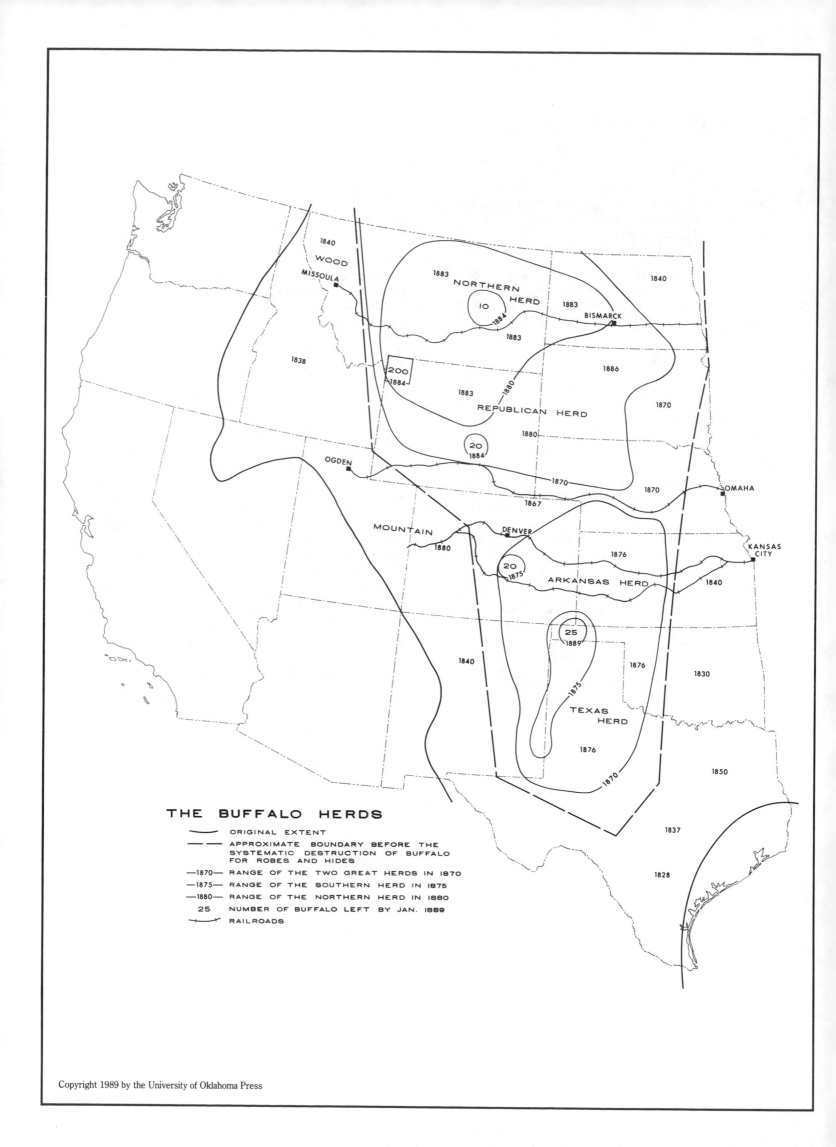

THE BUFFALO HERDS

——— ORIGINAL EXTENT

— — APPROXIMATE BOUNDARY BEFORE THE
SYSTEMATIC DESTRUCTION OF BUFFALO
FOR ROBES AND HIDES

—1870— RANGE OF THE TWO GREAT HERDS IN 1870

—1875— RANGE OF THE SOUTHERN HERD IN 1875

—1880— RANGE OF THE NORTHERN HERD IN 1880

25   NUMBER OF BUFFALO LEFT BY JAN. 1889

+—+—+ RAILROADS

10. THE BUFFALO HERDS

THE BUFFALO was one of the most important animals in the history of the American West. This shaggy beast could weigh as much as a ton and stand over six feet tall. Plagued by a combination of dim eyesight and wits to match, buffaloes were depicted in the early white chronicles as the most stupid of animals. Yet when aroused, they could be ferocious adversaries because of their great size, speed, and, above all, numbers.

It is not possible to determine exactly how many plains buffaloes there were in the midnineteenth century, but the figure of seventy-five million is probably a reasonable one. In 1889, William T. Hornaday observed that "of all the quadrupeds that have lived upon the earth, probably no other species has ever marshaled such innumerable hosts as those of the American bison." From the first report of Coronado, the Spanish explorer, who in 1540 told his king, "it is impossible to number them," to the late nineteenth century, men found it hard to estimate the size of the herds. One commented that "there is such a quantity of them that I do not know what to compare them with, except the fish of the sea." Another found them to be as "numerous as the locusts of Egypt." One railroad surveyor in North Dakota estimated that from a high hill he could see half a million.

As Wayne Gard puts it, "On the western plains the buffalo and the Indian were linked as closely as they would be later on a nickel coin." In fact, it is doubtful that any other animal in the world has ever matched the buffalo in providing so many commodities of prime importance to any one people. The fatty meat of the hump and the tongue was a treasured delicacy, but it was buffalo meat in general which sustained life. It was preferred fresh, but it was also cut into strips and dried for the day that buffaloes were not immediately available. The bones provided material from which implements and weapons could be fashioned. Buffalo hides furnished blankets, clothing of all kinds, boats, rope, and a warm tepee; hooves produced glue, and sinews were used for bowstrings. Horns furnished drinking vessels and spoons, and even the dried manure was used for fuel on the treeless prairies.

But buffaloes were more than the Indians' commissary; the native plainsmen developed their very culture, their daily thought and ceremonial practices, around these shaggy beasts. In short, the Indians of the plains were spiritually and materially dependent on the buffalo.

When settlers moved into the plains after the Civil War, they found their way blocked by the Indians and the buffalo. Both had to go before the land could be claimed by ranchers and farmers. Columbus Delano, secretary of the interior, spoke for many when in 1871 he advocated the slaughter of the buffalo as a means of controlling the Indians. However, the destruction of the great herds took place in a short period of time because of the glamour attached to hunting buffalo, the coming of the railroad, and improvements in tanning techniques which made it profitable to use buffalo leather for many purposes. Hunting buffalo was depicted as a romantic pastime in the American press because of the exploits of foreign "sportsmen." Sir William Drummond Stewart was the first of such men to slaughter buffaloes in 1843. Sir St. George Gore came west in 1854 and spent half a million dollars over a three-year period killing two thousand buffaloes. The Russian Grand Duke Alexis arrived in 1872 and was accompanied by George A. Custer, William F. Cody, and Gen. Phillip Sheridan on a well-publicized hunting expedition.

Buffalo meat was a staple food for the railroad crews. The buffalo robe had long been a popular trade item, and Indians had sold thousands of them. But with the railroads to transport hides worth a dollar or more apiece, the great slaughter began in the 1870s. After the herds in Kansas had been wiped out by 1873, the railroad built to Fort Worth, and the buffalo hunters followed, killing off most of the Texas herd by 1875. By 1881 the Northern Pacific had reached Montana, and in the following year five thousand hunters bagged a quarter of a million hides. By 1884 the great herds of the north had virtually been killed off. Disease brought onto the plains by cattle from Texas and the Midwest was also an important factor in destroying the buffalo herds.

Seasoned pioneers found it hard to grasp that the once limitless herds that had roamed the plains for ages could vanish within a single decade. And with the demise of the buffalo, the way of life of the Plains Indians soon followed.

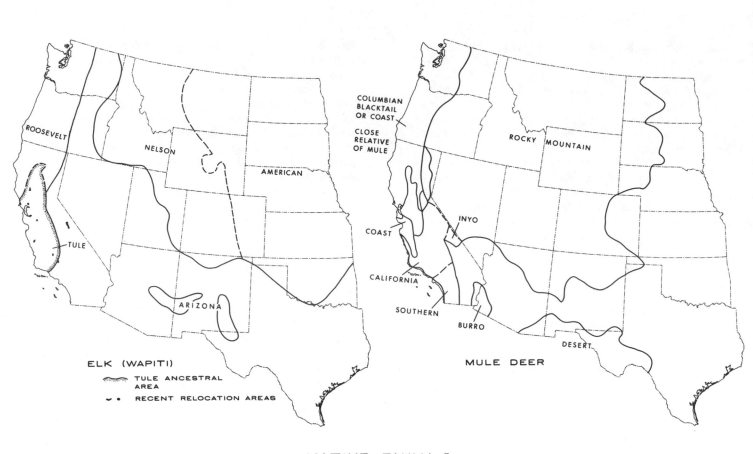

ELK (WAPITI)

ROOSEVELT
NELSON
AMERICAN
TULE
ARIZONA

 — TULE ANCESTRAL
    AREA
 •— • RECENT RELOCATION AREAS

MULE DEER

COLUMBIAN
BLACKTAIL
OR COAST
CLOSE
RELATIVE
OF MULE
ROCKY MOUNTAIN
INYO
COAST
CALIFORNIA
SOUTHERN
BURRO
DESERT

NATIVE FAUNA I

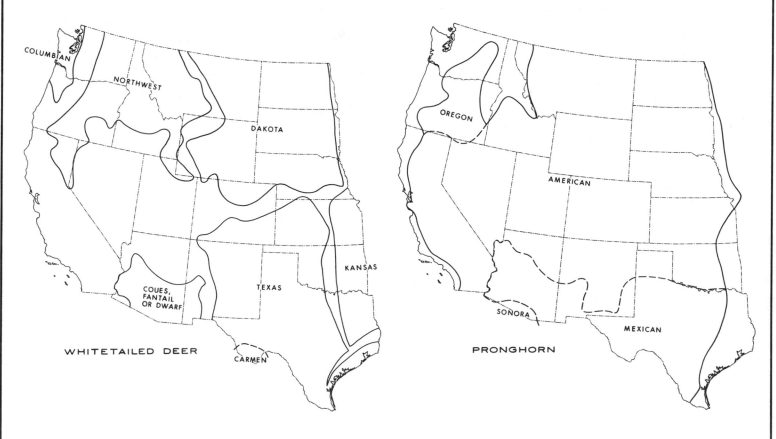

WHITETAILED DEER

COLUMBIAN
NORTHWEST
DAKOTA
COUES,
FANTAIL
OR DWARF
TEXAS
KANSAS
CARMEN

PRONGHORN

OREGON
AMERICAN
SONORA
MEXICAN

11. NATIVE FAUNA I

As the Anglo-American frontier moved westward from the Atlantic Coast, pioneers found wild mammals indispensable to their existence. They were sustained by the meat until, and even after, crops could be harvested, and the hides and skins were an important source of clothing. The Great Plains of the American West may have been initially looked upon as a desert useless for agriculture, but the early travelers were uniformly fascinated by the diversity and abundance of native fauna. Meriwether Lewis was one of the first to observe that the grasslands of the Dakotas were teeming with wild game, which increased in numbers as they went westward.

Lewis found "a great number of elk" (*Cervus canadensis*), or wapiti, as the Indians called this noble animal, which was once abundant from the Alleghenies to the Pacific Coast, equally at home on the plains or in the mountains. The Roosevelt elk is native to the rain forests of the Northwest Coast. Elk are the second largest of the deer family, with bulls weighing up to eight hundred pounds (only moose are larger). Tule elk, dwarfs found only in California, are the exception.

The mule deer was first recognized as a distinct species by William Clark, the partner of Lewis in the famed westward exploration. It was named for the obvious reason that its ears resembled those of the mule. It is similar to its cousin, the black-tailed deer. In fact, one observer notes, "mule deer and black-tailed deer are sufficiently different to justify common names, yet similar enough to be included in one species." The black-tailed deer is found on the Pacific Coast, while the mule deer is found throughout the American West. The mule deer prefers to feed in open parks and meadows but was once at home on the plains. In more recent years it has been forced into mountains or foothills and even into the semidesert shrub habitats of the Southwest.

The white-tailed deer is believed to have evolved in the deciduous forest areas of the eastern part of the continent, while the mule deer was a product of the dry, rugged areas of the American West. Ultimately, the two species overlapped, as the map suggests. To native Americans and to pioneers, deer were second only to buffalo in value. Venison was a basic staple, and deerskins were a universal item of attire. Deer neared extinction by 1900, but since then have grown in numbers so fast that in some areas they are agricultural pests. Controlled hunting, the destruction of predatory animals, and better forage have brought about this change.

The pronghorn (*Antilocapra americana*) is native to America and is not to be confused with the European antelope. It is believed that forty million of these animals roamed the plains from Canada to Mexico as well as the valleys of the coastal states. Some even contend that they were more numerous than the buffalo. One reason for their great numbers was that they eat virtually everything; sagebrush, cacti, weeds, and even plants poisonous to livestock are a part of their diet. In addition, they are the fastest wild animal in North America, with speeds of forty miles per hour being common. They also have tremendous eyesight. As Walter Prescott Webb noted, the pronghorn is an animal "peculiarly well fitted for its chosen environment." Despite this, by 1908 pronghorns had dwindled to fewer than twenty thousand animals north of Mexico.

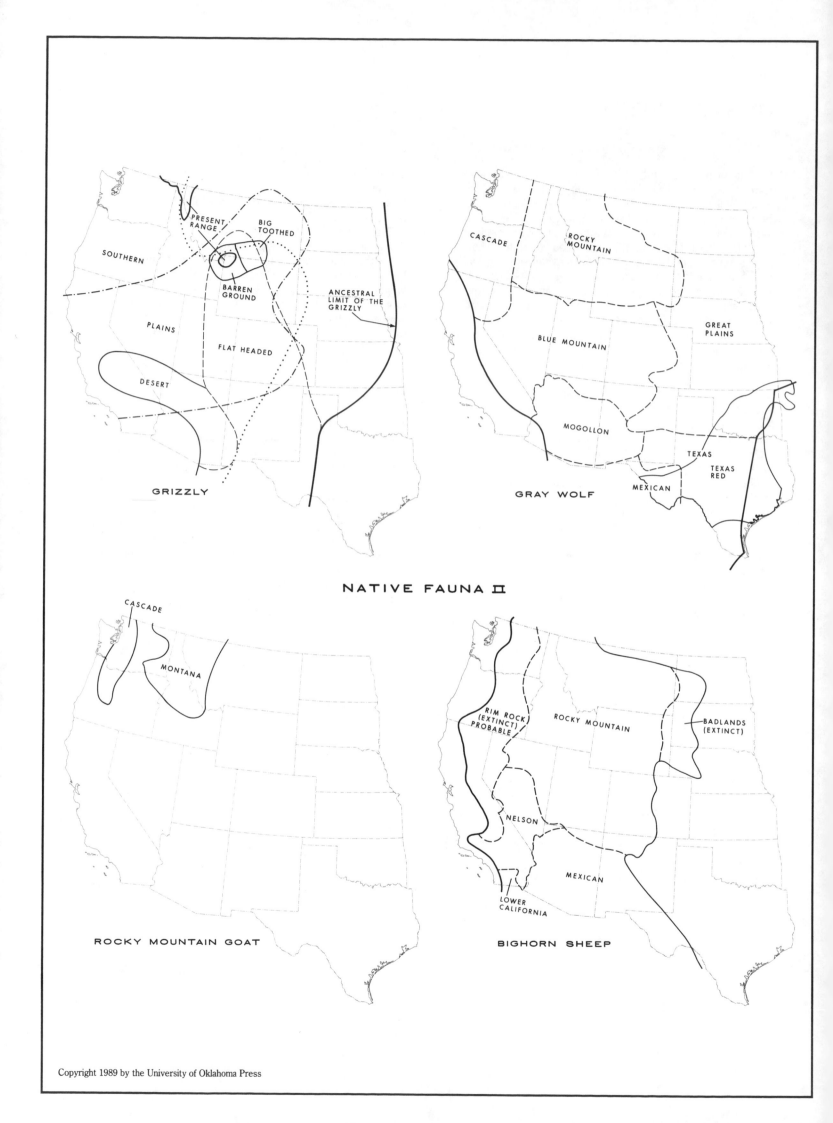

GRIZZLY

SOUTHERN

PLAINS

DESERT

PRESENT
RANGE

BIG
TOOTHED

BARREN
GROUND

FLAT HEADED

ANCESTRAL
LIMIT OF THE
GRIZZLY

GRAY WOLF

CASCADE

ROCKY
MOUNTAIN

BLUE MOUNTAIN

GREAT
PLAINS

MOGOLLON

TEXAS

TEXAS
RED

MEXICAN

NATIVE FAUNA II

ROCKY MOUNTAIN GOAT

CASCADE

MONTANA

BIGHORN SHEEP

RIM ROCK
(EXTINCT)
PROBABLE

ROCKY MOUNTAIN

BADLANDS
(EXTINCT)

NELSON

MEXICAN

LOWER
CALIFORNIA

12. NATIVE FAUNA II

THE GRIZZLY BEAR occurred mainly in the foothills and valleys of the Rocky Mountains. Among the more intelligent of wild animals, grizzly bears have been greatly feared because of their ferocity and great size (adult males may reach one thousand pounds). Indians feared these animals, yet many tribes also worshiped them as sacred and sought their claws as a symbol of prowess as a great hunter. The Anglo pioneers also feared grizzly bears but killed them for food and hides as well as to protect livestock. The grizzly bears often relied on grasses, berries, pine nuts, and root crops as their basic foods. They ate fish and all kinds of rodents. They are capable of killing adult moose, buffalo, and mountain sheep, but most often they obtain their meat as scavengers. Although they avoid man when possible, there are many examples of their willingness to attack when surprised or frightened. Once numerous, especially in California, they are mainly found in parks or in the less accessible regions of Montana and Idaho.

The European settlers brought from their homeland an antipathy for the gray wolf. As a result, this largest of the canine family has been shot, poisoned, and trapped to the point of extinction. Because the wolf preferred domestic livestock as its main food, farmers felt justified in trying to eliminate this able predator. In its wild habitat the wolf eats mainly rodents and rabbits or even insects and berries. When wolves attack herds of deer, elk, pronghorns, or other animals they make a wild dash to panic their prey. When an animal falters or falls behind, the wolves move in for the kill. As Walter P. Webb points out, "The wolf's impudence, cunning, and cautious opportunism which induced him to prey on those in misfortune led the tactless Greeley to denominate him the prairie lawyer." In recent years the wolf has had many defenders, who claim that it performs a service by reducing the herds of wild animals by removing the unfit.

The coyote, a cousin to the wolf, is found throughout the West. Horace Greeley described this animal as "a sneaking, cowardly little wretch." It lives on insects, rodents, prairie dogs, jackrabbits, and the helpless young of all animals. Its appetite for lambs and calves is enormous. Coyotes have shown tremendous ability to adapt to a changing environment, and efforts to eliminate these cunning predators by trapping and poison have been futile. In fact, in recent years coyotes have invaded urban areas, carrying off pets and attacking children—in one instance killing a child.

The bighorn or mountain sheep originally roamed from Canada south into Mexico. Bighorns were not only found in the mountains, but were equally at home in the foothills and on the plains. In some areas the sheep migrated seasonally from the mountains to winter in the lowlands. The animals on the plains were eliminated by human beings early in the twentieth century. These sheep were frequently victims of infectious diseases and parasites carried by domestic livestock introduced by Euro-Americans. In recent years efforts have been made to reintroduce them into ranges where they were once numerous. The horns of the adult ram are one of the most sought after big game prizes in the American West. Today, in most parts of the West, bighorns are an endangered species.

Despite its goatlike appearance and name, the Rocky Mountain goat is not really a goat but an antelope related to the Alpine chamois. This surefooted animal probably migrated from Asia over the Bering land bridge. Today it is found in Washington, Oregon, Idaho, and Montana, as well as in Canada and Alaska. Small numbers have also been successfully introduced into Nevada, Utah, Colorado, Wyoming, and South Dakota. This agile animal is able to survive because it inherited an area not coveted by human beings. In the lofty mountain peaks that they inhabit, these handsome two to three hundred pound goats have few predators. Snowslides and landslides are their greatest enemies.

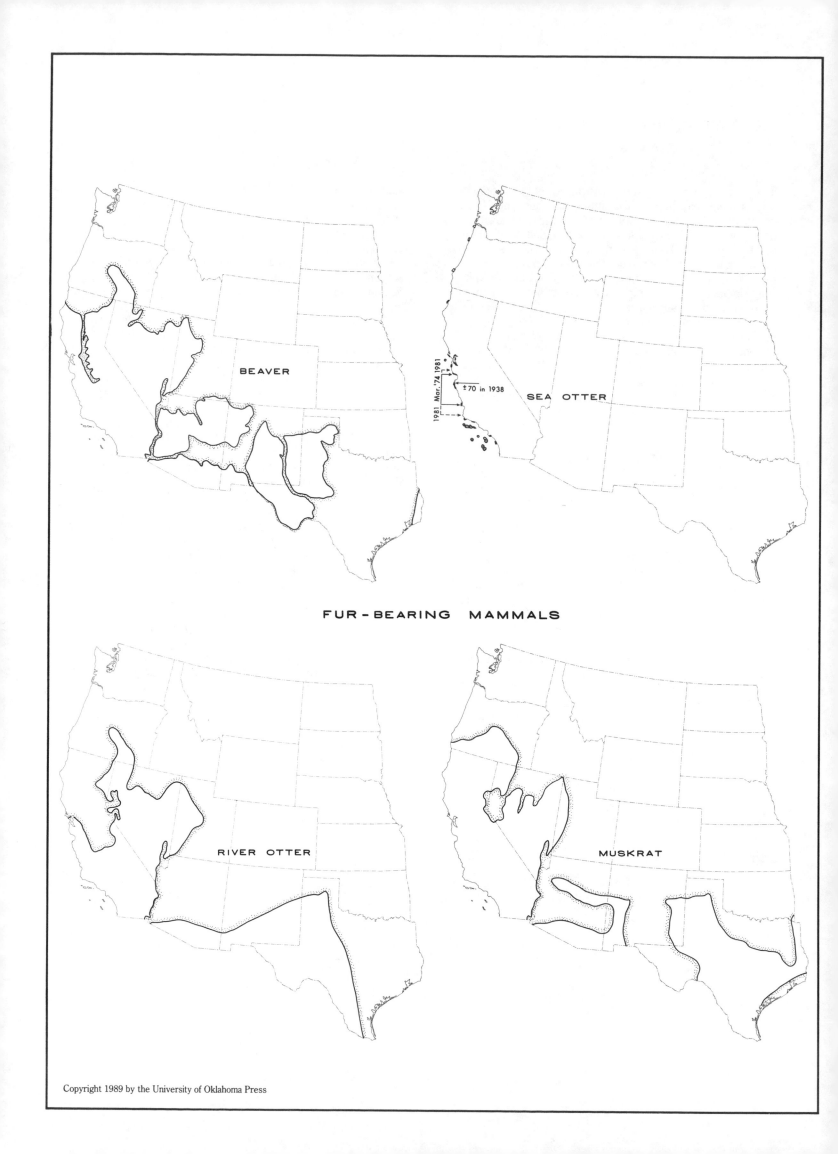

BEAVER

SEA OTTER

1981 Mar. '74 1981

±70 in 1938

FUR-BEARING MAMMALS

RIVER OTTER

MUSKRAT

13. FUR-BEARING MAMMALS

THE BEAVER (*Castor canadensis*) has influenced American history, and especially that of the West, more than any other wild animal, for with the exception of human beings, the beaver is the only species that can significantly alter its environment. Beavers were found anywhere in the United States and Canada where there was sufficient water to enable them to live in ponds or to dam streams so they could escape predators. In the American West they were absent only in the most arid regions, as indicated on the map. Beavers were sought by trappers because of their thick, lustrous fur, which was used for hats, coats, and robes. Hunters roamed every corner of the West in their efforts to find virgin beaver territory. As a result, this largest of the North American rodents,—some weighing sixty-five pounds—became almost extinct.

The sea otter (*Enhydra lutris*) is another of the remarkable animals to figure prominently in the history of the American West. Sea otters can attain five feet in length and weigh up to eighty-five pounds. They are found only in the North Pacific as far south as Baja California. They live exclusively in shallow salt waters, usually on rocky, open coastline but seldom on inside passages. They only infrequently leave the water, and they subsist on a diet of crabs, clams, mussels, abalones, and other shellfish. Intelligent, curious, and friendly creatures, they were prized for their extremely thick and dense fur. In fact, their fur is the most beautiful of any marine animal's. One hunter claimed that "there are only two objects in the world which could rival the sea otter in appearance—a beautiful lady and a lovely infant." Otter pelts were especially prized in China, where well-dressed ladies wore otter capes. In the late eighteenth century, Russians and Americans eagerly sought sea otter pelts, which could bring up to $100 apiece in Oriental markets. As a result, the animals were soon almost extinct, but as the map indicates, their numbers are slowly increasing along the California Coast.

The river otter (*Lutra canadensis*), also a member of the weasel family, attains a maximum weight of twenty-five pounds. Highly intelligent animals, river otters can be taught to retrieve like dogs. One observer describes the river otter as the "acknowledged playboy of the mammal world." Unlike other animals that have to struggle to survive, otters play for hours until hunger prompts them to seek fish, frogs, crayfish, turtles, snakes, birds, or eggs. They are found in the American West wherever there is enough water for their food. As the map illustrates, they are only absent from the arid regions.

The muskrat (*Ondatra zibethicus*) is another semi-aquatic mammal found throughout the West except in the most arid lands. It must have enough stream water to burrow into the bank or enough swamp or lake water so that it can build a reed or mud mound with an underwater opening. Its food consists mainly of aquatic plants or fish. Because of their availability, beauty, and durability, muskrat pelts have, since colonial times, been a staple of the fur industry. In fact, some thirteen million pelts were harvested in one year recently, and despite their small size, three pounds, they are the most valuable fur on the American market in most years. In some regions muskrat flesh is sold as food.

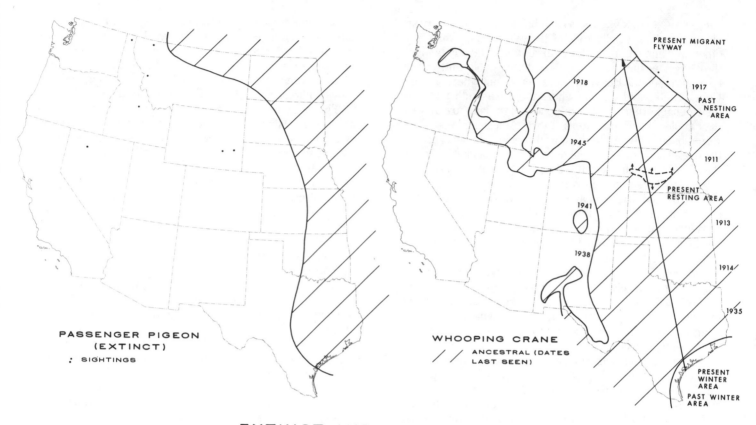

PASSENGER PIGEON
(EXTINCT)

: SIGHTINGS

WHOOPING CRANE

// ANCESTRAL (DATES
   LAST SEEN)

PRESENT MIGRANT
FLYWAY

1918

1945

1941

1938

1917

PAST
NESTING
AREA

1911

PRESENT
RESTING AREA

1913

1914

1935

PRESENT
WINTER
AREA

PAST WINTER
AREA

EXTINCT AND RARE BIRDS

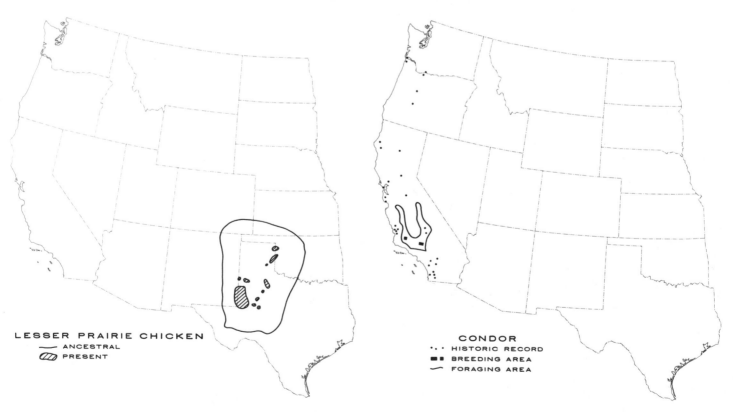

LESSER PRAIRIE CHICKEN
— ANCESTRAL
▱ PRESENT

CONDOR
· · · HISTORIC RECORD
■ ■ BREEDING AREA
— FORAGING AREA

14. EXTINCT AND RARE BIRDS

BIRDS PLAYED A LESSER ROLE on the frontier, and especially in the American West, than did mammals. In a land of large game, the hunting of birds, except for pheasants, turkeys, geese, ducks, and prairie chickens, was neglected. One exception was the passenger pigeon, which was so numerous in early colonial days that a flock would darken the sky. So many would alight on the branches of apple trees that the limbs would snap from the weight. This pigeon was considered to be the food of the poor because so many could be obtained with ease. It is reported that twelve hundred could be netted at a time. The passenger pigeon was shot so easily that up to the middle of the nineteenth century it was not considered a game bird. However, the expansion of the railroads made it possible to profitably market the birds, and by the 1860s single individuals were commonly killing twelve hundred birds a day; one man even claimed to have shot this total before breakfast.

The passenger pigeon abounded from the Atlantic coast to the middle plains, but a few were sighted farther west. With hunters killing such large numbers in the 1870s, these pigeons' days were numbered despite efforts to save them. The last one in the wild state was killed in 1899. President Theodore Roosevelt wrote of the loss: "The destruction of the wild pigeon . . . has meant a loss as severe as if the Catskills or the Palisades were taken away. When I hear of the destruction of a species I feel just as if all the works of some great writer had perished; as if we had lost all, instead of only part, of Polybius or Livy." To many people today the extinction of the passenger pigeon is not of great importance. However, it can be hoped that the words of conservationist Aldo Leopold represent the views of most Americans today: "For one species to mourn the death of another is a new thing under the sun. We, who have lost our pigeons, mourn the loss. Had the funeral been ours, pigeons would hardly have mourned us. In this fact, rather than in nylons or atomic bombs lies evidence of our superiority over the beasts."

The whooping crane has very nearly gone the way of the passenger pigeon. Near extinction but a generation ago, it has been saved through the concerted efforts of a few conservationists, and its numbers have slowly grown both in captivity and in its habitat. The whooping crane is the tallest and most imposing of North American birds. An adult male is five feet tall, has a wingspread of seven and one-half feet, and may weigh twenty-five pounds. Whooping cranes once were common in the American West in the areas noted on the map. The basic problem has been that their natural breeding grounds have been sloughs or the reed areas along the edges of the lakes. Their wintering area has been along the Gulf Coast. Human beings have destroyed this environment besides shooting the cranes for food or "sport." Fortunately, these remarkable birds are protected today, and it is possible that they can make a comeback.

The lesser prairie chicken is slightly smaller than the greater prairie chicken found throughout the Great Plains. Its range was formerly from the Arkansas River in southeastern Colorado eastward to south central Kansas and southward through northeastern Oklahoma, the Texas Panhandle, and eastern New Mexico. It was probably never present in large numbers even in its ancestral home, and with the dwindling of the open prairie it has become even rarer. In the past, lesser prairie chickens were desirable game birds and were overhunted. Today, game management has been able to increase their population.

The California condor is another of the world's rarest birds, with about twenty-eight known to exist. It is black with white wing linings and a yellow head. It weighs about twenty pounds and has a wingspread of nine feet. It feeds on meat, and one reason for its decline in numbers is that human beings have reduced its foraging area. Condors were first sighted in California by members of the Vizcaino expedition in 1602 and then by the Serra-Portola party in 1769. The Lewis and Clark expedition found them on the lower Columbia River in 1805. However, as the map illustrates, they were largely confined to the California coast and the foothills of the Sierra Nevada. Today, it is believed that all condors are in captivity. In fact, in April, 1988, a condor chick was hatched in captivity for the first time.

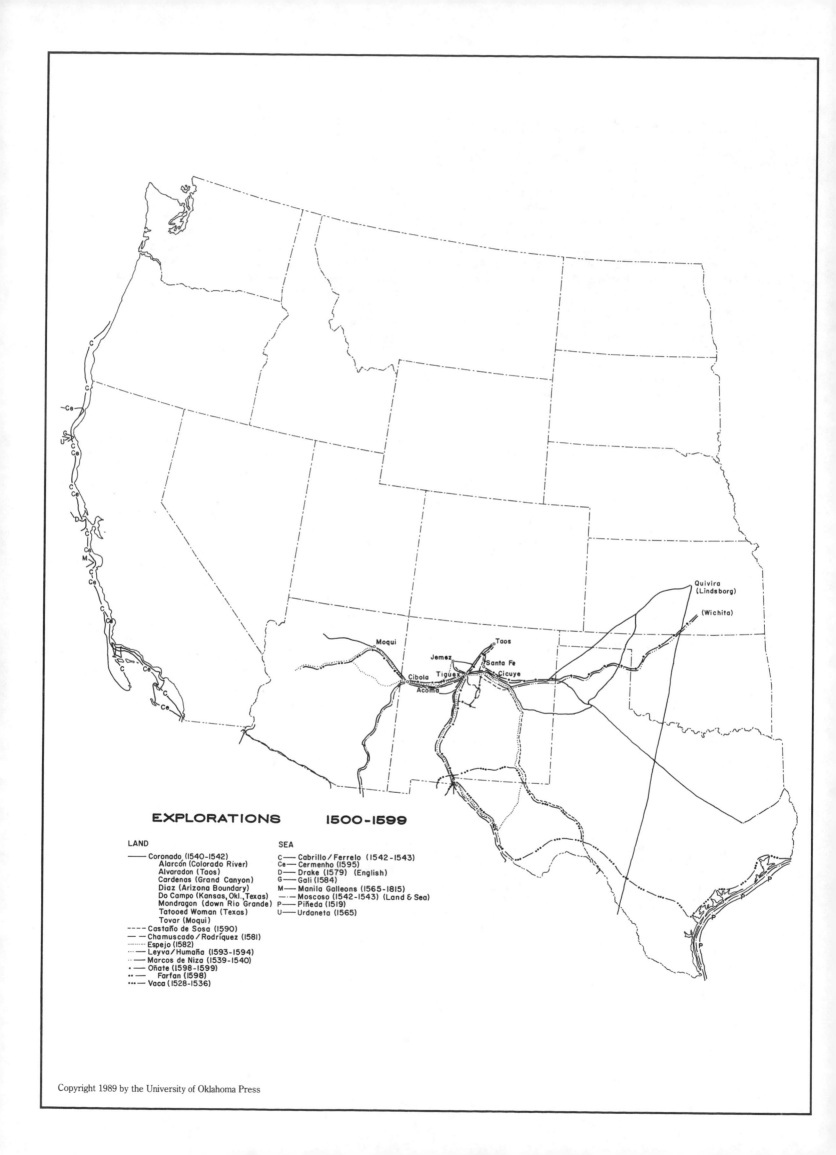

EXPLORATIONS   1500-1599

LAND

—— Coronado (1540-1542)
     Alarcón (Colorado River)
     Alvaradon (Taos)
     Cardenas (Grand Canyon)
     Diaz (Arizona Boundary)
     Do Campo (Kansas, Okl., Texas)
     Mondragon (down Rio Grande)
     Tatooed Woman (Texas)
     Tovar (Moqui)
- - - Castaño de Sosa (1590)
— — Chamuscado / Rodríquez (1581)
········· Espejo (1582)
—·— Leyva / Humaña (1593-1594)
—— Marcos de Niza (1539-1540)
·—· Oñate (1598-1599)
··—·· Farfan (1598)
···— Vaca (1528-1536)

SEA

C —— Cabrillo / Ferrelo (1542-1543)
Ce —— Cermenho (1595)
D —— Drake (1579) (English)
G —— Gali (1584)
M —— Manila Galleons (1565-1815)
—·— Moscoso (1542-1543) (Land & Sea)
P —— Piñeda (1519)
U —— Urdaneta (1565)

Moqui   Taos   Quivira (Lindsborg)   (Wichita)
Jemez   Santa Fe
Cibola   Tiguex   Cicuye
Acoma

15. EXPLORATIONS, 1500–1599

THE INITIAL EUROPEAN EXPLORATIONS along the southern fringe of what is today the American West were dictated by the Spanish experience in Mexico. The fabulous treasure found in the Aztec Empire fueled the explorers' imaginations; they dreamed that similar riches could be found elsewhere. Fantastic stories of wealth circulated throughout all Spanish America. The wilder the tale, the easier it was to believe. One enduring myth was of the seven cities of Cibola. This legend, originating about 1150, was a tale of seven bishops and their congregations who fled from the Moors. They were reputed to have sailed westward and to have founded seven cities which became fabulously wealthy. When Spanish explorers asked the Indians about their location, native Americans hastened to oblige, perhaps in the hope that these strange invaders would move on.

Cabeza de Vaca, a member of a Spanish expedition to explore Florida, spent eight years trying to return home after being shipwrecked on the Texas coast. Upon his return to Mexico in 1536, he brought tales of wealthy Indian cities. Fray Marcos de Niza was sent northward in 1539–40 on an exploratory trek into Arizona and New Mexico. The positive reports of the good father led to the most extensive expeditions of the century—the group led by Francisco Vásquez de Coronado, who went as far as central Kansas, and whose lieutenants in addition roamed over most of the Southwest. Coronado found numerous reports of gold-rich Indian cities, but all proved false.

Coronado's expedition was basically a business enterprise, and the investors who financed the venture expected to profit from the gold of Cibola. The failure of the explorers to return with precious metals consequently discouraged other financial supporters, so land exploration was curtailed after Coronado's effort. However, in the following decades the Mexican frontier slowly moved northward. Missions, mines, farms, and stock ranches were the basic institutions of expansion. In 1548 the rich silver mines opened at Zacatecas. Others followed in quick succession; Guanajuato, San Luis Potosí, and Durango brought wealth. More important, they excited the interest of others in finding silver that would enrich them.

In 1579 a captive Indian from the northern frontier told exciting tales of the wealth to be found along the Rio Grande, whereupon Spanish officials, who paid at least lip service to the necessity of advancing settlements in order to Christianize the natives, gave permission to Fray Agustín Rodríguez for a missionary reconnaissance. On his trip to the New Mexico pueblos in 1581 he was accompanied by Captain Francisco Sánchez Chamuscado. Upon their return to Mexico, they left behind three friars who were subsequently killed by the Indians. One Antonio de Espejo financed an expedition to rescue the three, but after learning of their deaths his group explored for mineral wealth before returning along the Pecos River.

Reports of precious metals led to renewed interest in the settling of New Mexico, and in 1590 Gaspar Castaño de Sosa led a colony into the region by way of the Pecos but was forced to turn back, as he lacked proper permission. In 1593–94 another unauthorized quest for New Mexico's mineral riches was launched by Francisco Leyva de Bonilla and Antonio Gutiérrez de Humaña. Although this group may have reached eastern Kansas, they were killed in internal quarrels or in conflicts with the Indians. The contract to settle the Rio Grande region and exploit the reportedly profitable mines there went to Juan de Oñate, who accomplished the task in 1598 and explored extensively.

Explorations by sea were usually taking place concurrently with the land expeditions. In 1519 Alonso Álvarez Piñeda coasted the Gulf of Mexico from Florida to Vera Cruz, discovering the mouth of the Mississippi. His was also the first European group to visit Texas. After Hernando de Soto died, Luis de Moscoso took over his command and crossed Arkansas, entering Texas perhaps as far as the Brazos River. The group then retraced their steps on land and built boats to descend the Mississippi and skirt the Texas coast, reaching Pánuco in 1543.

Most of the Spanish sea explorations were in the Pacific Ocean and resulted from an effort to find mineral wealth, to discover a passage through North America to Europe (the legendary Northwest Passage), and to find a port of call for the Manilla Galleon. Juan Rodríguez Cabrillo and his lieutenant, Bartolomé Ferrelo, coasted California from San Diego to Oregon in 1542–43. The quest for a port of call for the Manilla Galleon was led by Andrés de Urdaneta in 1565, Francisco Gali in 1584, and Sebastian Rodríguez Cermenho in 1595. Spanish sea exploration was intensified as the result of Sir Francis Drake's visit to California in 1579. After raiding the Spanish treasure fleet off Peru, the English captain paused to refurbish his ships in California near San Francisco Bay.

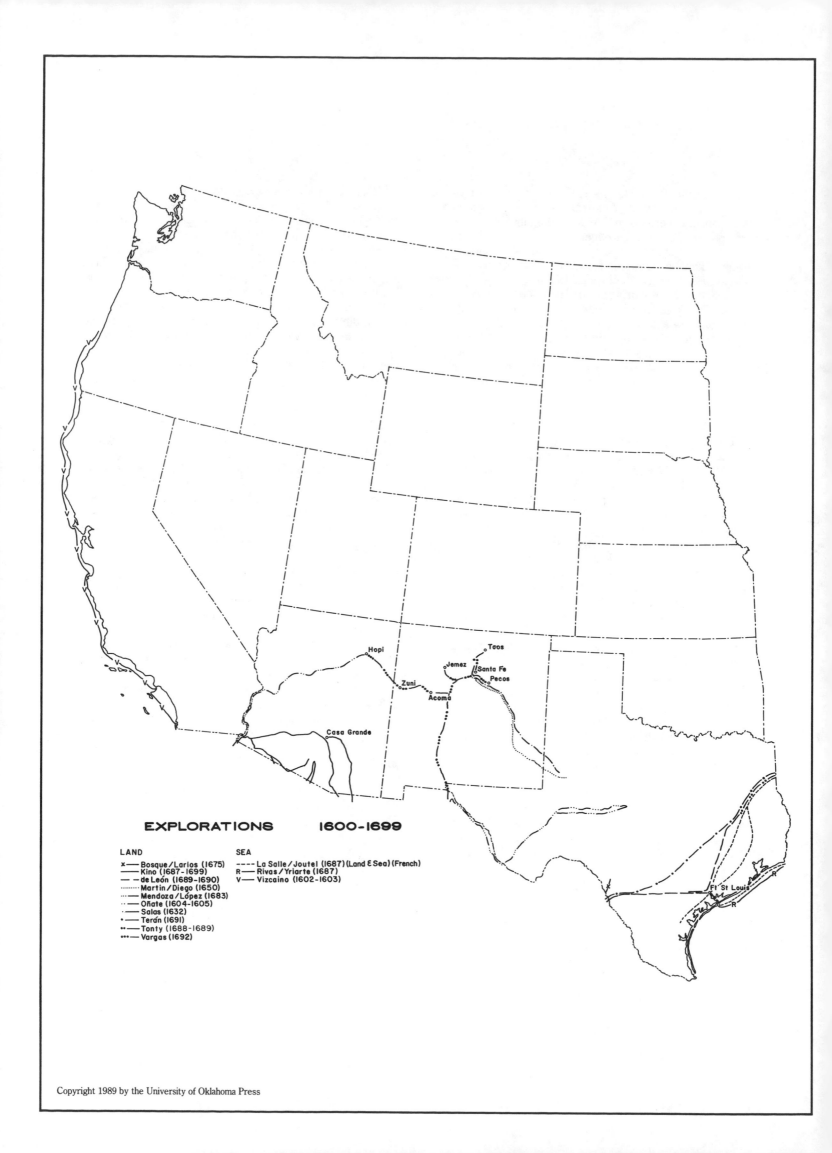

EXPLORATIONS   1600-1699

LAND

x——— Bosque/Larios (1675)
——— Kino (1687-1699)
——— de León (1689-1690)
·········· Martín/Diego (1650)
·—·—·— Mendoza/López (1683)
·—·—·— Oñate (1604-1605)
·—·—·— Salas (1632)
•——— Terán (1691)
••——— Tonty (1688-1689)
•••——— Vargas (1692)

SEA

·——— La Salle/Joutel (1687) (Land & Sea) (French)
R——— Rivas/Yriarte (1687)
V—— Vizcaíno (1602-1603)

Hopi
Zuni
Acoma
Jemez
Taos
Santa Fe
Pecos
Casa Grande
Ft St Louis

16. EXPLORATIONS, 1600–1699

THE PURPOSE OF SPANISH EXPLORATIONS continued to be the quest for precious metals. In addition, information about the terrain was sought, and missionaries were constantly looking for new mission fields. After initially exploring the upper reaches of the Rio Grande, Juan de Oñate led a force in the winter of 1604–1605 across Arizona to the head of the Gulf of California. His report helped convince the Spanish that this new land was poor in all respects.

In 1632 Father Juan de Salas, who had previously visited the eastern plains of present-day New Mexico, crossed the Llano Estacado to visit the Jumanos. This tribe had requested a missionary and told of having first been converted by a mysterious man. Eighteen years later Captains Hernando Martín and Diego del Castillo followed a similar route also to visit the Jumanos, and they returned with a few pearls, which aroused interest in further trade.

Father Juan Larios has been called "the founder of Coahuila." After establishing missions in that Mexican province on the Texas frontier, in 1675 he and Fernando del Bosque crossed the Rio Grande. Nothing came of their recommendations at the time, as resources were not then available, but their expedition prepared the way for future Texas missions.

The Spanish situation in the Southwest was dramatically changed by the revolt of the Pueblo Indians in 1680. All of the Spaniards were forced to flee from the upper Rio Grande region and retreat to what is today El Paso. From this base in 1683 Juan Domínguez de Mendoza and Fray Nicolás López led another exploratory venture to visit the Jumanos. These Indians had apparently requested missionaries several times and continued to have trade relations with the Spanish. In fact, this expedition brought five thousand buffalo robes back. But, owing to the tumult in New Mexico and fear of the French in eastern Texas, no further action was taken. The New Mexico situation was resolved in 1692 when Diego de Vargas was able to subdue the rebellious Pueblo Indians and reassert Spanish authority.

Spain also faced a serious threat in Texas as the French began exploring in that area. Moving into Texas was France's greatest explorer, Robert Cavelier, Sieur de la Salle, who had already explored the Ohio and Mississippi valleys. Returning from France, La Salle's party missed the mouth of the Mississippi and instead established a settlement at Fort Saint Louis in Texas. In 1687, while exploring, La Salle was murdered, and the remnants of his party were led by Henri Joutel. Henri de Tonty, another French explorer, came down the Mississippi from Illinois searching for La Salle and followed the explorer's footsteps through eastern Texas in 1688 and 1689.

While the French were exploring eastern Texas and trading with the Indians, Spanish officials tried to keep informed about their activities. The first exploration by sea was the Rivas/Yriarte expedition, which left Vera Cruz on December 25, 1686. This group carefully explored the Gulf Coast as far as Mobile and in Texas discovered the wreckage of the *Belle,* La Salle's ill-fated vessel. In 1688, on orders from Madrid, Alonso de León, governor of Coahuila, led an expedition across southern Texas to find the abandoned French fort of Saint Louis. In 1690, de León helped establish Spanish missions in eastern Texas. However, the Indians proved hostile, and the Spanish abandoned Texas for a time.

During the seventeenth century, New Mexico was the center of Spanish exploration. However, Jesuit missionaries had advanced up the West Coast corridor, thrusting the Hispanic frontier ever northward. Perhaps the most remarkable of these Jesuits was Father Eusebio Francisco Kino, who personally founded twenty-nine missions and led more than fifty overland expeditions. Kino explored Arizona and laid the foundation for the ultimate settlement of the area.

The most important sea exploration of the century was led by Sebastián Vizcaíno in 1602–1603. A successful merchant in the Manilla trade, this explorer hoped to find riches in pearls along the California coast. This expedition mapped the coast and gave most of the place names in use today. They went as far north as 42° north latitude but missed San Francisco Bay, as had all earlier voyagers.

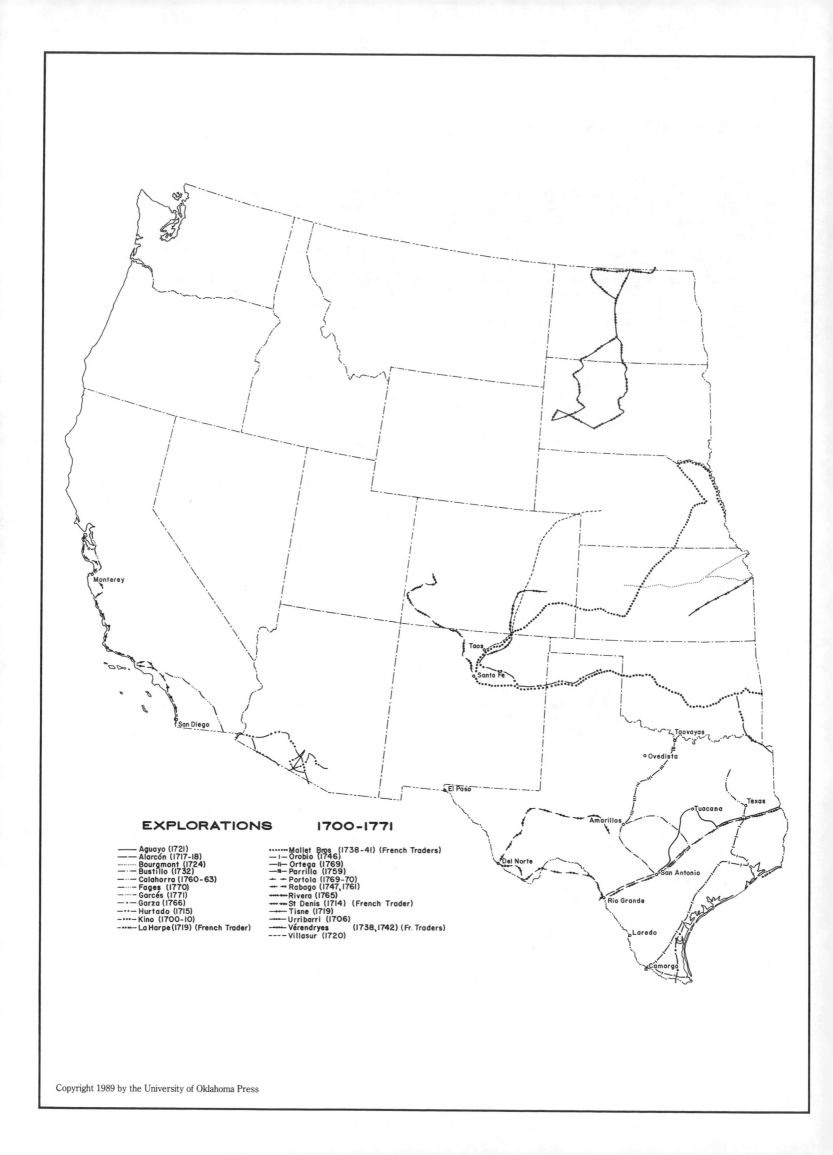

EXPLORATIONS   1700-1771

——— Aguayo (1721)
— — Alarcón (1717-18)
·········· Bourgmont (1724)
—·—·— Bustillo (1732)
—··—··— Calahorra (1760-63)
·····:···· Fages (1770)
—·—·— Garcés (1771)
—·—·— Garza (1766)
— — — Hurtado (1715)
···•···•··· Kino (1700-10)
—··—··— La Harpe (1719) (French Trader)

•••••••• Mallet Bros (1738-41) (French Traders)
—I— Orobio (1746)
—II— Ortega (1769)
—■— Parrilla (1759)
—+— Portola (1769-70)
—••—••— Rabago (1747,1761)
•••••••• Rivera (1765)
—•••—•••— St Denis (1714) (French Trader)
—•—•— Tisne (1719)
——— Urribarri (1706)
•—••—••— Vérendryes   (1738,1742) (Fr. Traders)
— — — — Villasur (1720)

Monterey
San Diego
El Paso
Taos
Santa Fe
Taovayas
○ Ovedista
○ Tuacana
Texas
Amarillos
Del Norte
San Antonio
Rio Grande
Laredo
Camargo

17. EXPLORATIONS, 1700–1771

IN THE EIGHTEENTH CENTURY, Santa Fe was no longer the center of Spanish exploratory efforts. Spanish officials did send a few ventures forth from New Mexico, but their overland probing was concerned mainly with the settlement of Texas and California and the growing threat from other nations.

Juan de Urribarri was sent from Santa Fe in 1706 to ransom Christian Indian captives from the plains tribes. He crossed the Arkansas River near the present site of Pueblo, Colorado, and turned eastward toward the Kansas border. In 1715 Juan Páez Hurtado was sent eastward into the Texas Panhandle in pursuit of raiding Apaches. Although this officer left a careful record of his travels, he had little luck in his efforts to chastize the natives. The Spanish continued to search for precious metals, and in 1765 Juan María Rivera went into southwestern Colorado to the junction of the Uncompahgre River with the Gunnison.

In Texas, Spanish exploration was usually a reaction to the growing French threat. Between 1699 and 1703, three missions and a presidio were established at San Juan Bautista, below modern Eagle Pass and opposite today's Rio Grande City. This was the first step in an effort to occupy Texas and keep the French out. Louis Juchereau de St. Denis was the most able of the French traders, and in 1714 he made his way across Texas to San Juan Bautista, ostensibly to trade, but instead he was arrested. Prison in Mexico City was followed by a stint in the Spanish service, after which he returned to the French. The Spanish reacted by sending out Martín de Alarcón to establish San Antonio and inspect possible mission sites. In 1719 a French trader from Illinois, Charles Claude du Tisne, moved into the Osage country of eastern Kansas. In the same year there was further French encroachment when Bénard de la Harpe surveyed potential trading post locations in eastern Oklahoma. When Pedro de Villasur was sent from Santa Fe in 1720 to warn the French away, most of his force was slain in an encounter with the Indians on the South Platte. In 1721 the Marqués de Aguayo was sent from Coahuila with a large force across Texas to strengthen Spanish control of the area.

The French continued to be a threat to the Spanish, however, because of their superior ability in trading with the Indians. Étienne Veniard, Sieur de Bourgmont, took his extensive experience in dealing with Indians in the Old Northwest to establish trade with the Indians in eastern Kansas in 1724. Further north, the French were also exploring. With extensive experience in the Great Lakes and Mississippi Valley areas for years, Pierre Gaultier de Varennes, Sieur de La Vérendrye, came down from Canada to visit a Mandan village near present-day Bismarck, North Dakota. In addition to trade, La Vérendrye sought a water route that would carry him to the Pacific Ocean. The French explorer left a detailed account of his route and of the Indians. Age kept him from continuing his travels, so he sent his two sons, Louis Joseph and François, who in 1742 followed his route and then explored farther into South Dakota, possibly as far as the Black Hills. The French shocked Spanish officials when the brothers Pierre and Paul Mallet came from Illinois to trade with Santa Fe. They left for New Orleans by way of the Canadian and Arkansas rivers.

Meanwhile, fear of the French and hostile Indians prompted the Spanish to continue to explore Texas. In 1732 the Texas governor, Juan de Bustillo y Zevallos, led a punitive raid against the Apaches from San Antonio by way of the San Saba River. In 1746, Joaquín de Orobio Bazterra moved from Coahuila along the Texas coast. He found no French, but he did find ample evidence that they had traded with the natives. In 1748 and 1761, Pedro de Rábago y Terán explored into Apache country. Colonel Diego Ortiz Parrilla in 1758–59 led a force across Texas to a village of the Taovayas on the Red River. Father José de Calahorra y Sáenz made a number of journeys from 1760 to 1763 on the upper Sabine River and was successful in keeping the Indians at peace. In 1766 the Spanish governor sent a party under José de la Garza to inspect the lower Texas Coast.

On the West Coast the Spanish profited from the continued explorations of Father Eusebio Kino in Arizona to prepare the colonization of California. Gaspar de Portola led a party north from San Diego to the San Francisco Bay area in 1769. A detachment from his larger group, under José Francisco Ortega, found the San Francisco Bay. Pedro Fages successfully scouted the region around the bay in 1770. Fray Francisco Garcés recognized that the successful settlement of California was dependent upon an overland route, and he charted one in 1772.

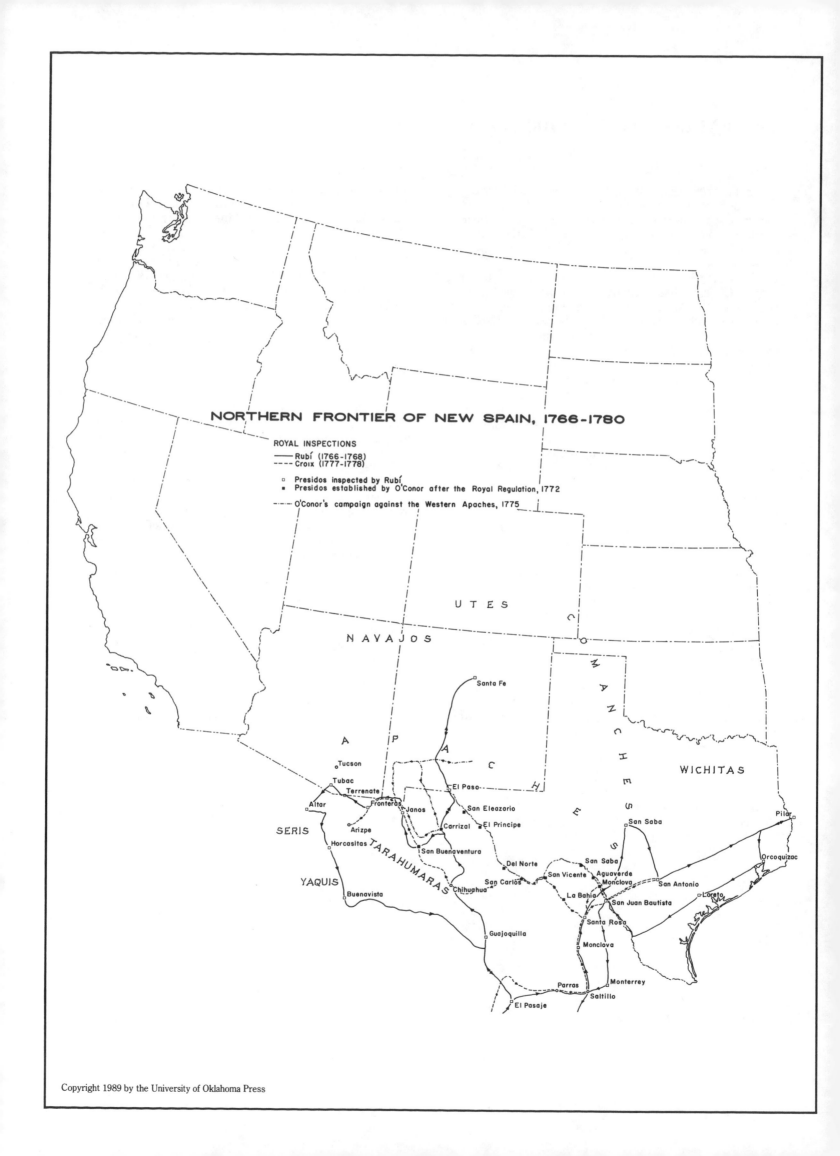

NORTHERN FRONTIER OF NEW SPAIN, 1766-1780

ROYAL INSPECTIONS
——— Rubí (1766-1768)
- - - - Croix (1777-1778)

□ Presidos inspected by Rubí
■ Presidos established by O'Conor after the Royal Regulation, 1772

—·—·— O'Conor's campaign against the Western Apaches, 1775

UTES

NAVAJOS

SERIS

YAQUIS

TARAHUMARAS

APACHES

COMANCHES

WICHITAS

Santa Fe

Tucson
Tubac
Terrenate
Altar   Fronteras
Arizpe   Janos
Horcasitas
San Buenaventura
Buenavista
Chihuahua
Guajoquilla

El Paso
San Eleazario
Carrizal   El Principe
Del Norte
San Carlos   San Vicente
              La Bahía
El Pasaje   Santa Rosa
              Monclova
Parras   Monterrey
    Saltillo

San Saba
San Saba
Aguaverde
Monclova   San Antonio
San Juan Bautista   Loreto

Pilar
Orcoquizac

18. NORTHERN FRONTIER OF NEW SPAIN, 1766–1780

IN 1763 THE TREATY OF PARIS eliminated the French threat to Spain in America; that threat was replaced by fear of the English. In 1759, Charles III became king of Spain, and once peace came to Europe he instituted a large number of reforms in his American colonies. The purpose of these changes was to strengthen the defense of Spanish America, to reduce administrative costs, and to improve mineral production. Inevitably, the reformist impulse reached the trouble-plagued northern frontier of New Spain, where Indian attacks had closed many mines and the cost of military defense soared.

Spain's problems in the area flowed from a continued dependence on the mission and presidio, institutions that had worked well in the past but did not fit the changing situation. The purpose of the mission was not only to Christianize the natives but also to Hispanicize them so they could be good, tax-paying citizens. The nomadic Plains Indians, mainly the Apaches and the Comanches, refused to settle down to the discipline of mission life. There was so much game available that they did not need the security the mission offered. Then too, the horse had so altered their life-style that they were not willing to become sedentary farmers.

The presidio was a fortress with walls at least ten feet high and two hundred to eight hundred feet in length. When first built, the presidio could withstand a siege, but the forts were not well maintained, and the troops who garrisoned them were usually poorly trained and ill equipped to fight the mounted Plains Indians. In fact, Spanish soldiers feared to leave the safety of the presidio.

In 1765 the first step in the overhaul of the defenses of the northern frontier was taken; the Marqués de Rubí was appointed to make an inspection of the military organization and the state of defenses on the northern frontiers and make recommendations for their improvement. Rubí set out on his tour on March 10, 1766, to review the presidios, their administration, the fitness of officers and men, and the state of their finances. He went first to Santa Fe by way of El Pasaje, Chihuahua, and El Paso. After a brief stay in the New Mexico capital, he retraced his steps through El Paso to San Buenaventura to Janos and on to Tubac. From that point Rubí went south to Buenavista and then east across the mountains and on into Texas to Pilar, where he turned back. In his two-year journey Rubí learned much about the northern Spanish frontier, and in his final report he recommended the closing of many presidios, the relocation of others, and the building of several new ones. Furthermore, he urged that more men be assigned to garrison these frontier outposts.

Most of Rubí's recommendations were put into effect in the Royal Regulations of 1772. One of the regulations was that an inspector-general of the frontier be appointed, and the first appointment went to Hugo O'Conor, whose task was to build the new presidios and relocate the others. However, O'Conor had to begin with an immediate effort to pacify the Apaches. In carrying out his difficult duties, he traveled over ten thousand miles, but he never reached California.

Further changes came to New Spain's northern frontier in 1776, when the area was removed from the administrative authority of the viceroy and was made a separate political unit. The first comandante-general of the new area was Teodoro de Croix, who had held several posts in New Spain. He pushed north vigorously in 1777, holding a number of councils of war on how best to deal with the Apache threat. Croix gathered much information from these councils and planned to strip the Apaches of their Indian allies. At Chihuahua in June and July, 1778, most of the key frontier figures of the day were present at one of these meetings. Much was accomplished, and the Indian threat was lessened for a time, but Spain's involvement in the American Revolution meant Croix would receive no more soldiers. Then in 1781 the Yuma uprising, which closed the land route to California, set back his policy. In 1783, Croix was promoted to be viceroy of Peru, so he was not on hand when relative peace came to the northern frontier.

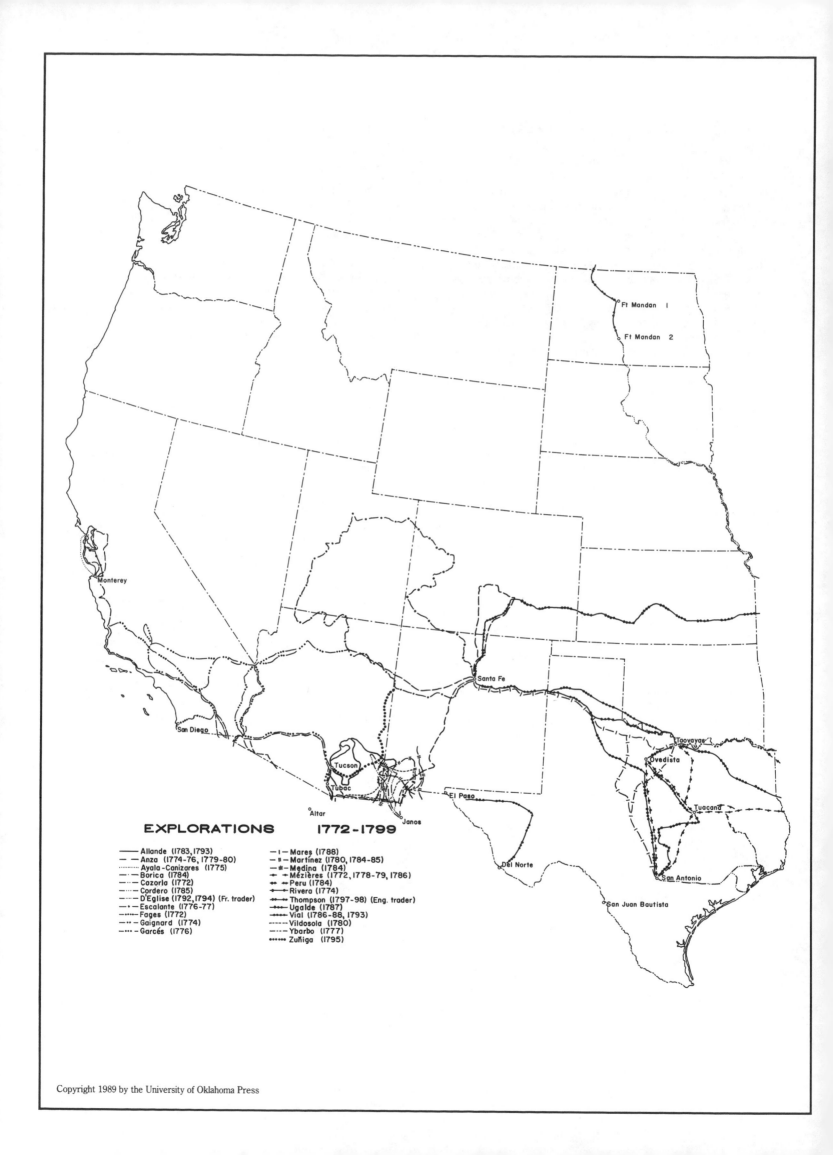

EXPLORATIONS   1772-1799

——— Allande (1783, 1793)
— — Anza (1774-76, 1779-80)
·········· Ayala-Canizares (1775)
—·—·— Borica (1784)
—··—··— Cozorla (1772)
—···—···— Cordero (1785)
—·—·—· D'Eglise (1792, 1794) (Fr. trader)
—·—·— Escalante (1776-77)
·········· Fages (1772)
—··—··— Gaignard (1774)
—···—···— Garcés (1776)

—ı—ı— Mares (1788)
—ıı—ıı— Martínez (1780, 1784-85)
—ııı—ııı— Medina (1784)
—•—•— Mézières (1772, 1778-79, 1786)
—••—••— Peru (1784)
—•—•—• Rivera (1774)
—•—•—• Thompson (1797-98) (Eng. trader)
—•••—•••— Ugalde (1787)
—•••••—•••••— Vial (1786-88, 1793)
————— Vildosola (1780)
—·—·—· Ybarbo (1777)
•••••• Zuñiga (1795)

Ft Mandan 1

Ft Mandan 2

Monterey

Santa Fe

San Diego

Tucson

Tubac

°Altar

Janos

El Paso

Del Norte

San Juan Bautista

Toovayas

Ovedista

Tuacano

San Antonio

19. EXPLORATIONS, 1772–1799

THE EXPEDITIONS TO EXPLORE the American West grew in number in the closing decades of the eighteenth century. Several military forays went into southwestern New Mexico and adjacent Arizona in an effort to control the growing Indian threat. Similar ones were launched in various directions from Santa Fe for the same purposes. Many took place in an effort to link both the Texas and California settlements with New Mexico. There was also some exploration for trading with the Indians.

One of the key figures in the attempt to connect New Mexico with Sonora was Juan Bautista de Anza. In 1774 he had led a California colony overland; in 1777 he became governor of New Mexico; and in 1779–80 he had led an expedition into north central Arizona and then northward into Colorado. He understood the Indian threat on the southern flank, and in 1780 he had explored extensively in southwestern New Mexico and nearby Arizona, searching for the best land route to Sonora. He was assisted by separate detachments commanded by Captains José Antonio Vildosola and Francisco Martínez. Much was learned of the area in 1780, but the hostility of the Apaches limited the effort. Explorations were continued in 1784 led by Roque de Medina, Diego de Borica, Antonio Cordero, Juan Bautista de Anza, and also by Francisco Martínez. Pedro de Allande proceeded northward to a rendezvous with the other forces in 1784 and in 1793 made a more thorough investigation northward and eastward. However, it was not until 1795 that José de Zúñiga charted the route from Tucson to the New Mexico pueblo of Zuñi.

The road from Santa Fe to California proved even more difficult for the Spanish. Pedro Fages in 1772 had blazed an inland trail through California, and de Anza and Garcés had charted a trail overland through Yuma only to see it closed by an Indian uprising in 1781. Fray Silvestre Vélez de Escalante in 1776 attempted to find a northern route which would connect Santa Fe with Monterey, California. Going northwestward across Colorado into central Utah, the party turned back without success but did return with knowledge of the Great Basin. In 1775, Manual de Ayala and José Canizares completed an extensive nautical survey of San Francisco Bay.

The English had replaced the French as the major threat to the Spanish in Texas, and in 1772 Luis Cazorla was sent with a party from San Antonio to the Gulf Coast to investigate their presence. He found only evidence that English guns had been traded to the Indians. The Indians continued to be a problem, and in the fall of 1773 a trader named J. Gaignard was sent from Natchitoches up the Red River to make peace with the Comanches. Although the Indians were hostile, a treaty was signed in early 1774. Gil Ybarbo in 1777 made a reconnaissance of the Gulf Coast between the Trinity and Neches rivers and reported an English vessel that had been grounded and abandoned.

Athanase de Mézières, a Frenchman in the service of Spain, made numerous explorations in central Texas in 1772, 1778–79, and 1786. Another Frenchman who transferred his allegiance to Spain after the cession of Louisiana in 1763 was Pedro Vial. He was commissioned in 1786 by the governor of Texas to find a direct route from San Antonio to Santa Fe. After reaching New Mexico, Vial was sent east to lay out a route to Natchitoches. In 1793 this able Frenchman traveled from Saint Louis to Santa Fe along the trail later made famous. As Vial's initial route between San Antonio and Santa Fe was not direct, José Mares was selected in 1788 to improve upon it, and perhaps did in a small way. Meanwhile, the Apaches were a constant threat to the Spanish frontier and had even raided far into New Spain. To punish them, Juan de Ugalde, an old warrior, was sent into their territory. In 1787 he mounted a successful offensive in the Big Bend country of the Rio Grande.

Explorations were also going on far from Texas. Jacques d'Eglise, who explored along the Missouri River, went up that stream in 1792 and 1794 into the Mandan country. This made him the first Spanish subject in the area, and he reported that the Indians he traded with told of English contacts.

In 1797–98, David Thompson, the famed English explorer who was just beginning his career, came into the Mandan country from the north.

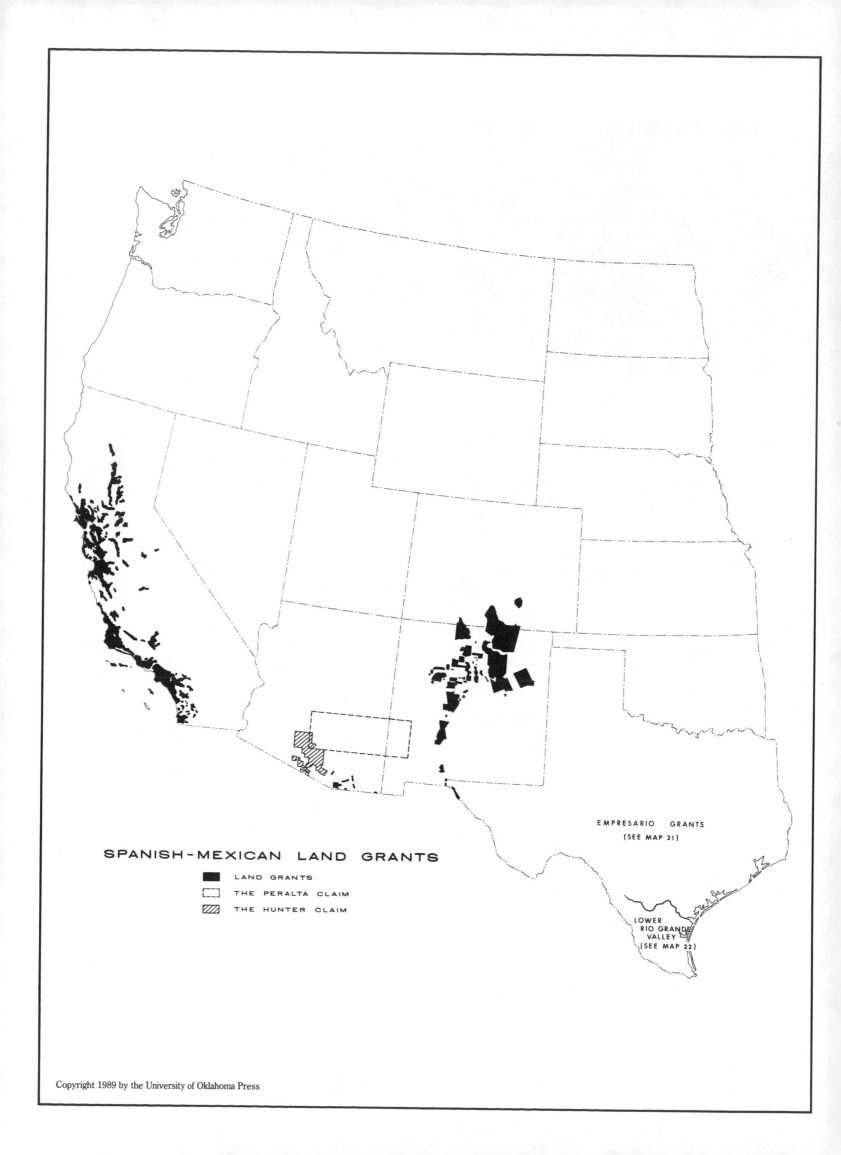

SPANISH-MEXICAN LAND GRANTS

◼ LAND GRANTS

▢ THE PERALTA CLAIM

▨ THE HUNTER CLAIM

EMPRESARIO   GRANTS
(SEE MAP 21)

LOWER
RIO GRANDE
VALLEY
(SEE MAP 22)

20. SPANISH-MEXICAN LAND GRANTS

THE GRANTING OF LAND in the southwestern states of Texas, New Mexico, Colorado, Arizona, and California has seen a major influence on the history of those states down to the present. Under both Spain and Mexico, land was granted to individuals or groups for government services or in lieu of money owed. The granting of land was controlled by a code of laws not unlike the homestead laws of the United States. The grantee was required to describe the land he desired in his initial petition. Before the title was made final, the grantee was required to erect a permanent building or fence or otherwise mark boundaries of the land and have the local magistrate define boundaries by the act of juridical possession, the closest thing to an actual survey. Unfortunately, this measurement was often not carried out, or if it was, documentation to prove it was not filed with the proper authorities. In many cases the records were destroyed, making proof of ownership difficult.

These circumstances made speculation and fraud in land grants the region's largest "industry" once the Americans took over. One original grant in New Mexico was for 32 acres and "pasture enough for small stock and horse herd," but it was surveyed for 104,554 acres. One authority estimates that 80 percent of the old Spanish and newer Mexican grants in New Mexico went to American lawyers and settlers. It was claimed that in Texas the words "lands" and "fraud" were almost synonymous. Today it is impossible to accurately gauge the amount of land claimed by illegal means, but the figure is undoubtedly enormous. Neither is it possible to estimate the number of claims taken from the innocent by ruthless lawyers and speculators without intervention by the territorial governors.

There were a few large land claims in the southwest which were such complete swindles that they were denied title. One of these was that of José Y. Limantour in California. A French citizen who had been a merchant in Monterey, this wily operator had two of his claims initially upheld by the land commissioners. These lands included large portions of San Francisco and the surrounding area. Businessmen and settlers began paying rent to and buying quitclaim deeds from Limantour. However, government officials were convinced that "the most stupendous fraud ever perpetrated in the history of the world" was being attempted. Investigation revealed that the paper used in the claims was manufactured at a later date than that on the documents. In addition, the seal used was a counterfeit, and examination of the Mexican archives revealed that there was no record of the supposed grants.

Arizona contained two of the largest land claims that disrupted titles and made settlement difficult for many years. The first of these was the Hunter claim to some 2,600,000 acres, or about 4,071 square miles, in the Papago Indian country west of Tucson. Robert Finley Hunter, an Ohio graduate of West Point, was cashiered from the army in November, 1861, for drunkenness, and he led a checkered career until 1880, when he filed the claim. At the time, he was a Washington, D.C., attorney for the Bureau of Catholic Indian Missions to protest an application for a mining patent in southern Arizona. He advised the leaders of the sixteen Papago villages to protect their land by filing as a Spanish and Mexican land grant. Hunter's fee would be one-half the land. The General Land Office rejected the claim, and it went to the courts for years; the U.S. Supreme Court finally dismissed the case in 1927. Hunter had died in 1912, but Robert Martin, his partner, pursued the case.

The most famous, or rather the most infamous, land swindle attempted in the American West was the Peralta claim, embracing some seventeen thousand square miles mainly in Arizona but extending into New Mexico. James Addison Reavis, a Missourian who trained as a con man working in a Saint Louis land office, specialized in "creating" Spanish land grants and also forging checks. He created a Spanish nobleman who was supposed to have received an eighteenth-century grant from the crown, and he even inserted forged documents into the Mexican and Spanish archives. After marrying a Mexican orphan, he created a role for her as the descendant of Miguel Peralta de Córdoba. Reavis's claim was so persuasive that settlers, mine owners, and even the Southern Pacific Railroad paid tribute to the "Baron of Arizona." Investigation ultimately revealed that the ink and paper used in the documents were of recent manufacture and that the Spanish language used was not that of the eighteenth century. Reavis went to jail for fraud.

EMPRESARIO GRANTS, 1833

DOMINGUEZ

PADILLA & CHAMBERS

WILSON & EXETER

CAMERON

TRES ALAMOS
(1831)

CAMERON

FILISOLA

AUSTIN & WILLIAMS

BURNET

WOODBURY & CO

ZAVALA

S.F. AUSTIN

VEHLEIN

DE WITT

AUSTIN

McMULLEN & McGLOIN

LEON

POWERS

21. EMPRESARIO GRANTS, 1833

SPAIN, AND ITS SUCCESSOR MEXICO, had a basic problem in dealing with frontier Texas: the non-Indian population of that vast land was sparse, perhaps 3,500 in 1821, and there was little likelihood it would increase, given the Indian menace and the region's remoteness from Mexico. Empresario grants were the Mexican government's attempt to solve this problem. The empresario was simply a contractor who acted as land agent for the Mexican government. For settling a specified number of families he would receive a certain amount of land. In addition, the incoming colonists had to pay him for surveying and other services. In practice, the empresario acted as intermediary between the settler and the Mexican government, and in effect he was the political leader of the community.

The first empresario grant in Texas was made to Moses Austin of Missouri, but it passed to his son, Stephen F. Austin, when Moses died in 1821. The younger Austin apparently had the ability to win the friendship of Mexican officials as well as the respect of the American frontiersmen who came to take up land in Texas. Each family of farmers could purchase 177 acres at prices much lower than public lands opened for settlement in the United States, while those in ranching could buy 4,428 acres. In ten years (1825–35) Austin located more than fifteen hundred families and received three additional grants.

Once the tide of immigration began in 1825, other contracts were made, but many of the empresarios were unsuccessful in bringing in settlers. Others had moderate success, but none of their attempts could compare to the accomplishments of Austin. Green De Witt, also of Missouri, received a grant south of Austin's in 1825. However, his grant overlapped that of Martín de León, who had obvious advantages as a Mexican citizen. De Witt brought in 166 families, but their land titles were in jeopardy in the quarrel with de León until 1831. Lorenzo de Zavala, David G. Burnet, and Joseph Vehlein in 1826 secured the rights to settle colonists near the eastern border of Texas. Their rights were later acquired by the Galveston Bay and Texas Land Company. James Powers in 1828 was given a contract to bring in Irish families but had boundary difficulties with the de León grant and health problems on the coast. Most of his two hundred settlers were Americans.

John McMullen and James McGloin founded an Irish colony south of and isolated from the Anglo-American settlements. They were only able to attract eighty-four families. Mexican General Vicente Filisola contracted in 1831 to settle six hundred families, but like most of the empresarios, he was unsuccessful. John Cameron obtained two large grants in 1827 and 1828 but had little success.

In 1831 the Tres Alamos empresario grant in Arizona, near present-day Tucson, consisted of 251,604 acres (393 square miles). An Apache uprising prevented the occupation of the land. In 1852 one José Antonio Crespe, a Spaniard residing in Guaymas, received a grant to settle one hundred or more Catholic families from South America or Spain. The Gadsden Purchase in 1853 stopped the surveying or settlement of this land, and American land speculators bought the rights to the grant, which was rejected by the Court of Private Land Claims in 1893.

The Wilson-Exeter grant was another interesting empresario contract that was never consummated. In 1826 a North Carolinian, Stephen Julian Wilson, who was a partner in a Mexico City mercantile firm, filed for and was granted land as follows:

> Beginning at the point of intersection of the 32nd degree of north latitude and the 102nd meridian, thence west on the 32nd parallel to the eastern boundary of New Mexico (not otherwise defined), thence north along that boundary to a point 20 leagues south of the Arkansas River, thence east along a line parallel to and 20 leagues south of the Arkansas River to the 102nd meridian, thence south to the point of commencement.

A few months later a half-interest was sold to British merchant Richard Exeter, who died in 1829. A survey of the tract was arranged, but there is no evidence it was carried out. Neither was the stipulation that two hundred families had to settle on the land within six years. The Exeter widow married a British physician, Dr. John Charles Beales, who actively promoted the grant until his death in 1878. The heirs continued efforts to obtain confirmation through friends in the U.S. Congress or in the American courts until 1902.

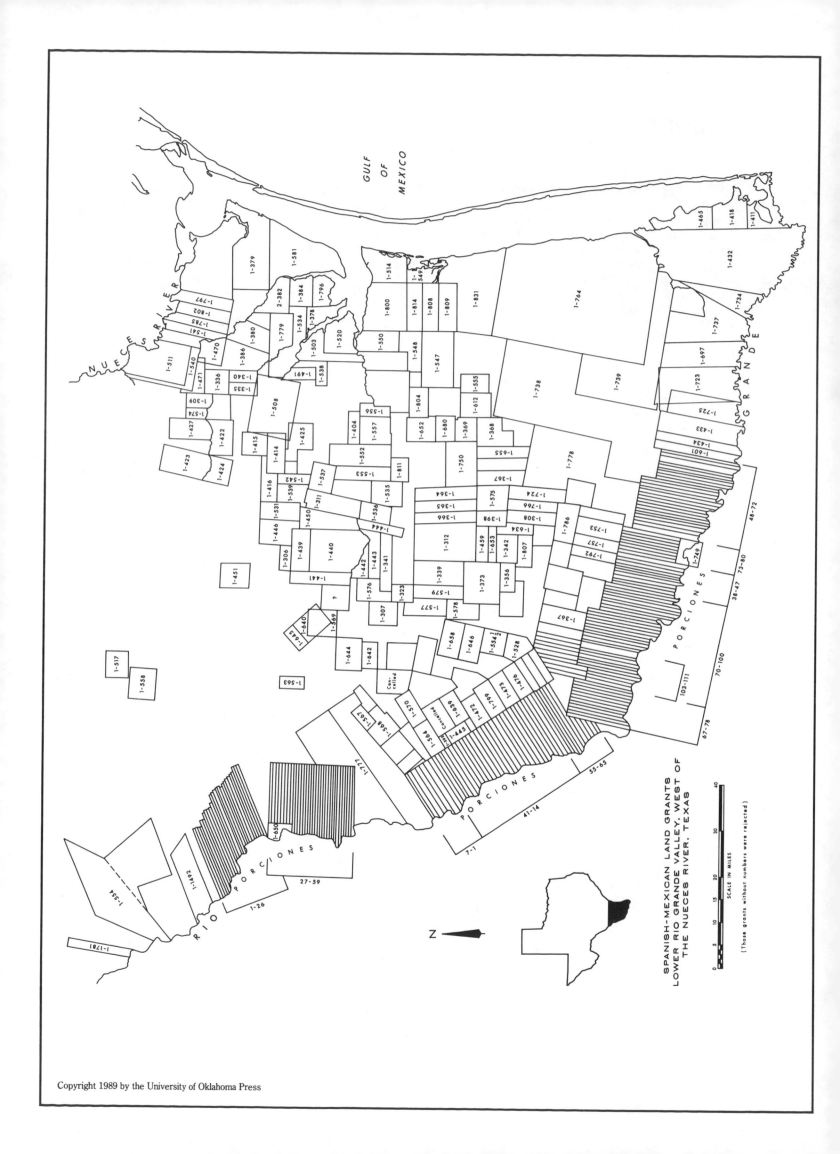

SPANISH-MEXICAN LAND GRANTS
LOWER RIO GRANDE VALLEY, WEST OF
THE NUECES RIVER, TEXAS

SCALE IN MILES

(Those grants without numbers were rejected)

22. SPANISH-MEXICAN LAND GRANTS, LOWER RIO GRANDE VALLEY, WEST OF THE NUECES RIVER, TEXAS

THE LAND GRANTS located between the Nueces River and the Rio Grande were in a different category from those in the rest of Texas. The first congress of the Republic of Texas laid claim to all territory to the Rio Grande, but possession did not come until the Treaty of Guadalupe Hidalgo in 1848. The area in dispute was a part of the Mexican state of Tamaulipas, where officials issued grants until the end of the Mexican War. Once Texas took possession of this area, a major responsibility was to prove the validity of Spanish and Mexican land claims. A commission was appointed to examine titles in Mexican archives, if they were available, and if not, to obtain oral evidence upon which claims could be accepted or rejected. Through the years legislation was enacted to enable Mexican and Spanish grantees to prove title to their land. It was a slow process, with the latest court approval of a grant coming in 1944.

The *porciones*,[1] or "portions," was a special kind of land grant along the banks of the Rio Grande. Some 300 were laid out, with about 170 ultimately titled by Spanish authorities. They had an average area of about 6,400 acres and were laid out "so that a watering place at the river be given to everyone, otherwise the cattle will certainly perish and the *porciones* of land become useless." The surveyors were instructed to begin their survey at the river and extend the land to a depth that would form "a prolonged quadrangle." No river frontage could be less than one thousand varas wide (a vara was about 33⅓ inches). Ultimately, the *porciones* covered all the land along the lower Rio Grande in this area.

The *porciones* were devised by the able Spanish leader Colonel José de Escandón, who laid out towns along the Rio Grande between 1748 and 1755. The area settled was away from the fever-plagued coast but was also intended to establish a bulwark against the hostile Indians of the region, which it did. Escandón was easily the most successful Spanish colonizer of eighteenth-century Texas.

Among the more notable of these huge grants was San Juan de Carricitos (General Land Office no. 1-764), made to José Narciso Cabazos. At 601,657 acres, it was the largest. Juan José Balli received 315,341 acres in his El Sal del Rey (no. 1-738). The rancho Espiritu Santo (no. 1-432) of José Salvador Garza embraced 284,418 acres (no. 1-432). The grant "Padre Island" to Nicholas Balli and his nephew, Juan José Balli, was made by Mexico in 1829. Although it was only 50,925.80 acres, it is unusual in that it was finally confirmed by the Texas Supreme Court in 1944. It has no land office file number.)

These vast landholdings were to be the spawning grounds of the West's cattle raising industry. The grassy savannahs north of the Rio Grande were seldom raided by the Apaches and Comanches, because game was scarce in the area. Neither did the buffalo come that far south. So the cattle grew by natural increase, and the Hispanic settlers slowly evolved many of the techniques of ranching that ultimately spread throughout the American West.

[1] A listing of the *porciones* is found in the Appendix.

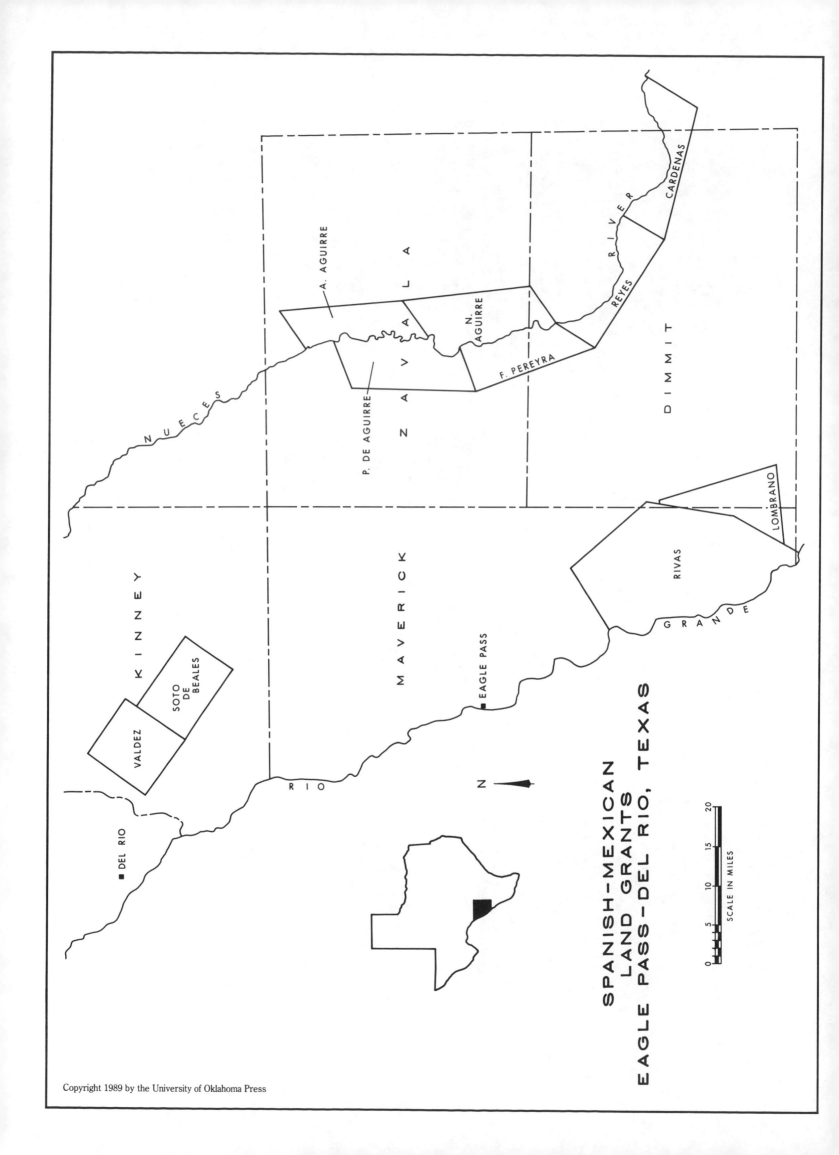

A. AGUIRRE

Z A V A L A

N. AGUIRRE

P. DE AGUIRRE

F. PEREYRA

REYES RIVER

CARDENAS

D I M M I T

N U E C E S

K I N N E Y

SOTO DE BEALES

VALDEZ

■ DEL RIO

M A V E R I C K

■ EAGLE PASS

R I O

RIVAS

LOMBRANO

GRANDE

N

SPANISH-MEXICAN
LAND GRANTS
EAGLE PASS-DEL RIO, TEXAS

20

15

10

5

0

SCALE IN MILES

23. SPANISH–MEXICAN LAND GRANTS, EAGLE PASS–DEL RIO, TEXAS

THE AVAILABILITY OF INEXPENSIVE LAND was a magnet that drew ever more settlers into Texas. Land grants made in Texas by Spain and Mexico up to 1835 amounted to 26,280,000 acres. Between 1764 and 1800 most of the present Lower Rio Grande Valley was parceled out to individuals either as *porciones* or in larger tracts. In fact, all of the desirable land of the lower delta on the north side of the Rio Grande was claimed and deeds were given for the land in the years from 1777 to 1808. The result was that those still in quest of land began to seek it farther inland, especially during the period of the Republic of Mexico from 1828 to 1836.

The area of present-day Maverick County was traversed by more Spanish explorers and settlers than any other part of Texas in the early days. The Old San Antonio Road passed just below Eagle Pass and San Juan Bautista, the first mission in the area. Thus, the region was well known, and a narrow strip along the river could be easily cultivated and was most productive in mission days. However, rough hills limited the productive area, and much of the land was suited only for grazing. Even then, the inland areas were subject to periodic drought. In the area of present-day Val Verde County (Del Rio is the county seat), the land was covered with semiarid grasses and thorny shrubs. To this day sheep and goats have been the chief source of income there.

In the area of Dimmit County land grants were made in 1834, as this region was also traversed by the Old San Antonio Road. All of the grants made along the Nueces River failed, despite the excellent grasslands that supported large herds of cattle after 1865. In addition to the problems of drought, Indians, often from Mexico, raided this region. Not until 1878 was the threat of the settlers ended so they could safely live in these counties.

In making grants in these outlying areas, the entire Spanish approach to distributing land to its citizens was brought into play. In arid regions land was classified either as (1) *de riego* or *de regadío*, arable land permanently irrigable or with facilities for irrigation; as (2) *de temporal*, arable land dependent upon rainfall for moisture, literally dry-land farming; or as (3) *de agostadero* or *de abrevadero*, land suitable for grazing only. The right to irrigate was usually granted separately, but many grantees on the frontier proceeded to irrigate illegally, knowing that it would be a long time before their actions were discovered.

The size of the grant naturally reflected the use intended for it. A league of land was 4,428.4 acres, and in theory, at least, the maximum grant was eleven leagues. A *sitio de ganado mayor* was 4,338 acres; a *sitio de ganado menor* was 1,928 acres. These grants were normally made for grazing purposes. A labor of land was 177.1 acres, a *caballería* was 105 acres, and a *suerte* was a garden plot of 26 acres; these last three types of grants were intended for farming.

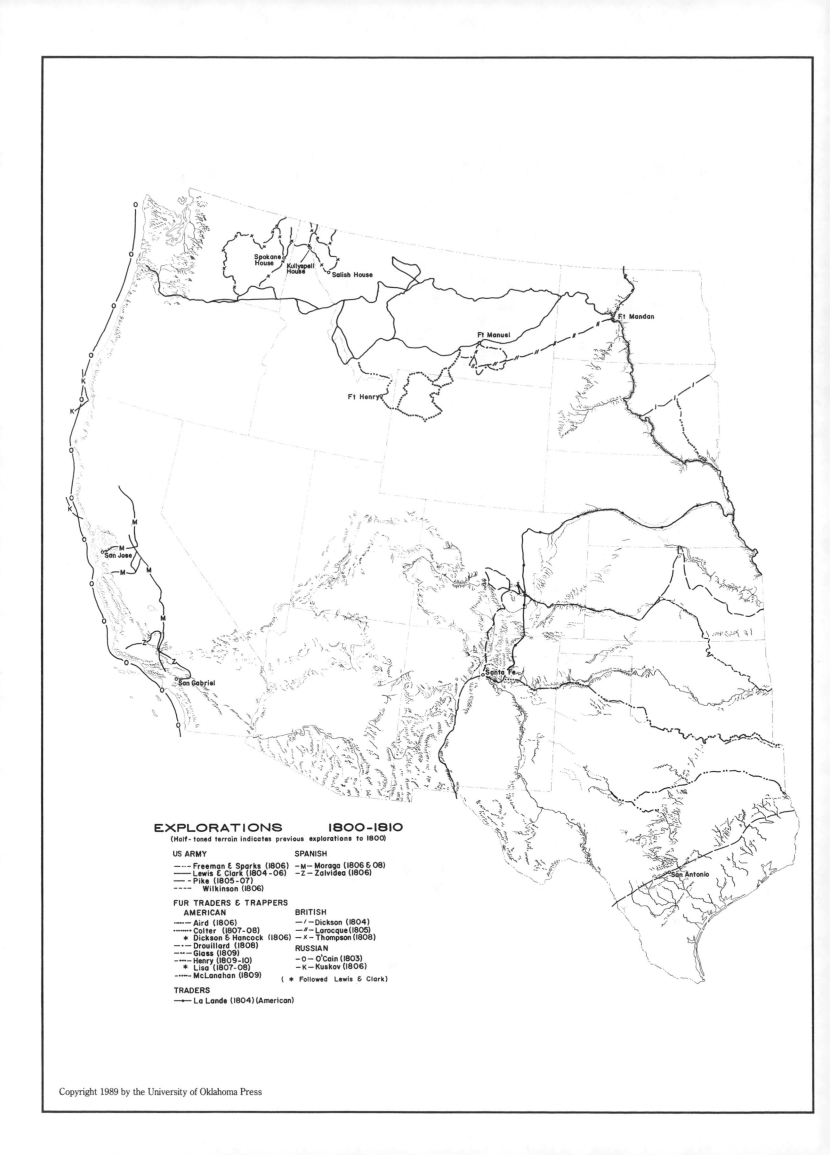

EXPLORATIONS 1800-1810
(Half-toned terrain indicates previous explorations to 1800)

US ARMY
- ----- Freeman & Sparks (1806)
- ——— Lewis & Clark (1804-06)
- —-— Pike (1805-07)
- ----- Wilkinson (1806)

FUR TRADERS & TRAPPERS

AMERICAN
- ---·-- Aird (1806)
- ········· Colter (1807-08)
- ✳ Dickson & Hancock (1806)
- ---·--- Drouillard (1808)
- ---·--- Glass (1809)
- ----- Henry (1809-10)
- ✳ Lisa (1807-08)
- ----- McLanahan (1809)

SPANISH
- —M— Moraga (1806 & 08)
- —Z— Zalvidea (1806)

BRITISH
- —/— Dickson (1804)
- —//— Larocque (1805)
- —x— Thompson (1808)

RUSSIAN
- —O— O'Cain (1803)
- —K— Kuskov (1806)

(✳ Followed Lewis & Clark)

TRADERS
- —•— La Lande (1804) (American)

24. EXPLORATIONS, 1800–1810

BY 1800 THE SPANISH had roamed over the American Southwest and the French had made a tentative entry into Texas, the central plains, and the Missouri Valley. The Anglo-Americans, on the other hand, knew little about this vast area; President Jefferson was certainly speaking the truth when he told Congress that the West was "not as well known as is desirable." This situation changed soon after the Louisiana Purchase of 1803.

Meriwether Lewis, Jefferson's secretary, and Lieutenant William Clark led the reconnaissance into the vast territory recently acquired. On May 14, 1804, the expedition started up the Missouri River, and for two years, four months, and ten days the explorers were on their own. In the autumn they prudently made winter camp among the Mandan Indians in North Dakota. One stroke of good luck during the idle months was the addition to the group of a French-Canadian whose wife, Sacajawea, was to be indispensable as an interpreter. On April 7, 1805, the party again headed west. Finally, on November 7, 1805, they reached the Pacific Ocean. After wintering on the Columbia River, they headed homeward on March 23, 1806. On their return journey the leaders separated so they could reconnoiter fresh territory. Lewis explored the Marias River, while Clark and the main group went down the Yellowstone River to its meeting with the Missouri. From that point the two parties joined for the return to Saint Louis.

The explorers did not find the stream that would carry them easily to the Pacific Ocean, but they brought back much information about the flora and fauna and the terrain of the territory they had traversed, as well as much knowledge about the Indians. Their report excited the imagination of others, making them eager to see this strange and wonderful land. More importantly, their description of the abundance of beaver and other fur-bearing animals was the stimulus to start many fur trappers westward.

Washington officials also sought to learn more about the Southwest, partially because there was some doubt about whether it was included in the Louisiana Purchase. In 1806 the army sent Captain Richard Sparks, with Thomas Freeman as surveyor, up the Red River some 635 miles until the presence of a Spanish force compelled them to retreat. Far more important were the explorations of Lt. Zebulon M. Pike. Starting in the summer of 1806, Pike went up the Missouri into Kansas and then up the Osage River and southward and then westward until he reached the Arkansas River in eastern Colorado. At that point he sent Lt. N. G. Wilkinson with four men down the Arkansas. Pike continued on, discovering the peak in the Rockies that bears his name. While traveling south along the Rio Grande, he was captured by a Spanish force, which escorted his group into Mexico, from whence they returned across Texas. Pike's writings about his travels excited great interest in fur trappings and in trade with Santa Fe.

In 1809, Joseph McLanahan led a group of traders up the Red River and across the plains to Santa Fe, where they were promptly jailed. In 1806, Jean Baptiste la Lande was supplied with trade goods by a Kaskaskia merchant and was able to sell them in Santa Fe despite the Spanish prohibition of such trade. And in 1809 a party led by Anthony Glass traded with Indians as far west as present-day Big Spring, Texas.

On their return trip Lewis and Clark met Joseph Dickson and Forest Hancock, who were headed up the Missouri to trap beaver. The two men were able to entice John Colter away from the main expedition. In 1807–1808 Colter made a remarkable journey alone through Wyoming, Montana, and Idaho in search of beaver. Colter was employed by Manuel Lisa, who was one of the first to grasp the opportunity in fur trapping. Lisa established Fort Manuel at the mouth of the Big Horn River, and his partner, Andrew Henry, set up Fort Henry at the Three Forks of the Missouri. Earlier, George Drouillard, a victim of the Blackfeet in 1810, had explored and mapped some of the area.

British explorers, mainly interested in the fur trade, were also active in the American West from 1800 to 1810. By the end of 1805 Antoine Larocque had explored the valley of the Yellowstone River on one of many trips south from Canada into North Dakota. The most famous of the British explorers was David Thompson, who traveled extensively in the Rocky Mountains near the Canadian border from 1807 to 1810. Traversing the states of Washington, Idaho, and Montana, he established a number of trading posts and brought many of the Indians under British influence.

In California the Spanish continued to explore the interior to learn more about the natives and to seek possible mission sites. Father José María de Zalvidea left Santa Barbara on July 19, 1806, and moved northward before turning eastward and crossing the mountains into the Great Central Valley. He probably went around the north side of Buena Vista Lake. The group then went south through the Tehachapi Pass and reached San Gabriel on August 14.

Gabriel Moraga left San Juan Bautista on September 21, 1806, and divided his party into two groups after crossing the San Joaquin River. After traveling a short distance north, the group turned south and, skirting the Sierra Nevada, reached Tejon Pass on November 1. In 1808, Moraga again explored the valley. After leaving San José on September 25, his party went south as far as the Merced River before turning northward.

Russian explorations along the California coast resulted from that nation's interest in the fur trade, and especially in sea otter. Joseph O'Cain, an American partner, sailed along the coast in 1803 using Aleut Indians to poach in Spanish territory. In 1806, Ivan Aleksandrovich Kuskov visited the coast to seek furs, to trade for food, and also to search for a possible site for a trading post.

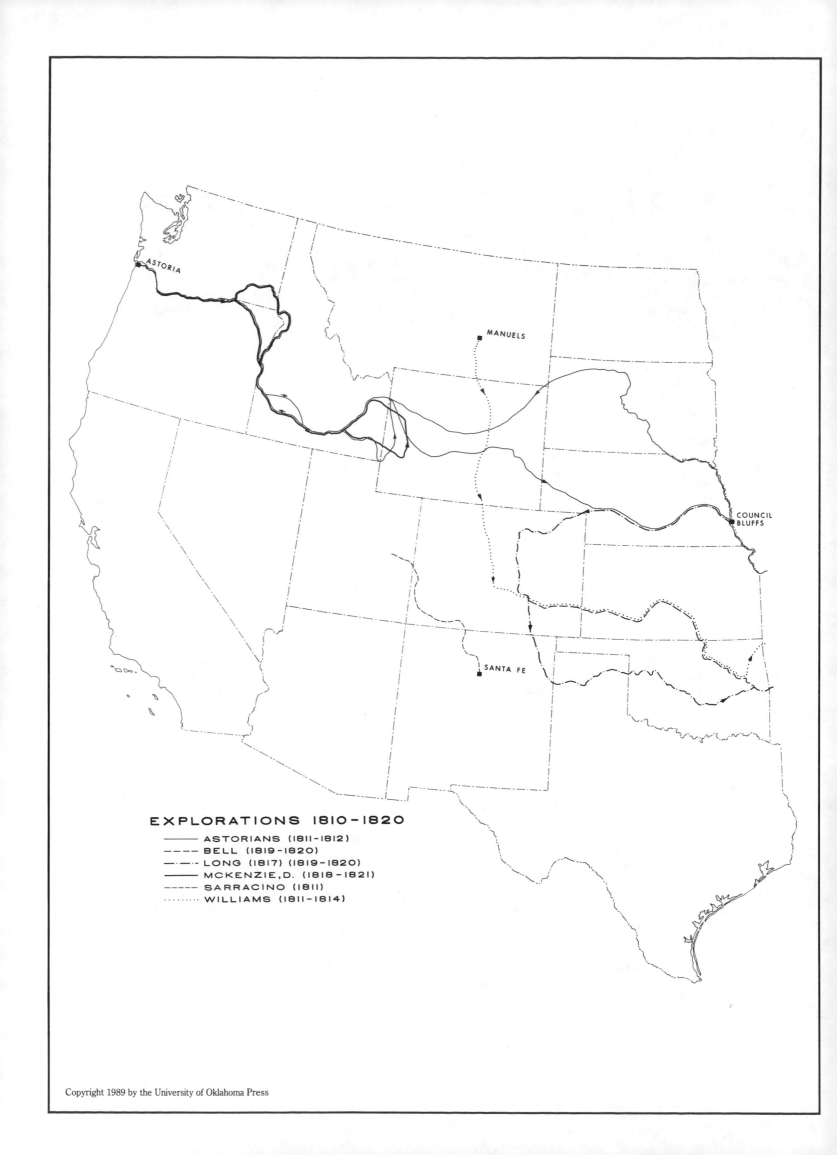

ASTORIA

MANUELS

COUNCIL
BLUFFS

SANTA FE

EXPLORATIONS 1810-1820

———— ASTORIANS (1811-1812)
- - - - BELL (1819-1820)
-··-··- LONG (1817) (1819-1820)
━━━━ MCKENZIE, D. (1818-1821)
– – – SARRACINO (1811)
·········· WILLIAMS (1811-1814)

25. EXPLORATIONS, 1810–1820

EXPEDITIONS CONTINUED TO ROAM over the West for all of the old reasons: to search the area out of scientific curiosity, to trade with the natives, and to trap fur-bearing animals. This last purpose became the most important from 1810 to 1820 because the Indians of the West, with their living assured by the buffalo, did little trapping. Hence, the whites were compelled, in most cases, to do their own work in obtaining the valuable pelts.

One of the most unusual influences upon exploration came from the activities of John Jacob Astor. This dynamic German immigrant sought to have his Pacific Fur Company dominate the Columbia Basin and the northern Rockies, with the trappers as mere hired hands. Astor hoped to ship his furs to Canton and profit again from the sale of Chinese luxury goods. In 1811 he established a base at Astoria in the Oregon Territory. In the same year, on July 18, a group of Astorians left the Arikara villages on the Missouri near the North Dakota state line. They were led by Wilson Price Hunt, assisted by Robert Stuart and, more importantly, Donald McKenzie. This was to be the first great overland crossing since that of Lewis and Clark. However, it was made unnecessarily difficult because the group abandoned their horses and tried to go down the Snake River in canoes. They soon found this impossible and were forced to go overland on foot, reaching Astoria on the verge of starvation. On June 29, 1812, Robert Stuart and six comrades started eastward on the return trip. They followed the route that would later approximate that of the Oregon Trail. The beginning of the War of 1812 saw Astoria soon fall to the British, thus ending Astor's dream of a fur empire.

With peace restored to the Northwest in 1815, Donald McKenzie, the former Astorian, had a vision of the possibility of fur trade along the Snake River. Unable to sell his idea to Astor, McKenzie went to work for the North West Company, a Canadian operation. He then spent the years from 1818 to 1821 exploring the Snake River area and establishing key trading posts.

Santa Fe, for so many years a focal point for the exploration of the American West, continued to send private traders among the Indians. However, the only significant expedition was that in 1811 led by José Rafaél Sarracino. He traveled northward and northwestward in an attempt to find a lost Spanish settlement isolated among hostile Indians. After a three-month journey he was forced to turn back when a large river blocked his way. Sarracino returned with valuable furs and evidence that there had been Spanish goods traded to the Indians.

A far more important reconnaisance was carried out by Ezekiel Williams. Leaving Manuel's Fort on the Yellowstone River, the party planned to trade with the Arapahoes on New Mexico's borders. Reaching the upper Arkansas River, they hunted and trapped during the winter. Trouble with Indians forced the group to separate, and many were killed or captured by the Spanish. Williams escaped and, after caching his furs, made his way down the Arkansas River, reaching Saint Louis in the fall of 1813. The next spring he returned to recover his cached furs. The importance of Williams's explorations lay in the discovery of the Central Rockies in Colorado north of the Spanish settlements. His reports of the richness of the beaver in that area brought many trappers in subsequent years.

The only scientific expedition of the period was that led by Maj. Stephen H. Long, an army reconnaissance financed by Congress in the hope that it could secure American control of the fur trade and end British dominance of the Indians on the Upper Missouri. A shallow-draft steamboat built for the expedition was defective, and in 1819 the group had reached only Council Bluffs, where it spent the winter. Disappointed over the meagre results, Long abandoned his plans to search the Yellowstone, and his party of "disgruntled career officers, eccentric scientists, and artist-playboys" struggled westward in 1820 along the Platte River. Reaching the Rockies, the group turned southward. At the Arkansas River, Capt. John R. Bell was sent down that stream while the main body continued southward to the Canadian River, which they mistook for the Red River. Going downstream under great hardship, Long met Bell at Belle Point on the Arkansas in Oklahoma. Long's expedition did report on the Indians and the flora and fauna, but in general it contributed little. Perhaps it is of most importance for having labeled the Great Plains the "Great American Desert," describing it as "unfit for cultivation and of course uninhabitable by a people depending upon agriculture for their subsistence."

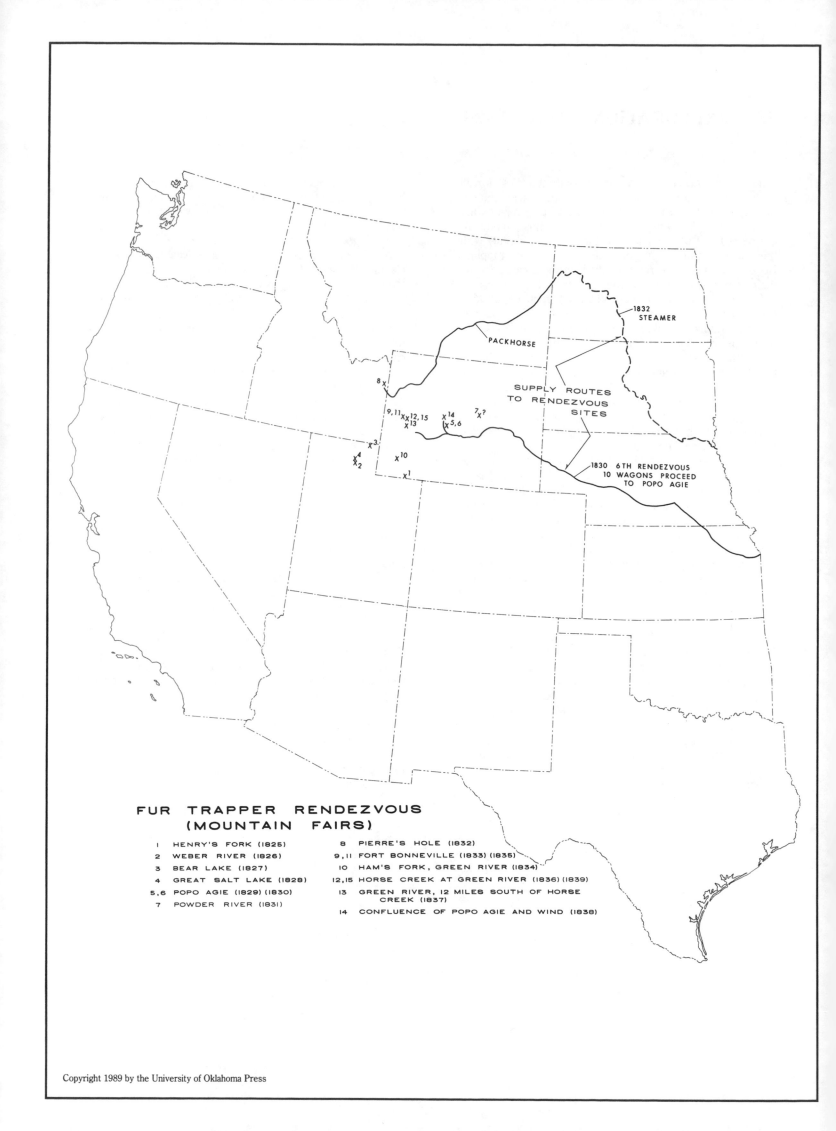

1832
STEAMER

PACKHORSE

8 x

9,11 x x 12,15
x 13

x 14
x 5,6

7 x ?

x 3

x 4
x 2

x 10

x 1

SUPPLY ROUTES
TO RENDEZVOUS
SITES

1830 6TH RENDEZVOUS
10 WAGONS PROCEED
TO POPO AGIE

FUR TRAPPER RENDEZVOUS
(MOUNTAIN FAIRS)

1	HENRY'S FORK (1825)	8	PIERRE'S HOLE (1832)
2	WEBER RIVER (1826)	9,11	FORT BONNEVILLE (1833) (1835)
3	BEAR LAKE (1827)	10	HAM'S FORK, GREEN RIVER (1834)
4	GREAT SALT LAKE (1828)	12,15	HORSE CREEK AT GREEN RIVER (1836) (1839)
5,6	POPO AGIE (1829) (1830)	13	GREEN RIVER, 12 MILES SOUTH OF HORSE CREEK (1837)
7	POWDER RIVER (1831)	14	CONFLUENCE OF POPO AGIE AND WIND (1838)

26. FUR TRAPPER RENDEZVOUS (MOUNTAIN FAIRS)

THE FUR TRADER AND THE TRAPPER had long been the cutting edge of the American frontier. Since the days of Puritan settlement they had blazed pathways through the wilderness, seeking furs and pelts. Permanent settlers followed these trails, slowly but surely extending the line of civilization westward. This continual process was repeated in the American West in the search for beaver, the most prized of fur-bearing animals. In the West the beaver was found mainly in the valleys of the Missouri, Columbia, and Colorado rivers and their tributaries, but it was also found along the banks of the Rio Grande, Arkansas, Humboldt, Sacramento, San Joaquin, and other streams. The trappers concentrated in the upper Missouri Valley, however.

Interest in the beaver of the American West was fanned by the reports of the Lewis and Clark expedition and, later, by that of Pike in the Southwest. The trappers, or mountain men, as they were called, were the precursors of the explorers, military men, miners, ranchers, and settlers who ultimately took over the West. They were men of all races, types, and cultural backgrounds, bound together by the opportunity for escape provided by the wild, free, and irresponsible life of the trapper. In addition to those who were fleeing the restraints of civilization there undoubtedly were many who sought the elusive beaver because they hoped to make money from the enterprise. The mountain men of the Southwest and the upper Missouri were on their own, although many were staked to supplied by entrepreneurs who were willing to advance them what they needed for a part of the catch. To survive in the wilderness the trappers often became more savage than their Indian enemies. This talent for shedding the trappings of civilization was evident when they gathered for their rendezvous after the spring catch had been completed.

In the past, Indians and trappers had brought their fur to permanent fortified trading posts. The situation in the West was unique in that the lack of navigable rivers made it hard to get merchandise in and furs out. Then too, the trapping frontier was constantly changing. William H. Ashley, the Saint Louis fur-trading entrepreneur, recognized the need for a new approach. His answer was a rendezvous held annually in early summer. The site had to have abundant game, grass, and water to accommodate the large gathering. It also had to be selected far enough in advance so word of its location could circulate to outfits scattered throughout the mountain West.

The trappers' rendezvous was something like the trade fairs of medieval Europe in that its basic purpose was to allow the exchange of merchandise—in this case beaver pelts for guns and ammunition, tobacco, coffee and sugar, blankets, trinkets, and liquor to trade with the Indians. It was also like the medieval fair in that it provided an opportunity for the trappers to relax—in their case from the rigors of months alone facing danger in the wilderness. Once the essential trading was finished and friends visited, there was resort to bacchanalian revelry, gambling, and an orgy of sexual abandonment in the arms of compliant Indian women. There were also moments of good, clean fun with horse races, shooting matches, wrestling bouts, and feasting and storytelling around the campfires. Sometimes, however, as at the eighth rendezvous at Pierre's Hole in 1832, pitched battles were fought, with many casualties.

Trade goods sold for higher prices at the rendezvous than the difficulty of hauling them up the Missouri or even overland would justify. Ashley, who originated the rendezvous idea, retired after operating the first two successful fairs, having cleared about eighty thousand dollars. Obviously there was great financial risk in bringing the essential trade goods far into the wilderness and getting the beaver skins safely to Saint Louis. But there was no question that the mountain men and the Indians were shortchanged.

The map shows the fifteen rendezvous that took place between 1825 and 1850. The location had to be convenient to the main trapping grounds and accessible to the supply trains that crossed the continental divide through the South Pass. In 1826, 1827, and 1828 the rendezvous were held in southwestern Idaho and northern Utah. After 1829 the rendezvous was shifted to the north and east as the beaver trapping area shifted. From 1834 to 1839, except for the 1838 meeting, the valley of the upper Green River was the site.

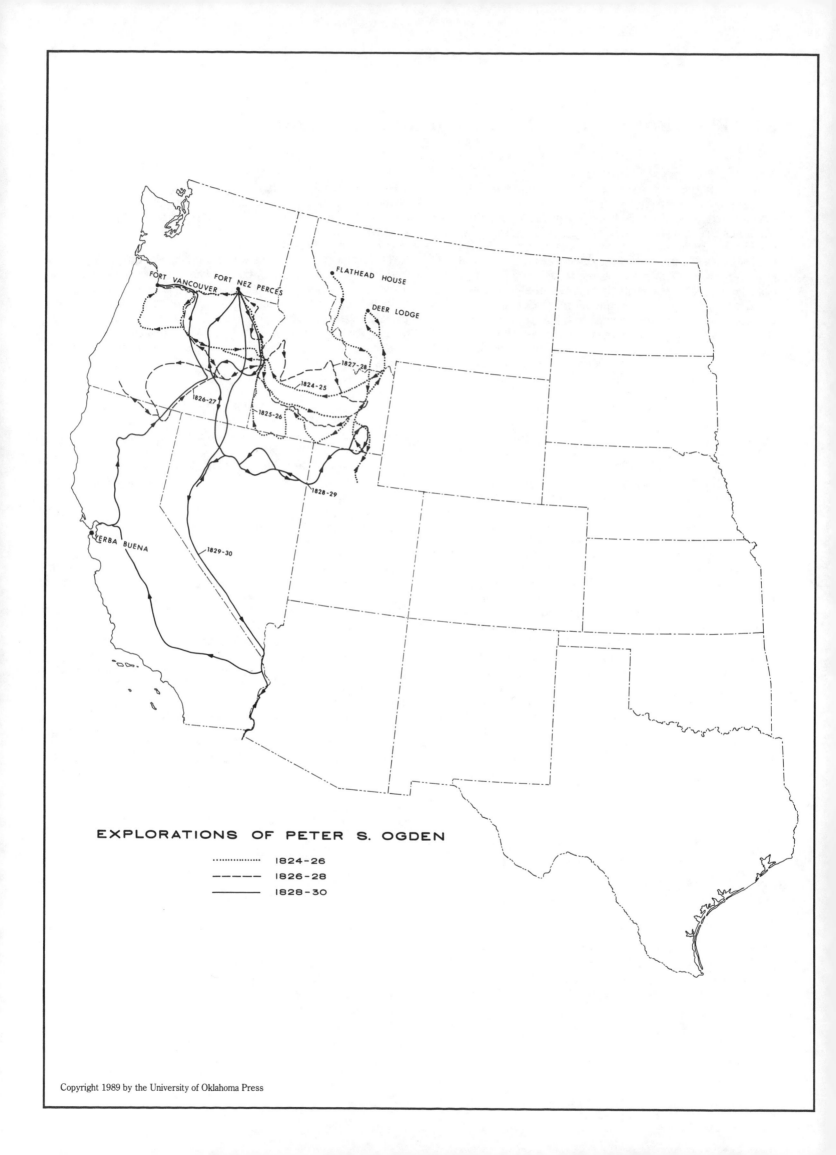

EXPLORATIONS OF PETER S. OGDEN

······· 1824-26
------- 1826-28
——— 1828-30

FORT VANCOUVER
FORT NEZ PERCES
FLATHEAD HOUSE
DEER LODGE
1827-28
1824-25
1826-27
1825-26
1828-29
YERBA BUENA
1829-30

27. EXPLORATIONS OF PETER S. OGDEN

PETER SKENE OGDEN was the greatest of the British fur trade explorers. Born in Quebec in 1792 of American loyalist parents, Ogden was better educated than most mountain men. Despite having been reared in an environment of culture, he was brash and ruthless and, according to some, downright mean. Ogden's reputation was so bad that after eleven years' service with the North West Company he was dismissed when that firm merged with the Hudson's Bay Company. Ultimately reinstated after a journey to London, he was made a brigade commander and led a series of important expeditions between 1824 and 1830.

On December 20, 1824, Ogden left Flathead House with a party of fifty-eight with orders to trap on the Colorado and then follow the Umpqua and Willamette rivers to the ocean. Naturally, such instructions were based on the geographical misconceptions of the day. On December 30 the party passed through the "Gates of Hell," a canyon east of Missoula, and for the next two weeks they trapped and traded up the Bitterroot Valley. On January 13, 1825, they reached Gibbons Pass and moved in a southerly direction along the Big Hole. About February 11, Ogden led the group through Lemhi Pass and over the Continental Divide and then went southeast up the Lemhi River. Heavy snow and tired horses slowed progress, and it was not until April 20 that the group reached the Portneuf River. Arriving at the Bear River on April 26, they went south and crossed into Utah near Franklin. There they left the main stream and trapped along Logan River and Blacksmith Fork, at which point they turned south again to the present town of Hyrum, and finally to Mount Green. The party neared Salt Lake but did not sight it. They were probably more concerned by a clash with a party of American trappers, who enticed away more than half of Ogden's group. After successfully trapping on the Snake, the British leader, because of the presence of Americans, decided to cross the mountains into Montana, probably to descend the Madison or the Gallatin River. Finally Ogden led the party west through the Beaverhead Country, over the mountains through Lemhi Pass, and arrived at Fort Nez Percé (Walla Walla) on November 3, 1825. In the eleven months of the journey Ogden probably saw more of that country than any other explorer.

Ogden's subsequent expeditions were just as extensive as the first and took him into Montana (clearly American territory) and often into Mexican areas. On his second expedition, 1825–26, he moved south from the Deschutes River into Oregon Territory and then went east into the Snake River area of Idaho. On his third trip he traveled from Fort Nez Percé to the vicinity of Klamath Lake in northern California. The following year, 1827–28, this intrepid explorer was back in the Snake River country searching for beaver. In 1828–29 he went back to northern Utah to the northern shore of the Salt Lake and then followed the Humboldt River across Nevada. The last expedition in 1829–30, south through Nevada to the Gulf of California, was the most remarkable of all of Ogden's exploratory ventures. Unfortunately, he lost a number of men and his valuable journals on his way home. However, his maps and reports on his extensive travels have been indispensable to subsequent mapmakers and explorers.

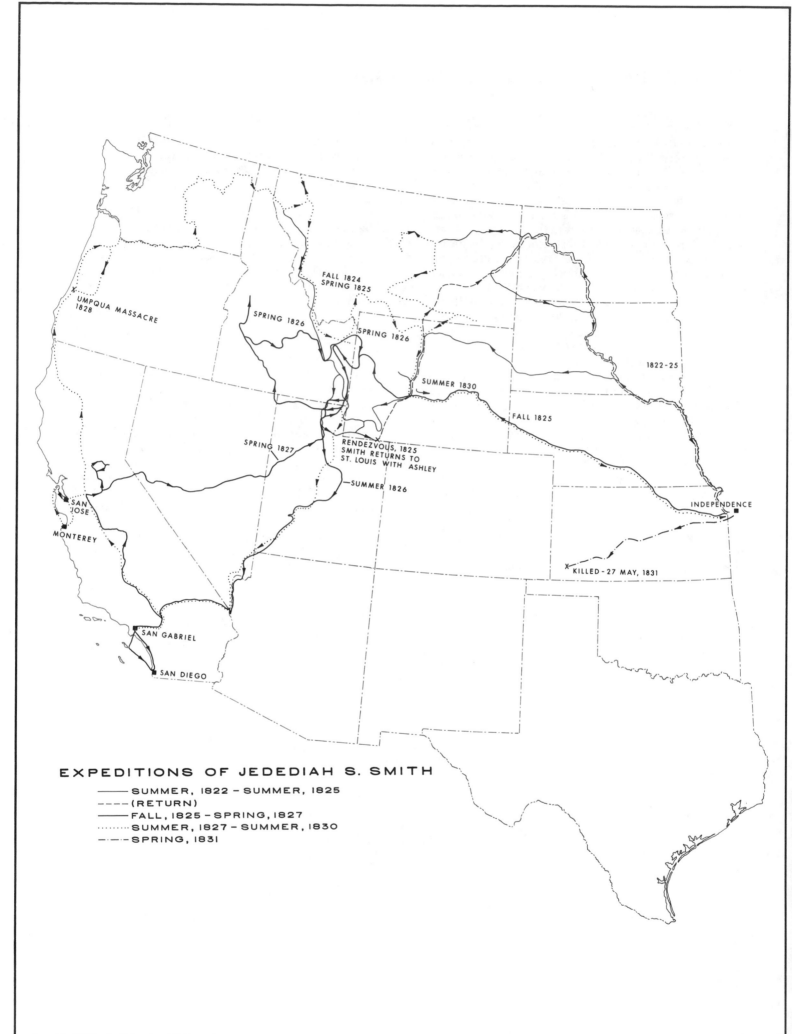

EXPEDITIONS OF JEDEDIAH S. SMITH

——— SUMMER, 1822 – SUMMER, 1825
----- (RETURN)
——— FALL, 1825 – SPRING, 1827
·········· SUMMER, 1827 – SUMMER, 1830
—·—·— SPRING, 1831

Map labels:

UMPQUA MASSACRE 1828
FALL 1824 SPRING 1825
SPRING 1826
SPRING 1826
SUMMER 1830
1822-25
FALL 1825
SPRING 1827
RENDEZVOUS, 1825 SMITH RETURNS TO ST. LOUIS WITH ASHLEY
SUMMER 1826
INDEPENDENCE
KILLED – 27 MAY, 1831
SAN JOSE
MONTEREY
SAN GABRIEL
SAN DIEGO

28. EXPEDITIONS OF JEDEDIAH S. SMITH

JEDEDIAH SMITH was the most remarkable explorer of the West. In only a few short years (1822–31), Smith saw more of the West than had any other single individual. Although he was recognized more as an explorer than a trapper, he took 668 pelts in 1824–25, perhaps a record for a single mountain man. In 1826 he joined William Sublette and David Jackson to buy out the entrepreneur William H. Ashley. While his partners worked the Central Rockies, Smith sought new beaver fields in the Southwest and on the Pacific Coast. Before the Indians cut short his life he was first to discover the natural gateway to the Oregon country. Smith was the first white overland explorer to reach California and the first to cross the Sierra Nevada. He was also the first to go overland from California to the Columbia River, and he was the first to cross the Great Basin on its most direct route.

This natural leader of men was different from most of the profane mountain men in that he was "a bold, outspoken, professing, and consistent Christian" who walked above the debauchery at the rendezvous. In the company of bearded comrades, he was clean shaven. His long hair covered the wounds left by a grizzly that had ripped open his scalp.

In the spring of 1822, Smith was a member of the first group Ashley led up the Missouri, reaching the mouth of the Yellowstone on October 1. In the spring of 1823, Smith was sent down the river with urgent messages for Ashley, and he returned a short time later. In September, 1823, Smith led a party from Fort Kiowa on the Missouri into the Black Hills, where the grizzly narrowly missed terminating his career. The group wintered near Dubois, Wyoming, and learned from friendly Crows of a river teeming with beaver. Following that stream, on March 19, 1824, they made the effective discovery of South Pass (first found in 1811 by the Astorians but soon forgotten). This discovery meant that it was no longer necessary to use the Missouri as a means of crossing the Rockies. The pass later became part of the Oregon Trail. In the fall of 1824, Smith helped a party of Hudson's Bay Company trappers through hostile Indian country to the company post. From December, 1824, to April, 1825, he accompanied Peter Skene Ogden's trapping party into the Snake River region. After the rendezvous in July at Henry's Fork, he returned with Ashley to Saint Louis.

Learning from other trappers that there were virgin beaver grounds in the Southwest, Smith and his party left Cache Lake in the summer of 1826 by way of Salt Lake and then went southward and followed the Colorado River to the Mohave Desert, where they crossed to San Gabriel Mission. The California governor ordered them to leave by the same way they had come. Instead, this first overland party went into the San Joaquin Valley, where they soon had 1,500 pounds of beaver pelts. Smith tried to cross the Sierra Nevada in April, 1827, but after first failing, he left his men and furs and with two companions made it eastward over the Sierra and through the Great Basin. After reaching the rendezvous at Bear Lake on July 3, 1827, and resting briefly, Smith headed again for California along the trail of the previous summer. However, he lost ten men when his group was attacked by the Mojave Indians. California officials were also more inhospitable than they had been the previous year, but Smith was finally able to rejoin his comrades and leave California for Oregon.

On July 13, 1828, Smith's group was attacked on the Umpqua River, and Smith lost fourteen of eighteen men. The survivors took refuge at Fort Vancouver, where Smith sold his beaver. The group stayed at the fort until March 12, 1829, when they began the ascent of the Columbia and Smith finally rejoined his partner, David Jackson, at Flathead Post. In 1829 and 1830 Smith led trapping parties into Wyoming and Montana, but at the rendezvous in 1830, Smith and his partners sold out. The great explorer bought a home in Saint Louis and entered the Santa Fe trade, only to be killed by Comanches on his first trip in 1831.

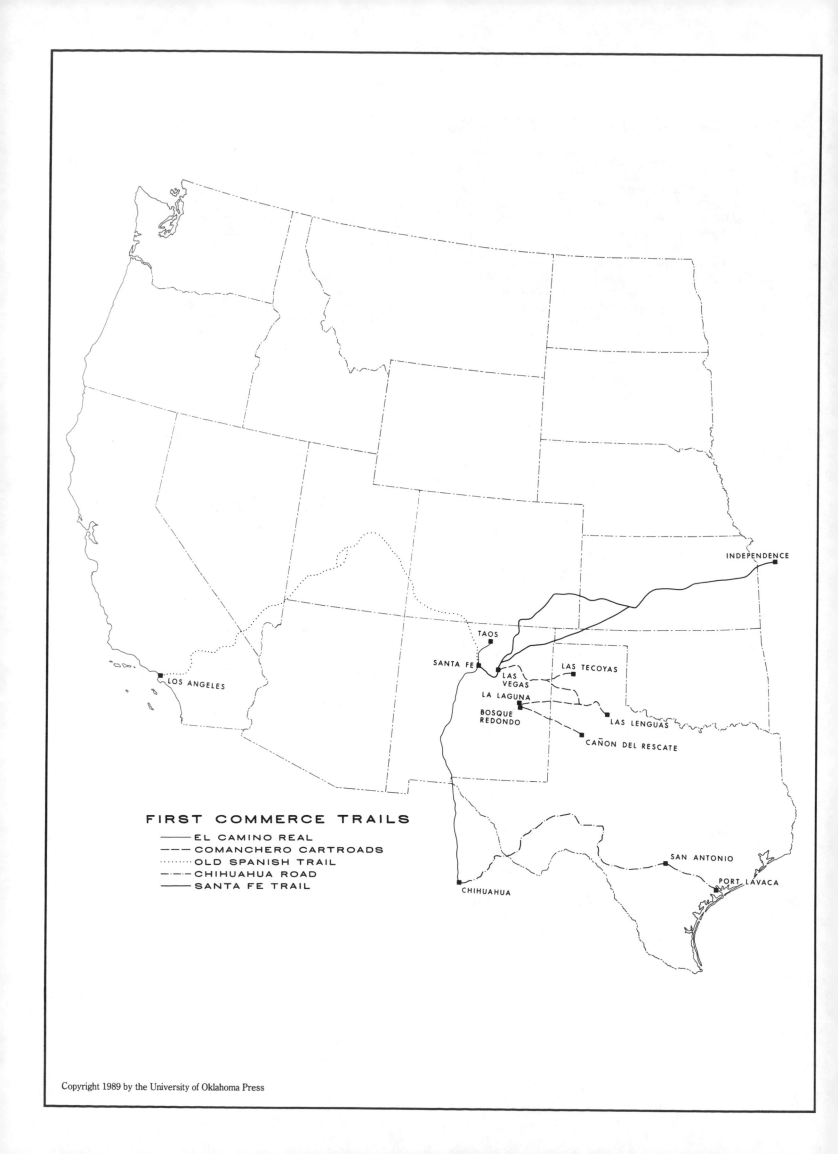

FIRST COMMERCE TRAILS

———— EL CAMINO REAL
– – – COMANCHERO CARTROADS
··········· OLD SPANISH TRAIL
–·–·– CHIHUAHUA ROAD
———— SANTA FE TRAIL

INDEPENDENCE

TAOS

SANTA FE

LAS VEGAS

LAS TECOYAS

LA LAGUNA

BOSQUE REDONDO

LAS LENGUAS

CAÑON DEL RESCATE

LOS ANGELES

SAN ANTONIO

PORT LAVACA

CHIHUAHUA

29. FIRST COMMERCE TRAILS

THE FIRST COMMERCE TRAILS in the West had Santa Fe as their hub, because New Mexico was the first populous area in the region. The first of these trails, El Camino Real, was originally intended as a road for government couriers and as a route for the mission supply service. It followed the Rio Grande south to El Paso and then on to Chihuahua along the route of present-day Mexican Highway 45. This route was intended to provide only for the missions, but it also handled most of the commerce of New Mexico in the seventeenth century. By the mid-eighteenth century, control had passed into the hands of the Chihuahua merchants, who shipped consumer goods such as tobacco, chocolate, sugar, imported fabrics, and trinkets for the Indian trade. New Mexico shipped south hides, blankets, Indian slaves, and sheep. An 1804 report indicated that the frontier province had a trade imbalance of $52,000, perhaps caused by the unscrupulous currency manipulation of the Chihuahua merchants.

An unusual commerce was carried on over cart roads that were described in the 1870s in the following words: "The roads of the Mexican trackers were almost as big and plain as the roads of today." Probably dating back to the mid-eighteenth century, these roads were the trails of the Comancheros, Mexicans from the small villages of northern New Mexico who traded with the Comanches. The Comancheros brought the Indians trinkets, knives, guns, ammunition, whiskey, and clothes and returned with buffalo robes, hides, horses, and even slaves captured in raids in Texas or south of the Rio Grande. The most southerly trail ran from Bosque Redondo to Cañon del Rescate near present-day Lubbock. The upper trail left from Las Vegas to Las Tecoyas on the Canadian River, with a fork going south. The central trail came from La Laguna, near today's Fort Sumner, and on to Las Lenguas.

Leroy Hafen has aptly described the Old Spanish Trail as "the longest, crookedest, most arduous pack mule route in the history of America." The trail was so rugged that wagons, when used at all, could only traverse short distances. The twelve-hundred-mile path was charted to link the old established settlements in New Mexico with the fledgling colony in California. Although the first effort to travel westward to connect Santa Fe and Los Angeles was made by Father Silvester Velez de Escalante in 1776, it was not until 1829 that Antonio Armijo made the route into a commercial trail. The New Mexicans carried westward serapes and blankets (it took two blankets to buy a horse) plus knives, guns, hardware items, and cloth bought in the Santa Fe trade. California mules were in great demand because they were larger and sturdier than their New Mexican cousins. Californios came to resent the traders from Santa Fe, as they obtained horses and mules by stealing them or by trading with Indians who had obtained them the same way. The trail wound northwestward from Santa Fe, through a pass in the Rocky Mountains, across the Colorado and Green rivers into Utah, and then down through the deserts from Las Vegas to Los Angeles.

The Chihuahua Road was a natural route used by marauding Indians for a long time. It ran from Chihuahua down the Rio Conchos, crossing the Rio Grande at Presidio del Norte, then ran northward and then eastward across the Pecos at Horsehead Crossing. It followed the Pecos southward a short distance before turning eastward through Uvalde and Castroville on into San Antonio. With the Santa Fe trade flourishing, efforts were made to connect landlocked Chihuahua with the Gulf Coast. The coastal portion wound southeast from San Antonio through Yorktown, Goliad, and Victoria to Port Lavaca. Silver, much of it smuggled, was the trade attraction in Chihuahua, and that city received all types of consumer goods. Portions of the route were used for freighting or staging between San Antonio and El Paso.

The Santa Fe trail ran some eight hundred miles westward from Independence, Missouri to the New Mexican capital. This trail was a part of a route to California and was also used to supply the army, but it was most important for trade. In 1821 one William Becknell brought consumer goods to Santa Fe to barter for gold, silver, and furs. The effort was so profitable that wagonloads of cotton goods, hardware items, guns, and glassware were soon being hauled westward across the prairie every spring. The trade lasted until the coming of the railroad in 1879.

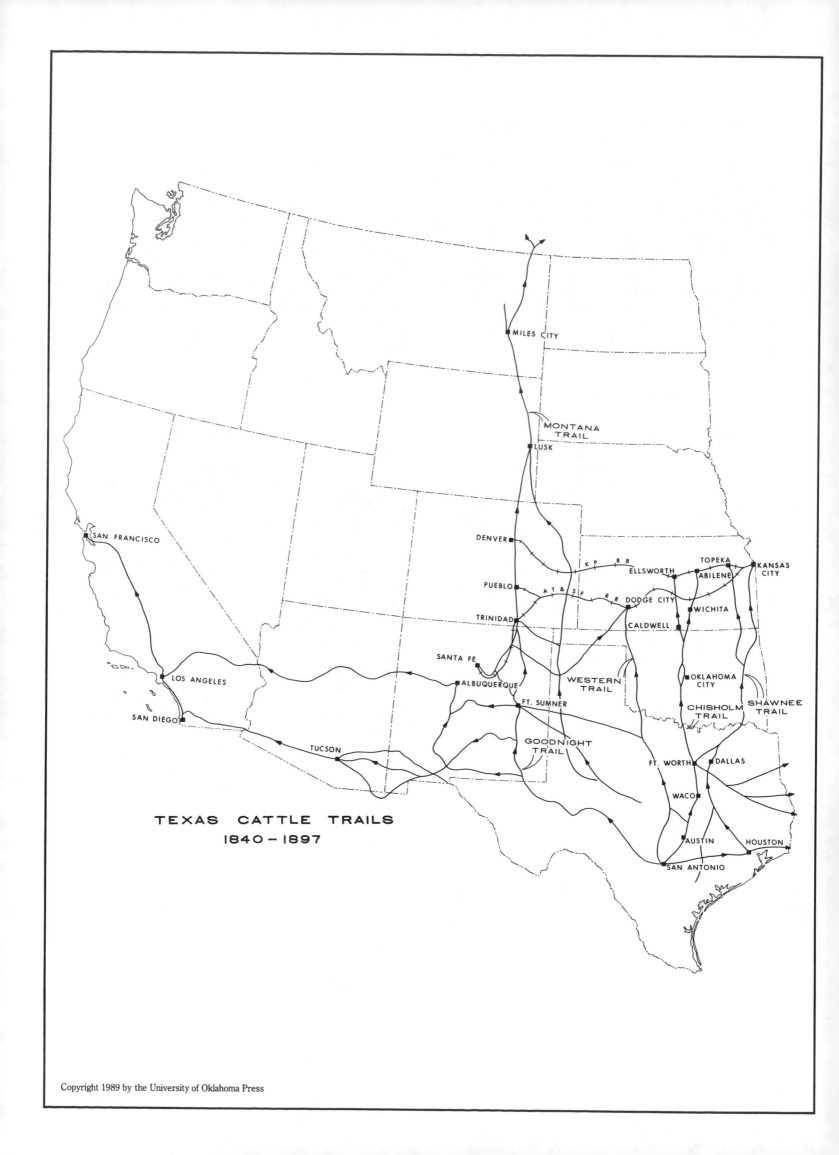

TEXAS CATTLE TRAILS
1840-1897

30. TEXAS CATTLE TRAILS, 1840–1897

THE CATTLE INDUSTRY OF THE WEST was developed from Spanish and Anglo-American practices in the triangle of Texas formed by the junction of the Rio Grande and the Gulf of Mexico. Conditions in that area were ideal. Plenty of rain and green grass the year around and few predatory animals allowed the animals to increase until uncounted millions roamed the open range. These wild cattle were a mixture of several breeds that finally emerged as the Texas longhorns, lean, tough, dangerous animals, some of which had horns that spread eight feet from tip to tip. To the Anglo farmer who came to this country, these animals were at first pests. A few longhorns were slaughtered for hides, which were shipped from Galveston. One adventurous herder drove a thousand head to the Ohio Valley in 1846, and others drove herds overland to California and the gold mines in the 1850s, but the difficulties of driving the cattle such long distances meant little profit.

During the Civil War years the cattle increased prodigiously, especially as the result of the isolation of Texas and the absence of herdsmen. By 1865 an estimated five million longhorns roamed Texas. In the Midwest, livestock were depleted by the war, and even range cattle sold for forty dollars a head, so if a herd could be rounded up at a cost of three or four dollars a head and driven to that market, the potential profits were enormous. By the end of the war the Missouri Pacific Railroad had reached Sedalia, Missouri, thus shortening the drive to market. In March, 1866, thousands of longhorns began the "long drive." By the end of the summer, 260,000 were headed towards Sedalia.

Profits were high in this first venture, but there were many problems along the way. Cattle used to the open range bolted in the forests, Indians stampeded the herds, and the farmers of Missouri tried to turn them back. A solution was provided by the westward expansion of the railroads. One Joseph G. McCoy laid out a better route to the railroad at Abilene, Kansas, in 1867. The herds followed the Chisholm Trail, blazed by Jesse Chisholm, a Cherokee, which ran along the 98th meridian. Although the main objective was Abilene, branches went to Wichita, Newton, and other towns. Abilene was succeeded in 1871 by Ellsworth, which in turn was succeeded by Dodge City in 1876 as the rails moved westward.

Not all the herds were headed for Kansas. One Texan, Charles Goodnight, decided to drive his cattle in a different direction, believing "the whole of Texas would start north for market" toward Kansas and that greater opportunities existed to the west. Gold mining had just started booming in New Mexico, and Goodnight was sure there would be a market for his herds. The Goodnight Trail mainly followed the Pecos River to Fort Sumner, New Mexico, where it branched out in several directions. Goodnight succeeded beyond his wildest dreams. Not only were the miners eager to purchase all of his cattle, but he also found a tremendous market at the numerous forts. In addition, the trail was pushed northward to Montana and even into Canada, where the cattle fed miners and soldiers, and large numbers of cattle were sold for breeding purposes to the emerging ranches on the plains.

Texas cattle drives were in their heyday for only a short time, but between 1866 and 1886 some ten million longhorns walked the trails to Missouri and Kansas or to more distant points in New Mexico, Colorado, Wyoming, Montana, and Canada. The cattle drives may have lasted but a few years, but they have remained an integral part of the nation's western folklore. Ernest S. Osgood expressed some of the reason for this fascination with the drives:

> To those who took part, accustomed as they became to all the possible incidents of the drive, near as they were with the solitudes over which they passed, each drive was a new adventure and its successful completion always brought to the most experienced, something of the thrill of achievement. . . . To all those who saw that long line of Texas cattle come up over a rise in the prairies, nostrils wide for the smell of water, dust caked and gaunt, so ready to break from the nervous control of the riders strung out along the flanks of herd, there came the feeling that in this spectacle there was something elemental, something resistless, something perfectly in keeping about the unconquered land about them.[1]

[1] Ernest S. Osgood, *The Day of the Cattleman* (Chicago, 1937), p. 26.

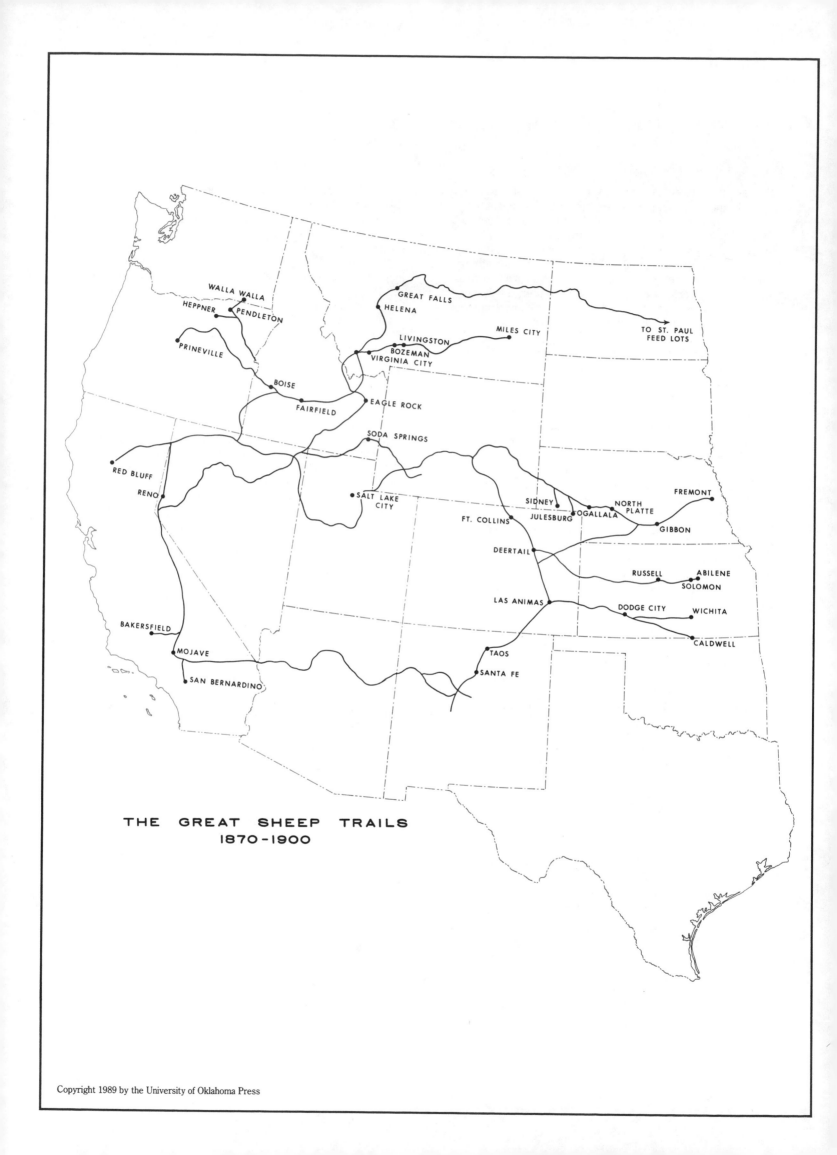

THE GREAT SHEEP TRAILS
1870-1900

31. THE GREAT SHEEP TRAILS, 1870–1900

THE COWBOYS WHO "headed them north" in the great cattle drives from Texas have been well remembered in both history and folklore. Their counterparts, the sheepherders, who performed an equally important task in trailing some fifteen million sheep from the Pacific states eastward, have been usually ignored. Perhaps the cowboy trail drivers have been immortalized as virtual knights of the prairie because Americans are steak eaters and have seldom developed a taste for mutton. It is also possible that the sheepherders have never won a lofty status in the popular mind because they were early forced to abandon horses and tend their charges on foot. A sheepherder and his dog have never fired the imagination as have the cowboy and his horse. Thus, sheepherders have seldom been fictional heroes of novels and movies.

The first great sheep drives in the American West resulted from the demand for food created by the California gold rush. Sheep worth a dollar a head in the Golden State rose to fifteen dollars a head a few months after gold was discovered. In the summer of 1849, Miguel A. Otero and Antonio José Luna drove some twenty-five thousand head in ten bands to the gold fields. Starting from near Santa Fe, New Mexico, they followed the route of the later Santa Fe Railway to the Mojave River before turning north for central California. Before the Civil War, as Edward Norris Wentworth puts it, "more than a million sets of bovine hooves beat their way through the Arizona dust en route from New Mexico to the California gold fields." Not all of this number came from New Mexico. One drive by Colonel W. W. Hollister brought nine thousand Merinos from Ohio to the Pacific shore. The basic result of this early westward sheep movement was that it improved the quality and quantity of the flocks in the coastal region, setting the stage for the massive drives eastward after the Civil War.

The early bands on the trail came from the swollen flocks in California. Major Gorham Gates Kimball, of Red Bluff, was perhaps the first to trail a band, totaling 3,700 head, to Boise in 1865. Unable to sell his sheep in Idaho, Kimball continued the drive into Montana. Several others followed his lead and drove sheep to the mining areas and also to stock the ranges of Idaho, Montana, Wyoming, Colorado, and Utah. Large numbers were trailed into the mesas of western and central Arizona. In the 1880s the development of irrigated agriculture left farmers with surplus feed, especially in Colorado and Nebraska; sheep were driven in to be fattened on the refuse left over from the processing of sugar beets. They were also used to forage for food after grain had been harvested.

Trail bands numbered from three thousand to seven thousand, and often a single owner had enough bands on the trail to total twenty-five thousand. Each band required three men, "one at the point, or lead, one at the swing or about the center, and the other bringing up the trail." Cattlemen on the trail had to worry about flooded rivers, stampedes in storms, bandits, and Indians. Sheepmen on the trail had all of these concerns plus fear of poisonous weeds, wolves, bobcats, coyotes, and eagles. Their job was made more difficult because sheep are more temperamental and harder to handle than cattle. To drive these bands of sheep, experienced hands were required. Many of them were Basques from France and Spain, and others were of Portuguese or Mexican origin.

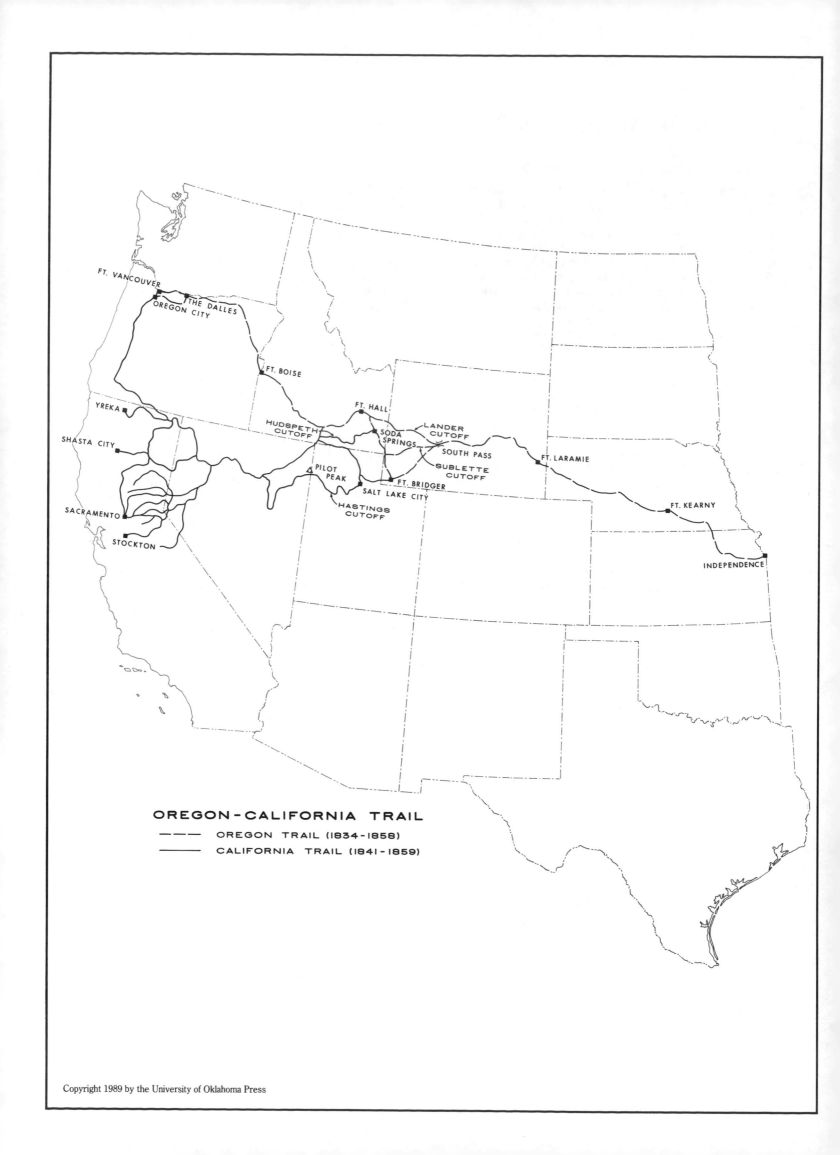

FT. VANCOUVER
THE DALLES
OREGON CITY

FT. BOISE

YREKA

SHASTA CITY

SACRAMENTO

STOCKTON

FT. HALL

HUDSPETH
CUTOFF

SODA
SPRINGS

LANDER
CUTOFF

SOUTH PASS

FT. LARAMIE

SUBLETTE
CUTOFF

PILOT
PEAK

FT. BRIDGER

SALT LAKE CITY

HASTINGS
CUTOFF

FT. KEARNY

INDEPENDENCE

OREGON-CALIFORNIA TRAIL

— — — OREGON TRAIL (1834-1858)

———— CALIFORNIA TRAIL (1841-1859)

32. OREGON-CALIFORNIA TRAIL

THE OREGON-CALIFORNIA TRAIL was the most important route for emigrants moving westward. Actually, a more accurate name would have been the Oregon-California-Utah Trail, as the first half of the journey to Mormon country followed almost the same route. From its beginnings in 1834 until it was made obsolete with the completion of the transcontinental railroad in 1869, this trail served as the route for some 350,000 people traveling to Oregon and California and for perhaps another 40,000 Latter-Day Saints making their way to Utah. Portions of the trail were undoubtedly first used by Indians and then by the explorers who traversed the area in the early nineteenth century. By 1810 a party of the Missouri Fur Company discovered the South Pass, and two years later a group of returning Astorians followed the route that became the Oregon Trail. In the 1830s several fur trading parties went over the trail; many traders from these groups would later guide emigrant wagons westward.

The departure point for the two-thousand-mile trek westward to either Oregon or California was Independence, Missouri. This site was selected because it had long outfitted the wagons rolling westward over the Santa Fe Trail and was the logical starting point at the eastern edge of the plains. By going up the Missouri to Saint Joseph to begin their journey, overland travelers could reduce time on the trail by four days, and by going as far north as Nebraska City or Council Bluffs, they could save even more time.

Although the Bidwell-Bartleson party went to California in 1841, most westward-bound emigrants headed first for Oregon; one thousand went over the trail in 1843, and this rate of migration continued for another six years. Gold in California shifted the migration in 1849. In 1847 the Mormons began using the eastern half of the trail en route to Utah.

For the first fifty miles after leaving Independence, the route followed the well-worn Santa Fe Trail. After the Oregon-California Trail turned to the right, the first significant milestone was the ferry across the Kansas River. From that point the trail headed for the Platte River; there, on the south bank, Fort Kearney provided a chance to stop for re-outfitting or repair. From Fort Kearney the travelers usually followed the south bank of the Platte (although there was a trail on the north side of the river). When they reached Fort Laramie the distance traveled was only 635 miles, and geography had played a mean trick on the migrants: they had come over the easiest part of their journey when they and their animals were fresh; the most challenging terrain lay ahead.

West of Fort Laramie the rolling prairies gave way to hills that slowed the wagons. At South Pass, at 7,550 feet elevation, the trail went over the Continental Divide. Just beyond that point the trail divided. Originally it turned south to Fort Bridger, where emigrants for Utah and those headed for California who wanted to use Hastings Cutoff turned to the left. The Sublette Cutoff avoided Fort Bridger, and in 1858, Frederick W. Lander cut a road suitable for wagons through the wilderness to Fort Hall.

The Lander Cutoff substantially shortened the route for Oregon-bound travelers. At Fort Hall, in the Snake River country, the first emigrants gave up their wagons and packed their belongings on horses. A few determined individuals, however, soon proved that wagons could get through, especially if time were allowed for their teams to recoup their strength in the lush grasslands. After passing through the rugged Blue Mountains, the migrants followed the Umatilla River to the Columbia, where wagons were often rafted downstream.

As difficult as the Oregon trek was, it was not nearly as formidable as the trail to California. Actually, there were many trails to California once the migrants reached South Pass, and some even went to Oregon and then turned south. In 1841 the Bidwell-Bartleson party left the Oregon Trail at Soda Springs, going southwest following the Humboldt River to its sink and then along the Carson River to the Walker River, crossing the Sierra Nevada between the Walker and Stanislaus rivers. Later parties followed the Humboldt to its sink and then went westward along the Truckee River, which became the favored route. In 1853 a northern cutoff went to Yreka, and in 1852 Noble's road went over the mountains to Shasta City. Of the great variety of trails through the eight to ten mountain passes that were used, some were feasible but some brought disaster.

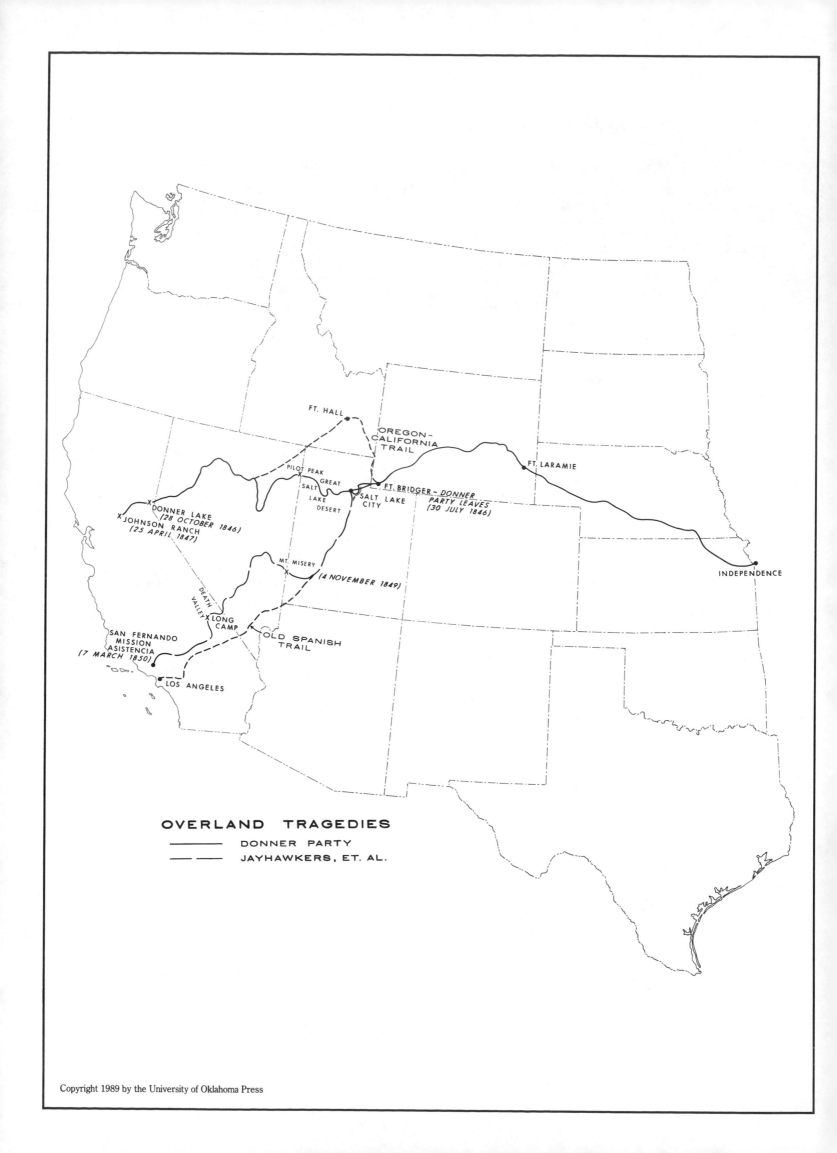

FT. HALL

OREGON-
CALIFORNIA
TRAIL

FT. LARAMIE

PILOT PEAK
X
SALT
GREAT
FT. BRIDGER - DONNER
PARTY LEAVES
(30 JULY 1846)

X DONNER LAKE
(28 OCTOBER 1846)
LAKE
SALT LAKE
CITY
X JOHNSON RANCH
(25 APRIL 1847)
DESERT

MT. MISERY
X
(4 NOVEMBER 1849)
INDEPENDENCE

DEATH
X LONG
CAMP
VALLEY

SAN FERNANDO
MISSION
ASISTENCIA
(7 MARCH 1850)
OLD SPANISH
TRAIL

LOS ANGELES

OVERLAND TRAGEDIES

—————— DONNER PARTY
— — — — JAYHAWKERS, ET. AL.

33. OVERLAND TRAGEDIES

WHEN ONE CONSIDERS the lack of experience of the thousands who crossed the American West, it is truly remarkable that most arrived at their destination only a little thinner than when they left home. However, there were two notable exceptions: the Donner party in 1846 and the tragedy in Death Valley in 1849.

The Donners, George and Jacob, wealthy Illinois farmers, were in their sixties when they organized a group headed for California, and their party suffered from a disproportionate number of elderly people and women and children, which slowed their progress on the trail. The group also suffered from more than the normal number of quarrels, one of which resulted in death.

The trip, however, went well as far as Fort Bridger. A messenger from Lansford Hastings, author of the *Emigrants Guide to Oregon and California,* informed them they could save four hundred miles by taking the Hastings Cutoff south of Great Salt Lake. About half of the group heeded the advice of veteran guides to take the trail to Fort Hall. The other group (eighty-seven or eighty-nine people), including the Donners themselves, elected to take the "shortcut" despite their lack of guides and ignorance of the area. They wandered aimlessly through the Utah wilderness for weeks (it took them twenty-one days to go thirty-six miles), and it was September 30 before they reached the well-marked California Trail on the Humboldt River. The group that had separated from the party had passed the same point forty-five days earlier.

Not until October 28 did the Donner party reach the base of the Sierras. Even then, had they hurried, they might have been able to go through the pass. But they took five fatal days to rest and were snowed in on Truckee Lake by November 5. Poor management permitted their livestock to wander off, thus depriving them of much-needed food.

A party of fifteen, equipped with snowshoes and with rations for six days, started from the lake camp on December 16 to cross the Sierras. Their journey lasted thirty-two days. As members died, they were eaten by the survivors, a practice also in effect at the lake cabins.

Once word reached Johnson Ranch (and Sutter's Fort) of the plight of the Donner party, four relief expeditions came through the snow to the aid of the beleaguered group. However, of the Donner group that had chosen the "shortcut," only forty-eight reached California.

An entirely different situation was created by the Argonauts stranded in Utah in the fall of 1849. It was too late in the season for them to continue on the direct western route. The Donner tragedy was still fresh in their minds, and no one desired to risk a similar fate, but neither was it desirable to winter among the Mormons. An alternative was suggested by Jefferson Hunt, a prominent Mormon who had led some mustered-out members of the Mormon Battalion over the Old Spanish Trail and the Mormon Corridor from Los Angeles to Salt Lake City the year before. Hunt pointed out that pack animals had ordinarily used the trail, but that wagons could also traverse it. He offered to lead the 107 wagons to Los Angeles for ten dollars apiece. It is estimated that there were four hundred persons in the group, although no one is in agreement on the exact number. The offer was accepted, and the large wagon train broke camp from near Provo on October 2, 1849. The first 208 miles of the trek, to the Beaver River, went well. However, another group, led by one Capt. O. K. Smith, had joined the party, and several from the new contingent argued that there was a route westward over the Walker Pass that would cut four hundred miles from the journey and get the group to the mines in twenty days. A week was spent in looking futilely for this better route, which was shown on a map one member of the group had. Hunt insisted on going on the trail he knew, but when the group divided, only seven wagons elected to stay with the Mormon leader. The going was rough over the snow-covered pass beyond Bitter Springs and in the desert, but Hunt led the wagon party along the Mojave River and over the Cajon Pass to arrive at Williams's Ranch (near Cucamonga) on Christmas Eve. Some who had gone with the larger group thought better of it, and the Rich-Bigler party returned to the Old Spanish Trail and caught up with Hunt.

After going westward for three days, the large group camped for several days at a point named Mount Misery, which probably reflected their condition. On November 7, a Mr. Rymerson convinced most of the group (some seventy wagons) to return to the Old Spanish Trail and follow Hunt. The remainder of the group (122 by the best count), with twenty-seven wagons and a number of pack animals, made their way westward into Death Valley. One member described the area as "dubious looking country." The going was so rugged that for the ninety-seven days from their leaving Hunt's party until they reached California, they averaged only six miles a day; in addition they zigzagged so much they only averaged three and a half miles a day toward their destination. This stupid effort to improve upon the Old Spanish Trail ended in failure. Even at this late date it is not possible to count the fatalities among the group that entered Death Valley, but they undoubtedly were numerous. An estimate has been made difficult by their division into seven separate parties, the largest being one called the Jayhawkers, with forty members.

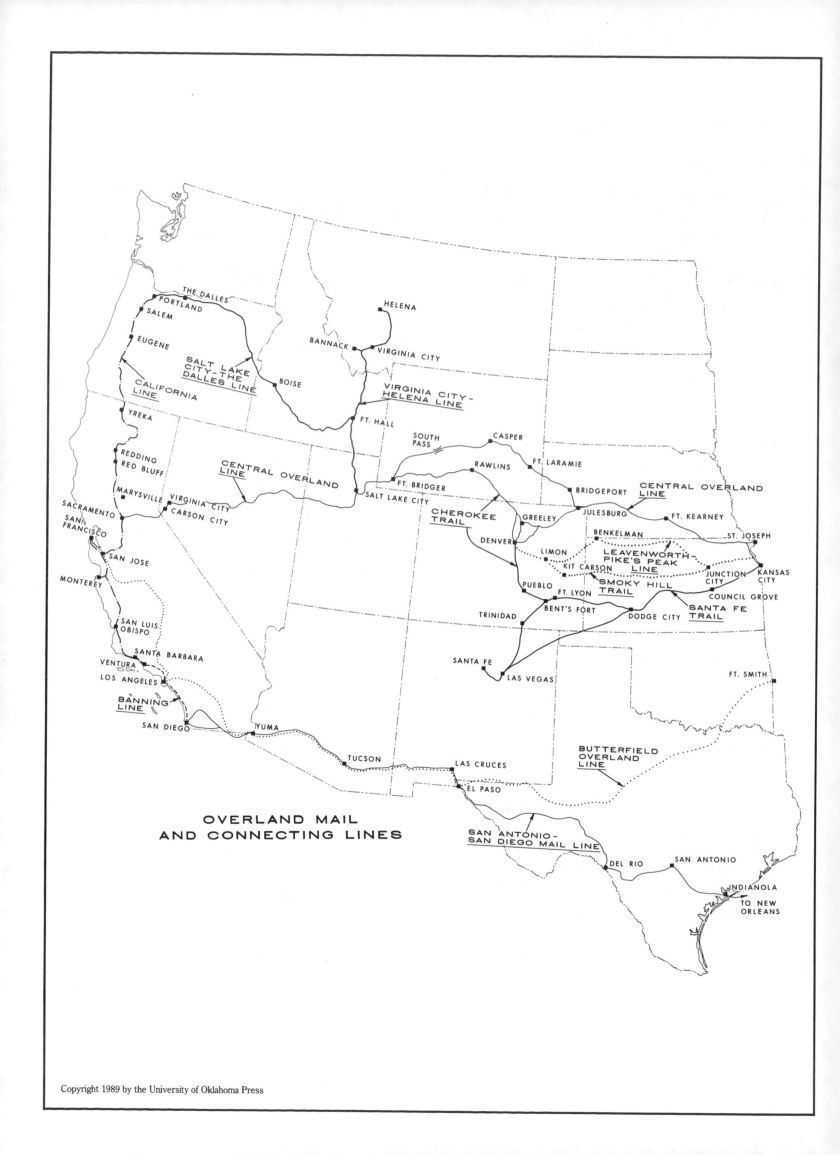

OVERLAND MAIL
AND CONNECTING LINES

34. OVERLAND MAIL AND CONNECTING LINES

As THE FRONTIER slowly edged westward from the Atlantic Coast, the mail service accompanied it. Even in the colonial period the government had assumed responsibility for this indispensable service. Mail meant letters from home, but it also brought newspapers and government-printed matter. By the midnineteenth century the area east of the Mississippi was covered with a network of roads, rails, riverways, and canals that made possible an effective mail service. Westerners expected the government to make comparable mail delivery available as soon as possible.

That federal authorities understood the importance of easing the isolation of westerners was reflected in President James K. Polk's message to Congress on August 5, 1846, in which he recommended legislation for the recently acquired Oregon Territory: "It is important that mail facilities, so indispensable for the diffusion of information, and for binding together the different portions of our extended Confederacy, should be afforded to our citizens west of the Rocky Mountains." In 1847, Congress passed a subsidy making possible semimonthly mail service to the Pacific Coast by way of Panama. However, the gold rush and the resulting flood of migrants to California created dissatisfaction with the slowness of the sea route and led to a clamor for a faster overland mail.

The first pioneer route was launched between Kansas City and Salt Lake City on July 1, 1850. Monthly service was promised over a twelve-hundred-mile route for a modest subsidy. Another company ran from the Mormon capital to Sacramento, completing the first full transcontinental mail service. Despite untold hardships, caused mainly by the weather, the mail usually went through, usually by pack animal. However, it did not satisfy Californians, and when Senator Weller presented a petition with seventy-five signatures, Congress responded by subsidizing a stage coach route with a mail contract. This stage line, described as going "from noplace through nothing to nowhere," ran from San Antonio to San Diego and was also contemptuously dubbed "the jackass line" because of the mules that drew the coaches. James Birch, its promoter, a prominent California stage entrepreneur, died at sea as the project got underway, and it soon became a complete disaster.

One estimate claimed it cost sixty-five dollars for every letter sent from San Antonio to San Diego. Another route from Independence, Missouri, to Santa Fe through Bent's Fort was then designated a post route, and regular stagecoach service was begun along it on July 1, 1850.

The southern route that Congress imposed upon Birch reflected efforts of southerners to route stagecoaches south in the hope that a transcontinental railroad would someday follow the same route. A far more successful operation, the Butterfield Overland Mail, also was forced to follow a southern route, entering the West at Fort Smith and, after dipping south in an "oxbow," following the path of the San Antonio–San Diego line from El Paso west. The Butterfield kept a semiweekly schedule between Saint Louis and San Francisco in twenty-five days. In 1861, the pending outbreak of hostilities led to the transfer of the line to the central route running from Saint Joseph to Sacramento.

Until the government-subsidized Butterfield line moved to the central areas, a group of entrepreneurs led by Alexander Majors had dominated freighting and staging in that region. In 1859 this group established the Leavenworth and Pike's Peak Express Company, hoping to profit from the Colorado gold rush. Service was soon extended to Salt Lake City to connect with the Overland Line to California. But Majors's line was not profitable, and when the Butterfield Line, with its one-million-dollar annual government subsidy, moved into competition, the Central Overland failed.

In 1861 the bankrupt Central Overland Line came under the control of Ben Holladay, who soon dominated western mail and staging. The new lines to Montana and to the northwest also came under his control. In California, Wells, Fargo & Co. controlled most of the stages except for local lines like that of Phineas Banning.

The building of the transcontinental railroad sounded the death knell for long-distance staging, but in regions not serviced by train, stagecoaches continued to carry letters, in some cases into the twentieth century. Without the necessity of getting the mail through to its destination, no matter how remote, the settlement of the West would have been slower and more difficult.

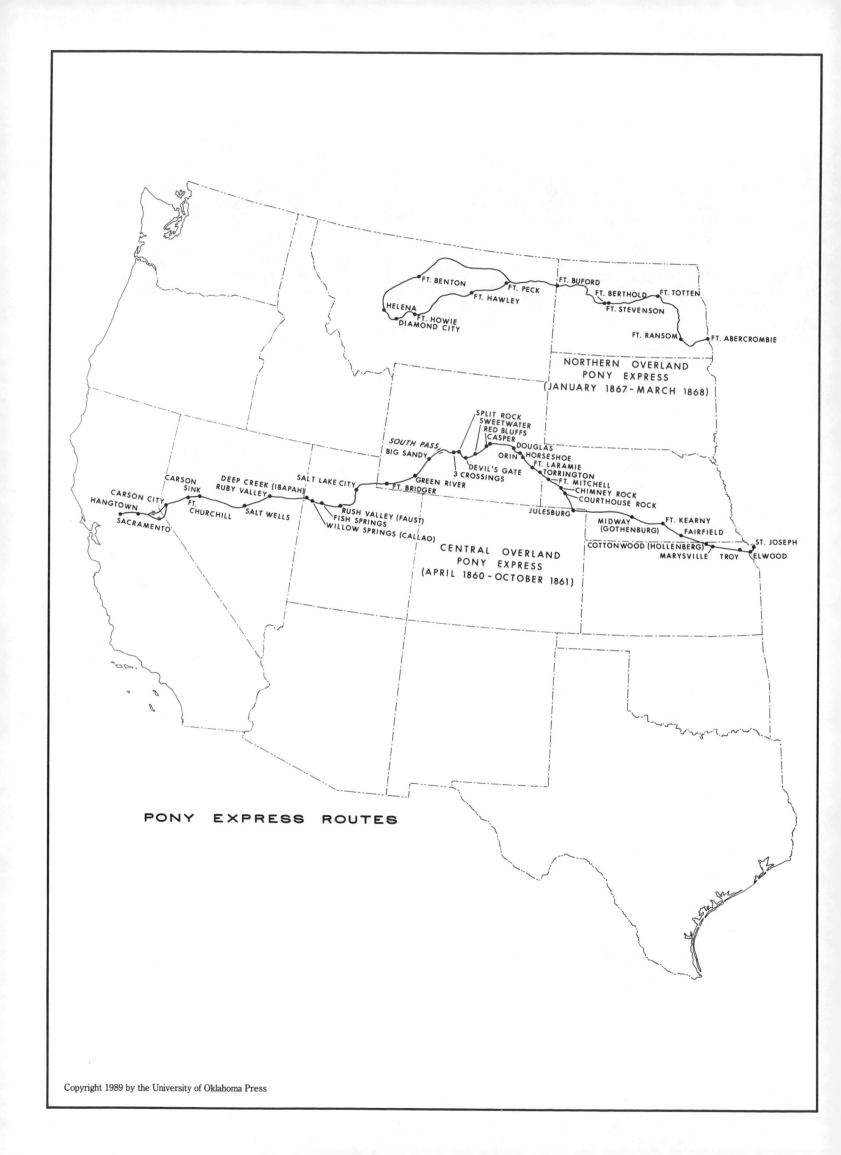

PONY EXPRESS ROUTES

NORTHERN OVERLAND
PONY EXPRESS
(JANUARY 1867 - MARCH 1868)

CENTRAL OVERLAND
PONY EXPRESS
(APRIL 1860 - OCTOBER 1861)

FT. BENTON
HELENA
FT. HOWIE
DIAMOND CITY
FT. HAWLEY
FT. PECK
FT. BUFORD
FT. BERTHOLD
FT. STEVENSON
FT. TOTTEN
FT. RANSOM
FT. ABERCROMBIE

SPLIT ROCK
SWEETWATER
RED BLUFFS
CASPER
DOUGLAS
SOUTH PASS
BIG SANDY
ORIN
HORSESHOE
FT. LARAMIE
DEVIL'S GATE
TORRINGTON
3 CROSSINGS
FT. MITCHELL
GREEN RIVER
CHIMNEY ROCK
FT. BRIDGER
COURTHOUSE ROCK
JULESBURG

CARSON
SINK
DEEP CREEK (IBAPAH)
RUBY VALLEY
SALT LAKE CITY
CARSON CITY
HANGTOWN
FT.
CHURCHILL
SALT WELLS
SACRAMENTO
RUSH VALLEY (FAUST)
FISH SPRINGS
WILLOW SPRINGS (CALLAO)

MIDWAY
(GOTHENBURG)
FT. KEARNY
FAIRFIELD
ST. JOSEPH
COTTONWOOD (HOLLENBERG)
MARYSVILLE   TROY   ELWOOD

35. PONY EXPRESS ROUTES

THE PONY EXPRESS remains the most fabled of all forms of western communication, despite the fact that it lasted only from April, 1860, to October, 1861. The dramatic vision of the lone rider galloping over rugged terrain night and day, braving rain and snow and Indian attacks to get the mail through, has always fired the popular imagination. Even when the Pony Express first began service, newspapers everywhere, even in Europe, uniformly praised the endeavor. In fact, writers from Mark Twain to the present have added to its romance.

The use of relay riders as military couriers goes far back in time and was used by American military authorities in the early period of the occupation of California to carry the mail between San Diego and San Francisco. California was a unique area because of its geographic isolation from the rest of the nation. The clamor of California residents for improved mail service grew as a result of the Gold Rush. Initially, a government subsidy helped bring mail to the Pacific Coast by ship via the Panama route. Other subsidies were granted for overland routes, the most successful being that awarded the Butterfield Overland Mail. But even that route took twenty-five days from Saint Louis to San Francisco.

The Pony Express probably was created as a result of Senator William Gwin's recommendation to William H. Russell, senior partner of the leading freighting firm of Russell, Majors and Waddell. Gwin, it is claimed, pointed out that an express route over the central trail to California would prove the feasibility of that route for transport in winter weather. Once that was proved, government subsidies would be forthcoming, ensuring the success of the venture.

The route ran 1,966 miles from Saint Joseph, Missouri, to Sacramento. Relay stations to supply fresh horses were stationed about ten miles apart. Eighty riders (as in the case of jockeys, smaller ones were preferred), half going east and half going west, were employed. Each rider normally rode 50 to 60 miles, but could ride 100 miles if necessary, and in an emergency one rider once rode 280 miles. In its sixteen months of operation these riders traveled 650,000 miles and lost only one shipment, while successfully delivering 35,000 pieces of mail. The mail was wrapped in oiled silk to protect it from the elements. Initially as many as 350 letters were carried at a time at ten dollars an ounce, but the rate was later reduced to two dollars an ounce. It took ten to eleven days to get the mail through.

While most attention has always been focused on the pony express route to California, there were many comparable services scattered throughout the West. Often these ventures lasted but a short time. In July, 1863, a weekly pony express was established between Fort Bridger and Bannock City in Montana, but there is no record of how long it operated. A far more important effort was the northern pony express route from Fort Abercrombie (near present-day Fargo, North Dakota) to the mining fields of Helena, Montana.

The unreliability of steamboat traffic on the Upper Missouri (there was none in winter and little in late summer) made essential a more dependable means of communication. In 1867 the postmaster general awarded a contract for triweekly mail service across 450 miles of a North Dakota prairie devoid of a single settlement and 500 miles of Montana that was even more desolate and dangerous. The contractors tried to fulfill their obligation to begin mail service on July 1, 1867, and made delivery in fourteen days, but during the summer Indian raids delayed the riders, although service never totally stopped. Promised military escort was usually inadequate or even unavailable. One report was that "the Indians have been raising h..l and frightening all the mail riders here so they dare not go out the door." The ferocity of winter storms intimidated riders to a point that the infrequent mail service came to a halt and was discontinued on March 12, 1868, when the contractors went bankrupt.

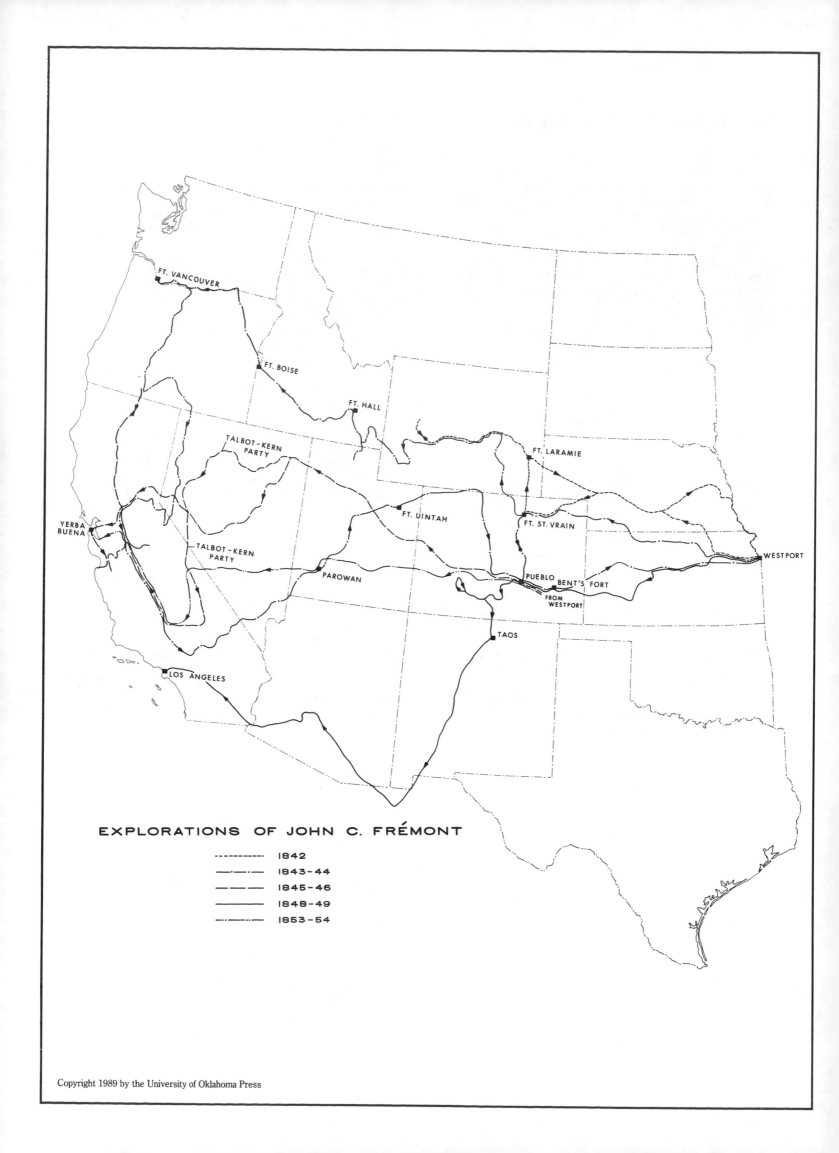

EXPLORATIONS OF JOHN C. FRÉMONT

-----------	1842
—·—·—	1843-44
— — —	1845-46
————	1848-49
—··—··—	1853-54

FT. VANCOUVER

FT. BOISE

FT. HALL

TALBOT-KERN
PARTY

TALBOT-KERN
PARTY

YERBA
BUENA

FT. UINTAH

FT. LARAMIE

FT. ST. VRAIN

WESTPORT

PAROWAN

PUEBLO BENT'S FORT

FROM
WESTPORT

TAOS

LOS ANGELES

36. EXPLORATIONS OF JOHN C. FRÉMONT

JOHN CHARLES FRÉMONT was famed as an explorer, soldier, and politician. He was, without question, the most renowned explorer of the American West despite the fact that he found few new paths himself. His great contribution was that he popularized the West at a time when the American people were caught up in the throes of expansionism and Manifest Destiny.

Frémont was aided by two powerful patrons. Joel R. Poinsett obtained a commission for him in the elite Topographical Engineers, and Senator Thomas Hart Benton, his father-in-law, rescued him from many a crisis. More importantly, his wife, Jessie Benton, rewrote his prosaic reports so that his exploits became high drama and thus made him one of the most popular men of the age. Although Frémont had been well trained by French scientist Joseph Nicollet on two expeditions, Frémont was often careless in reporting on the lands he explored.

Frémont's first venture westward came in 1842. Its purpose was to aid emigration to Oregon by advertising the ease of the Platte River–South Pass route. Departing from Westport, Missouri, the party, including Christopher ("Kit") Carson as guide, Lucien Maxwell as hunter, and Charles Preuss as topographer, followed the Oregon Trail to the South Pass in what is today western Wyoming. Upon reaching the Wind River Range, Frémont decided to climb what he believed was the highest peak in the Rocky Mountains (Frémont Peak, elevation 13, 785 feet). In fact, fifty-five peaks in the central Rockies are higher, and the ascent of Frémont Peak was not especially difficult.

After the descent the party headed east. The main group, under Clement Lambert, went overland, while Frémont and six others sought to descend the Platte River at flood stage in a collapsible boat. Amid rocks in a narrow canyon, the boat capsized. Many scientific records were lost and instruments damaged, but despite a close call, no lives were lost. Frémont's report, ably ghostwritten by Jessie, made popular reading with the renewed national interest in Oregon.

In 1843, Frémont was charged with continuing his explorations westward to the Pacific along the route of what later approximated the Oregon Trail. On September 6, Frémont reached the Great Salt Lake, and it was his exaggerated reports of the area that possibly convinced Brigham Young later to settle there. On reaching Oregon, Frémont had completed the task he had been assigned. However, he decided to follow the Deschutes River through Oregon in the hope of finding the legendary Buenaventura River, which supposedly flowed from the Rockies to the Pacific. His party went south to Klamath Lake, mistook the Klamath River for the Sacramento, and then went south along the Sierra Nevada. On January 19, 1844, Frémont decided to cross the Sierras in midwinter, and did so with great hardship. After resting at Sutter's fort,

he went south in the San Joaquin Valley over the Tehachapi Pass until he struck the Old Spanish Trail eastward through Fort Uintah and then to Bent's Fort.

Frémont's third western expedition into California was his most controversial, and many have speculated that he was instructed to seize the Mexican province. From Bent's Fort the party went up the Arkansas and through the Rockies and Utah. After exploring both Utah Lake and the Great Salt Lake, they pushed westward into Nevada, where the party was divided to cover as much area as possible. Theodore Talbot and Edward Kern led the larger group, assisted by Joseph R. Walker. Both parties met at Walker Lake only to continue their separate ways. Frémont, with a small group, went through what the next year became known as the Donner Pass, while the larger party came north through the San Joaquin Valley. After reuniting, the Americans defied the Mexican authorities from their camp at Gavilan Peak. Finally, after moving northward into Oregon, Frémont returned to California as a result of messages carried by Lt. Archibald Gillespie.

Frémont's explorations in 1848–49 were a complete disaster. Eager to regain prestige lost in his army court martial, he led a privately financed party in an effort to find a pass through the Rockies for a transcontinental railroad. Leaving Westport on October 20, 1848, Frémont followed the Kansas River and then its Smoky Hill Fork and then journeyed up the Arkansas River. He went over the Sangre de Cristo Range at Mosca Pass and down into the Upper Rio Grande in the San Luis Valley. By then it was December, and the experienced men in the group warned Frémont to turn back. Disaster hit after a snowstorm in the San Juan Mountains, and before the party could extricate itself ten men were dead; later there were charges of cannibalism against the group. Frémont then returned to Taos, where he continued on to California and even claimed: "The result was entirely satisfactory. It convinced me that neither the snow of winter nor the mountain ranges were obstacles in the way of a railroad."

Despite the loss of one-third of his party in 1848–49, Frémont still believed that a railroad route through the mountains along the thirty-eighth parallel was feasible and could be operated in winter, so in 1853 he again led an expedition westward from Westport by Bent's Fort and Pueblo despite being slowed by personal illness. On December 3 the group plunged into the mountains, reaching Cochetopa Pass on December 14. From there they moved westward along the Uncompahgre River, the Gunnison, and the Grand until they reached the Green River in Utah. Although it was very cold, the snow was usually passable. Nevertheless, the party lost one of its twenty-two men before finding food and warmth in the Mormon village of Parowan, Utah. After a period of rest, Frémont continued to California.

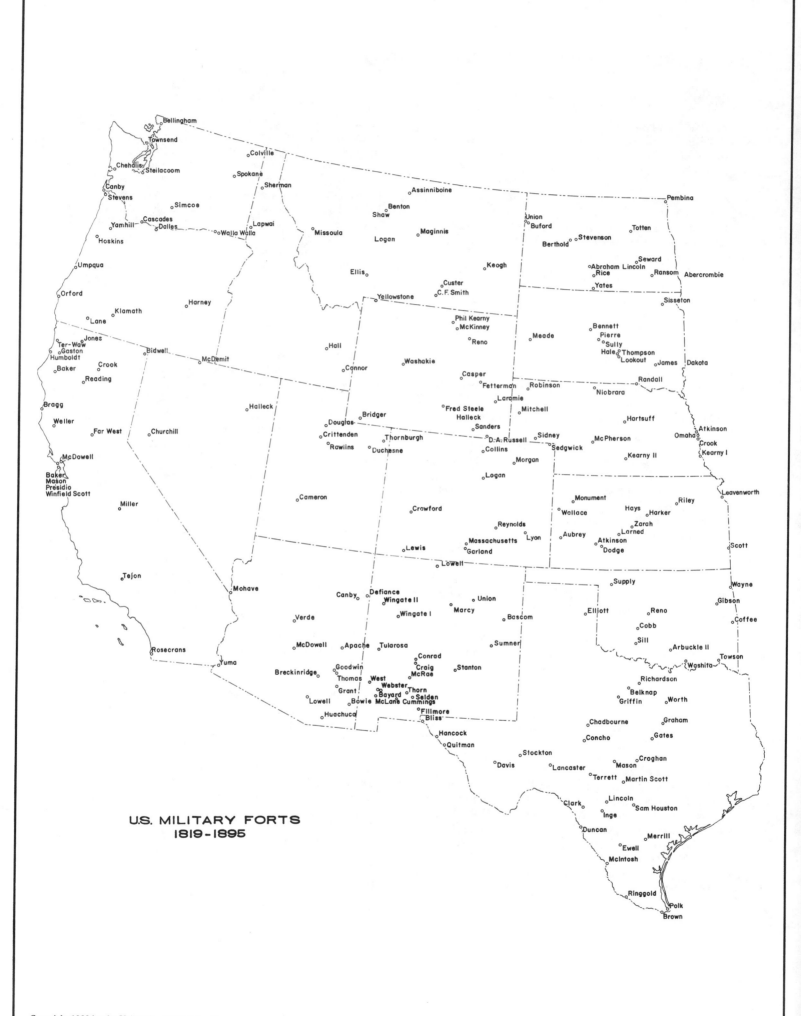

U.S. MILITARY FORTS
1819-1895

37. U.S. MILITARY FORTS, 1819–1895

As THE PIONEERS EDGED WESTWARD the U.S. Army was usually nearby. Its official purpose was to protect the pioneers from the Indians, and vice versa, under treaty obligations. In addition to their peacekeeping function, the army's forts became the harbingers of civilization in the wilderness. The first roads were usually charted by the military, while at the forts, gristmills, sawmills, and blacksmith shops were erected by the troops, often so serve the early settlers as well. The initial trade was created to fulfill the needs of the army. In other words, frontier military posts provided the nucleus around which civilized society emerged. In some cases, flourishing cities developed on the sites of former forts.

Forts were established to keep the Indians in check or to protect a mountain pass, a juncture of waterways, or an international border. Water was the prime essential for western forts; a stream, a lake, or even a spring was a minimum necessity. Pasture for horses and cattle had to be reasonably close, though at Fort Yuma the nearest hay was one hundred miles distant. Suitable building material in the form of stone, timber, or earth for adobe was also an absolute need. Often, suitable supplies of these essentials were soon depleted, and the post commander was forced to relocate. Thus, a fort could be established at one point and later be moved several times.

Forts were often called posts, cantonments, or barracks. The designation of fort indicated some degree of permanence. In actual practice, this was not a firm rule, and the same installation often was known variously as post, camp, or fort. The War Department issued regulations in 1832 and again in 1878 governing the naming of forts, but they usually were not followed. One reason for confusion was that forts were commissioned to serve a need, but once their purpose had been fulfilled, they were abandoned. Some lasted only a matter of months, while others were in use for several decades. The acquisition of Texas, Oregon, and the Mexican cession saw a flurry of fort building. This was also true in the 1840s and 1850s, when the plains were crowded with wagon trains en route west. The Indian wars of the 1850s, '70s, and '80s were likewise times of fort building. By 1891 the Indian wars were over, and in that year the secretary of war declared that a quarter of the posts occupied in 1889 had been closed and that it was planned to abandon a dozen more.

Forts were built of whatever materials were at hand. Logs chinked with a mixture of sand, mud, and lime were preferred, but in the Southwest adobe structures were common. Often the first sawmills in an area were operated by the army in an effort to get lumber to build proper frame dwellings. Some forts of stone and brick were handsome and pleasant places for the troops. Others, like Fort Ruby, Nevada, were so humble that the soldiers stationed there offered to surrender their back pay if they could be transferred out of such desolation to fight on Civil War battlefields. Few of the forts were surrounded by a stockade, because Indians seldom attacked a fort.

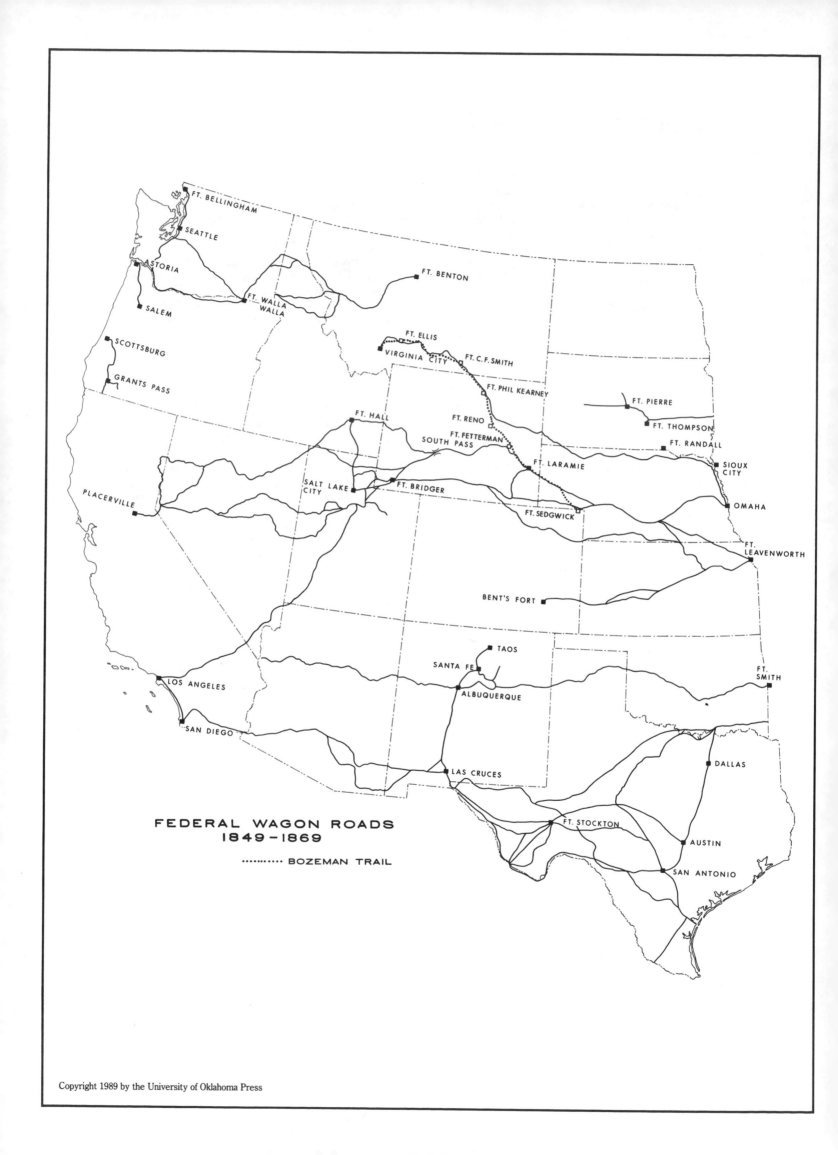

FEDERAL WAGON ROADS
1849–1869

·········· BOZEMAN TRAIL

38. FEDERAL WAGON ROADS, 1849–1869

THE MASS EXODUS WESTWARD in the early days of the nation was greatly facilitated by the roads built during the 1790s, when an enthusiasm for internal improvements swept the new republic. Most of those roads were not highways in the modern meaning of the term but were often charted paths; some were merely crudely cut slashes, dotted with stumps and interspersed with bottomless mudholes, through dense wilderness. But they were passable to the traveler of the day, and westward-moving Americans came to expect the federal government to ease their way by building roads.

As important as federal road building was east of the Mississippi, it was of even greater significance in the American West, where distances were much greater, navigable rivers fewer, and mountains so formidable that even the stout-hearted trembled before them. To cross the higher elevations it was often necessary to unload the wagons and pull them up by means of block and tackle, with the contents being hand-carried up the slope. Sometimes the trail was so steep it was necessary to put the two large hind wheels on one side and the two small front ones on the other to keep the wagon from tipping over. Even on the plains the going was difficult, especially in inclement weather, as most trails followed river valleys that quickly became bogs. Road building usually consisted of marking the trail and perhaps rolling a few rocks out of the way.

Federal road building in the West was triggered by military necessity after the Mexican War. It was essential that the army learn the most advantageous sites for forts, survey the best routes between them so wagons could haul essential supplies, and chart the best roads by which immigrants could settle the new territory. The discovery of gold in California speeded up this process. Even while the war was in progress, Capt. Philip St. George Cooke led the Mormon Battalion from New Mexico to San Diego.

Leaving the established trail, he swung southward in a wide; semicircular loop and effectively showed that wagons could traverse the Southwest. In 1849, Capt. Randolph B. Marcy charted a wagon road from Fort Smith to Santa Fe along the Canadian River. Other army surveys improved the Oregon Trail, laid out new wagon roads in Utah, and in general helped the rush across the plains to the gold fields. In the northwest the Mullen Road connected Walla Walla and Fort Benton.

While the building of federal wagon roads was ostensibly for military purposes, it worked to the advantage of settlers, who simply used the army-constructed routes. In fact, military use and civilian use were often identical. As William Goetzmann points out, "It was the nearest approach to federal planning for the development of the trans-Mississippi region that existed, and it had arisen out of the military necessity of binding the political Union closer together and the desire to facilitate the exploitation of the gold deposits in California." While the army built roads throughout the West, the most extensive network was in Texas, New Mexico, and Utah.

Although the army, as the government's road builder, was instrumental in opening the way for miners, ranchers, lumbermen, and settlers, there was always a clamor for more and better routes. California's Senator John B. Weller presented a memorial to the Congress on May 19, 1856, demanding the construction of a federal wagon road to the Mississippi River. Enthusiasm for the project was high on the West Coast, but it soon became entangled in sectional politics and failed to be passed. However, some of the planning for a road across the Sierra Nevada was of assistance in the ultimate building of the transcontinental railroad. In general, the federal wagon roads of the West blazed the trails that the railroads and, much later, the modern highways were to follow.

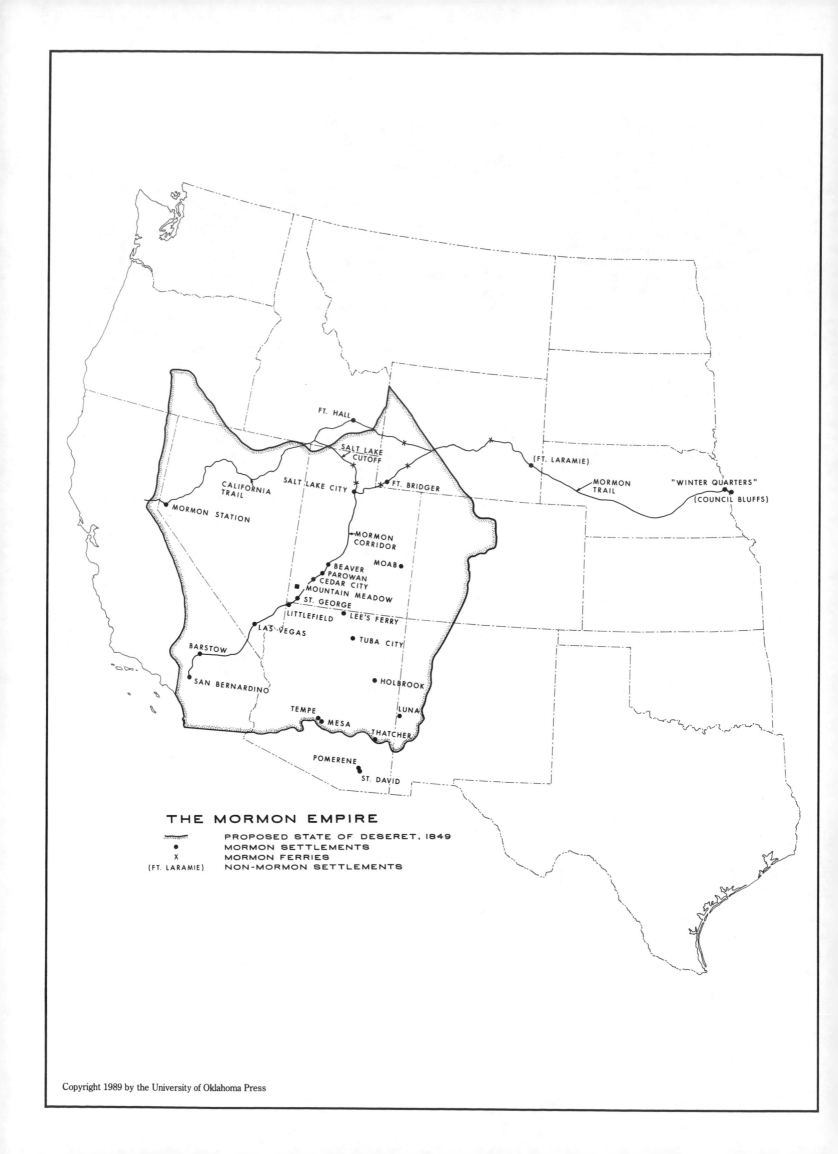

FT. HALL

SALT LAKE
CUTOFF

CALIFORNIA
TRAIL

SALT LAKE CITY

FT. BRIDGER

(FT. LARAMIE)

MORMON
TRAIL

"WINTER QUARTERS"

(COUNCIL BLUFFS)

MORMON STATION

MORMON
CORRIDOR

MOAB

BEAVER
PAROWAN
CEDAR CITY
MOUNTAIN MEADOW
ST. GEORGE
LITTLEFIELD   LEE'S FERRY
LAS VEGAS
BARSTOW   TUBA CITY
SAN BERNARDINO
HOLBROOK

TEMPE   LUNA
MESA
THATCHER
POMERENE
ST. DAVID

THE MORMON EMPIRE

PROPOSED STATE OF DESERET, 1849
•   MORMON SETTLEMENTS
X   MORMON FERRIES
(FT. LARAMIE)   NON-MORMON SETTLEMENTS

39. THE MORMON EMPIRE

FROM JULY 24, 1847, when Brigham Young led the first contingent of Latter-Day Saints into Utah, he dreamed of a mighty empire in the American West which would be the true "Kingdom of God on earth." The Mormons first proposed the state of Deseret (the *Book of Mormon* word for honey bee) for which they hoped to attain immediate statehood. The planned state embraced one-sixth of the entire modern United States. Included were present-day Utah and Arizona, most of Nevada, portions of Idaho, Wyoming, Colorado, and New Mexico, and southern California below 34° N. San Diego was to be the seaport for this vast inland empire.

Congress refused to approve so vast a state for the unpopular Mormons. Instead, the territory of Utah (named for the Ute Indian tribe), with boundaries which included all of the present state of Utah, most of Nevada, the western third of Colorado, and part of Wyoming, was approved. Through the years the territory of Utah lost 91,900 square miles to Nevada, 29,500 square miles to Colorado, and a smaller area to Wyoming.

The Morman Trail along the Platte River through Nebraska was initially established because so many of the faithful came from the Midwest. On the trail the Mormons, who counted among their converts some of the nation's ablest entrepreneurs, saw the potential gain in establishing ferries or other businesses catering to the needs of the overland travelers. And once the California Gold Rush of 1849 was on, profits were enormous.

To Brigham Young the future of his empire lay in establishing new settlements, as it was obvious that the Salt Lake Valley could support but a small number of people. Initially, "the inner cordon" of settlements was founded at Salt Lake and Weber valleys in 1847 and 1848, followed by colonies in the Utah, Tooele, and San Pete valleys the next year. Within ten years more than a hundred such settlements emerged. Once the "inner cordon" was successfully colonized, expansion southward along the Mormon Corridor took place. Near Cedar City a mountain of iron ore combined with limitless supplies of cedar wood for fuel was a boon to settlement.

The next step in Mormon expansion was to ring the inland empire with strategically located colonies. Parowan (Utah) was one of the early key points. Carson Valley, Nevada, was started in 1849–51; Las Vegas in 1855; Fort Bridger, Wyoming, in 1853. In 1852 a group of Mormons settled on the old San Bernardino Ranch below the strategic Cajon Pass in California. This expansive drive was checked in 1857 as a result of the troubles culminating in the Mountain Meadows Massacre, after which most settlers in distant villages abandoned their homes and heeded the call to return to Utah.

Once the threat of hostilities was removed, expansion from the core of Mormon settlement in Utah was renewed. In one respect the threat of conflict in 1857–58 aided the establishment of new colonies. Brigham Young, fearing an invasion by the U.S. Army, sent out exploring parties to the vast areas southwest of Salt Lake City to look for isolated valley oases that could be used for farming but that could also be easily defended. Several new settlements were founded as a result of this exploration, but the large number of people called in during the threat of war demanded immediate action. Then too, two thousand to four thousand immigrants were brought to Utah annually by the church wagon trains. Between 1858 and 1868, 150 new towns were founded. The 1850 Utah population of eleven thousand grew to eighty-six thousand by 1870.

The struggle over polygamy also acted as a catalyst to further the expansion of Mormon settlements. Once the U.S. Supreme Court had affirmed the constitutionality of federal antipolygamy laws, it was obvious that Utah would be denied statehood until the matter was resolved. Therefore, in 1890 the church withdrew its approval of plural marriages, and in 1896 Utah became the forty-fifth state.

Many Mormons, unwilling to surrender the practice of polygamy, sought refuge from the law in isolated valleys of Utah and Arizona as early as the 1870s. Lee's Ferry across the Colorado River facilitated Mormon movement southward into Arizona. From that crossing the settlers went along the Little Colorado River, founding a number of towns with Holbrook as the hub. The Mormons usually had excellent judgment in locating where there was an opportunity for survival. For example, a settlement near Saint David sold farm produce to the mining camps of Tombstone and Bisbee, the railroad town of Benson, and the nearby military forts.

The Mormons' very success may have triggered some persecution from the non-Mormon community, but most opposition to them arose from their practice of polygamy. This pressure caused their expansion first northward into Idaho and then into Canada. However, Mexico was considered the best refuge. In 1886 the main Mormon exodus took place mainly to the northwestern part of the state of Chihuahua, but with two colonies nearby in Sonora. By 1912 the Mexican colonies had 4,225 people. However, the prosperous Mormons suffered during the Mexican revolutions, and most were forced to flee in poverty to El Paso. A few hardy souls returned once the turmoil had died down, and in 1980, Colonia Juárez and Colonia Dublán had a combined population of seven hundred.

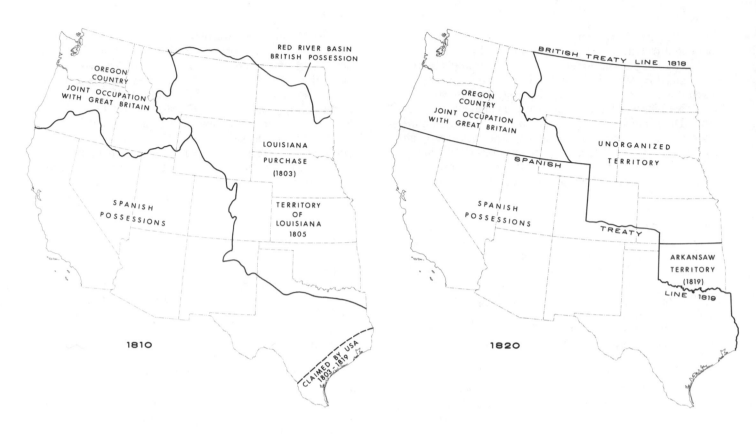

TERRITORIAL EXPANSION I

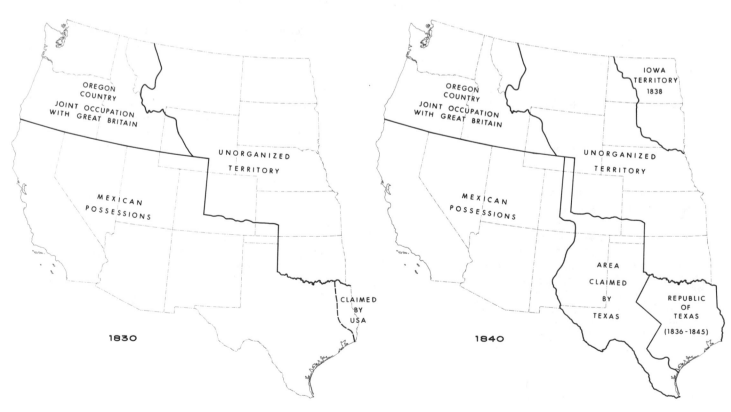

40. TERRITORIAL EXPANSION I

MOST OF THE VAST EXPANSE of the American West was first created by the Louisiana Purchase in 1803. This area had been transferred by France to Spain in 1763, but a secret treaty returned it to Spain in 1800. When news of the transfer emerged, the normally pro-French President Jefferson wrote that if it were true, "we must marry ourselves to the British fleet and nation." The presidential concern came from the need of western farmers for a trade route with European markets via New Orleans. Jefferson, for political reasons, was prepared to go to any length to protect the economy of the Mississippi Valley. So he attempted to buy New Orleans. When Napoleon countered by offering all of Louisiana, Jefferson accepted.

One problem of the Louisiana Purchase was that it had not been surveyed, and its boundaries were vague. They were defined as the same as they had been under Spain in 1800 and the same as they had been under France in 1762. When Robert Livingston, an American negotiator, pressed for a clarification of the southwestern boundary with Spanish territory, he was told by Talleyrand, the French foreign minister, "I do not know . . . I can give you no direction; you have made a noble bargain for yourselves, and I suppose you will make the most of it." With such vague limits to their purchase, the Americans were to lay claim to Texas. However, in 1819 they surrendered this shadowy title in the Adams-Onís Treaty with Spain.

The boundary of the Louisiana Territory as fixed in the 1819 treaty followed the Sabine River from the Gulf of Mexico to parallel 32° N and then ran due north to the Red River, following that stream to the meridian 100° W. From there it turned due north to the Arkansas River and ran along that stream to its source, and then again due north to the parallel of 42° N and west along that line to the Pacific Ocean.

By the Convention of 1818 the northern boundary of the American West was established at the parallel of 49° N from Lake of the Woods to the Rocky Mountains. American efforts to extent that line to the sea and thus settle the Oregon question were rejected by the British. Instead, agreement was reached in the Convention of 1818 to continue for ten years what had, in effect, become a joint occupation of the Oregon territory.

However, many alterations were to occur in the next decades. Arkansas Territory was created in 1819, and Iowa Territory in 1838. Texas became an independent republic from 1836 to 1845, then in late 1845 was annexed to the United States, with its western boundaries still claimed as the Rio Grande to its source and then north to the parallel of 42° N.

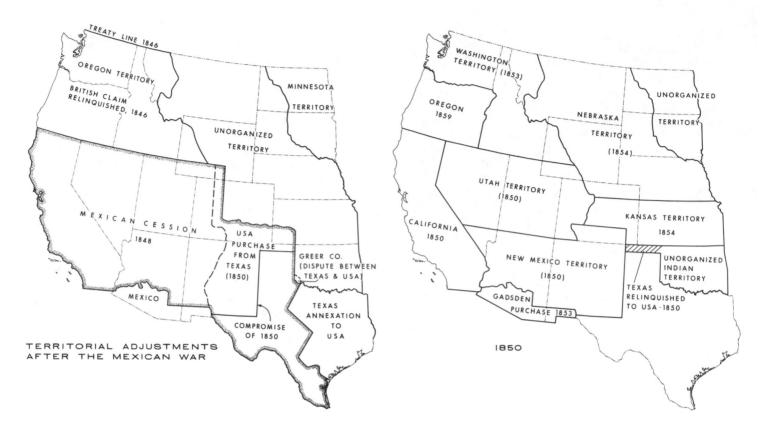

TREATY LINE 1846

OREGON TERRITORY

BRITISH CLAIM
RELINQUISHED, 1846

MINNESOTA
TERRITORY

UNORGANIZED
TERRITORY

M E X I C A N   C E S S I O N

1848

USA
PURCHASE
FROM
TEXAS
(1850)

GREER CO.
(DISPUTE BETWEEN
TEXAS & USA)

MEXICO

COMPROMISE
OF 1850

TEXAS
ANNEXATION
TO
USA

**TERRITORIAL ADJUSTMENTS
AFTER THE MEXICAN WAR**

WASHINGTON
TERRITORY (1853)

OREGON
1859

NEBRASKA
TERRITORY
(1854)

UNORGANIZED

TERRITORY

UTAH TERRITORY
(1850)

CALIFORNIA
1850

KANSAS TERRITORY
1854

NEW MEXICO TERRITORY
(1850)

UNORGANIZED
INDIAN
TERRITORY

GADSDEN
PURCHASE 1853

TEXAS
RELINQUISHED
TO USA·1850

1850

TERRITORIAL EXPANSION II

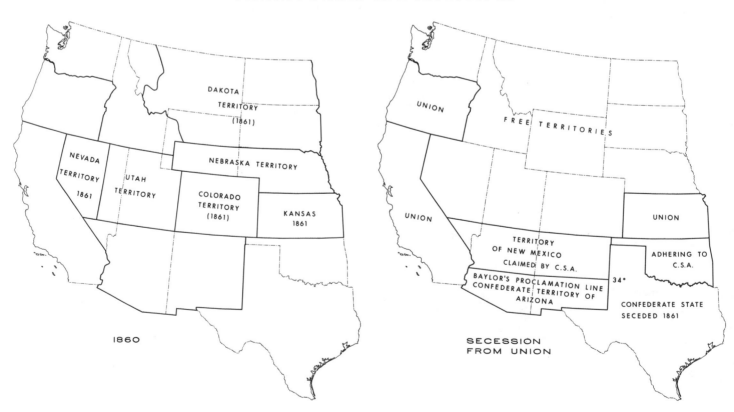

DAKOTA
TERRITORY
(1861)

NEVADA
TERRITORY
1861

UTAH
TERRITORY

NEBRASKA TERRITORY

COLORADO
TERRITORY
(1861)

KANSAS
1861

1860

UNION

F R E E   T E R R I T O R I E S

UNION

UNION

TERRITORY
OF NEW MEXICO
CLAIMED BY C.S.A.

ADHERING TO
C.S.A.

34°

BAYLOR'S PROCLAMATION LINE
CONFEDERATE TERRITORY OF
ARIZONA

CONFEDERATE STATE
SECEDED 1861

**SECESSION
FROM UNION**

41. TERRITORIAL EXPANSION II

THE MEXICAN CESSION after the war between the United States and that country expanded the American West to almost its present size. The Treaty of Guadalupe Hidalgo, signed in 1848, gave the United States the present-day states of California, Nevada, Utah, most of Arizona and New Mexico, and parts of Colorado, Wyoming, Kansas, and Oklahoma. In addition, American title to Texas was confirmed. As a part of the Compromise of 1850, the Lone Star State surrendered its claim to the upper Rio Grande for a cash settlement.

A curious dispute arose over Greer County, a fertile 2,300-square-mile area which soon attracted many settlers. The difficulty arose because surveys as far back as 1852 designated the North Fork of the Red River as the main branch of that stream, placing Greer County in Texas by terms of the Adams-Onís Treaty of 1819. Later federal surveys discovered that the original mapping was in error and that the North Fork was only a tributary of the Red River. Therefore, Greer County belonged to Indian Territory. A U.S. Supreme Court decision confirmed this in 1896.

The rapid influx of settlers into Oregon in the 1840s prompted the British to relinquish their claim to the region south of 49° N latitude in 1846. In 1848 Oregon was organized as a territory. In 1853 the area north of the Columbia River was detached and became part of Washington Territory. Minnesota Territory was formed in 1849, extending to the Missouri River.

The present area of the American West was completed by the Gadsden Purchase from Mexico in 1853. This vast area below the Gila River was coveted because it provided an excellent route for a transcontinental railroad. Except for Texas, California was the first trans-Mississippi state to be admitted to the Union, in 1850. It was followed by Oregon in 1859. Utah and New Mexico became territories in 1850, and Nebraska and Kansas were organized as territories in 1854. Kansas was admitted as a state in 1861. In the same year, several territories were organized or had their boundaries adjusted: Dakota, Nevada, Colorado, and Nebraska.

The Civil War had a limited effect upon the American West. Texas was the only western state to secede and join the Confederate States of America. Oregon, California, and Kansas remained as free states in the Union. Although several tribes remained loyal to the United States, Indian Territory was organized into a military district of the Confederacy. On March 16, 1861, a secessionist convention was held at Mesilla which declared Arizona to be a territory of the Southern states. After his victory over Union forces in southern New Mexico, Col. John R. Baylor proclaimed the Confederate Territory of Arizona. This vast area included all of New Mexico south of the parallel 34° N and extended from Texas to California. It ultimately became the only territory of the Confederacy. However, the officers of this new territory fled when the Confederate troops were driven from all of New Mexico in 1862.

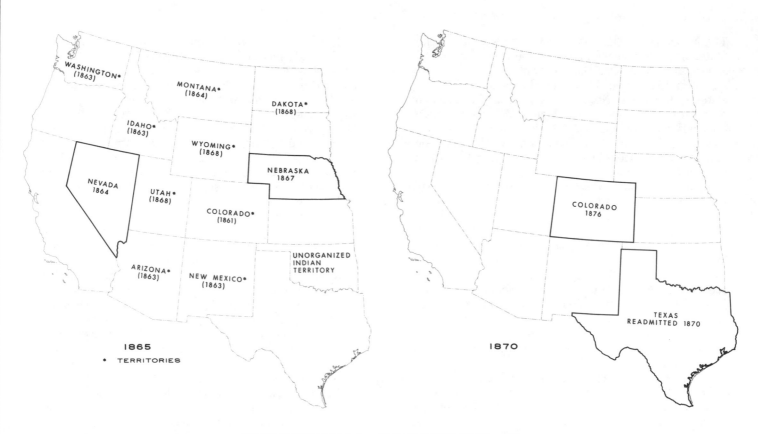

WASHINGTON (1863)

MONTANA (1864)

DAKOTA* (1868)

IDAHO* (1863)

WYOMING* (1868)

NEBRASKA 1867

NEVADA 1864

UTAH* (1868)

COLORADO* (1861)

ARIZONA* (1863)

NEW MEXICO* (1863)

UNORGANIZED INDIAN TERRITORY

1865

• TERRITORIES

COLORADO 1876

TEXAS READMITTED 1870

1870

TERRITORIAL EXPANSION III

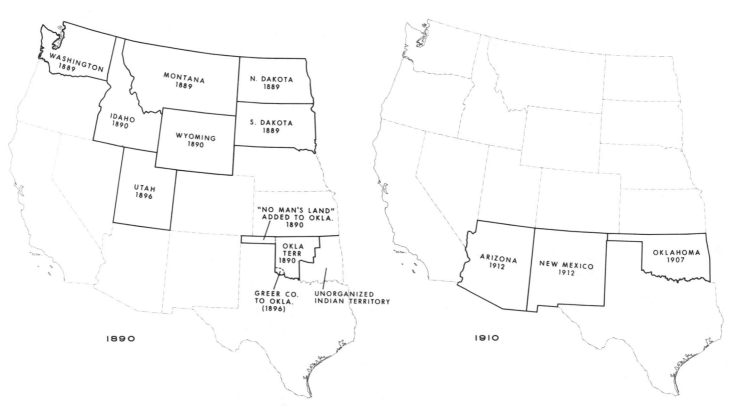

WASHINGTON 1889

MONTANA 1889

N. DAKOTA 1889

IDAHO 1890

WYOMING 1890

S. DAKOTA 1889

UTAH 1896

"NO MAN'S LAND" ADDED TO OKLA. 1890

OKLA TERR 1890

GREER CO. TO OKLA. (1896)

UNORGANIZED INDIAN TERRITORY

1890

ARIZONA 1912

NEW MEXICO 1912

OKLAHOMA 1907

1910

42. TERRITORIAL EXPANSION III

AFTER THE CIVIL WAR extensive changes took place in the American West. In 1864, Nevada was admitted to the Union as a state, followed by Nebraska in 1867 and Colorado in 1876. Texas was readmitted in 1870. Idaho and Arizona were organized as territories in 1863. Montana became a territory in 1864 and Wyoming in 1868.

Change in the West came more slowly after the flurry of activity following the war. In 1890 the western portion of today's state of Oklahoma became a territory and received the panhandle strip known as "No Man's Land" that had originally been a part of Texas.

Statehood was often determined by politics. Nevada had too small a population to justify it but was nevertheless granted it to ensure that Lincoln had enough electoral votes in 1864. The rapid influx of settlers in the northern part of the American West in the 1880s brought frequent demands for statehood. These demands went unheeded, however, because the states would have been Republican states, and the Democrats who controlled one house or the other during the decade did not want to upset the delicate balance. Not until 1888, when the Republicans controlled the House and Senate, was action on statehood possible. To assure themselves of two additional Senate seats, the Republicans even divided Dakota Territory into North and South, a move that is questionable to this day. By means of an "omnibus bill," North Dakota, South Dakota, Montana, and Washington were admitted as states in 1889. Idaho and Wyoming were accepted as states the following year. Utah, which had long had more than enough population to qualify for statehood, had been denied admission ostensibly because of the practice of polygamy. After the Mormon leaders banned this practice, Congress admitted Utah as a state in 1896.

From the first land rush in 1889, the people of Oklahoma Territory worked for statehood. Every year from 1889 to 1907 delegates to Congress lobbied for statehood bills. The territory had a population of 400,000 by 1900, more than enough to qualify it for statehood. The relationship of Oklahoma to Indian Territory was one cause of delay. Most assumed that the two territories would be fused into a single state. The leaders of the Five Civilized Tribes vigorously opposed statehood and worked to delay it as long as possible. They even proposed a separate state of Sequoyah, held a convention, and ratified a constitution. Their efforts were in vain, as Congress insisted on the single state of Oklahoma, which was admitted to the Union in 1907.

The struggle of Arizona and New Mexico to be admitted as states lasted from 1850 to 1910, during which period fifty bills requesting admission were introduced into Congress. The two territories had sufficient population, but statehood was delayed because of partisan politics and the question whether they should be admitted as a single state or two. Unfortunately, religious bigotry, racial discrimination, and general ignorance of the Southwest were more important obstacles. When these two states were finally admitted in 1910, all of the American West was in the Union.

1800-1820

1820-1835

EUROPEAN   SETTLEMENT

1835-1850

1850-1890

43. EUROPEAN SETTLEMENT

ALTHOUGH MUCH OF THE SOUTHWEST and the California coast had been explored by the middle of the sixteenth century, European development took place slowly. The region was distant from Spanish-held Mexico, the closest center of European settlement, and the failure to discover gold or silver left no incentive for settlers to move into such an inhospitable land. Therefore, Spain first settled in New Mexico, and the basic reason for that action was religious. The mission was used to convert and Hispanicize the Indian. Settlement began in Santa Fe in 1610, but the white man was driven out by the Indians in 1680, only to return in the 1690s.

The settlement of Texas was even more difficult, with San Antonio, first founded in 1718, the only significant settlement still in existence by 1800. The first Spaniards moved into California in 1769. In all of the Spanish colonies by 1800 there were probably only 4,000 Europeans in San Antonio and the surrounding area, perhaps 2,130 in California, and possibly 28,000 in New Mexico. (Exact figures are impossible to determine, as Indians were counted as Europeans in some colonies but not in others.)

European settlement of Spain's northern frontier was partially a result of accident; church leaders would have preferred keeping the area as an exclusive Indian region controlled by the missions. However, church leaders needed the military for protection against the Indians, and the Spanish fort, or presidio, often became the nucleus around which towns grew. The poorly paid soldiers often took Indian wives and then tilled the soil or kept livestock to support their families. When retired, the soldiers would usually stay near the presidio or obtain a rancho in the area. Thus, European settlement grew unplanned. In California, pueblos or towns were established at San José in 1777 with sixty-six persons, and in 1781 at Los Angeles with forty-six persons. The purpose of these towns was to have people who would raise food for the military and also to provide extra hands for defense.

Between 1820 and 1835 there was a slow but steady growth of European settlements. The development of population clusters along the coast in California resulted from the growing importance of the hide and tallow trade and, to a lesser extent, of lumbering. New Mexico's population also expanded between 1820 and 1835 but was still confined to towns and ranchos along the Rio Grande or its tributaries. Texas, in this same period, went through extensive changes. The Hispanic population grew slowly and was only four thousand by 1835, but thirty thousand Anglo whites and five thousand black slaves were added to the total.

From 1835 to 1850, New Mexico's European settlement showed a small growth. Texas and California, however, experienced dramatic change. The Lone Star State counted 154,034 whites and 58,161 black slaves concentrated in the eastern third of the state. California underwent even more extensive population growth. As late as 1848 there were only some 14,000 Europeans in the state, most of whom were Hispanics. By 1850 the total was about 100,000, and two years later it was estimated to be 250,000, most of whom were Anglos concentrated in the central portion of the state.

In the years from 1850 to 1890 the American West was rapidly filled by Europeans, most of whom actually came between 1870 and 1890. What happened in Montana was repeated many times in different parts of the West. In 1880 central and eastern Montana were practically uninhabited, with buffalo, antelope, deer, and elk plentiful. Three years later the wild animals were gone, replaced by range cattle. Settlement followed river valleys and railroad lines. This "last frontier" was settled by miners, ranchers, and farmers lured by rich mineral deposits and the chance to exploit free grass and free land. The rapid settlement was speeded by favorable land laws, immigration, and especially by the building of the railroads. In addition, the invention of barbed wire and the production in quantity of cheap windmills helped the process. Several years of above-average precipitation also convinced the settlers that bonanza farming would make them rich.

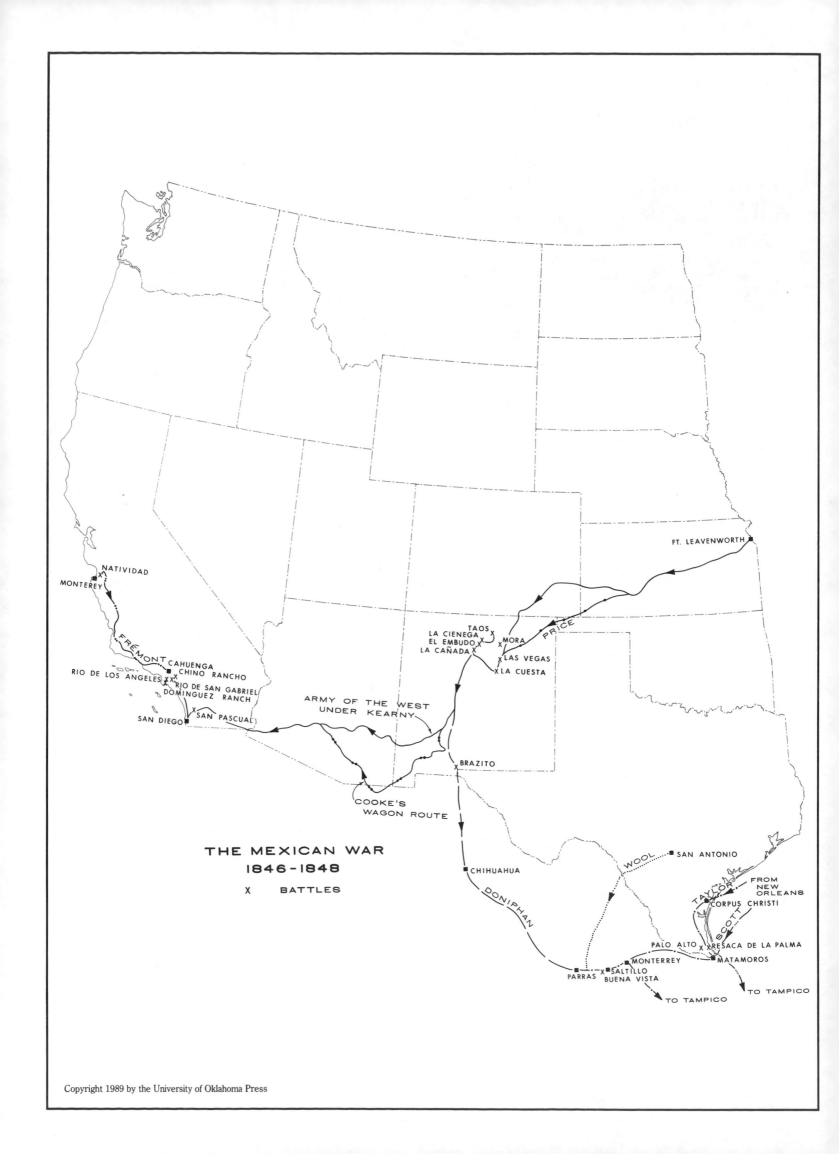

THE MEXICAN WAR
1846-1848

X   BATTLES

NATIVIDAD
MONTEREY
FRÉMONT
CAHUENGA
CHINO RANCHO
RIO DE LOS ANGELES
RIO DE SAN GABRIEL
DOMINGUEZ RANCH
SAN DIEGO
SAN PASCUAL

ARMY OF THE WEST
UNDER KEARNY

TAOS
LA CIENEGA
EL EMBUDO
LA CAÑADA
MORA
PRICE
LAS VEGAS
LA CUESTA

FT. LEAVENWORTH

BRAZITO

COOKE'S
WAGON ROUTE

CHIHUAHUA

DONIPHAN

WOOL   SAN ANTONIO

TAYLOR
CORPUS CHRISTI
FROM
NEW
ORLEANS
SCOTT

PALO ALTO
RESACA DE LA PALMA
MATAMOROS

MONTERREY
SALTILLO
BUENA VISTA
PARRAS

TO TAMPICO

TO TAMPICO

44. THE MEXICAN WAR, 1846–1848

ANTICIPATING THE OUTBREAK OF HOSTILITIES with Mexico, Gen. Zachary Taylor, with a small army, arrived on the Nueces River at Corpus Christi in July, 1845. This placed him on the edge of the territory in dispute between the United States and Mexico, while making it possible to supply his force by sea. When the Mexican government refused to negotiate, President Polk ordered Taylor to the Rio Grande in April, 1846. Hostilities began on April 24 when an American patrol blundered into a superior Mexican cavalry unit. On May 7, Taylor marched towards the Rio Grande, and although outnumbered two to one, he defeated the Mexicans at the Battle of Palo Alto on May 8 and at Resaca de la Palma the next day. After these victories Taylor crossed the river and occupied the Mexican river town of Matamoros.

With reinforcements pouring in and men dying of disease en masse, the American leader marched his force toward Monterrey, an old fortified city. After bitter and costly fighting, the Mexicans surrendered. Meanwhile, Washington officials had decided that the war could be won only by an assault on Mexico City and ordered Taylor to remain in Monterrey. Instead, the American general led his forces to Saltillo, which guarded the Rinconada Pass. Gen. John E. Wool, with 2,400 men, had marched from San Antonio, bringing Taylor's force of mainly volunteers to 6,000. Mexican General Santa Anna attacked the Americans at Buena Vista. The main battle was fought on February 23, 1847, with the Mexicans winning the day. However, short of supplies and poorly organized, they fled the battlefield, allowing Taylor his greatest victory.

While Taylor was engaging the major Mexican forces in the lower Rio Grande Valley and on to Buena Vista, an Army of the West, commanded by Gen. Stephen Watts Kearny, was sent from Fort Leavenworth. Sterling Price, a Missouri politician, organized a thousand men for the army and received the rank of colonel. Despite good natural defences at Glorieta Pass, near Las Vegas, the Mexican force offered only token resistance. Believing that New Mexico had surrendered, and informed that California had ceased resistance, Kearny dispatched Colonel Alexander William Doniphan's force to help Taylor, left Price in command at Santa Fe, and led only a small force to the Pacific Coast. Doniphan fought battles at Brazito and Chihuahua and arrived too late to help at Buena Vista. However, a revolt in Taos in January, 1847, provoked considerable fighting at La Cienaga, El Embrudo, La Cañada, Mora, Las Vegas, and La Cuesta.

En route to California, Capt. Philip St. George Cooke charted a wagon route through Guadalupe Pass into Arizona. Kearny, with only some hundred men in his command, met a superior Mexican force at San Pascual, California, on December 6, 1846. Twenty-one Americans were killed and eighteen wounded, but that was the last Mexican victory in California.

Before the arrival of Kearny, Americans in California, assisted by Capt. John C. Frémont, started a revolt against Mexico on June 10, 1846. A number of skirmishes were fought, including one at Natividad in the Salinas Valley. After first laying down their arms, the native Californios revolted against the Americans and won minor clashes at Chino Rancho and Dominguez Ranch. However, Kearny's force, greatly strengthened, routed them at battles on Rio de San Gabriel on January 8, 1847, and on Rio de Los Angeles the next day. Meanwhile, a force from northern California under Frémont moved southward, and on January 13, 1847, the Californios capitulated at Cahuenga, formally ending hostilities.

While most of the fighting in the West was on a limited scale, the decisive battles of the Mexican War were fought to the south. In March, 1847, Gen. Winfield Scott landed an army that captured Vera Cruz, fought its way overland, and on September 14, 1847, captured Mexico City. By the Treaty of Guadalupe Hidalgo, signed on February 2, 1848, Mexico ceded a huge expanse of territory to the United States.

LAWRENCE

MINE CREEK X

DRUM CREEK—X

COWSKIN
PRAIRIE—X

CHUSTENAHLAH—X X—CABIN CREEK
CAVING BANKS—X   X—FT. WAYNE
ROUND MT.—X   X—LOCUST GROVE
FT. DAVIS—X
HONEY SPRINGS—X X—WEBBER'S FALLS
X GLORIETA PASS   X
X—TONKAWA   BACKBONE MT.
X PERALTA   X—PERRYVILLE
X—MUDDY BOGGY
X VALVERDE   X—BOGGY DEPOT

X PICACHO PASS

BATTLES OF THE CIVIL WAR

---- QUANTRILL'S RAID, AUGUST, 1863

X DOVE CREEK

SABINE
PASS X

X NUECES
GALVESTON X

X FT. ESPERANZA

X—PALMITO RANCH
BROWNSVILLE X (LAST BATTLE OF
CIVIL WAR)

45. BATTLES OF THE CIVIL WAR

COMPARED WITH THE BATTLES in the Mississippi Valley and those in Virginia, the Civil War fighting in the American West was on a very small scale. At the beginning of the conflict, though, the stakes in the West were high, and if the Confederate plans had been successful, they could have changed the course of the war. Some Southern leaders hoped to capture Arizona and New Mexico as a prelude to taking California. The seizure of such a vast territory would have enhanced the prestige of the South and perhaps have gained diplomatic recognition from England. The gold of California would have helped finance the war.

The initial campaign was carried out by Col. John R. Baylor, who invaded New Mexico from the El Paso area in July, 1861, capturing many Union soldiers and causing the evacuation of two forts. Baylor also helped Southerners at Mesilla to organize the Confederate Territory of Arizona, embracing the area west of the Rio Grande and south of the Gila River. (Arizona was then a part of New Mexico.)

The next step in this grand design was for a Texas force under Gen. Henry H. Sibley to complete the conquest of New Mexico. The Confederates defeated Col. E. R. S. Canby's Union force at Valverde on February 16, 1862. After taking Santa Fe, Sibley pushed eastward to capture Fort Union. However, the Texans were outflanked at Glorieta Pass and soundly defeated March 26–28. With their supplies gone, they retreated. The Texans were surprised by Union forces after a night of revelry at Peralta on April 15 and were being defeated when a sandstorm halted the battle. Meanwhile, the California Column, a Union force under Gen. James Henry Carleton, moved eastward. An advance unit of this column met and defeated a small detachment of Confederates on April 15, 1862, at Picacho Pass in the westernmost battle of the war.

Texas was the only state of the American West to join the Confederacy, but even in its area there was little fighting. In the western part of the state Comanche-Kiowa bands raided at will, driving settlers from the frontier. Texas lacked the manpower to handle the Indian threat, and when they did attempt to battle the Indians, they blundered. In January, 1865, a unit of Texas state troops attacked a well-armed and large group of Kickapoos at Dove Creek. The Indians repulsed the Texans and inflicted heavy losses. On August 10, 1862, a detachment of Texas Rifles surprised a mounted group (reportedly of German Texans), killing thirty-two while suffering only two dead themselves. This engagement on the Nueces River was fought twenty miles from Fort Clark. Although their coast was blockaded, the Texans won a naval battle at Sabine Pass on September 8, 1863, sinking two of four Union gunboats and driving off a landing force with heavy casualties. Federal forces captured Galveston in October, 1862, but were driven out December 29–31. An excellently defended Fort Esperanza was captured by Union troops on the night of August 29–30, 1863, but not before the Confederates were able to blow up most of it. The Battle of Palmito Ranch on May 12–13, 1865, was one of those battles that had best be forgotten. A Union force had occupied Brownsville since November, 1863, but with the Confederates in nominal control of the countryside. In May, 1865, Col. Theodore H. Barrett, an officer who had seen no combat, and desiring battlefield glory to further a future political career, attacked a superior Confederate force. Perhaps two-thirds of the Union force were casualties in this rout, and even prisoners were shot by the victorious Texans.

Kansas, which had figured so prominently in events leading to the Civil War, saw little fighting during the conflict. The worst time of the war occurred when William Quantrill raided Lawrence on August 21, 1863, murdering some 150 male civilians and burning about two hundred buildings. The most important battle was at Mine Creek on October 25, 1864, when the Confederates were already in full retreat. At Drum Creek, on May 15, 1863, a number of Confederate officers were massacred by Osage Indians.

Indian Territory (now eastern Oklahoma) suffered heavily from the raiding of irregular groups. The Choctaws and Chickasaws, located on the Texas border, mainly supported the Confederacy. Some Cherokees, Creeks, and Seminoles were at first in favor of the South, but many cast their lot with the Union after early Southern setbacks. Confederate plans to seize the territory were thwarted on November 19, 1861, when they were defeated at Round Mountain; on December 9 at Caving Banks (Christo Talasah) Union forces were again victorious. At Chustenahlah on December 26 the Confederates won, driving many Union Indians into refugee camps in Kansas. However, on July 3, 1862, Union forces won at Locust Grove, and they never again lost their dominance in Oklahoma, though they were to lose some skirmishes. As a result, many Indians repudiated their Confederate allegiance and changed sides.

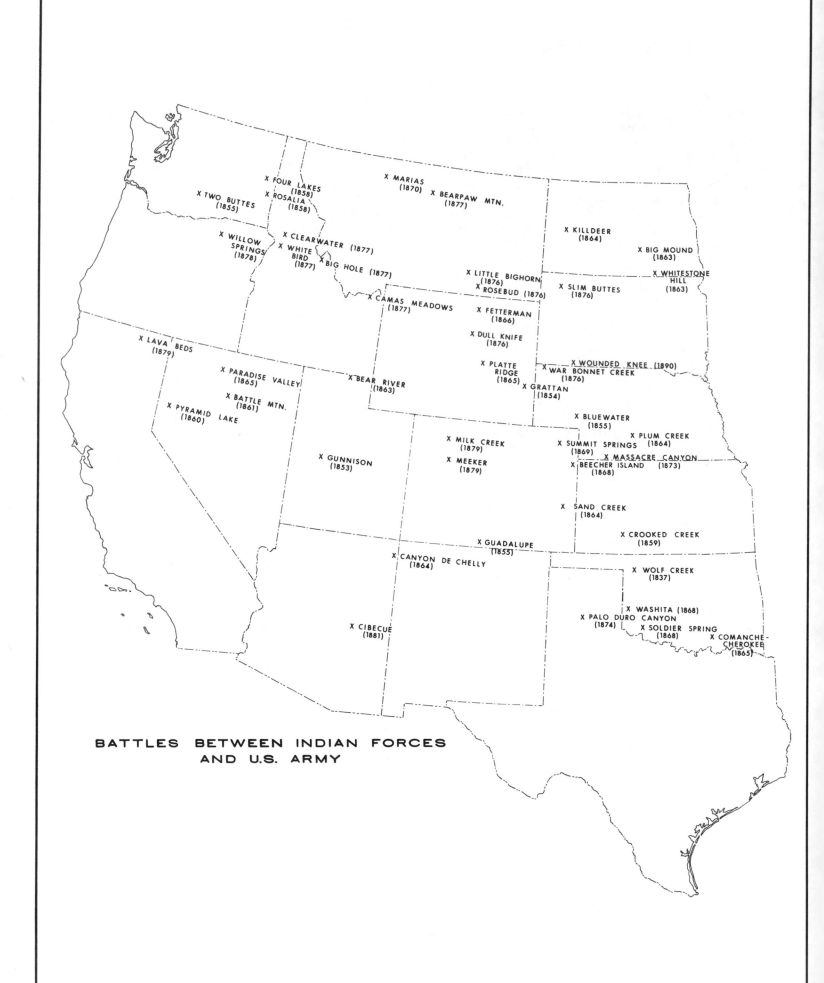

BATTLES BETWEEN INDIAN FORCES
AND U.S. ARMY

46. BATTLES BETWEEN INDIAN FORCES AND THE U.S. ARMY

THE AMERICAN WEST WAS THE SCENE of countless battles between Indians and the U.S. Army. Between 1866 and 1891 more than one thousand engagements were fought, with 2,571 whites, both military and civilian, and an estimated 5,519 Indians killed. The conflict was simply a continuation of the contest for control of the Americas that was begun between the natives and invading whites when Columbus first landed.

In 1866, all of the West had an estimated 270,000 Indians in 125 distinct groups. In the Southwest, the Comanches and Apaches, who had so harassed the Spanish, were intractable in their resistance to the Americans. However, the more pacific California mission Indians, who had been a threat to peace in the Mexican period, were no longer a menace. Neither were the Pueblo tribes of Arizona and New Mexico, and most of the mountain tribes had also made peace with the whites. Some, like the Navajos, had fought and lost and then accepted their situation. Many tribes, like the Utes, Crows, and Pawnees, not only were friendly with whites, but also provided the army with much-needed scouts.

After the Civil War only a few tribes fought most of the battles. They were the Sioux, Cheyennes, Arapahos, Kiowas, and Comanches on the Great Plains and the Apaches in Arizona and New Mexico. In the Rocky Mountains there were brief battles with the Nez Percés, Utes, and Bannocks; in the Northwest it was the Paiutes and Modocs that resisted the invaders.

These Indians were mostly nomads, dependent on hunting and fishing for their livelihood. Under the best circumstances it has historically been difficult to turn such people into sedentary farmers or herdsmen.

Unfortunately, the government's efforts to restrict the Plains Indians to reservations were poorly conceived and haphazardly executed. The problem for the whites was that most of the western tribes had developed cultures that produced effective warriors. The result was that these Indians could effectively resist efforts to drive them from their ancestral homes, and the battles between the Indians and the army were often fiercely contested.

In addition, by that time many Indians looked upon the whites with contempt, and when one considers the usual failure of poorly mounted cavalry to catch them after one of their raids, that is understandable. In addition, the Indians looked upon the whites' proffer of treaties as an indication of weakness. The native Americans assumed that their enemies were afraid of them and hence wanted peace by means of a piece of paper. Isolated and lacking geographical knowledge, they could not comprehend the number of whites and believed themselves to be more numerous.

Unfortunately, the Indians of the American West did not have a monopoly on misunderstanding. The battles fought were caused, in part, by Washington officials' failure to understand the American Indian, despite the fact that the conflict in the West was but a continuation of that which had begun shortly after the English landed on the Atlantic seaboard. The government's lack of a policy made the army's role as peacemaker more difficult. General Sherman outlined the closest to a policy the national government was ever to have for dealing with the Indians. He suggested about all the army could do was to protect the settlers "till time and events settle this . . . time is helping us and killing the Indians fast, so that every year the task is less."

But neither did the U.S. Army develop a policy to deal with the Indians. Military leaders simply did not foresee the years it would take to settle the problem and trained soldiers to fight in the conventional manner. The Indians, however, fought in a most unorthodox fashion—in essence, a guerrilla war.

What was needed in fighting the Indian was a highly mobile force that could respond rapidly to the warriors' threats. A police force was more in order than the conventional military. Though poorly equipped and ill-trained to fight Indians, the army usually gave a good account of itself. Furthermore, many soldiers came to respect their aboriginal foe.

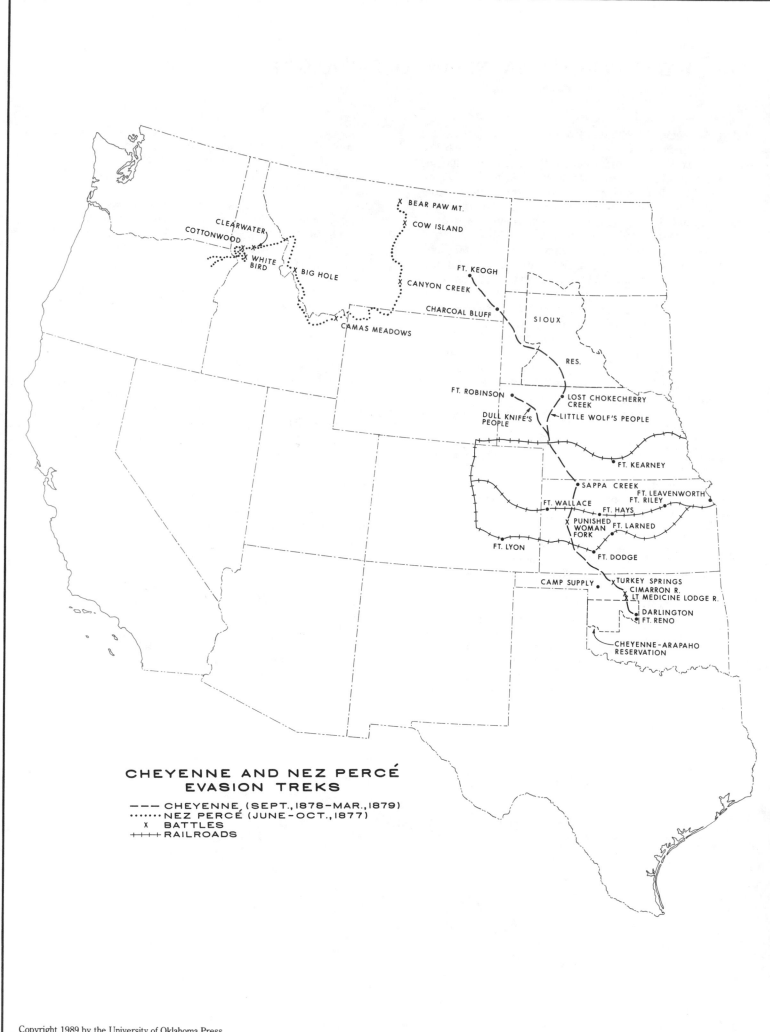

CHEYENNE AND NEZ PERCÉ
EVASION TREKS

– – – CHEYENNE (SEPT., 1878–MAR., 1879)
········· NEZ PERCÉ (JUNE–OCT., 1877)
X   BATTLES
++++ RAILROADS

X BEAR PAW MT.
X COW ISLAND
CLEARWATER
COTTONWOOD
X WHITE BIRD
X BIG HOLE
FT. KEOGH
X CANYON CREEK
CHARCOAL BLUFF
SIOUX
X CAMAS MEADOWS
RES.
FT. ROBINSON
LOST CHOKECHERRY CREEK
DULL KNIFE'S PEOPLE
LITTLE WOLF'S PEOPLE
FT. KEARNEY
SAPPA CREEK
FT. LEAVENWORTH
FT. RILEY
FT. WALLACE
FT. HAYS
X PUNISHED WOMAN FORK
FT. LARNED
FT. LYON
FT. DODGE
CAMP SUPPLY
X TURKEY SPRINGS
X CIMARRON R.
X LT MEDICINE LODGE R.
DARLINGTON
FT. RENO
CHEYENNE–ARAPAHO RESERVATION

47. CHEYENNE AND NEZ PERCÉ EVASION TREKS

THE NORTHERN CHEYENNES were sent to a reservation in Indian Territory on May 28, 1877. A total of 937 people were removed as a part of the army's effort to control the tribes involved in Custer's defeat. The Cheyennes hated their new home. They suffered from malaria and other illnesses and had inadequate medical care. Used to hunting buffalo and elk in the north, they were often hungry on the short rations provided. They refused to learn farming, and after a year and a half of longing for their homeland, they fled northward, led by Chiefs Dull Knife and Little Wolf. On September 9, 1878, a total of 92 men, 120 women, and 141 children slipped by the army sentries. They were armed, as they had been permitted to keep their guns for hunting when they had surrendered two years earlier.

The trek of the Northern Cheyennes was complicated by the fact that much of the area they traveled was settled, three railroad lines made it easy for the army to move reinforcements, and telegraph lines made it possible for army units to communicate the movements of the fleeing Indians. Telegrams quickly alerted all the forts in the area. On September 12 the Cheyennes killed three ranchers, and the following day they fought a battle with pursuing troops at Turkey Springs, east of Camp Supply; the army lost three dead and three wounded. After other skirmishes, the Cheyennes attempted to trap their pursuers in a canyon near Punished Woman's Fork on September 27. They were unsuccessful, but the army commander was one of the casualties. The Indians traveled without rest and again were able to evade the troopers. On Sappa Creek they raided a number of ranches, killing an estimated forty men and raping several women; only the young children were spared.

After crossing the tracks of the Union Pacific, the Cheyennes split into two groups. The band under Little Wolf settled down on Lost Chokecherry Creek for the winter and then continued on to Fort Keogh in the spring. The others, led by Dull Knife, encountered cavalry on October 23, 1878, not far from Fort Robinson. They surrendered, but gave up only their old weapons. Dull Knife requested that they be allowed to join the Sioux at the Pine Ridge Agency, but they were kept at Fort Robinson. At first they were allowed moderate freedom, but when numerous restrictions were enforced, they decided to escape on January 9, 1879. Of the 150 at the fort, 64 were killed in the attempted breakout, many of them women and children. Many cases of indiscriminate killing of men, women, and children or the wounded were committed by settlers.

The Nez Percé Indians were found in the southeastern corner of Washington and nearby Oregon and Idaho. They were known for their skill as horse breeders and for their friendship with whites. Unfortunately, gold was discovered in their lands in 1860, starting an influx of Anglos who endeavored to push the Indians out. A long dispute came to a head in 1877 when the Nez Percés were ordered out of their ancestral home and forced onto a reservation. Vio-

lence erupted when a few young braves, fueled by liquor, went on a rampage, killing nineteen settlers. Nez Percé bands that had nothing to do with this outrage fled, fearing that the army would punish the innocent as well as the guilty.

The Indians took refuge at White Bird Creek, where they were soon joined by Chief Joseph, who was to play a vital role in the evasion trek. Friendly Indians had apparently convinced the Nez Percés that if they surrendered those guilty of the massacre, the rest would be allowed to go free. But when an Indian group approached under a white flag, civilians with the army opened fire on them. Thus began the Nez Percé War. When the battle ended, thirty-four whites, mostly settlers, had been killed, and four wounded, while the Nez Percés suffered two wounded.

The army, though chastened, was soon in the field under Gen. Oliver Howard with four hundred men. Meanwhile, the Nez Percés could count three hundred fighting men and five hundred women and children as more bands joined the Indians on Cottonwood Creek. On July 3 a scouting party of ten troopers was surprised and wiped out. At Clearwater a pitched battle was fought on July 11–12, with the army losing fifteen dead and twenty-five wounded; the Nez Percés had four killed and six wounded. The Indians next crossed the rugged Bitterroot Mountains into Montana. After a most arduous retreat over difficult terrain, they were caught by surprise in their camp at Big Hole. The army's losses were twenty-nine dead; Indian casualties were eighty-nine, many of them women and children. On August 13 the Indians raided the army camp on Camas Meadow and ran off 150 mules. They next invaded Yellowstone Park, frightening and scattering tourists and killing two.

The Nez Percé band then turned north into Montana, raiding and pillaging as they went. But the army was using telegraph and rails to marshal its resources against the Indians. At Canyon Creek on September 13 the army caught up with the fleeing tribe but again let them escape after a skirmish. On September 25 the Nez Percés crossed the Missouri River and raided an army depot at Cow Island for supplies. Pausing to hunt buffalo at the Bear Paw Mountains, the tribal leaders knew that General Howard's army was far behind. They did not know that Col. Nelson Miles's force was close at hand. On September 30 the final battle began; it lasted until the Indians surrendered on October 5.

The captives numbered 418—87 men, 184 women, and 147 children. It had taken the army four months to halt this great trek of the Nez Percés. The campaign was also costly; the military estimated it had spent $931,329.02 on the pursuit. Casualty lists showed 127 soldiers and perhaps 50 civilians killed; 147 soldiers were wounded. The Nez Percés counted 151 dead and 88 wounded.

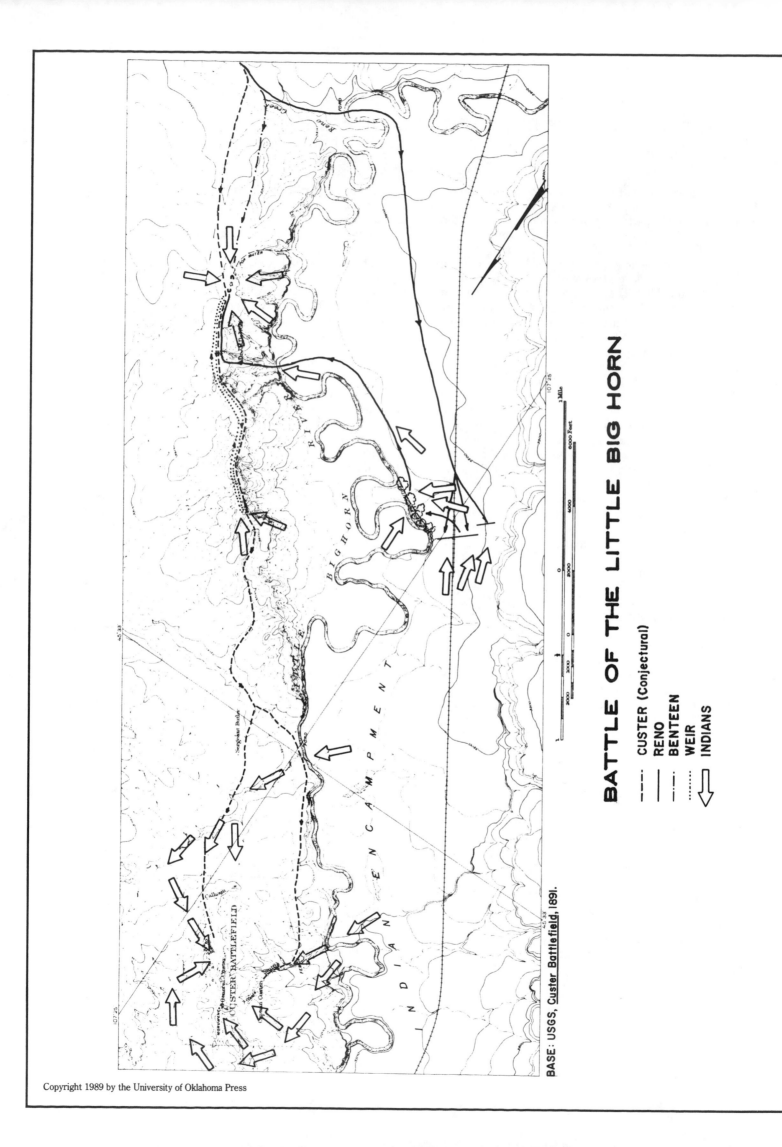

BATTLE OF THE LITTLE BIG HORN

CUSTER (Conjectural)
RENO
BENTEEN
WEIR
INDIANS

BASE: USGS, Custer Battlefield, 1891.

THE MOST FAMOUS, OR INFAMOUS, depending upon one's point of view, of the clashes between the U.S. Army and the Indians of the American West was the one that took place on the Little Big Horn River. This battle captured the national imagination as few incidents have. More has been written about this encounter than perhaps any other in the history of the American West. To this day it is not possible to pierce the clouds of fiction and state with certainty what did happen on the banks of this small Montana stream on June 25, 1876. Reporters and dime novelists poured forth misinformation about the battle. Reputations were made and lost as a result of the affair. Indian and white relations have been studied with this battle as a focal point, and a recent book on this subject had the interesting title of *Custer Died for Your Sins*. The controversy over events on the Little Big Horn has been fueled by the dominant personality of George Armstrong Custer, the most famed of those who died there.

The battle was an outgrowth of white violation of the 1868 treaty with the Sioux. That tribe had been granted a "permanent" reservation in Dakota Territory west of the Missouri River. Unfortunately, promised supplies were too few and consisted of moldy flour, spoiled beef, and motheaten blankets. The Sioux were also justifiably alarmed over the incursion of the Northern Pacific Railroad into territory they considered theirs. Worst of all, by the summer of 1875 the discovery of gold in the Black Hills brought in hordes of prospectors to disrupt their lands. Angry young braves slipped away to join bands of nontreaty Indians and prepared to fight.

When these Sioux men refused an order to return to the reservation, the army was given the problem in the spring of 1876. Three columns of converging troops were sent against the Indian camps. One, under Gen. George Crook, moved northward from Fort Fetterman on the upper North Platte; a second, commanded by Gen. Alfred H. Terry, started westward from Fort Abraham Lincoln on the Missouri; and a third, led by Col. John Gibbon, advanced eastward from Fort Ellis in Montana. When scouts finally reported the presence of Indians on the Little Big Horn, General Terry, overall commander, outlined a campaign against them. It called for Colonel Custer to lead twelve troops of the Seventh

Cavalry in an encircling movement intended to cut off the retreat of the Indians.

The vain and foolhardy Custer chose to disobey orders and not wait for the convergence of the three armies; he decided to attack on his own. The Indians were discovered on the south bank of the Little Big Horn, so Custer sent Major Marcus A. Reno with three troops of cavalry to attack the Sioux camp. Captain Frederick W. Benteen, with three troops, was sent to the left of Reno's line of march. One troop was detailed to guard the pack animals. Custer then led five troops across the hills and down the river to a ford in order to attack the Indian camp from the opposite side of the river from Reno.

As the battle began, Reno became convinced that the Indian force outnumbered his, and he retreated to the bluffs of the river with heavy losses. This enabled the Indians to concentrate their attack on Custer's force. Despite being joined by Benteen's troopers, Reno failed to come to Custer's rescue. (In fact, this small besieged force expected Custer to come to their aid.) Capt. Thomas B. Weir, on his own initiative, started downstream to assist, but he was driven back by superior numbers. Meanwhile, Custer was trapped and annihilated in a few minutes. The next day the forces of General Terry arrived to rescue the survivors, but Terry was too late to save Custer's command.

Efforts to understand the Battle of Little Big Horn continue today. In the summer of 1983 a grass fire burned some 600 acres of the battlefield. The destruction of underbrush and grass accumulated over more than a century cleared the ground for a systematic investigation. In 1984 an archaeological team unearthed some four thousand artifacts, including brass blouse buttons, iron pants buttons, hook-and-eye fasteners from shirts, and an assortment of bullets. The location where these items were found helps fill out details of the battle. Discovery of a large number of bullets from Indian rifles has prompted some to conclude that Custer was not just outnumbered but outgunned as well. Naturally, many students of the battle minimize the importance of these new findings and dents of the battle minimize the importance of these new findings and conclusions. Thus, the controversy surrounding the battle of the Little Bighorn continues.

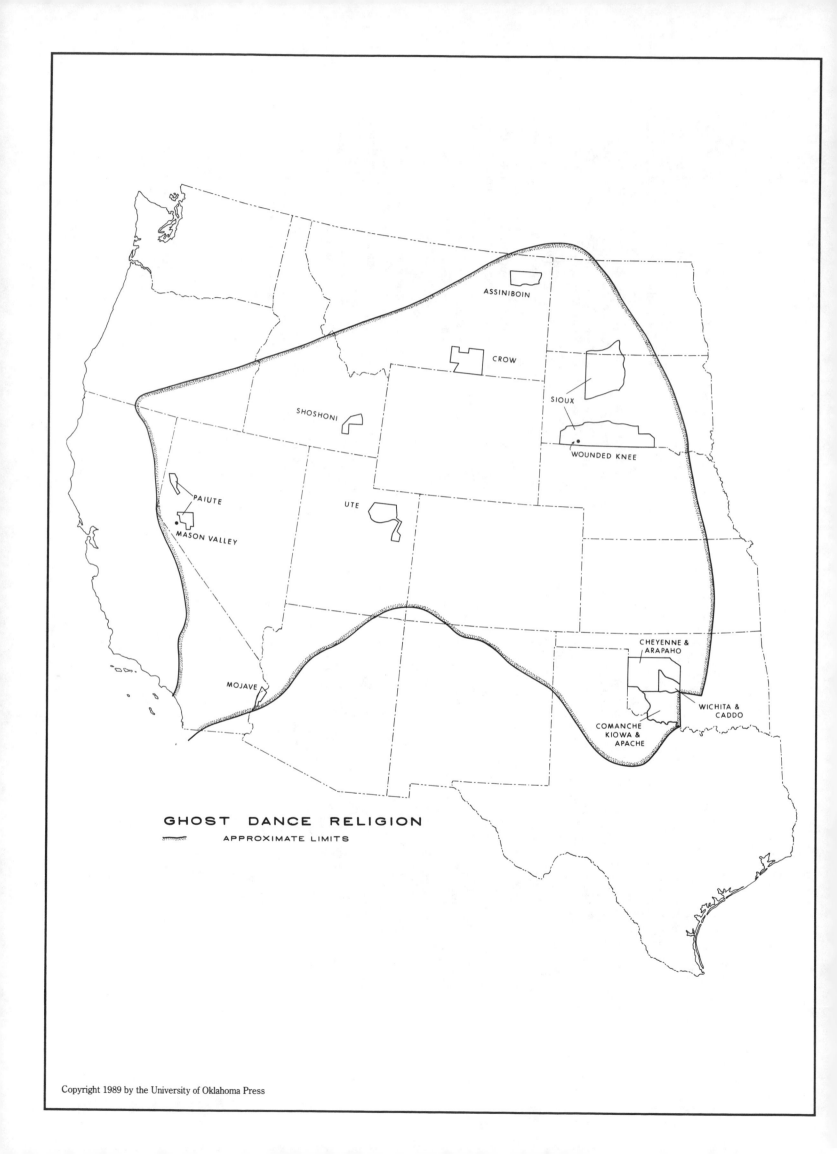

GHOST DANCE RELIGION

APPROXIMATE LIMITS

49. GHOST DANCE RELIGION

THE GHOST DANCE RELIGION was a messianic movement that spread among many of the tribes of the West but is most remembered in connection with the tragedy that struck the Sioux in 1890. This cult had its inception among the Pauites of the Mason Valley in Nevada about 1870 through the Indian prophet Tavibo, who taught that all the whites would suddenly disappear as a result of some undefined cataclysmic event. At the same time, all dead Indians, and even the dead buffalo, would return to the earth and live happily ever after. A dance called the Ghost Dance was the means by which contact with the dead was established. The movement spread quickly among the Indians of Nevada, California, and Oregon but died soon after Tavibo's death, probably in 1870.

A new Paiute prophet named Wovoka emerged in 1889—some even claimed that he was the son of Tavibo. In any event, this handsome, charismatic thirty-five-year-old preacher accepted the older man's teachings but added many more ideas of his own. Residence with a Christian rancher helped him learn basic Christianity, and he incorporated the ethical message of the Ten Commandments and the messianic concepts of Christianity into his new religion. It is also alleged that he absorbed much from Mormonism. On January 1, 1889, a major eclipse of the sun occurred, and Wovoka was stricken with fever. According to his followers, he was taken up to Heaven by God, who revealed the teachings Wovoka was to follow. Above all, the Indian was to live in peace with the whites and do good. He was also given a number of songs which he was to use to perform miracles. One of the key doctrines was a dance to be held every six weeks. This dance became something of a seance in which many fell into a trance and communicated with the dead. Some contend that the inspiration for these wild dances may have come from the Shakers. In any event, such dances were to be the prelude to the new world, wherein the whites would disappear and the Indian dead would be resurrected to join the living and inherit the earth.

These teachings spread among western tribes at a time in which their natural world was disintegrating. The traditional way of life built around hunting had been destroyed, and in warfare with the white invaders of their homeland the Indian had lost. Worst of all, the diseases brought by this alien foe had devastated many tribes. Confinement to reservations was the final blow to these proud native Americans, who had once roamed the open land. Unable to check their enemies in the natural world, they turned to the supernatural in an effort to beat them. In this the Indians were no different from people throughout the world and down through the pages of history who turned to religious cults in time of disaster and calamity.

Most Indian tribes turned to this new messiah and accepted his teachings, even those of pacifism and living in harmony with the whites. The Teton Sioux of South Dakota were to be the tragic exception. This once great tribe had been hard hit by the severe winter of 1889–90, which brought hunger and disastrous epidemics, and finally, much of their land had been taken from them unfairly. So the Tetons sent eleven emissaries to the Paiutes to learn about the new religion, which promised so much to the Indian. They returned and enthusiastically endorsed this new faith. Unfortunately, the Teton Sioux rejected the pacifist part of Wovoka's teachings, and many of them openly preached hatred against the whites and even talked of a war of extermination. Soon the Ghost Dance became a preparation for battle. The Ghost Shirt was to be worn as a magic charm that promised to halt the white man's bullets. The dances spread rapidly, with men, women, and even children taking part. At first the Indian agents applauded the new religion, which had so many tenets of Christianity, but when the songs that were chanted began to speak of a predicted Indian millennium when the whites would be annihilated, alarming reports began to reach responsible officials even in Washington, D.C. The Ghost Dance led to an outbreak of violence that cost the life of Chief Sitting Bull and caused the tragedy at Wounded Knee.

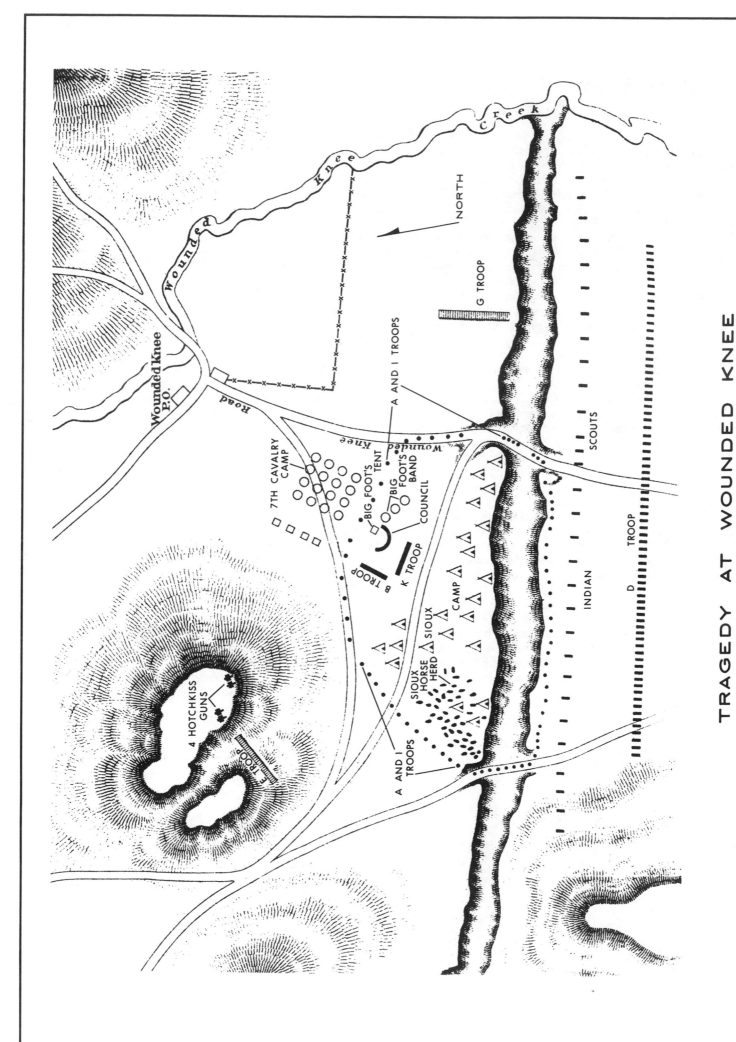

TRAGEDY AT WOUNDED KNEE
DECEMBER 29, 1890

BASE: FROM JAMES MOONEY,
THE GHOST-DANCE RELIGION

Wounded Knee Creek

NORTH

G TROOP

A AND I TROOPS

SCOUTS

INDIAN

D TROOP

Wounded Knee P.O.

Road

Wounded Knee

7TH CAVALRY CAMP

BIG FOOT'S TENT

BIG FOOT'S BAND

COUNCIL

B TROOP

K TROOP

A AND I TROOPS

SIOUX CAMP

SIOUX HORSE HERD

4 HOTCHKISS GUNS

E TROOP

50. TRAGEDY AT WOUNDED KNEE, DECEMBER 29, 1890

THE LAST MAJOR MILITARY CONTEST of the nineteenth century between the Plains Indians and the U.S. Army took place along Wounded Knee Creek on the Pine Ridge Reservation in South Dakota on December 29, 1890. And, as is true of most such encounters, much controversy surrounds what actually happened.

This clash resulted from the army's attempts to disarm the Miniconjou Sioux and transport them by rail to Omaha. The Indians were nervous as the result of the death of Sitting Bull, the famed chief, in a clash with reservation police the week before. The Miniconjous were also aroused because their rifles were their most prized possessions, and surrendering them represented a loss of manhood. Then too, the braves had been told that they would be slaughtered as soon as their weapons were surrendered. They were also on edge because they had only 120 men (220 women and children) against some 500 military.

Col. James W. Forsyth, commanding the Seventh Cavalry, deployed his units to disarm the Indians, not to fight them. Two troops, A and I, surrounded the Indian village. Troops B and K were dismounted and formed in front of the council ring. The cavalry camp was north of the council ring. Troop E was stationed on a hill where they could guard the field artillery, four Hotchkiss guns, located there. Troop G lined up east of the agency road. Troops C and D formed a long line south of the creek behind the Indian scouts. The reserve was stationed near the artillery. At most, the soldiers were no more than three hundred yards from the Indians.

When the weapons search began, the soldiers were initially given broken carbines and obsolete weapons, but no one surrendered any Winchester repeating rifles the Indians were known to possess. Indian women apparently concealed the better weapons under their skirts, and as the soldiers pressed their search, tempers flared. Yellow Bird, a medicine man attired in Ghost Dance dress, danced about and urged an attack on the soldiers. A gun accidentally discharged in a scuffle, and the result was general firing from both sides.

In the chaotic wild melee that followed it was difficult to tell friend from foe. In addition to the shooting, stabbing, and clubbing going on at close range, the artillery fired shells at the fleeing Sioux. Before the carnage ceased, at least 153 Indians were dead, including 44 women and 18 children. At least 50 Indians were wounded. The army had 25 dead and 39 wounded.

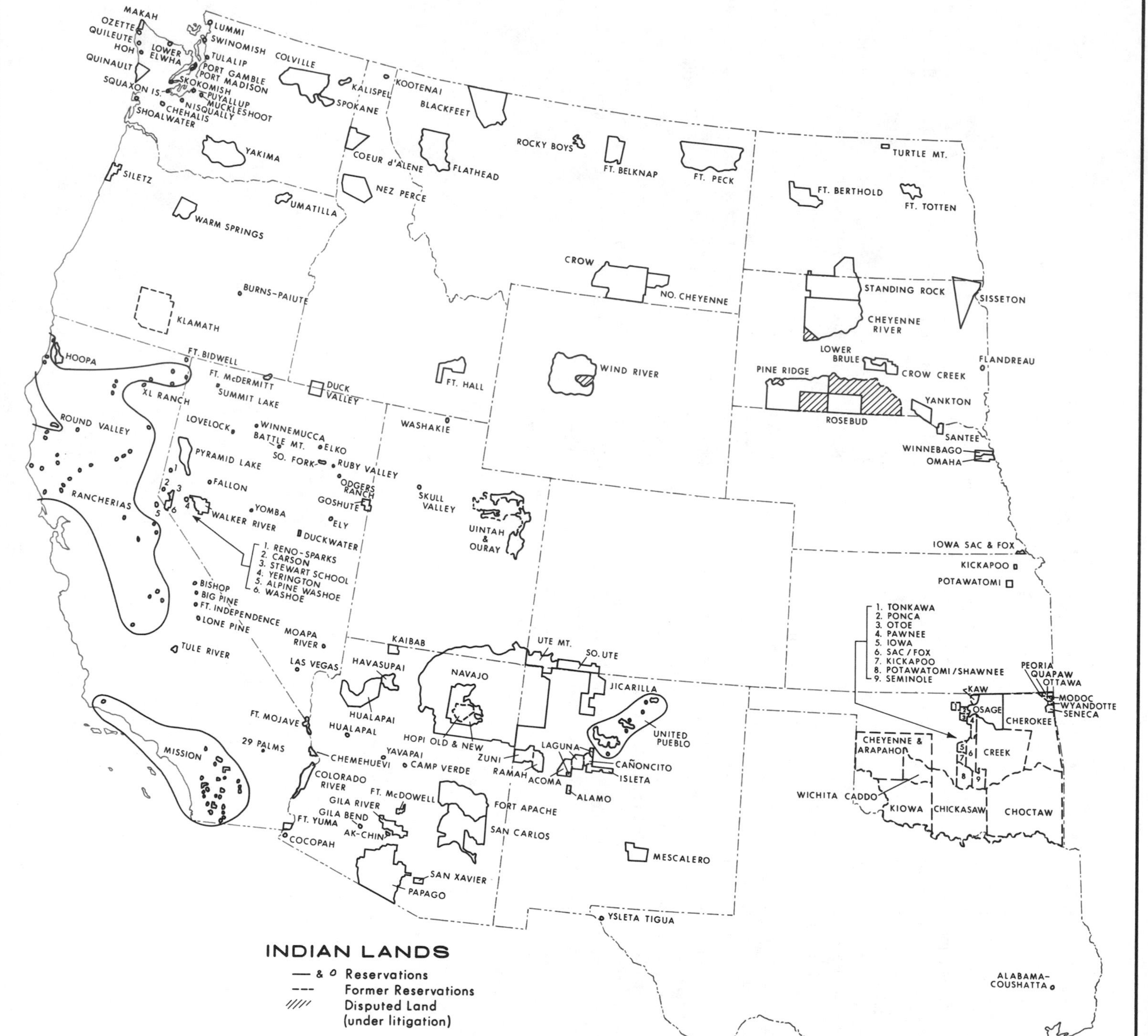
INDIAN LANDS
— & ○ Reservations
--- Former Reservations
//// Disputed Land (under litigation)
MAKAH
OZETTE
QUILEUTE
HOH
QUINAULT
LOWER ELWHA
LUMMI
SWINOMISH
TULALIP
PORT GAMBLE
PORT MADISON
SKOKOMISH
SQUAXON IS.
PUYALLUP
MUCKLESHOOT
NISQUALLY
CHEHALIS
SHOALWATER
COLVILLE
KALISPEL
SPOKANE
KOOTENAI
BLACKFEET
YAKIMA
COEUR d'ALENE
FLATHEAD
ROCKY BOYS
FT. BELKNAP
FT. PECK
TURTLE MT.
SILETZ
NEZ PERCE
FT. BERTHOLD
FT. TOTTEN
UMATILLA
WARM SPRINGS
CROW
NO. CHEYENNE
STANDING ROCK
SISSETON
BURNS-PAIUTE
CHEYENNE RIVER
KLAMATH
LOWER BRULE
FLANDREAU
HOOPA
FT. BIDWELL
FT. McDERMITT
DUCK VALLEY
FT. HALL
WIND RIVER
PINE RIDGE
CROW CREEK
XL RANCH
SUMMIT LAKE
YANKTON
ROSEBUD
ROUND VALLEY
LOVELOCK
WINNEMUCCA
BATTLE MT.
ELKO
WASHAKIE
SANTEE
WINNEBAGO
OMAHA
PYRAMID LAKE
SO. FORK
RUBY VALLEY
FALLON
ODGERS RANCH
GOSHUTE
SKULL VALLEY
RANCHERIAS
YOMBA
WALKER RIVER
ELY
DUCKWATER
UINTAH & OURAY
1. RENO-SPARKS
2. CARSON
3. STEWART SCHOOL
4. YERINGTON
5. ALPINE WASHOE
6. WASHOE
IOWA SAC & FOX
KICKAPOO
POTAWATOMI
BISHOP
BIG PINE
FT. INDEPENDENCE
LONE PINE
MOAPA RIVER
1. TONKAWA
2. PONCA
3. OTOE
4. PAWNEE
5. IOWA
6. SAC / FOX
7. KICKAPOO
8. POTAWATOMI / SHAWNEE
9. SEMINOLE
TULE RIVER
LAS VEGAS
KAIBAB
UTE MT.
SO. UTE
HAVASUPAI
NAVAJO
JICARILLA
PEORIA
QUAPAW
OTTAWA
KAW
MODOC
WYANDOTTE
SENECA
OSAGE
CHEROKEE
HUALAPAI
FT. MOJAVE
HUALAPAI
HOPI OLD & NEW
UNITED PUEBLO
CHEYENNE & ARAPAHO
CREEK
MISSION
29 PALMS
CHEMEHUEVI
YAVAPAI
CAMP VERDE
ZUNI
LAGUNA
RAMAH
ACOMA
CAÑONCITO
ISLETA
COLORADO RIVER
ALAMO
WICHITA CADDO
FT. McDOWELL
GILA RIVER
FORT APACHE
KIOWA
CHICKASAW
CHOCTAW
GILA BEND
FT. YUMA
AK-CHIN
SAN CARLOS
COCOPAH
MESCALERO
SAN XAVIER
PAPAGO
YSLETA TIGUA
ALABAMA-COUSHATTA

51. INDIAN LANDS

THE PRACTICE OF setting aside land for Indian occupancy and use dates back to 1786. Most reservations are found in the American West, partially because belief in the Great American Desert suggested in the early nineteenth century that the area was unsuitable for whites. In addition, westward migration meant that the solution to the problems of white-Indian relations had to be resolved in the West.

Indians from the eastern United States were moved during the 1820s and 1830s to the present states of Nebraska, Kansas, and finally Oklahoma, where, it was assumed, the whites would leave them alone. However, during the 1820s fur trappers and traders were already entering Indian lands and preparing the way for more numerous intruders. The acquisition of the Northwest Territory from England and the Southwest from Mexico in the 1840s made the Great Plains into a highway through Indian country. The discovery of gold in California exacerbated the situation. Native Americans were not to be left undisturbed on the Great Plains, nor in the mountains, nor even upon the Pacific Coast.

In 1851 the chiefs of the main Plains tribes gathered at Fort Laramie, and in return for gifts, annuities, and bounties agreed to accept definite tribal limitations. Despite promises that these lands were theirs for all time, with the organization of Kansas and Nebraska territories in 1854 their removal was foreordained. Between 1854 and 1859 they were forced to surrender their large reserves for ever smaller reservations. By 1860 most of Kansas and Nebraska and a part of Dakota Territory were freed of Indians. Most of the tribes of the Great Plains were skilled warriors, and, as the land base for their way of life constantly diminished in size, they defended their rights by force. The bloody Indian wars were the result, but the flood of migration doomed the native occupants. The destruction of the buffalo removed their food supply, thus forcing their acceptance of reservation life.

The nation rationalized, forcing the first Americans to surrender their basically nomadic hunting and fishing way of life and to be incarcerated on reservations on the grounds that what counted was "the greatest good for the greatest number." President James Monroe stated in 1817: "The earth was given to mankind to support the greatest numbers of which it is capable, and no tribe or people have a right to withhold from the wants of others more than is necessary for their own support and comfort."

It was for the common good that the way of life of the first Americans had to be destroyed. As one observer bitterly puts it:

It was for the common good that the western lands were opened up for settlement, even as the eastern lands had been settled; it was for the common good that treaties were signed, and often broken, and that provision was made in these treaties for roads, way stations, trading houses and forts, which could be built at governmental whim on lands reserved for Indians; it was for the common good that rail and road links were established through Indian lands to link east and west; it was for the common good that Indian hunting and fishing rights, guaranteed by treaty or solemn promise, were revoked to make room for people, or things (such as dams) to serve people, or programs (such as conservationist schemes) to satisfy people; it was for the common good that the Indians were herded like cattle, treated like children, swatted like flies and quarantined like animals suspected of having rabies.[1]

[1] *Toward Native Americans* (New York, 1975), pp. 8–9.

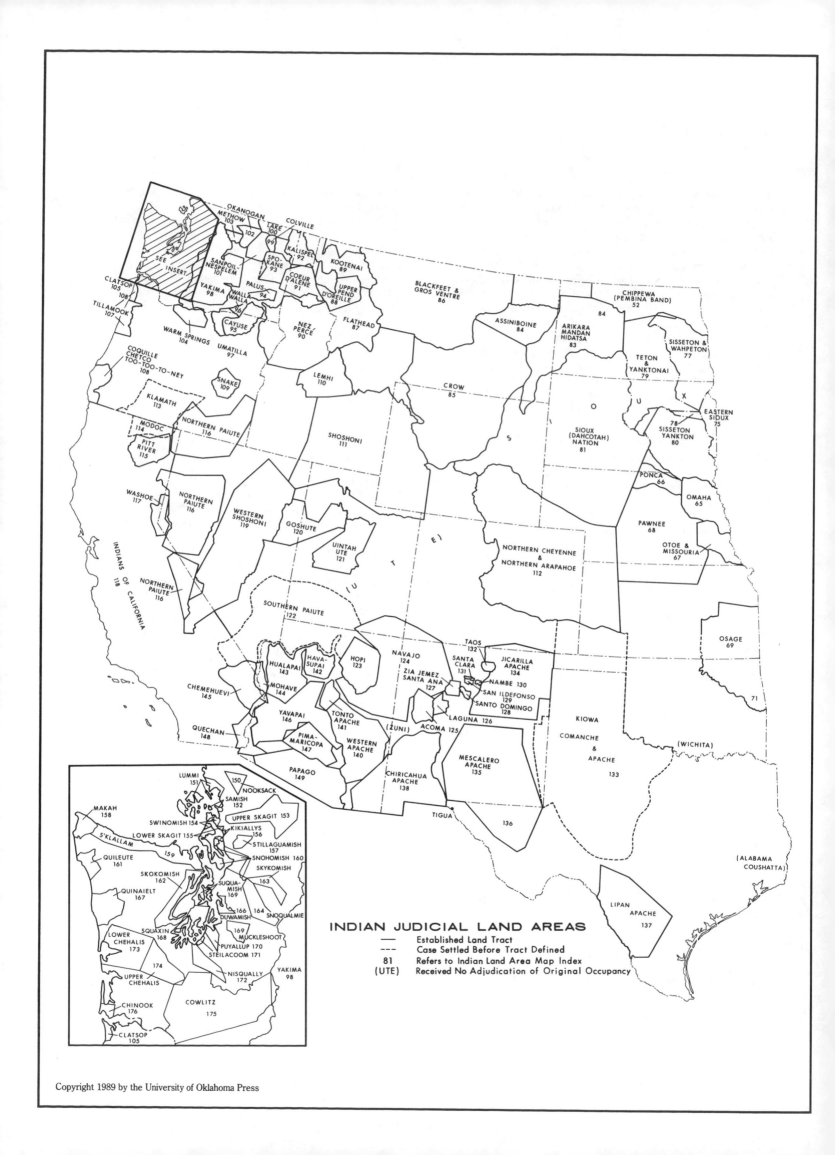

INDIAN JUDICIAL LAND AREAS
—— Established Land Tract
- - - Case Settled Before Tract Defined
81 Refers to Indian Land Area Map Index
(UTE) Received No Adjudication of Original Occupancy

52. INDIAN JUDICIAL LAND AREAS

THIS MAP SHOWS THE RESULT of cases before the U.S. Indian Claims Commission in which federally recognized American Indian tribes had the opportunity to prove original tribal occupancy within the United States and to request compensation for treaty violations. The story of Indian land claims against the federal government goes back many years. In 1831 the Cherokees were the first native Americans to appeal to the whites' court. Initially, the Indians had little success, but after 1881 they were at least granted access to the courts.

The number of claims against the U.S. government grew with the passing years and finally led Congress to set up the Indian Claims Commission, which heard cases from 1946 to its termination in 1978. Many of the claims filed were for compensation for Indian title lands lost without adequate payment being made. The commission heard the testimony of expert witnesses such as anthropologists, historians, ethnohistorians, and geographers in an effort to determine if the particular tribe actually did occupy the land they were claiming. Occupancy was normally recognized if a tribe used land for agriculture, hunting, gathering, or religious purposes over a long time.

By the time the Indian Claims Commission had completed its work, more than six hundred claims had been heard, and the Indians had won some 60 percent of the cases presented and had been awarded several hundred million dollars. Not all claimants were satisfied with the work of the commission and have retained legal counsel to further pursue their cases. Nevertheless, the Indians finally had "their day in court" and thus helped publicize some of the past wrongs in the federal government's relations with their tribes. In addition, the massive ethnohistorical research conducted as a basis for the legal proceedings has provided an important source for Indian-white relations.

The work of the Indian Claims Commission was only a part of the long quest of native Americans for justice. It was not the final one. Perhaps it will take another 150 years to resolve the position of the Indian in American society.

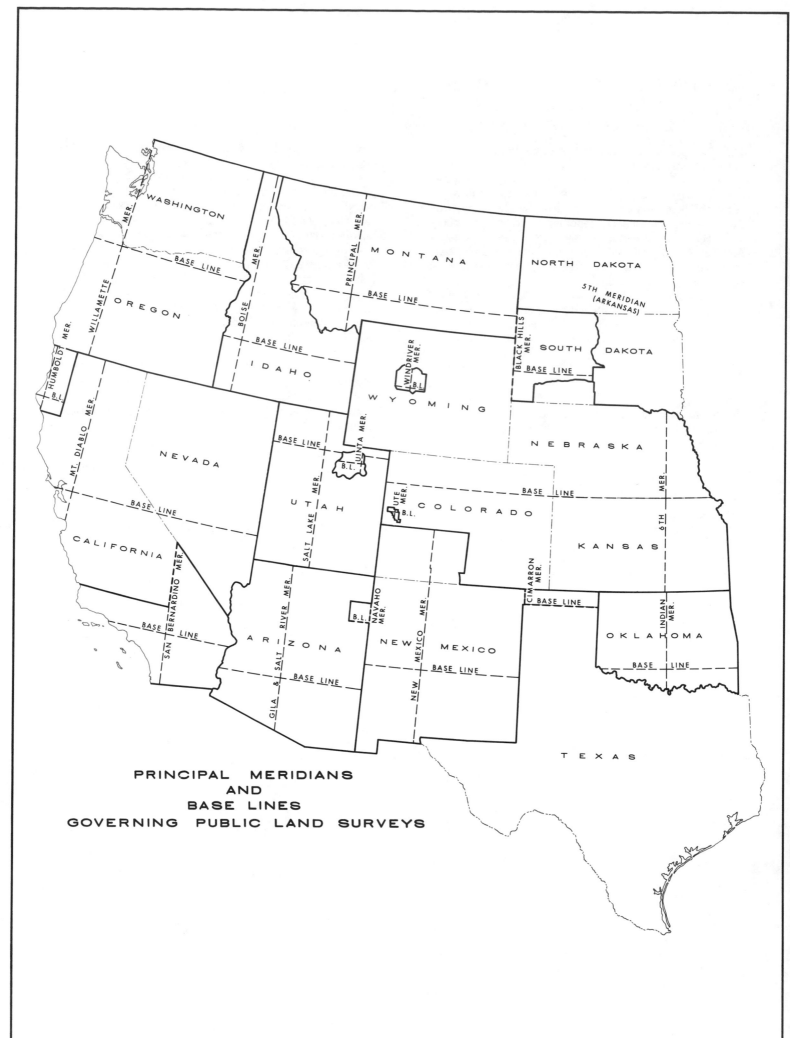

PRINCIPAL MERIDIANS
AND
BASE LINES
GOVERNING PUBLIC LAND SURVEYS

53. PRINCIPAL MERIDIANS AND BASE LINES GOVERNING PUBLIC LAND SURVEYS

THE PRINCIPAL MERIDIANS AND BASE LINES of the west are a product of the Northwest Ordinance of 1785. This measure provided for the orderly survey and sale of public lands. During the colonial period, New England had disposed of public lands by surveying them first and then selling them in orderly blocks. A system of "indiscriminate locations and subsequent survey" prevailed in the southern colonies. This permitted settlers to lay out the land they desired where they wished and then have it surveyed. The southern system bred a welter of conflicting titles as pioneers laid out irregularly shaped plots to claim the most fertile land and made it impossible for the government to dispose of the less desirable tracts. The survey of public lands was originally evolved in Ohio and was well developed by the time the West was settled.

The Ordinance of 1785 provided that the public lands of the United States be divided by lines intersecting true north and at right angles to form townships six miles square, the townships to be marked with progressive numbers from the beginning. Such townships were to be divided into thirty-six sections, each one mile square and containing 640 acres. The sections were to be numbered respectively, beginning with the number one in the northeast section and proceeding west and east alternately through the township with progressive numbers to thirty-six.

To carry the foregoing requirements into operation, it was necessary to establish independent initial points to serve as bases for surveys. Principal meridians and base lines were then surveyed from these initial points. Guide meridians were initiated at base lines, and standard parallels were initiated at principal meridians to form townships.

Meridians and Base Lines in the American West

Meridians	Governing Surveys (wholly or in part) in States of	Longitude of Initial Points West from Greenwich			Latitude of Initial Points		
		°	′	″	°	′	″
Black Hills	South Dakota	104	03	16	43	59	44
Boise	Idaho	116	23	35	43	22	21
Cimarron	Oklahoma	103	00	07	36	30	05
Fifth Principal	Arkansas, Iowa, Minnesota, Missouri, North Dakota, and South Dakota	91	03	07	34	38	45
Gila and Salt River	Arizona	112	18	19	33	22	38
Humboldt	California	124	07	10	40	25	02
Indian	Oklahoma	97	14	49	34	29	32
Mount Diablo	California and Nevada	121	54	47	37	52	54
Navajo	Arizona	108	31	59	35	44	56
New Mexico Principal	Colorado and New Mexico	106	53	12	34	15	35
Principal	Montana	111	39	33	45	47	13
Salt Lake	Utah	111	53	27	40	46	11
San Bernardino	California	116	55	17	34	07	20
Sixth Principal	Colorado, Kansas, Nebraska, South Dakota, and Wyoming	97	22	08	40	00	07
Uintah	Utah	109	56	06	40	25	59
Ute	Colorado	108	31	59	39	06	23
Willamette	Oregon and Washington	122	44	34	45	31	11
Wind River	Wyoming	108	48	49	43	00	41

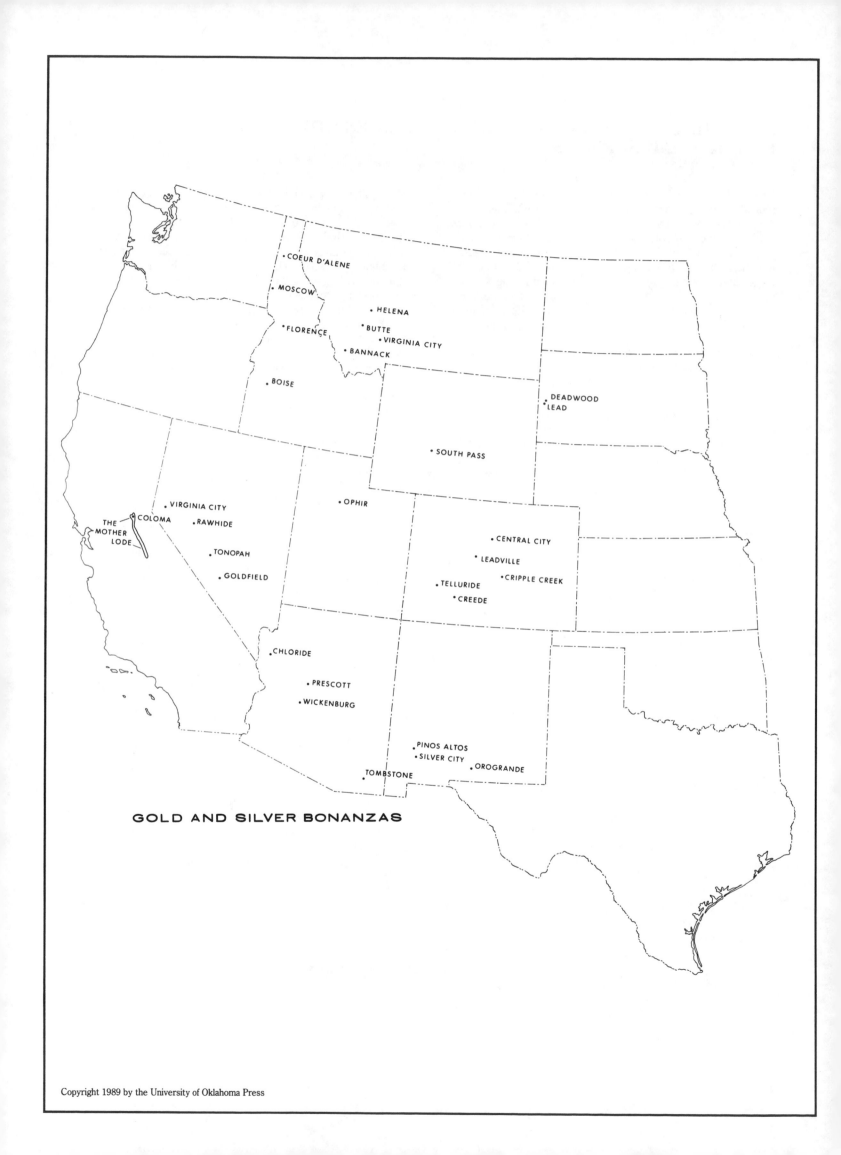

GOLD AND SILVER BONANZAS

54. GOLD AND SILVER BONANZAS

MANY OF THE RICH LODES of gold and silver in the American West were discovered by individual prospectors who roamed in the second half of the nineteenth century with their mule, washing pan, gun, and too few supplies. However, once the placer deposits had been worked, they were forced to move on, for most of the gold was locked in quartz lodes or buried deep beneath tons of debris that had accumulated for thousands of years. To reach the gold in the quartz, tunnels had to be dug deep into the ground. Huge mills had to be built to crush the ore. Hydraulic mining which uncovered the gold necessitated the damming of streams to build water pressure. Dredges were used to process tons of ore to obtain only a small quantity of gold. All of this cost a great deal of money that could only be raised from individuals far from the mining scene. And it was these capitalists who were made rich from the gold and silver bonanzas of the West. To entice the necessary investment, there had to be enough ore present to be worked for a period of time. The result was that permanent, or at least semipermanent, towns were built near the mines. Some had all the amenities of the day, and some even had a disproportionate number of wealthy, who erected fine homes.

Silver, even more than gold, required elaborate facilities for processing the raw ore, because silver was seldom found in easily mined placers. It was more likely to occur in combination with other minerals, especially lead and gold. To extract the silver was a slow and complex process requiring substantial investment and a large labor force. Supplying such installations became big business, often attracting road builders and then railroads to serve the needs of the mining community.

A brief but wild gold rush to the Pike's Peak region in 1859 turned into a complete fiasco, with little gold being found and most miners soon returning home without riches. Prospectors in California paid no attention to silver ore if they even recognized the blue muck in which it was found. Some miners wandered into Nevada seeking gold and met with some success. However, in 1859 near Virginia City, the Comstock Lode, the world's most productive silver mine, was discovered, and Nevada was soon rich, populous, and a state.

Some of the miners who stayed in Colorado after the failure to find precious metals at Pike's Peak were rewarded by both gold and silver strikes near Denver in 1859. Some gold was prospected on the Gila River in 1858, but it was in the Northwest that the real discoveries were made. From 1861 to 1866 gold and silver were located in enough quantity to trigger a stampede into Idaho and Montana. South Pass in Wyoming became a gold center in 1867. The army tried to prove there was no gold in the Black Hills of South Dakota—they did not want to see the Indians aroused—but managed to prove otherwise, causing a stampede to the area and the trouble they had feared with the Sioux.

Today, the West is dotted with ghost towns that once flourished during the flush period of mining, and towns are even being closed down along with the mines in the 1980s. But the following description by F. L. Paxson suggests that even the prosperous mining town left something to be desired:

A single street meandering along a valley, with one story huts flanking it in irregular rows, was the typical mining camp. The saloon and the general store, sometimes combined, were its representative institutions. Deep ruts along the streets bore witness to the heavy wheels of the freighters, while horses loosely tied to all available posts at once revealed the regular means of locomotion, and by the careless way they were left about showed that this sort of property was not likely to be stolen. The mining population centering here lived a life of contrasts. The desolation and loneliness of prospecting and working claims alternated with the excitement of coming to town. Few decent beings habitually lived in the towns. The resident population expected to live off the miners, either in way of trade or worse. The bar, the gambling house, the dance hall have been made too common in description to need further account. In the reaction against loneliness, the extremes of drunkenness, debauchery, and murder were only too frequent in these places of amusement.[1]

[1]Frederic Logan Paxon, *The Last American Frontier* (New York, 1924), pp. 171–72.

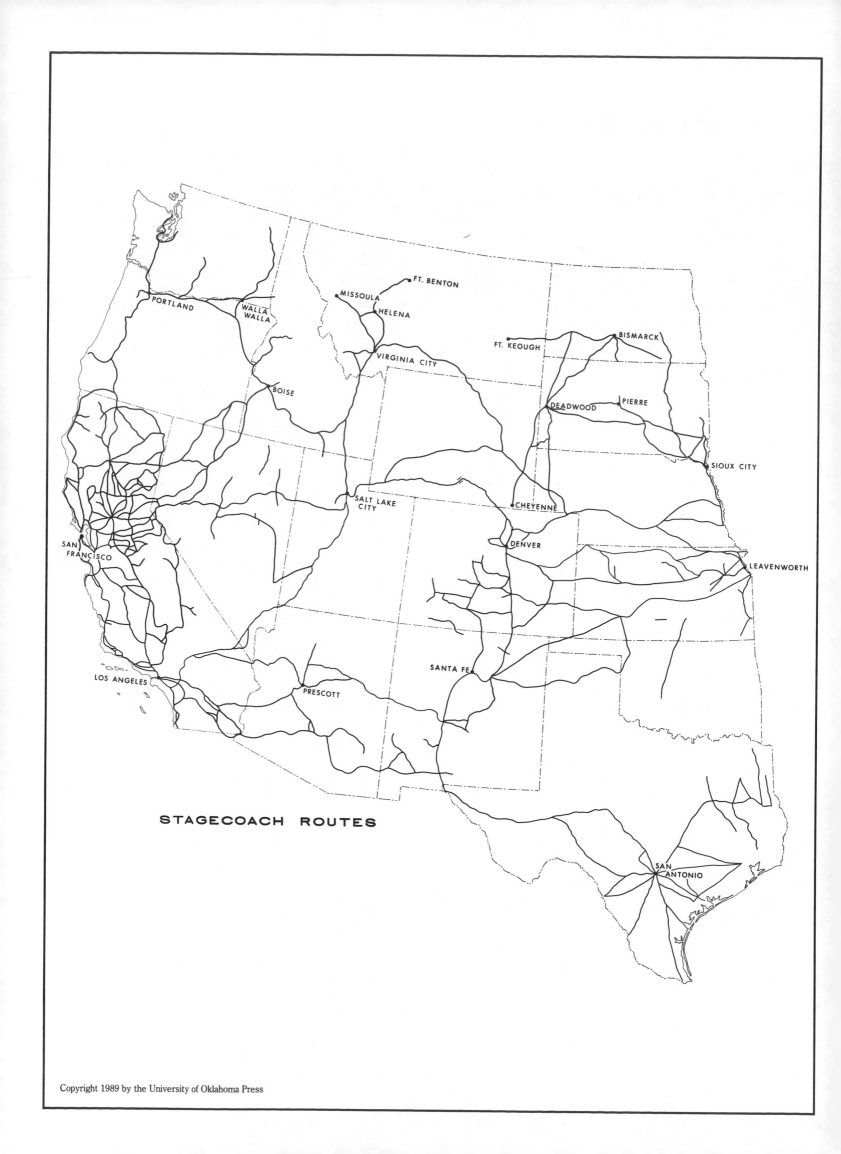

STAGECOACH ROUTES

55. STAGECOACH ROUTES

AFTER THE AMERICAN PIONEERS began their westward trek, they desired to keep in touch with family and friends back home. The stagecoach was an important means by which letters and newspapers could be received, valuables exchanged, and even an occasional visit arranged. So long before the geographic West had been settled, the rocking Concord coach was a well-established part of frontier transportation. In fact, the stagecoach was to be far more important west of the Mississippi River than east of it, because in the West there were fewer navigable rivers and canals to compete with land transport.

In the American West travel by stagecoach was facilitated by the wide expanse of prairie but made most difficult by transit through mountainous terrain. It was also difficult for drivers to adjust to distances far greater than those found east of the Mississippi. Ironically, western stagecoach routes profited from the transition from horse-drawn transportation to the railroad that was taking place in the east before 1850. Displaced stagecoach operators and workers moved westward in search of opportunity. Equipment could also be acquired more cheaply than might otherwise have been the case.

Stagecoach beginnings in the West usually followed established trails in an effort to connect frontier settlements, or often forts, with established communities. Attempts to link Santa Fe with Independence before the Civil War were one example of this effort. A mail contract was indispensable to such an operation, but there were also government express and passengers, either military personnel or their dependents, to be hauled. In many cases stage lines acted as feeders to navigation on rivers like the Missouri, the Columbia, or the Sacramento. Whenever settlement began, small operators tried to make a living by transporting goods and passengers. The key to the success of these "one man–one horse" operations was a contract to carry the U.S. mail.

San Antonio was one of the earliest hubs of stagecoach routes, and between 1847 and 1881 more than fifty different lines operated out of this Texas city. Here, as elsewhere, the trend was toward consolidation, with the smaller operators soon absorbed by one or two companies that came to dominate the area. As early as 1850 a mail subsidy was granted on a route from San Antonio to El Paso and on to Santa Fe. This route helped James E. Birch get a contract in 1857 for a semimonthly mail service between San Antonio and San Diego. The use of mules prompted the line to be known as the "Jackass Mail."

All types of settlement in the American West attracted local stagecoach operators, but the most important to stagecoaches were the mining communities. The California gold rush was hardly underway when stagecoach service was launched in 1849 between San Francisco and San Jose. In little more than a year the major river ports of Sacramento, Stockton, and Marysville were linked with the gold mining camps despite formidable road building problems. In fact, in a short time the Golden State had the most complete stagecoach network in the west. Mining communities in Colorado, Montana, Idaho, Arizona, and South Dakota briefly had numerous stagecoach lines. Even with competition from railroads, many lines served as feeders into the twentieth century.

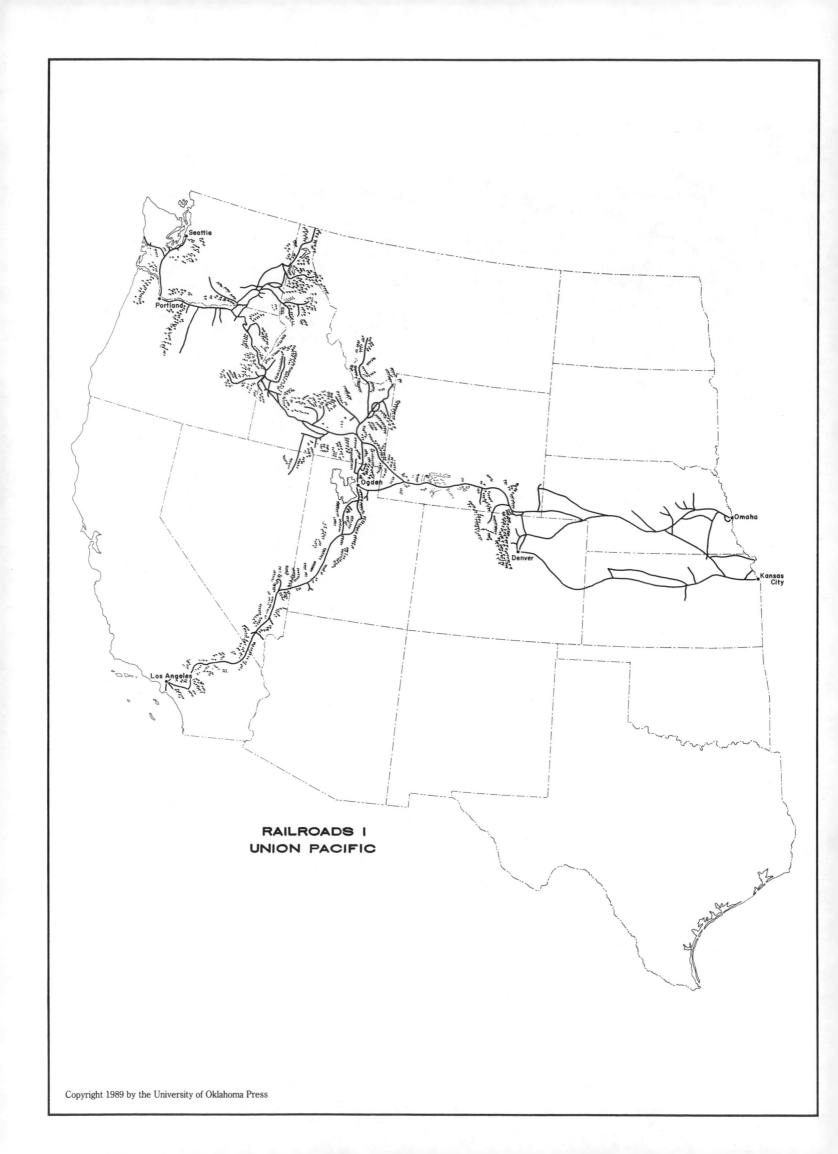

RAILROADS 1
UNION PACIFIC

56. RAILROADS I—UNION PACIFIC

THE OFFICIAL PRONOUNCEMENT by the Census Bureau of the closing of the frontier in the West in 1890 would have been almost impossible without the railroad. As the nation's pioneers pushed the frontier westward, they followed water routes. In the American West only the Missouri River was a significant navigable waterway. Wagon roads were built and freight was hauled by the romanticized covered wagons, but such transport was simply too expensive between distant points. Western pioneers had to be quickly and cheaply hauled to their destination. In addition, the settlers had to be able to market their crops and to obtain the manufactured goods of the East at a fair price. Steamboats and canals may have fulfilled the transport needs east of the Mississippi, but railroads were essential in the settling of the West. And the building of the western railroads between the Civil War and 1890 was one of the great feats of all time.

Visionaries promoted a transcontinental line as soon as railroads began to be built in America. However, the vast open spaces devoid of either people or goods to transport provided no incentive for such a project. The acquisition of the Oregon Territory in 1846, the Mexican Cession in 1848, and the California gold rush provoked interest in a railroad. Congress authorized a series of surveys in the 1850s but took no further action, as it was impossible to select a route in the midst of the sectional strife. The outbreak of the Civil War settled the question whether the railroad would follow a northern or southern route. The Pacific Railroad Act of 1862 gave the line to the Union Pacific, then building westward from Omaha, and to the Central Pacific, which would build eastward from Sacramento. The federal government subsidized the project with land grants and loan bonds for each mile of track laid.

Work on the Union Pacific roadbed west of Omaha began in earnest during July, 1865. Obtaining necessary supplies in the war economy was a herculean task, and rails had to be imported from England. Since none of the Iowa railroads had reached across the state at this time, goods and construction supplies had to shipped up the Missouri River and then hauled overland. Once in full operation, the Union Pacific building project needed supplies for ten thousand animals and eight thousand to ten thousand men. To supply one mile of track with materials took forty railroad cars—and the gangs built an average of a mile a day. As the line inched westward, the difficulty of obtaining ties (twenty-four thousand were needed for each mile) was a major obstacle on the treeless prairie. Sufficient wood for locomotive fuel was also a constant worry. Shortages in the labor force were filled with Civil War veterans and Irish immigrants. Indian attacks, however, took their toll, especially of the survey parties and bridge construction crews, which were out ahead of the main building operation. The statement that a man died for every mile of track laid was no exaggeration. But under the dynamic leadership of Grenville M. Dodge, the Union Pacific met its prescribed one thousand miles of track in January, 1869.

The Union Pacific was not initially a productive enterprise, partially because of the lack of profitable freight to be hauled in its hinterland. In the 1870s Jay Gould acquired control and merged the Kansas Pacific into the system, producing a route to Denver. This gave the Union Pacific another gateway to the East via Kansas City. Gould, however, failed in his effort to acquire the Wabash and the Missouri Pacific, which would have made the Union Pacific a true transcontinental railroad. Under Edward H. Harriman's control in the 1890s, the road acquired the Oregon Short Line Railroad, giving it a route to the Pacific Northwest. In addition, Harriman acquired the Salt Lake route running from Salt Lake City to Los Angeles. This southwest expansion turned the Union Pacific into one of the most important railroads in the West.

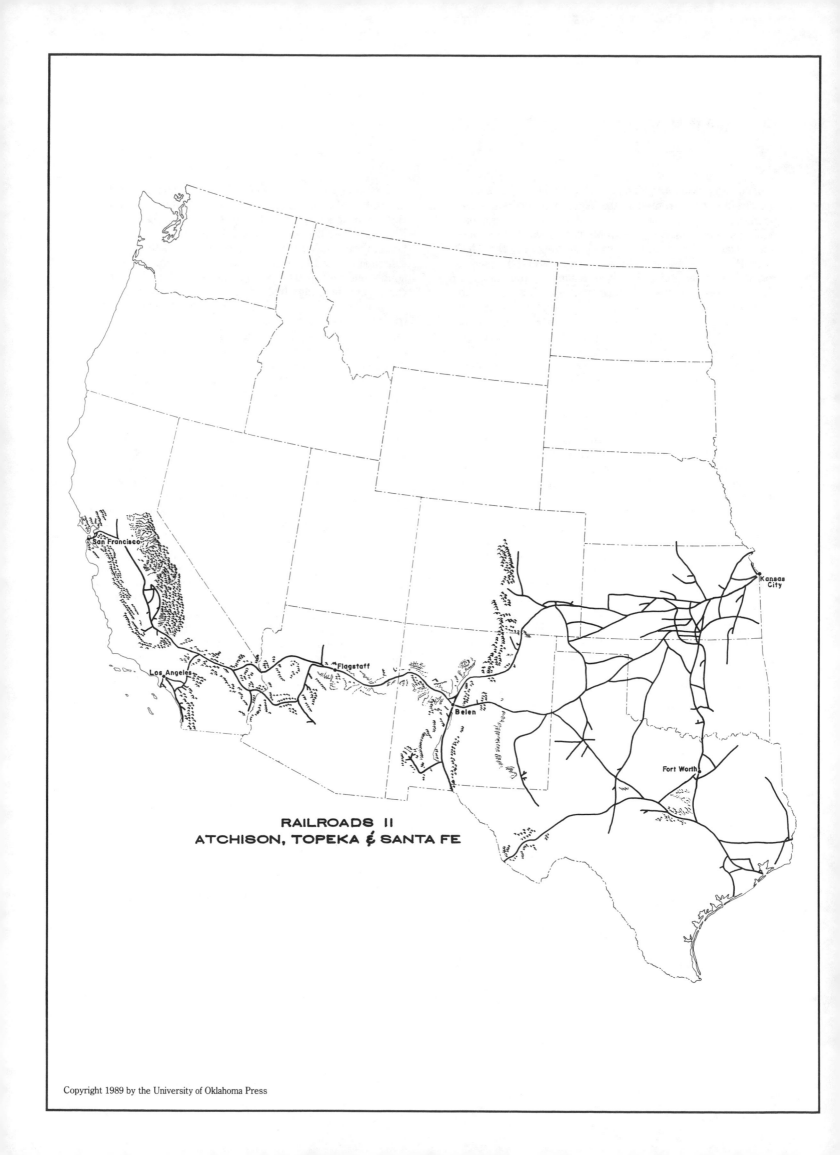

RAILROADS II
ATCHISON, TOPEKA & SANTA FE

57. RAILROADS II—ATCHISON, TOPEKA & SANTA FE

THIS LINE, more popularly known as the Santa Fe, was and still is the most important railroad in the Southwest. Originally chartered as the Atchison & Topeka Railroad by Cyrus K. Holliday in 1858, the Santa Fe was added to the name in the hopes that the mystique of the Santa Fe trade would attract investors. It was 1868 before construction began, and even with a very generous land grant, progress was slow. Road building on the treeless prairie was aided by the ability to float ties, cut in the forests of the Colorado Rockies, down the Arkansas River. However, investors were frightened off by the Credit Mobilier scandals, which hampered railroad financing in general. The new road, inching westward through the empty land, was constantly on the verge of bankruptcy.

The Santa Fe was saved between 1871 and 1885 by revenue from the range cattle industry. In 1871 over 600,000 Texas cattle were shipped from Abilene, and until 1885 the road averaged some 90,000 head per year. The cattle trade also helped balance the company's traffic, as most goods at the time moved from east to west, but beef moved from west to east. In addition to this important cattle trade, the road made money from the wanton slaughter of the buffalo. Hides and bones were shipped east, the former to provide buffalo robes in carriages and sleighs, the latter to be processed for fertilizer.

The Santa Fe reached La Junta and Pueblo, Colorado, in 1876. This destination was vital, as the road needed the coal mined there for fuel. Armed conflict with the Denver & Rio Grande Railroad nearly erupted over who should have control of the vital Raton Pass into New Mexico. The Santa Fe won on both the battlefield and in the courtroom. It is ironical that the town of Santa Fe was initially bypassed because of its mountainous location, with passengers having to take an eighteen-mile stagecoach ride in order to reach the New Mexican capital. A spur line was later built into the town.

The Santa Fe Railroad had planned to use the southern route westward to California, and it constructed its road south from Albuquerque to Deming. However, the Southern Pacific had already reached El Paso in 1881 and did not take kindly to a parallel route. In its effort to reach the Pacific, the Santa Fe first worked with and then acquired the Atlantic & Pacific charter, which ran westward from New Mexico along the 35th parallel. Again, blocked by the Southern Pacific at the California border, the Santa Fe traded a line into Mexico, built from Deming to Guaymas, for a roadbed the Southern Pacific had built from Mojave to Needles. During the 1880s the Santa Fe built or acquired railroad lines in Texas which linked it to Amarillo, Fort Worth, Dallas, Houston, and Galveston, and by 1887 the road had reached the nation's railroad hub, Chicago.

The Santa Fe has always been one of the most progressive and innovative of the western railroads, and therefore one of the most successful. The leaders of the railroad realized from the very inception of the line that if they were to prosper they needed a blend of passengers and freight for their trains and, above all, settlers who would raise crops on the fertile Kansas prairie. Therefore, they established a colonization office which distributed attractive brochures in various European languages to entice farmers. They even had agents in Europe, some of whom may have exaggerated farming prospects on the Great Plains. But they were successful, and empty lands were quickly filled. To attract passengers as tourists, they glorified the uniqueness of the Southwest. They even hired the great artist of the West, Thomas Moran, to paint beautiful pictures of the scenery, the Indians, and the architecture. These pictures were then distributed by the thousands on calendars that helped to create the romantic image of the southwest held by the rest of the nation. To keep the tourists who did come happy, the Fred Harvey organization served them excellent food and built luxurious lodges, called Harvey Houses, many of which still exist.

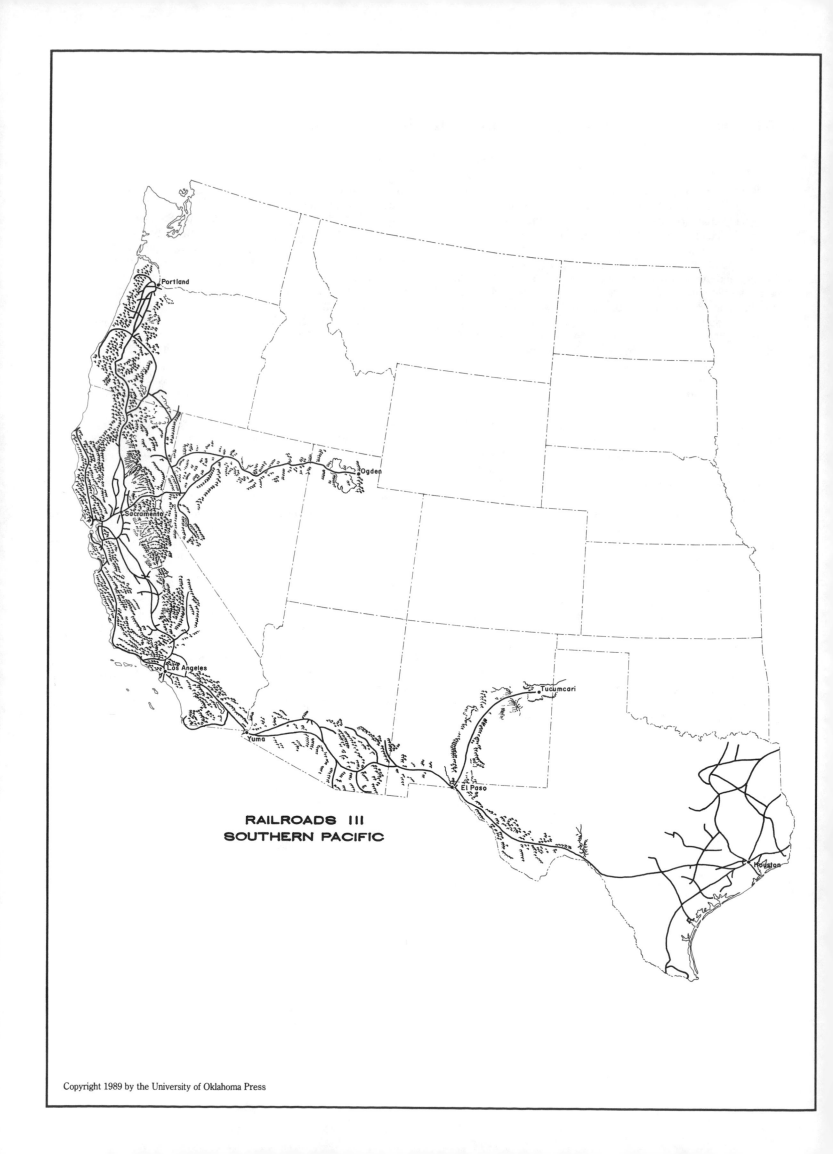

RAILROADS III
SOUTHERN PACIFIC

58. RAILROADS III—SOUTHERN PACIFIC

THE WESTERN HALF of the first continental railroad was the Central Pacific, the precursor of the Southern Pacific. It was built from Sacramento eastward until it linked up with the Union Pacific at Promontory, Utah, on May 10, 1869. The construction problems of the Union Pacific were minor compared to those of the Central Pacific. It had to build a railroad through mountains that most experts considered impassable; the basic problem was that grades could be no steeper than 116 feet to the mile. Then too, everything needed to build a railroad—from spikes to rails, from shovels to locomotives—had to be shipped from the East, across Panama or around Cape Horn. Rails that cost $91 a ton in New York were $141 a ton delivered in San Francisco.

That the road was successfully built was because of several outstanding individuals. Theodore D. Judah first proved by surveys that a railroad could be built over the Sierra Nevada, and he initiated the company to survey the route. Death took this competent engineer before the railroad was finished. James Harvey Strobridge was in charge of construction and was able to solve the many day-by-day challenges. Charles Crocker, the overall supervisor of building the line, was described as "a living, breathing, waddling monument to the triumph of vulgarity, viciousness and dishonesty." Collis P. Huntington was in control of the eastern office, which raised money, bought supplies, and bribed congressmen. He was often labeled as "scrupulously dishonest, and having no more soul than a shark." Leland Stanford and Mark Hopkins were a little less picturesque but also manipulative. This was an age of unscrupulous business practices, and perhaps it took men of little ethics to accomplish the herculean task of building the railroad.

When labor was scarce, Crocker tried Chinese, and when they proved their worth as laborers, he imported some seven thousand. Hundreds of these hardworking "celestials" died in scraping the dirt away or blasting tunnels and cuts through the mountains. Building in the Sierra Nevada was painfully slow. The first track was laid in 1863, twenty miles in 1864; twenty more in 1865; thirty in 1866, and forty-six in 1867. Once the steep mountain grades had been mastered, however, track-laying moved at a fast pace.

Before the transcontinental lines met in May, 1869, the Central Pacific controlled all rail lines radiating out of San Francisco. Through its subsidiary, the Southern Pacific Railroad, it was building south to Los Angeles and east to Yuma, El Paso, and ultimately to New Orleans. In 1884 the Central Pacific and its various subsidiaries combined under the corporate name of the Southern Pacific Company.

Although this line was one of the better operated railroads in the West, it engaged in practices which earned it the name of "octopus," and it was depicted as strangling the economic lifeblood of California. By 1877 the road controlled 85 percent of the railroad mileage within the state and bought politicians of both parties to do its bidding. The railroad squeezed special subsidies out of towns along its route, and when rights-of-way demanded were not forthcoming, the towns were bypassed and left to languish. Settlers were sold land at an agreed price, only to have this figure escalated after improvements were made. Farmers who failed to meet the new charge for the land were evicted. Violence attending such an eviction resulted in seven deaths at Mussel Slough in California in 1880 and further sullied the reputation of the railroad.

Extensive changes took place after the turn of the century, when control of the railroad passed into the hands of Edward H. Harriman. Unlike many Wall Street financiers, Harriman upgraded the railroads he ran instead of milking them. The roadbed was greatly improved, and a line was built north to Portland. The coastal route through Santa Barbara was completed in 1901. When Hiram Johnson's Progressives did "kick the railroad out of politics," they made it possible for company executives to concentrate on running the railroad—and this they have done very well. The Southern Pacific today is one of the better operated and one of the more profitable railways in the nation. It has been helped, to a certain extent, by the fact that the economy of the Southwest, which it services, continues to flourish. Efforts to merge the Southern Pacific and the Santa Fe railroads in the late 1980s have been blocked in the courts.

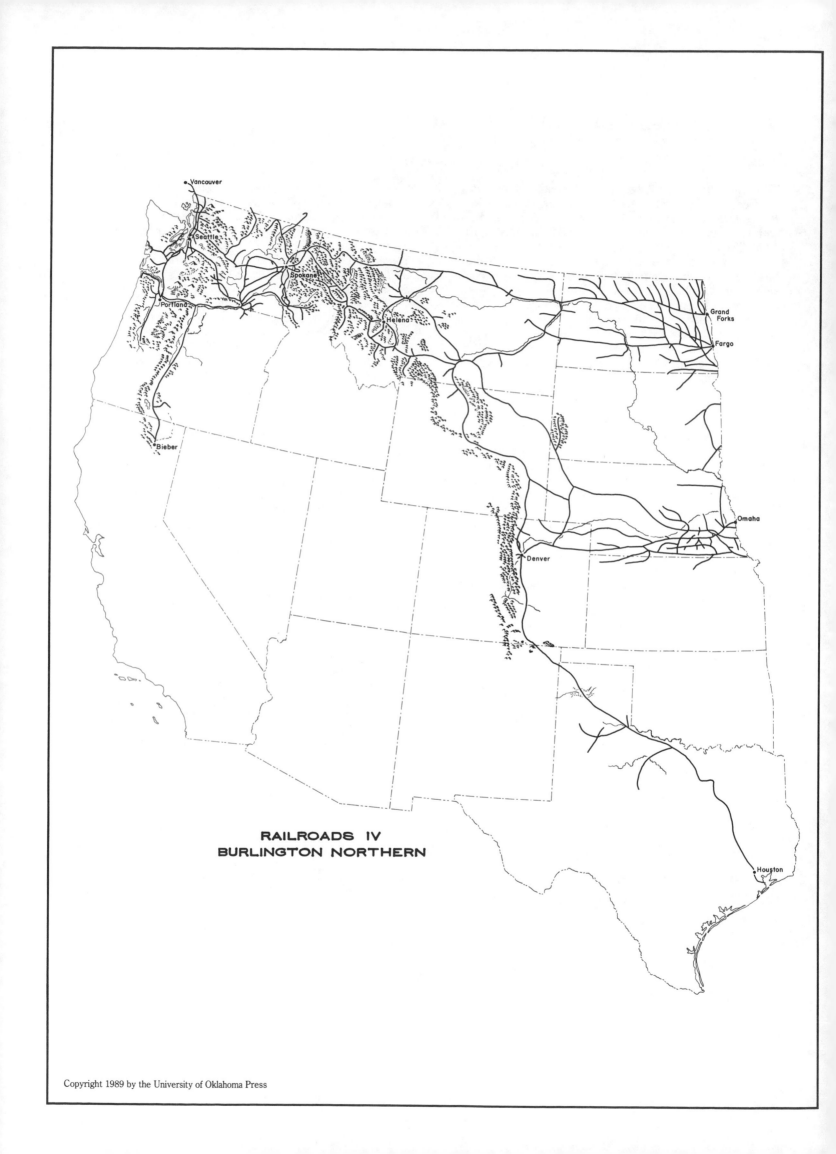

RAILROADS IV
BURLINGTON NORTHERN

59. RAILROADS IV—BURLINGTON NORTHERN

MOST AMERICAN RAILROADS are an amalgam of several roads. The Burlington Northern was formed in 1970 from the merger of the Burlington, Northern Pacific, Great Northern, and several smaller roads. With twenty-six thousand miles of track, it is the longest railroad line in North America. The original claim of the Burlington as the road to "everything West" has certainly been realized in the formation of the new carrier, for this railroad services the Pacific Northwest, Denver, Minneapolis–Saint Paul, Chicago, and all points in between with a connecting line from Denver to Houston.

The original line was put together between 1849 and 1850 with the joining of four small carriers in northern Illinois; it assumed the title "Burlington Route" in 1855. It slowly extended west of the Mississippi by construction and the purchase of 203 smaller roads. The Burlington played a key role in the development of the Midwest and the state of Nebraska. By 1882 the Chicago, Burlington & Quincy arrived in Denver, and two years later it began building across Wyoming with branch lines into the Black Hills. By 1894 the road reached Billings, Montana, where an agreement was reached with the Northern Pacific giving the Burlington access to the Pacific. The line was famed for its building of bridges across the Mississippi despite the bitter opposition of the steamship companies, who desired to snuff out competition from the railroads. Abraham Lincoln defended the railroad in a celebrated case that ended with the U.S. Supreme Court's upholding of the railroads' right to bridge a navigable stream.

The Northern Pacific was chartered by Congress in 1864 and given a fifty-million-acre land grant. This troubled line was the result of agitation in the Pacific Northwest for its own transcontinental route. Jay Cooke financed the road, with construction beginning in Minnesota and Washington in 1870. Bankruptcy during the Panic of 1873 halted work for a number of years. A major obstacle in the West was finding a suitable pass through the Cascades. Henry Villard, a German-born journalist, was retained to protect the interests of German investors, and he was mainly responsible for pushing the road to completion in 1883. Despite Villard's ability to bring settlers from Europe who developed farms and ranches along the railroad right-of-way, the route was repeatedly in and out of financial trouble. A two-mile-long tunnel in the Cascades was completed with great difficulty, thus shortening the route to Puget Sound.

Even with the rapid settlement of eastern Washington and Oregon, the Northern Pacific was seldom free of financial difficulties. Despite its tremendous land grant to sell, the Northern Pacific could not make money. Yet James J. Hill was determined to build another railroad to the Northwest without a land grant to raise money. Hill had obtained control of a small Minnesota carrier and then had driven a road north to Winnipeg. He now proposed to turn his railroad, the St. Paul, Minneapolis & Manitoba, into yet another transcontinental road. Hill knew that the Northern Pacific was overcapitalized and poorly built. Its steep grades made operation expensive, and its management was grossly inefficient. In other words, Hill determined to build a better railroad. He personally surveyed the land and insisted that the track be laid "to last a hundred years." He also personally searched out the gentlest grades so his operating costs would be minimal. In his construction Hill was greatly assisted by one of the nation's greatest railroad engineers, John Stevens. (After working on many difficult projects, including the building of the Panama Canal, Stevens ran the Russian railroads when the U.S. Army invaded Siberia in 1918.) The new road, the Great Northern, was completed in 1893. A few years later Hill and Harriman pooled the stock of the Great Northern Pacific and the Chicago, Burlington & Quincy. This, the Northern Securities Company, was later disallowed by the U.S. Supreme Court, so it is ironical that the final merger of these same three railroads should be permitted in 1970.

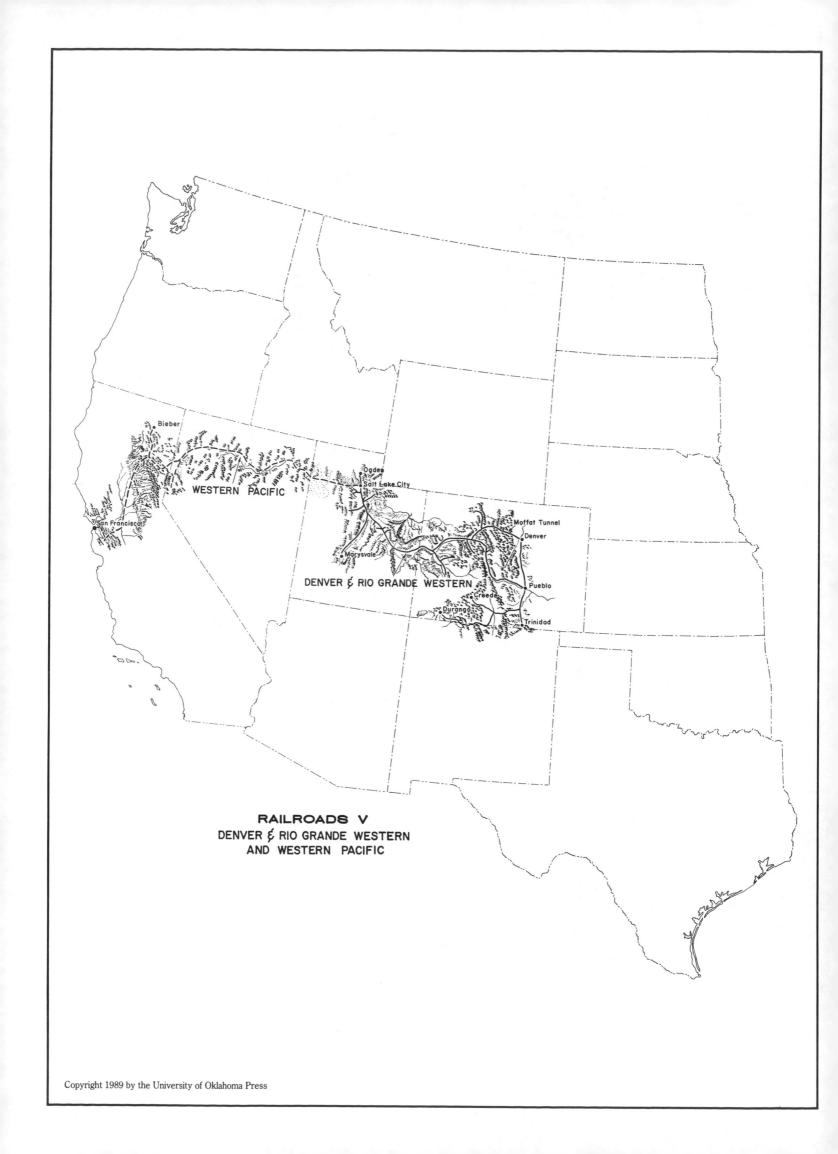

RAILROADS V
DENVER & RIO GRANDE WESTERN
AND WESTERN PACIFIC

60.   RAILROADS V—DENVER & RIO GRANDE WESTERN AND WESTERN PACIFIC

THE DENVER & RIO GRANDE WESTERN is mainly a Colorado and Utah railroad that ultimately linked Denver and Salt Lake City. The Western Pacific was built to complete the link to California. The Denver & Rio Grande was largely the creation of Gen. William Jackson Palmer, who before the Civil War had been secretary to the president of the Pennsylvania Railroad and after the war had been an executive of the Kansas Pacific. Palmer was obsessed with railroads and confided to a friend: "I had a dream last evening. . . . I thought how fine it would be to have a little railroad a few hundred miles in length, all under one's own control." He was also obsessed with the future potential of Colorado. The mines obviously provided a need for a railroad, but Palmer saw also the possibilities in irrigated agriculture, and he was one of the first to see the promise of Colorado's grandeur to the tourist trade, as his early development of Colorado Springs suggests.

The Denver & Rio Grande is the only leading carrier to adopt a narrow gauge (three feet between the rails), which caused it to be nicknamed "the baby road." The four-foot, eight-and-one-half-inch gauge had become standard as a result of the Pacific Act of 1862, and almost all railroads followed that size. The officers of the mountain railroad knew that many mines had their own narrow-gauge branch lines which they would be using. The narrow gauge would mean cheaper construction in mountain terrain, especially when they would be forced to tunnel. Setting such a standard might also discourage competition from entering Colorado. Finally, the narrow gauge might make the road more attractive to British investors, who were familiar with that gauge. The road began converting its heavily traveled line's gauge to the standard gauge in 1887, but there remained several hundred miles of narrow gauge into the 1980s.

Chartered in 1870, the Denver & Rio Grande built southward towards its destination, El Paso, in 1871. Pueblo, Colorado, was reached before the Panic of 1873 disrupted finances and halted construction for three years. The Santa Fe Railway had reached Pueblo in 1876, setting the stage for two major battles. Both railroads needed the Raton Pass in order to enter New Mexico. For a number of years, Richard L. Wooton had operated a toll road through the pass. Perhaps influenced by a promise of a pension of fifty dollars a month for life from the Santa Fe, Wooten sided with that road and guided their armed party into the pass the night before the opposition arrived. The Denver & Rio Grande engineers and roustabouts challenged them but retreated before blood was shed. Their court case also ended in failure. A similar confrontation took place in the Royal Gorge of the Arkansas River west of Pueblo. This canyon route was the most direct way to Salt Lake City at the time, and it was indispensable to the Denver road. On this occasion it was the Santa Fe which lost.

Through the years the Colorado railroad built to most of the key areas of the state, and in 1883 it finally reached Salt Lake City. The line was then extended to Ogden, where a linkup with the Union Pacific gave it a West Coast outlet. However, the road was in and out of receivership and seldom made a good profit, basically because of the lack of sufficient traffic and the cost of building and operating in the mountains. Not until the 1930s, when the seven-mile-long Moffat Tunnel west of Denver, a cutoff shortening the westward trip by 175 miles, was completed, did the road really start to turn reasonable profit.

In 1908, George Gould, heir to his father's railroad empire, merged the Denver & Rio Grande with the Rio Grande Western to form the Denver & Rio Grande Western. Gould also financed the building of the Western Pacific from the bay area over the Feather River route. This road, the dream of Arthur W. Kiddie, was in service by 1910 and for a brief period gave Gould control of the only coast-to-coast railroad. However, in 1911 the financier lost control of his empire. Despite teetering on the brink of bankruptcy many times, both the Western Pacific (now owned by the Union Pacific) and the Denver & Rio Grande Western remain a viable part of western railroading.

STATES AND THEIR CAPITALS

61. STATES AND THEIR CAPITALS

THE STATES OF THE AMERICAN WEST have been the bene-
ficiaries of the federal constitution's Great Compromise,
the measure which granted equal representation in the
U.S. Senate to all states. This has been true because most
of the western states have been, and still are, sparsely
populated, yet their senators in the nation's capital, in
theory at least, exert as much influence as those from the
largest states. This situation has helped keep western
states in a close relationship to the federal government. In
fact, these states are almost wards of Washington, which
owns some one-half of the land area in the region. Western
senators may see themselves as apostles of frontier rugged individualism, but that does not keep them from solic-
iting billions of dollars from the national treasury to spend
on land and forestry management, water resources, aid to
agriculture, or military installations. The West receives
much more in services from Washington than it pays in
taxes.

The states of the American West have other similari-
ties. Despite the small populations in most of them, those
populations are concentrated in a few cities. More than
one-half of the populations of Wyoming, Nevada, Colorado, New Mexico, and Utah are in one or two cities;
three-fourths of Arizonans live in Phoenix or Tucson.

The West has always suffered from extractive indus-
tries—those which strip the resources of the land. First it
was fur trapping; then it was mining—which is still important. Even its farming and ranching has been exploitive,
and thus extractive. In too many cases the control of the
economies of the western states is in the hands of out-
siders. Perhaps the only important industry that is locally
controlled is tourism. In all of the western states vast
spaces and great distances are the rule. As Western states
are simply too big for the number of people in them, and
as it is often a long way from one urban center to another,
transportation is expensive. Finally, as Walter Prescott
Webb so ably put it: "The heart of the West is a desert,
unqualified and absolute," a fact which westerners do not
like to be reminded of.

The capital cities of the states of the American West
have had, in most cases, tumultuous histories of their
own. The question of what town should be the seat of
territorial or state government was usually a most bitter
issue and one that was often fought over for years. The
reasons for this were essentially economic. Agricultural
success in the arid West was thought to be almost as big a
gamble as exploitation of minerals. A surer source of income was that obtained from trapping, Indian trade, land
speculation, and political office. These sources were all
tied to the patronage of the federal government, since it
controlled the territory and the various jobs associated
with the Indian Bureau, the Land Office, and the Departments of the Interior, Justice, and War.

Avery Craven described the fight over the capital issue
common to most states: "Kansas settlers, like other frontiersmen, usually found their funds exhausted before their
new land began to yield a surplus. The control of government and the salaries from public office often measured
the difference between failure and holding on. Control of
government also gave the power to locate county seats,
to determine the location of the territorial capitals, and to
influence the lines along which the railroads would run."

In the early years of California's statehood in the 1850s,
every legislative session was concerned with the location
of the state capital. As the historian Bancroft so ably put
it, "The seat of government was hawked about for years
in a manner disgraceful to the state." Numerous land
promoters made glowing promises to entice the capital to
their city, and it was moved from Monterey to San Jose to
Vallejo, back to Vallejo, to Benicia, and finally to Sacramento in 1854. Political intrigue and a ten-thousand-dollar
bribe may have been the deciding factors in the final location. In Montana the territorial capital site was only
decided in 1869, when an "accidental" fire destroyed
the ballots settling the matter. Most states had similar
experiences.

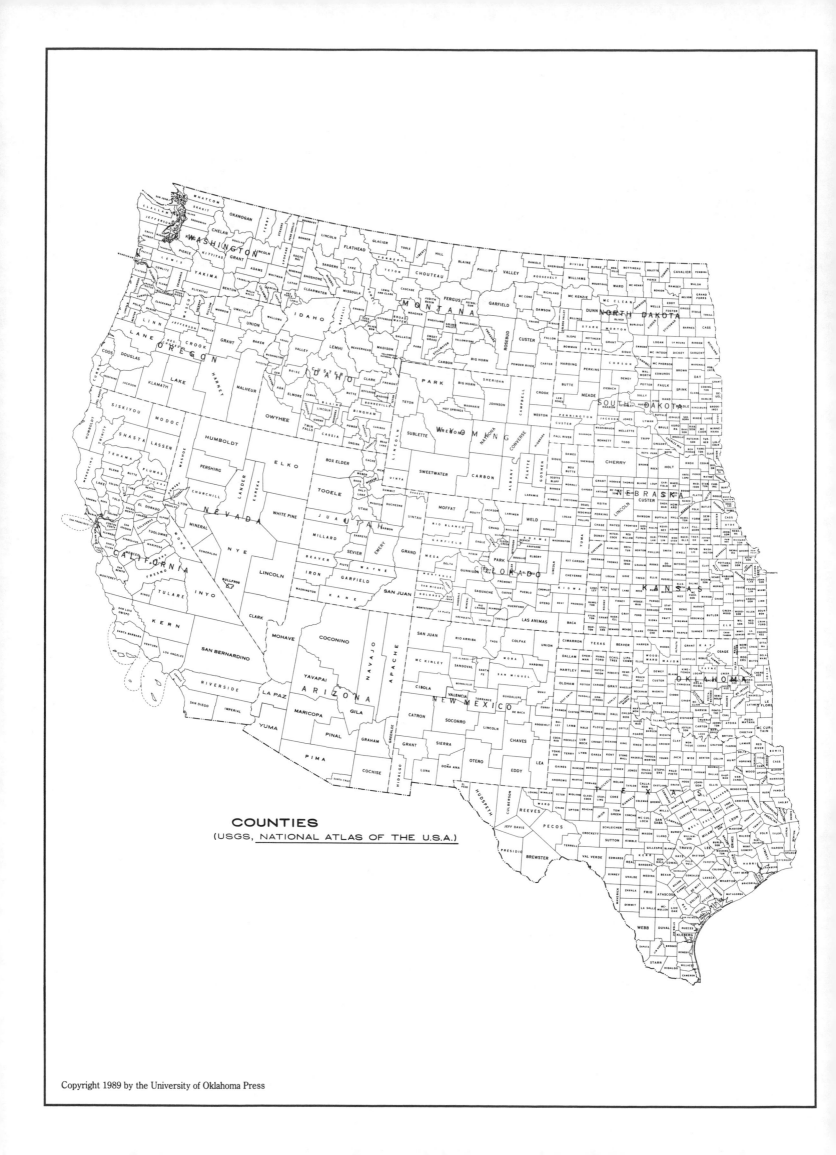

COUNTIES
(USGS, NATIONAL ATLAS OF THE U.S.A.)

62. COUNTIES

THE COUNTIES OF THE AMERICAN WEST had their origin in the system of English shires transplanted into Virginia by the early colonists. This institution of local government has been only slightly changed through the years by the settlers who came west, who favored it because it could be readily adapted to their predominantly agricultural society.

Initially, counties were arbitrarily formed when territorial governments were installed. In most territories or states too few counties were often the rule, and the result was that they were much too large and the county seat too remote to satisfy the needs of the people. So when a new area was settled it was often necessary to create a new county or move the county seat closer to the populace. The size of a typical county, it has been said, was determined by the distance that a person could travel between milking time in the morning and milking time in the evening, going and coming from the county seat. For example, initially Idaho had seven counties, but today there are forty-four. This was especially true in the mining communities, where large towns could rise and fall in a short period of time. A new railroad line was often followed by a row of new counties centered on the rail line, with county seats at important points on the railroad.

The largest county in the West, and in the nation, is California's San Bernardino County, with 20,131 square miles. The average county is about 1,000 square miles in size. There is also a great variance in population. For example, Los Angeles County has in excess of 7,500,000 people, while Loving County, Texas, has just over 200.

A glance at the map shows that the basic shape of counties in the American West, especially on the Great Plains, is rectangular. In fact, Kansas appears to be divided into 105 small squares. Where a county has an odd-shaped side, it is usually the result of a natural boundary, such as a stream or a mountain range.

While most counties of the West have been little changed in the twentieth century, there continue to be revisions. In 1983 the Arizona legislature created the new 4,430-square mile county of La Paz, with Parker as its county seat.

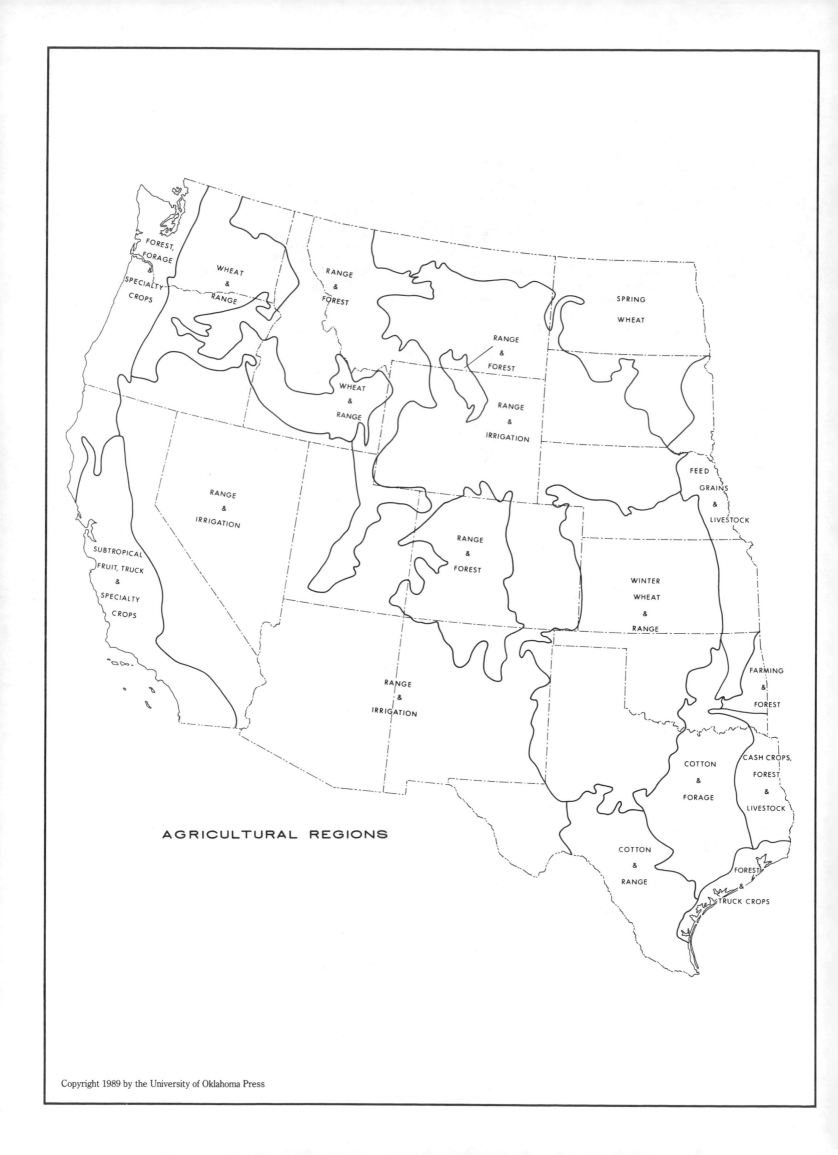

AGRICULTURAL REGIONS

FOREST, FORAGE & SPECIALTY CROPS

WHEAT & RANGE

RANGE & FOREST

SPRING WHEAT

RANGE & FOREST

WHEAT & RANGE

RANGE & IRRIGATION

FEED GRAINS & LIVESTOCK

RANGE & IRRIGATION

RANGE & FOREST

WINTER WHEAT & RANGE

SUBTROPICAL FRUIT, TRUCK & SPECIALTY CROPS

FARMING & FOREST

RANGE & IRRIGATION

COTTON & FORAGE

CASH CROPS, FOREST & LIVESTOCK

COTTON & RANGE

FOREST & TRUCK CROPS

63. AGRICULTURAL REGIONS

THIS MAP SUGGESTS one of the main characteristics of farming in the American West: through trial and error it has been learned that some crops prosper in certain regions, and thus many areas concentrate on a single one. Western agricultural regions are also determined by the availability of irrigation, the practice of dry farming, and the physical characteristics of the area.

Along the eastern edge of the American West is an extension of the Midwestern corn belt specializing in feeding grain to livestock. In eastern Texas the farmers raise crops common to the areas adjacent to the east. North Dakota and part of South Dakota are dominated by the spring wheat belt. In that region the grain is planted in the spring, grows all summer, and is harvested in late summer or early fall. To the south winter wheat is planted in the fall, begins growing with the fall rains, dies down under the winter snow, but grows rapidly with the spring rains and is ready for harvest in early summer. Another wheat growing region is on the Columbia Plateau of eastern Washington and Oregon, where both winter and spring wheat are grown. Where the rainfall is too scanty for normal cultivation, dry farming is practiced. This involves working the soil to best retain moisture and, in some cases, permitting the land to lie fallow for a year.

Where there is insufficient moisture for wheat or other grain, the land is used to pasture cattle or sheep; In many parts of the Edwards Plateau in Texas, only goats can find enough sustenance. Slopes of mountains receive more moisture and allow less evaporation, so the grasslands there are superior as animal feed. As one climbs higher, the pasturelands blend gradually into open pine forest. However, at the timberline the forest gives way to alpine pasture, where livestock are able to fatten on the lush grass during the summer months. In the Northwest and in other mountainous regions trees are a new and important crop.

Throughout the American West agriculture has been expanded by the use of irrigation. Perhaps the smallest amount of acreage is watered on the Great Plains, but even in that region the damming of mountain-fed rivers has supplied an increasing basis for irrigation. In the Texas Panhandle and the Staked Plains, improved pumping techniques have made it possible for farmers to draw water from ever deeper in the ground. The valleys of streams, however, are the main irrigated farming areas in the West. In most regions the main crop is alfalfa or other kinds of livestock feed.

The richest irrigated farming areas of the American West are in the Central Valley in California, in the lowlands in the southern part of the state, and in the nearby Imperial Valley. There, fruits, vegetables, vineyards, rice, cotton, and alfalfa abound. Fresno County is the richest single agricultural area in the nation.

WHEAT

BARLEY

FIELD CROPS I

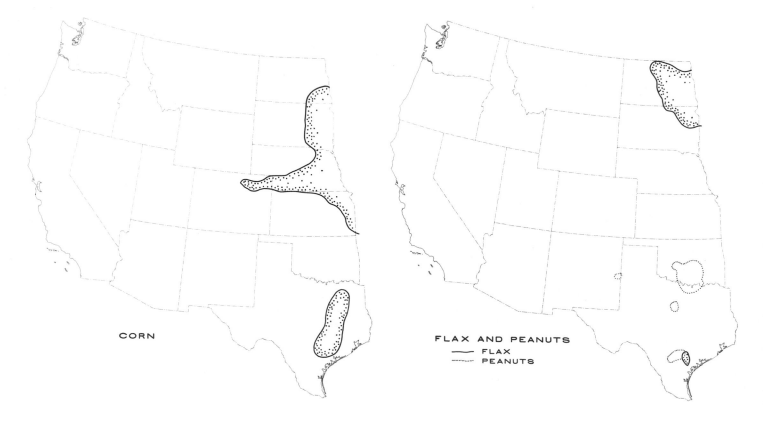

CORN

FLAX AND PEANUTS
—— FLAX
········ PEANUTS

64. FIELD CROPS I

SINCE EARLIEST TIMES wheat has been a preferred grain crop because it has had a higher value per unit of weight than other grains. Therefore, wheat could be transported some distance overland at a profit. The first great wheat producing state in the American West was California, which had to ship grain vast distances by sea. With irrigation, California found even more valuable crops for its land, but arid eastern Washington is still a leading wheat producer. Pioneer farmers of Nebraska and Kansas preferred corn, because it produced more bushels per acre and was favored as livestock feed, but by the 1880s they had shifted to wheat, because corn required greater rainfall. Winter wheat, planted in the fall and harvested in early summer, took advantage of the limited moisture and expanded in acreage with the introduction of superior varieties.

Hard, red "Turkey" wheat was introduced into Kansas in 1874 by French immigrants, but it was at first unsuccessful because it was difficult to mill with the procedures of the day. In the 1880s Russian Mennonites produced this type of wheat in such quantities that the millers had to solve the processing problem. Because this strain resisted winterkill and the destructive Hessian fly, it soon became the standard winter wheat of the Great Plains.

Spring wheat, planted in the spring and harvested in late summer, was common in North Dakota and Montana. Bonanza wheat growing flourished in the Red River valley of North Dakota and continues to this day, with many farms exceeding ten thousand acres. Improvements in technology helped expand acreage sown to wheat, but a successful crop normally requires fifteen inches of rainfall, and there were, and still are, dry years disastrous to wheat farmers.

As the map suggests, barley is usually grown in the same areas as wheat. In California, barley has gained importance as the state's leading grain crop and is grown as both a dry-farm crop and under irrigation. Acreage planted throughout the West has increased in recent years because of the government allotment program for wheat. The highest grade of barley is sold for malt, but about 90 percent is used as livestock feed.

America's farmers learned quickly that corn, or Indian maize, was their most valuable crop. In the East, trees could be girdled to clear plots and corn seed planted with little preparation of the soil. In the treeless prairie, before the chilled-beam iron plow was developed to break the heavy sod, the farmer could plant corn in holes chopped in the ground. Corn production was much higher per acre than wheat, and corn could be fed to both man and beast. As Nicolas Hardeman has pointed out, corn has many uses: "Most crops—wheat, barley, rye, potatoes, fruits—were harvested at one time or as individual plants or fruits ripened, that was that. Not so with Indian corn. There were suckers, baby ears, roasting ears, semihard grains, and mature ears, all with their own seasons." In addition, corn could be converted into liquor and either consumed at home or transported to market with only one-sixth the weight of the original product. It also had the advantage that it could be stored in its dry or liquid form for long periods of time.

With corn being such an integral part of frontier life, it was natural that farmers would attempt to grow it throughout the American West, usually with disastrous results, as the rainfall in most areas was simply inadequate for corn culture. The crop has proposed in Texas where there is sufficient precipitation, and in the past decade it has also been grown in the Texas Panhandle under irrigation. It also continues as a leading crop in the eastern portions of the Dakotas, Nebraska, and Kansas, where it supports the hog industry.

Flax was, until a few years ago, grown in many areas of the American West. Today there is a small producing area in Texas, but the most important region is in the spring wheat belt of northeastern South Dakota and the adjacent areas in Minnesota. Flax is primarily used for straw, for livestock feed, and for linseed oil. The decline in the use of linen has virtually ended its use as fiber in the United States.

Peanuts were at one time confined to the deep South. Union soldiers who invaded the area brought them to the North and made peanuts a national product after the Civil War. The crop prospers on the light soils of the coastal plain and was brought into Texas by early settlers. The peanut producing area has expanded into Oklahoma and New Mexico.

COTTON

IRISH POTATOES

FIELD CROPS II

RICE

SUGAR BEETS

65. FIELD CROPS II

THE QUEST FOR RICH VIRGIN SOIL to raise cotton was one of the primary reasons for the American acquisition of Texas. Cultivation of cotton in the coastal plain remained important, and in 1900 Texas became the leading cotton producing state. Today, California is the leader, which suggests the shift of cotton raising to arid irrigated lands where yields are more than twice that of the area along the Gulf Coast. Cotton raised in the Texas Panhandle and nearby New Mexico and Oklahoma is mainly irrigated by deep wells. In addition, the arid regions are preferable for cotton because the relative absence of rain simplifies harvesting with mechanical equipment—cotton can be left in the field until it is all ripe without threat of damage by moisture. While cotton production has been steadily declining in the states of the Old South, it has been increasing in the West.

The Irish potato is grown today in only a few selected areas of the West. In the era of subsistence farming most families planted an acre or two of potatoes for the table. But in this day of production for the market, only a few areas have been found to be suitable for the commercial production of this crop. The best example is the Snake River plains in Idaho, where there are more than 300,000 acres in potatoes. That area is responsible for about one-quarter of the annual U.S. output of this crop. It had long been known that a combination of proper irrigation, soil, and temperature could produce high-quality potatoes in eastern Washington, Idaho, and the mountain valleys of Colorado, but because of potatoes' low value per unit of weight, they could not be shipped any great distance to market. Efforts to preserve food for overseas shipment during World War II, however, resulted in the invention of methods to convert potatoes into dry flakes and frozen chips or slices. The result is a range of new products that can be profitably shipped and preserved indefinitely.

Rice production in the American West is an example of the most progressive agricultural engineering in the world. To produce rice in the Orient, labor requirements are about one person per acre; in the United States the ratio is one person per 100 acres. On the Texas Gulf Coast some 500,000 acres are planted in rice, and in the center of California's Great Valley about 330,000 acres. A special seed was developed for the California fields, which are flooded to kill the weeds, with seeding and fertilizing performed by low-flying, specially equipped airplanes. Self-propelled combines harvest the crop after the field has been drained, and complex machinery dries it, making the requirements of human labor minimal. The result is that both Texas and California can produce rice cheaper than the Orient; in fact, much of their crop is shipped to Asia.

Farmers in California first grew sugar beets as early as 1870, but they were dependent on sugar processing plants. Claus Spreckels built the first plant in the West in California in 1888, and Robert and Henry Oxnard built several at the turn of the century, making California the leading state in sugar beet production in 1910. Sugar beets are raised in North Dakota's Red River valley, Montana's Yellowstone Valley, northern Colorado, western Nebraska, and especially in the Snake River valley of Idaho, making the last-named state third in national production. Sugar beets were first grown in the Pacific Northwest in 1897, but the acreage has expanded in recent years in the Columbia Basin with the completion of the Grand Coulee irrigation project. Sugar beets produce more than sugar; beet pulp, molasses, and beet tops are used for livestock feed.

CITRUS

GRAPES

FRUITS AND NUTS

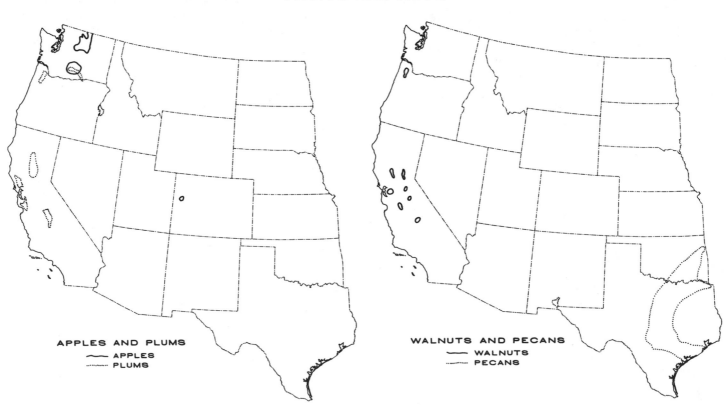

APPLES AND PLUMS
—— APPLES
········ PLUMS

WALNUTS AND PECANS
—— WALNUTS
········ PECANS

66. FRUITS AND NUTS

THE PRODUCTION OF CITRUS FRUIT—oranges, lemons, grapefruit, and tangerines—is concentrated in California. Only Arizona and Texas among western states have any such fruit at all. Oranges are grown as far north as Oroville in California, but because of urbanization they have been forced out of their traditional home in the Los Angeles Basin. Acreage in orange trees has steadily increased in the San Joaquin Valley, but even that has not made up for the losses in Los Angeles and Orange counties. From a position of national leadership California has fallen far behind Florida in orange acreage. Only in raising lemons has the Golden State continued to be first. Arizona has the essential warm and frost-free weather along with adequate water for irrigation to raise citrus, but that state is also busily uprooting trees to build new cities.

California is also the leader in the American West in grape production, accounting for some 90 percent of the nation's total. Again, the primary area of production is in the San Joaquin Valley. Only Arizona and Washington have significant acreages in grapes. Grapes are marketed fresh as a table fruit; as raisins; or as juice, either fresh or as wine. The profit per acre is greatest from table grapes. Surplus which cannot be marketed as table grapes or dried as raisins can be processed into wine. California also produces 90 percent of the nation's wine, some of it of very high quality. Washington has twenty-three wineries, but many are local and have limited production capacity. Most of the nation's supply of raisins also comes from California.

Washington is the nation's leading apple producing state and supplies most of the market demand in urban centers. Distance from markets dictates that only the best fruit be shipped and that it be attractively packaged and effectively marketed. The orchards are concentrated in the irrigated Yakima, Wenatchee, and Okanogan valleys east of the Cascade Mountains.

Plums have long been recognized as delicious fruits, and among stone fruits they are second only to peaches in popularity. Countless varieties of plums, European types as well as native ones, have been cultivated in the United States, and through the years more have been developed. Plums are found in most of the nation, but most of those grown commercially are in the Pacific Coast states. In addition to the fresh-fruit varieties, the Lombard and Italian varieties are dried and marketed as prunes.

Walnuts are another of the many crops with which California leads the nation, accounting for 96 percent of the total. Originally concentrated in Los Angeles, Orange, and San Diego counties, they are now grown in widely scattered areas of the state. Walnuts were probably first brought to California by the French explorer La Perouse in 1786. Early visitors to the missions record seeing walnut trees and being treated to the nuts. Walnut trees were planted near San Diego in 1843, and the nuts were exhibited at agricultural fairs in the 1850s. English soft-shelled walnuts were first planted in Santa Barbara in 1867 and were soon a commercial success. About 5 percent of the nation's walnuts come from a small region in the Willamette Valley of western Oregon.

The pecan is a member of the walnut family. Trees of this species flourish in the Deep South and commercial growing has expanded into Texas and Oklahoma, with a small producing area in southern New Mexico. The production and consumption of both walnuts and pecans has increased dramatically in recent years, mainly because improved technology has made it possible to process the nuts by machinery and thus keep the price within the reach of more consumers.

CATTLE

SHEEP

LIVESTOCK AND POULTRY

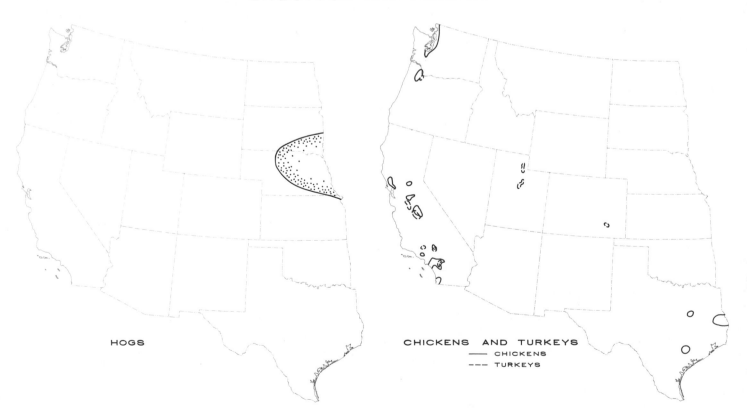

HOGS

CHICKENS AND TURKEYS
—— CHICKENS
--- TURKEYS

67.   LIVESTOCK AND POULTRY

THE ROMANTIC OPEN-RANGE PERIOD of the cattle industry ended by the 1890s, but the importance of cattle raising in the American West has remained and in fact continues to increase, basically because much of the West still is, and should continue to be, grassland. This land can raise cattle more cheaply than other regions of the nation. Yearlings are then shipped to the feed lots of the Midwest or near urban areas of the West to be fattened on corn for market. The map depicts this concentration in California, where thousands of head are prepared for market. In some states receipts from beef cattle and dairy sales are the leading form of agricultural income.

The first Spanish settlers of New Mexico, California, and Texas brought both cattle and sheep into the areas they settled, but they preferred sheep. Perhaps that was true because they raised sheep for both meat and wool production and because sheep had prospered in their arid homeland, so similar to the American Southwest. Because sheep have cleft lips and can graze closer to the soil than cattle can, and also because they need less water than cattle do, they have tended to take over the more arid regions, especially in Texas. In addition, sheep are found in rugged hill country along the California coast and in Oregon. The number of sheep has declined sharply in the twentieth century, partially because of the emphasis on synthetic clothing material. However, such material is derived from oil, and since the price of that commodity has risen rapidly from 1973 on, wool is back in favor and the raising of sheep is again flourishing.

Unlike sheep and cattle, which have a long history in the American West, hogs have only recently become a significant part of the agricultural scene. However, in the West they are confined to a relatively small area in southeastern South Dakota and the eastern half of Nebraska, where the primary fattening feed is the corn grown nearby. One advantage of raising hogs for market is that they make more pounds of meat in proportion to their feed than do cattle. Another advantage is that they are less speculative than beef; the farmer does not have a large investment in the feeders. With hogs the farmer can also react more quickly to market forces; he can rapidly cut back on hog production when corn is in short supply or commands too high a price and can increase hog production when corn is plentiful and cheap.

Chickens, a fowl whose origins go back to ancient China, were, until recently, a supplemental part of farming and ranching in the American West and were often left in female hands. However, even small-scale poultry farmers were superseded beginning in the 1950s by technicians who raised chickens on a production-line basis for either meat or eggs. As the map indicates, the chicken ranches are usually near the great urban centers, their markets. Petaluma, California, lays claim to being "the egg capital of the world."

Chickens and their eggs are consumed the year around. Turkeys, on the other hand, are produced mainly for sale in the holiday season at the end of the year. Although some Indian tribes had domesticated the turkey, which is native to America, it was not until the wild birds became scarce that New England farmers began breeding them in the nineteenth century. In recent years turkeys have been bred with a broad breast, thus providing the most desirable meat. Like chickens, turkeys are raised in the West near urban centers, with most of them in California and a few in Utah and Colorado. One reason the turkey has prospered in these areas is because it is subject to respiratory diseases and is therefore healthier in dry climates.

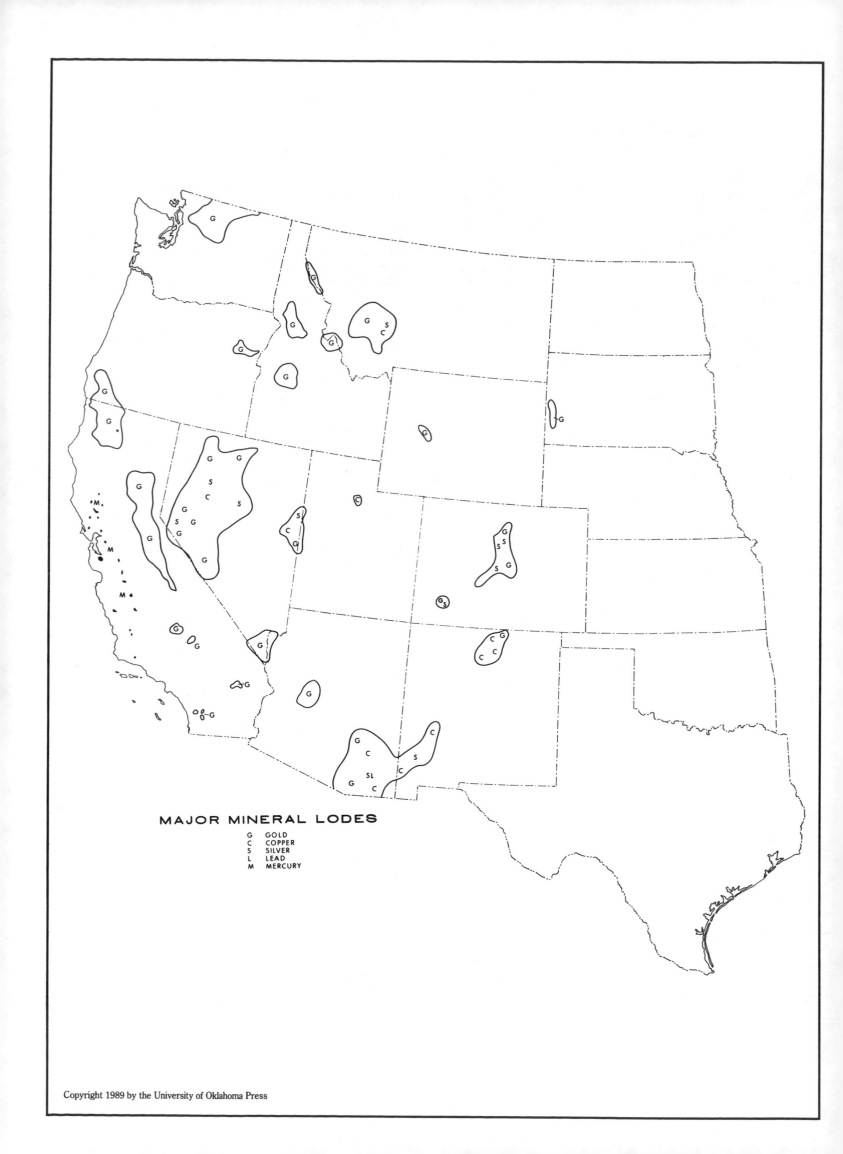

MAJOR MINERAL LODES

G   GOLD
C   COPPER
S   SILVER
L   LEAD
M   MERCURY

68. MAJOR MINERAL LODES

A FEW MINERALS, led by gold and silver, have been valued out of all proportion to their intrinsic value. Precious metals inspired the Spanish to conquer Mexico and explore much more of North America. The English settlers at Jamestown wasted precious time searching for gold and silver to no avail. As the American frontier slowly advanced westward, mining played little part, except for the exploitation of lead and zinc in Missouri and Wisconsin. In fact, the influence of precious metals on the economy of the United States, and on that of Europe, was declining until the discovery of gold in California in 1848, which completely transformed the development of the American West. Gold, as John Walton Caughey so ably put it, became the cornerstone.

After the events in California, the search for precious metals in the West became at times the prime determinant of settlement and operated in independently from the trappers' frontier or even that of the ranchers and the farmers. In the past, pioneer communities were relatively near the settled regions and could depend on them for their economic or social needs. But the miners' frontier was different; it went where the minerals could be found, no matter how distant, as in the case of California, or how remote, as in the case of Helena, Montana.

Miners were complete capitalists interested only in amassing wealth, and they searched even the most inhospitable lands. Ray Allen Billington and Martin Ridge describe the process:

> They occupied not fertile valleys or rich farmlands but often the unattractive portions of the Far West—steep mountainsides where roaring creeks covered deposits of precious metal, parched deserts where shifting sands hid beds of ore, and highlands where jagged rock outcroppings shielded mineral-bearing lodes. The prospectors scoured thousands of square miles of mountain and desert that would have been avoided had farmers been the only pioneers. They were unusual, moreover, in that they moved not from east to west in the usual frontier pattern, but initially from west to east. For prospectors in most goldfields came from California rather than the settled areas of the Mississippi Valley.[1]

Conditions in California tended to eliminate the lone prospector after 1852 and to drive him to seek his fortune elsewhere. Initially, gold had been easily obtained. The precious metal had been created when volcanic action forced hot liquid into the fissures and cracks on the earth's mantle. A subsequent series of geologic cycles after the veins were formed brought erosion, volcanic eruption, and an uplift of the mountains westward, increasing the erosive power of the westward-flowing streams. Therefore, gold was found along the banks of streams or in stream beds. These placer deposits could be easily obtained by panning, which was simply swirling the ore around in a pan to separate the gold from the sand and gravel. Being heavier, the gold would sink to the bottom of the pan, while the foreign matter was washed over the rim. When there was enough "pay dirt," other tools were used. The "cradle" was a wooden box which was rocked as water was led into it, washing the refuse away and catching the gold in cleats at the bottom. Where enough water was available to create a powerful stream, a larger separator called the "long tom" was used. All of these methods required little investment and only limited knowledge of mining. They worked only in rich virgin deposits, and once the cream had been skimmed, the miner was forced to move on. Often miners sought greener pastures even before placer deposits they had been working were played out.

[1] Billington, Ray Allan, and Martin Ridge, *Westward Expansion: A History of the American Frontier* (New York: Macmillan, 1982), p. 556.

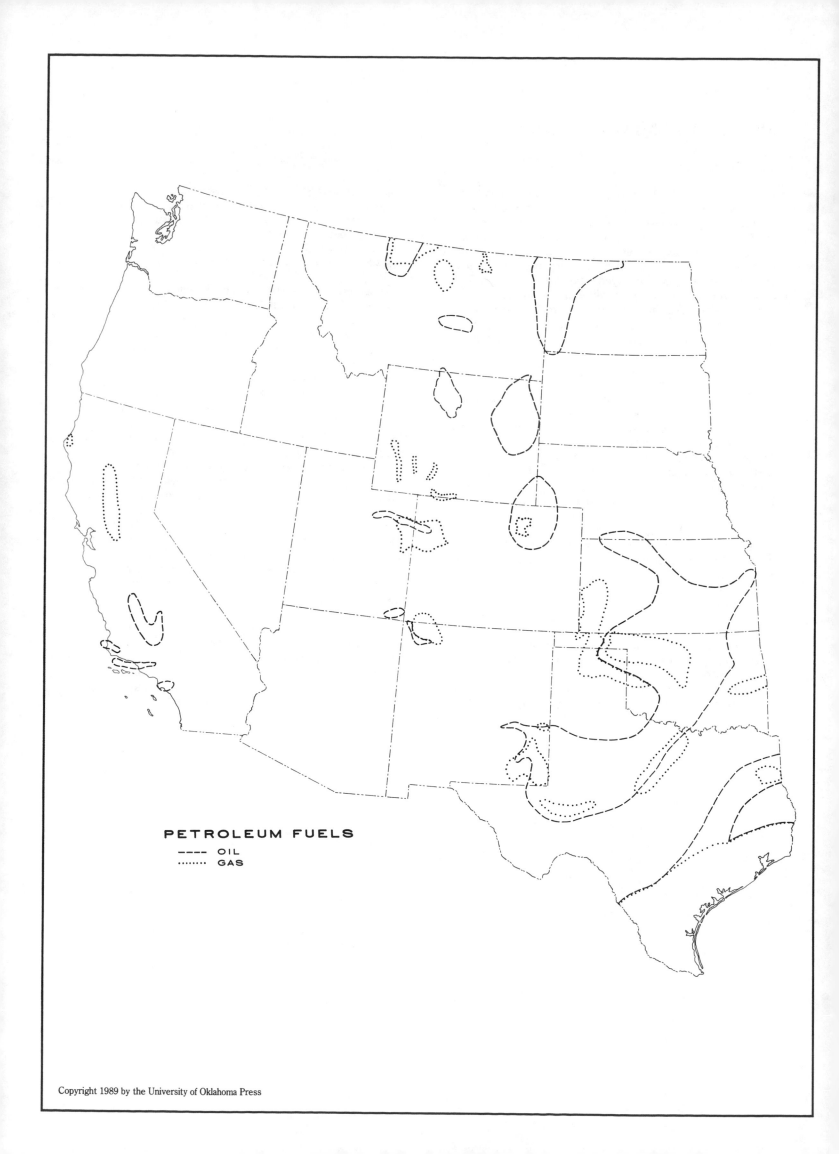

PETROLEUM FUELS

---- OIL

······ GAS

69. PETROLEUM FUELS

THE MODERN OIL INDUSTRY BEGAN in western Pennsylvania in 1859 and gradually moved westward; Ohio was the leading producing state by 1900. California was the only state in the American West to have a sizable oil production in 1900; in fact, the Golden State led the nation from 1903 to 1936. Since the beginning of the century petroleum fuels have been the most important mineral wealth produced in the American West, far surpassing in value and significance previous metals such as gold and silver. Oklahoma, Texas, and Kansas were soon leaders in the production of oil and gas, but, as the map indicates, there are rich fields in most western states.

The opening of new sources of oil in the American West coincided with increased demand resulting from the emergence of the automobile and the increased use of petroleum for many sources of energy. In addition, improved drilling techniques meant that production could be increased. Better geological knowledge made it easier for the trained eye to locate potential oil-producing areas in sedimentary rock formations. New refining processes also obtained a greater percentage of finished products from the crude oil.

As the map suggests, natural gas is usually found along with oil, although there are a number of gas fields alone. The natural gas that accompanies crude oil in the ground is usually under compression. Therefore, it often provides sufficient energy to move the oil through the porous rock to the bottom of the well, and sometimes up the well to the surface. For many years the gas was burned off as waste, but with the advent of pipelines it has become economically valuable.

The Gulf Coast of Texas is one of the richest fields in the nation and has the advantage of being able to ship oil by sea. The Permian Basin of West Texas and southeastern New Mexico and the area which extends through Texas and Oklahoma into Kansas is one of the great reserves. The Rocky Mountain province of Montana, Wyoming, Colorado, New Mexico, and Utah has been developed more recently but must ship its oil some distance by pipelines. California has three large producing areas: the Los Angeles Basin, the southern San Joaquin Valley, and the coastal district.

The search for and production of petroleum fuels has always been a high-risk venture. This has been especially true in the second half of the twentieth century, as they have become human beings' most favored source of energy. Shortages drove the per-barrel oil price to a high of $36 in 1985, bringing great prosperity to all associated with the petroleum industry. This high price was followed by a collapse which saw prices falling to $10 a barrel in only a few months and plunging the areas dependent upon oil into a deep depression. Prices will undoubtedly rise once again, but such fluctuations simply underscore the speculative nature of the industry.

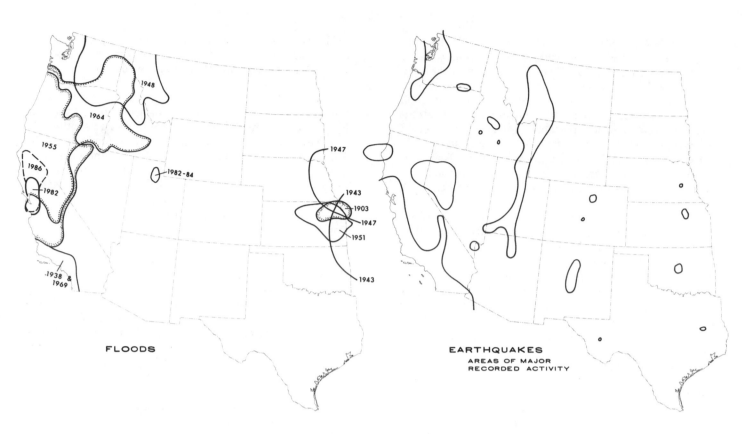

FLOODS

1948
1964
1955
1986
1982
1982-84
1938 &
1969

EARTHQUAKES
AREAS OF MAJOR
RECORDED ACTIVITY

1947
1943
1903
1947
1951
1943

CATASTROPHIC NATURAL EVENTS

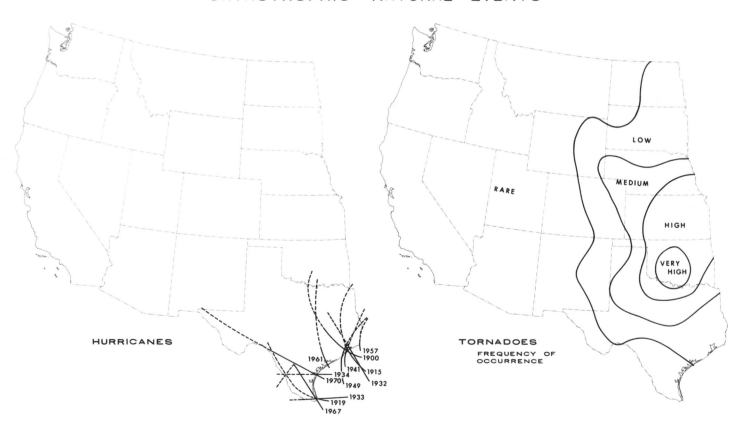

HURRICANES

1961
1957
1900
1941
1915
1934
1970
1949
1932
1919
1933
1967

TORNADOES
FREQUENCY OF
OCCURRENCE

LOW
RARE
MEDIUM
HIGH
VERY
HIGH

70. CATASTROPHIC NATURAL EVENTS

MANY SETTLERS IN THE AMERICAN WEST looked upon their new home, as Frederick Jackson Turner suggested, as "a gate of escape from the past," or in the words of the songwriter, as a place where "we'll find perfect peace, where joys never cease." As a result the West was widely promoted as a paradise. And it was true that many migrants, especially those with respiratory ailments, found improved health in the land. Those who settled the Great Plains, however, soon learned that there were also many things wrong with the new land: the scourge of grasshoppers, prairie fires, hailstorms that could devastate crops in minutes, and winds that could scorch the earth in summer and freeze both human beings and animals in winter. Above all, the West was cursed with drought and floods, earthquakes, hurricanes, and tornadoes.

Since Biblical times floods have been humankind's most frequently recorded natural catastrophe. In the American West the early travelers were plagued by high water, and in the nineteenth century floods were possibly even more damaging than they are today. Flood hazards are more of a danger in the arid West because the shortage of water prompts builders to locate along streams and upon alluvial fans and debris cones at the foot of mountains, thus putting their buildings at the mercy of desert cloudbursts. Los Angeles and Salt Lake City are examples of such cities: in fact, the Utah city experienced one of the worst floods in its history as late as the spring of 1983. Another reason why floods are common in the American West is because most of the region is arid, and when rainfall does occur, half the annual moisture may fall in a matter of hours. The frequency of flooding has caused governments to spend much of their tax dollars building reservoirs, levees, and flood control channels.

As the map indicates, earthquakes have occurred over widely scattered areas of the American West, with tremors in Missouri in 1811 and 1812 being the most severe in the history of the nation. The states closest to the Pacific Ocean have experienced the most quakes, though. As a part of the Pacific Basin seismic belt, which has 80 percent of the world's earthquakes, California records more earth tremors than any state except Alaska. Earthquakes have the potential to do more damage to man and the cultural landscape than any other natural catastrophe. Historian Will Durant expressed the problem well when he observed: "Civilization exists by geological consent, subject to change without notice."

Hurricanes, described as the greatest storms on earth, occur in the American West only along the Gulf Coast of Texas. Winds in this most violent of storms reach two hundred miles per hour. With such great velocity trees are uprooted, houses blown off their foundations, and even large buildings demolished. But nine out of ten hurricane victims drown in water that is piled up and swept ashore in storm surges twenty-five feet higher than normal or that is deluged in torrential rains. Hurricanes form out at sea between June and November. In September, 1900, six thousand people died in Galveston, Texas, in the worst such disaster in the nation's history. Fortunately, sophisticated storm warning systems developed since 1950 have led to a steady decline in the number of lives claimed by hurricanes. On the other hand, the cost of damage inflicted by these storms has risen sharply, perhaps because more people and more businesses are settling in the vulnerable coastal areas.

Tornadoes are common in the Great Plains in spring and early summer. They result from the collision of cold air masses from the north or west with warm, moist air from the south. The convectional activity that results triggers thunderstorms that occasionally develop into tornadoes, in which winds spiralling inward and upward reach great velocity as they near the center of the storm. The funnel-shaped cloud hangs below the violently agitated cloud mass, and with a frightful roar, "like 10,000 freight trains," its winds rotate at speeds up to three hundred miles per hour. The almost random march of the tornado is one of its most frightful aspects. It may devastate a single square mile and leave the surrounding area untouched. There are about fifty tornadoes a year, but only about twenty do much damage. Woodward, Oklahoma, was smashed in April, 1947, with 101 persons killed, another 1,000 injured, and property loss exceeding $10 million. Although tornadoes are greatly feared, a person could live a lifetime in the tornado country of Oklahoma and never see the dreaded funnel cloud.

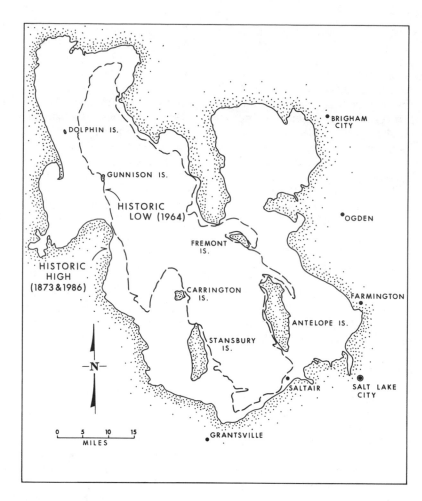

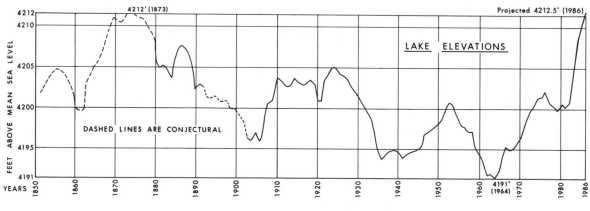

THE GREAT SALT LAKE
UTAH

71. THE GREAT SALT LAKE, UTAH

THIS LAKE IS THE MOST REMARKABLE aspect of the Great Basin and one of the most unusual and interesting geographic features of the American West. The lake has an average maximum length of about seventy-five miles and an average width of fifty miles. Early visitors to the lake believed it to be a trapped arm of the Pacific Ocean. However, scientific studies have concluded that this salt lake is a remnant of a vast inland sea, Lake Bonneville, which was almost as big as Lake Michigan. It once had an outlet to the north into the Snake River, but reduced precipitation caused it to shrink in size and recede until its outlet was lost. Without drainage, the Great Salt Lake's salt content has built to some 25 percent.

In the many years that have passed since the last glacial period, the area of the lake has probably fluctuated dramatically, but in the long run it has steadily shrunk to its present size. Its past history has prompted most geologists to predict its early demise. Many have based their conclusions on the continually increasing use of water for irrigation. One student of the lake, Dale Morgan, disagreed in his *The Great Salt Lake* (1947) and concluded that "although its level has exhibited a general downward trend, from time to time the lake has embarked on astonishing adventures." The map illustrates the manner in which these ups and downs of the lake have occurred.

At the time of the survey in 1849 by Capt. Howard Stansbury, U.S. Army, the lake's surface was 4,201 feet above sea level. Until 1874 exact data were not kept on the lake level, but enough information was available to have a reasonably accurate picture of its fluctuations, as indicated by the dotted line on the map. Through the years the lake has risen and fallen some 20 feet, as a result mainly of increased or decreased precipitation rather than of humans' use of the water. After the Stansbury survey the lake rose 4 feet, but in a few years it fell 5 feet. It reached its all-time high in 1873 of 4,212 feet above sea level. From that point it fell steadily until 1905, except for a brief rise in 1884–85. In this century the lake level rose gradually until the drought years of the 1930s. A few years of rising level since 1941 were followed by the all-time low of 4,191 feet above sea level in 1964. A steady elevation then took place until in 1984 the lake level neared its all-time high, reaching 4,209.25 feet above sea level. The two-year rise since 1982 of some ten feet has been the fastest in recorded history.

The last rise has meant a growth in the lake size of some 30 percent and has completely disrupted the ecological balance in the region. Freshwater marshlands protected from the saline lake by dikes have been flooded with salt water, which has killed fish and ruined the nesting areas of birds. Some 300,000 to 400,000 ducks which normally hatch each year have been lost, and the number of Canada geese in the region has been cut in half.

Human beings have also been hit hard by the rise in the lake level. Roads have been flooded out, an interstate highway and the Southern Pacific Causeway have had to be raised at great expense, tens of millions of dollars' worth of property have been destroyed, chemical and mining operations have been curtailed, and a once lucrative tourism industry has been all but shut down. Utah, a desert state, has become a water wasteland. Worst of all, politicians aware of the unpredictability of the Great Salt Lake are hesitant to spend money to control flooding when the lake level may once again recede and the area may suffer another period of drought.

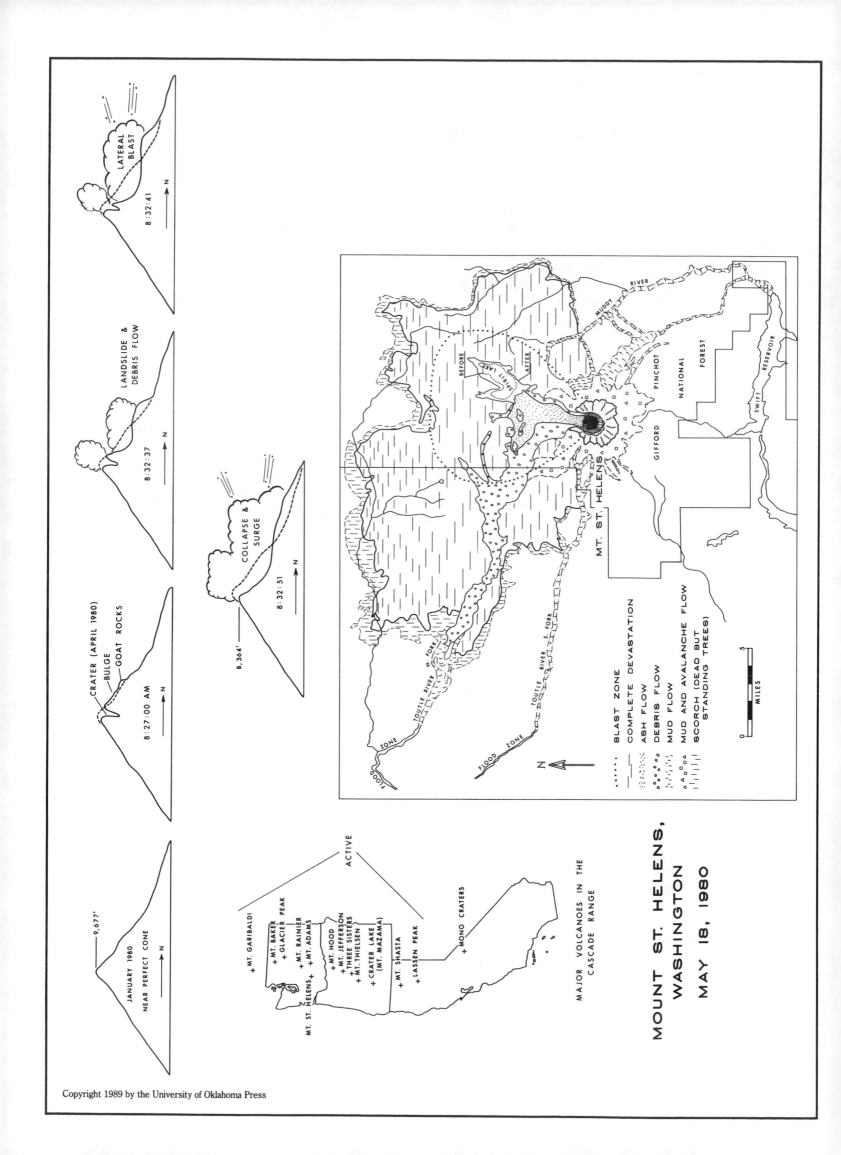

MOUNT ST. HELENS,
WASHINGTON
MAY 18, 1980

72.   MOUNT ST. HELENS, WASHINGTON, MAY 18, 1980

A VOLCANO is simply a place where magma, molten rock from the interior of the earth, is expelled through a vent to the surface, and much the American West was formed by such volcanic action. However, there is a temptation to think of our land as finished and complete, ignoring the fact that the earth is ever changing and the forces of nature are ever at work.

Most Americans who live in the western portion of the country like to stress the positive features of the natural environment. They like to ignore the catastrophic natural events that sometimes disturb this idyllic land. They especially have ignored the possibility of volcanoes, perhaps because volcanoes have erupted there so infrequently. Yet of 529 known active volcanoes in the world, 421 are located around the edge of the Pacific Ocean in what is known as the Ring of Fire. Fourteen of these are in the Cascade Range, and at least a dozen major eruptions have occurred in the area since the whites intruded on the scene. Mount St. Helens (named for an English nobleman by Vancouver) was active in 1835, with a major eruption in 1842 and minor ones until 1857. Before Mount St. Helens exploded in 1980, the last significant eruption in the West was that of Mount Lassen in 1914.

A minor earthquake on March 20, 1980, indicated that the 123 years of dormancy of Mount St. Helens were about to end. The seismic activity continued accompanied by the venting of steam until May 18, when the great eruption took place. This was followed by several minor eruptions, and most experts predict that the volcano will be heard from often in the immediate future.

The great blast was five hundred times more powerful than the atomic bomb dropped on Hiroshima. A mushroom-shaped cloud ascended to 63,000 feet, and ash rained down on most of three states. A DC-9 commercial airliner, flying at 33,000 feet, had the ash clog its engines and was forced to make an emergency landing. Rail, air, and highway traffic came to a halt in much of Washington, Idaho, and Montana. Ash settled in the fields and in orchards, doing incalculable damage. Mount St. Helens literally blew its top. It had been 9,677 feet high; after the explosion it was 1,277 feet shorter.

The greatest damage, naturally, was in the immediate area. A beautiful forested vacation paradise was transformed in minutes into a dull gray wasteland. The blast destroyed 156 square miles of timber in a fan-shaped swath. Trees fell like matchsticks, and many that did not fall were scorched dead by the hot gas that raced down the mountainside. Lightning, triggered by the friction between the hot gas blast and the cold air, started some two hundred forest fires, which had to be left to burn themselves out. The heat melted the mountain snow, adding to the problem. A wall of mud and debris, carrying millions of tons of timber and shattered wood, flowed down both the North and South Forks of the Toutle River, knocking out all bridges for miles. The mass flowed out into low-lands, inundating homes, campgrounds, and logging camps. The river was so hot that fish tried to leap out of the water. All fish and most wild animals in the area were killed. Insect life was destroyed for miles around, further upsetting the biological balance. At least fifty people were reported killed, but the real total will never be known. The cost of the cleanup was in the millions of dollars. Mount St. Helens was a grim reminder that not all of nature's ways are beneficial to humankind.

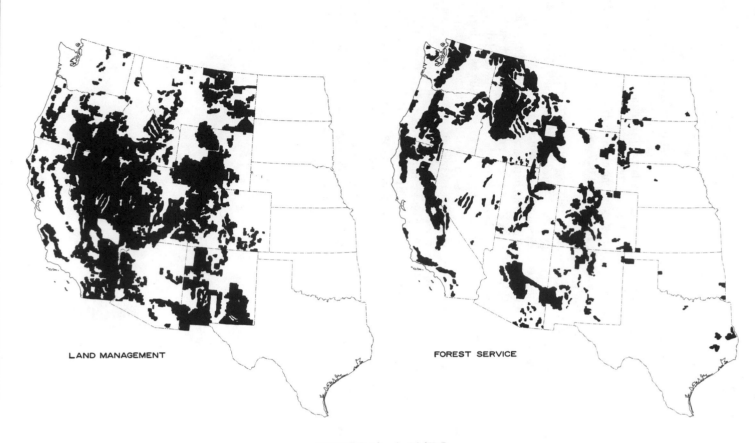

LAND MANAGEMENT

FOREST SERVICE

FEDERAL LANDS

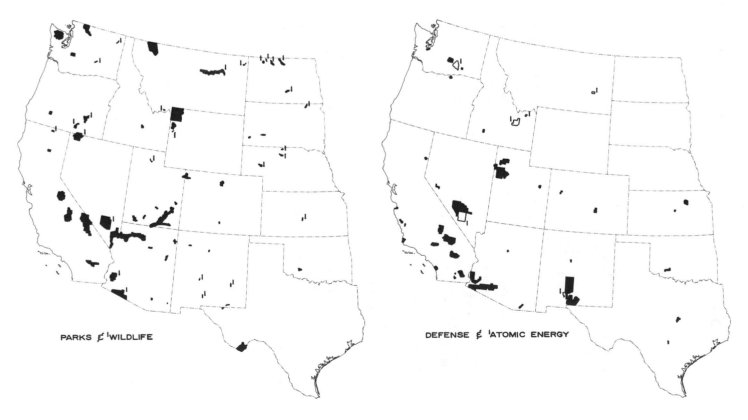

PARKS & WILDLIFE

DEFENSE & ATOMIC ENERGY

73. FEDERAL LANDS

FROM ITS BEGINNING, the federal government has been a substantial landowner, and the acquisition and disposition of those lands is an important part of our nation's history. The disposition of federal lands has always been controversial and complicated, but in the East and Midwest such lands were disposed of gradually. However, in the mountainous and arid West, huge areas were retained by the federal government because they were unfit for settlement and cultivation.

As new states entered the Union, they were granted federal lands to dispose of in order to support state services, mainly education. As part of the price for admission, they were required by Congress to surrender any future claims to federal lands within their borders.

Federally owned or administered lands constitute some 24 percent of the total land area of the United States; of this federal land, 89 percent is in the American West, and such lands constitute almost one-half of the total land area of the eleven most western states. Among the plains states only South Dakota, with 18 percent, has much federal land (mostly Indian reservations). Eighty-six percent of Nevada, 66 percent of Utah, 63 percent of Idaho, more than half of Oregon, and nearly half of Arizona, California, and Wyoming are federal lands. Colorado and New Mexico are about 35 percent federal, and Montana and Washington some 30 percent. There are virtually no federal lands in Texas because the treaty of annexation permitted the Lone Star State to retain title to all of its public lands. Four agencies control more than 99 percent of all federal lands. They are the Departments of the Interior, Agriculture, and Defense and the Atomic Energy Commission. The Department of the Interior's Bureau of Land Management controls about 60 percent of the total; the Agriculture Department's Forest Service has nearly 25 percent. Of the total federal lands, 44 percent is reserved for grazing and 42 percent for forests and wildlife. Less than 5 percent of the total is for defense or atomic energy. The public lands of the West are mainly public domain that has never left federal control, in contrast with acquired lands.

Most of the national parks are in the American West and are intended to safeguard some of the region's most beautiful and primitive scenery. The last such park was created in 1987, when 120 square miles of wilderness in Nevada were dedicated as Great Basin National Park.

Wildlife refuges are largely a product of the present century and grew out of opposition to the destruction of many birds and animals as people moved into their natural habitat. The growth of such refuges was made possible by sportsmen's organizations, which recognized that without government control there would soon be few game birds and animals to hunt. These groups were also assisted by a large body of the public interested in wildlife for its own sake and as a source of personal enjoyment and scientific study.

Since the early days of the republic there has been disagreement about the disposition of federal lands, with many powerful groups agitating for private exploitations. Until 1976, a total of 1.144 billion acres of federal lands were disposed of. From the tenure of President Theodore Roosevelt until the 1970s, environmentalists who favored Washington's control of the federal lands won most of the battles. Those who wanted these lands to pass into private ownership were alarmed when Congress passed a law in 1976 directing the Bureau of Land Management to hold land "in perpetuity" instead of systematically disposing of it. This triggered what was known as the "Sagebrush Revolt," which peaked in 1979. The so-called revolt was an effort by miners and ranchers to give control of the federal lands to the states. One Nevada legislator expressed their aims well: "It is time to wrest the land from the perfidious absentee landlord who resides along the banks of the Potomac."

This movement ran its course but was succeeded by "privatization" of the federal lands in 1982. Privatization was a plan by the Reagan administration to sell unneeded property to reduce the national debt. However, neither public nor political support for the privatization of federal lands in the West was forthcoming, so the movement lapsed. The debate over the Sagebrush Revolt and privatization sparked extensive discussion over the nature and purpose of federal landownership and will undoubtedly be renewed in the future.

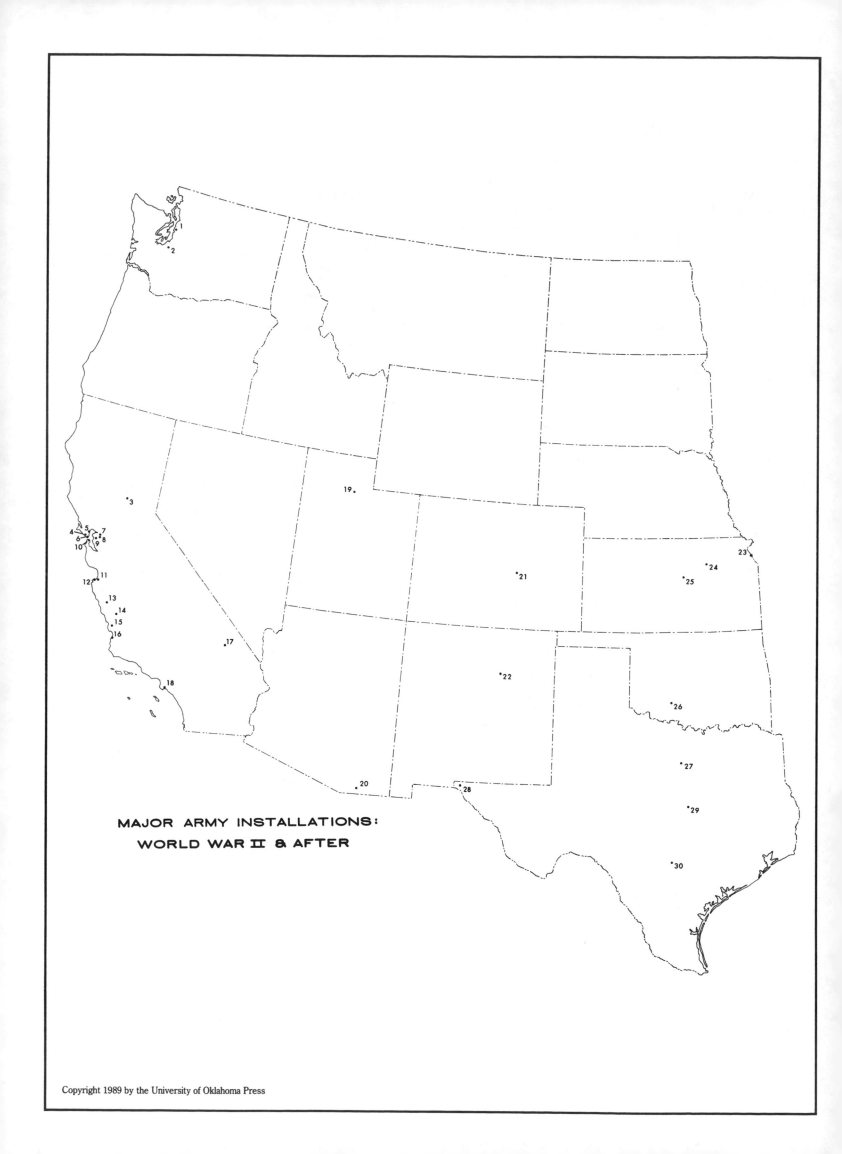

MAJOR ARMY INSTALLATIONS:
WORLD WAR II & AFTER

74. MAJOR ARMY INSTALLATIONS: WORLD WAR II AND AFTER

FORTS, CAMPS, AND CANTONMENTS of the U.S. Army once dotted most of the strategic locations of the American West. With a few exceptions, most of them were ephemeral. Built of logs, adobe, or stone, they were usually abandoned in a few years when the Indian threat in the area quieted or other reasons for their existence had passed. The army seldom thought of permanent facilities, or, for that matter, had the funds for them. World War I altered this thinking. The new technology of war made it necessary to build camps to house whole divisions, with warehouses, depots, and terminals to handle huge quantities of material. These new camps were, in effect, modern cities; in 1900, the largest army facility was at Fort Riley, Kansas, and accommodated thirteen hundred troops. The installations built in 1917 were for from thirty thousand to forty thousand men.

The onset of war in 1917 led to the construction of sixteen Regular Army cantonments, three of them in the West: Camp Funston at Fort Riley, Kansas; Camp Lewis in Washington; and Camp Travis at Fort Sam Houston, Texas. Of sixteen National Guard camps built in 1917, seven were in the West. The army cantonments survived the postwar era, but the National Guard camps did not. A few installations were built between the two world wars, but most of the modern army facilities were the product of a crash building program between 1939 and 1942. Since 1945, many of these camps were disposed of or put on inactive status, but army installations still dot the West.

Washington

1. Fort Lawton (inactive)
2. Fort Lewis

Oregon

None

California

3. Camp Beale
4. Fort Cronkhite
5. Fort Baker
6. Fort Barry
7. Camp Stoneman (inactive)
8. Camp Parks
9. Oakland Army Base
10. Headquarters VI Army, Fort Mason, Presidio, Fort Scott, Fort Miley, and Fort Funston
11. Fort Ord

12. Presidio of Monterey
13. Hunter Liggett (general officers' private hunting reserve)
14. Camp Roberts (inactive)
15. Camp San Luis Obispo (inactive)
16. Camp Cooke (Vandenburg Air Force Base)
17. Fort Irwin (inactive)
18. Fort MacArthur

Idaho

None

Utah

19. Fort Douglas (inactive)

Arizona

20. Fort Huachuca

Montana

None

Wyoming

None

Colorado

21. Fort Carson

New Mexico

22. Camp Luna
Fort Wingate Army Depot
White Sands Missile Range

North and South Dakota

None

Nebraska

None

Kansas

23. Fort Leavenworth
24. Fort Riley (Camp Funston)
25. Camp Phillips (inactive)

Oklahoma

26. Fort Sill

Texas

27. Fort Wolters
28. Fort Bliss
29. Fort Hood
30. Headquarters V Army, Fort Sam Houston

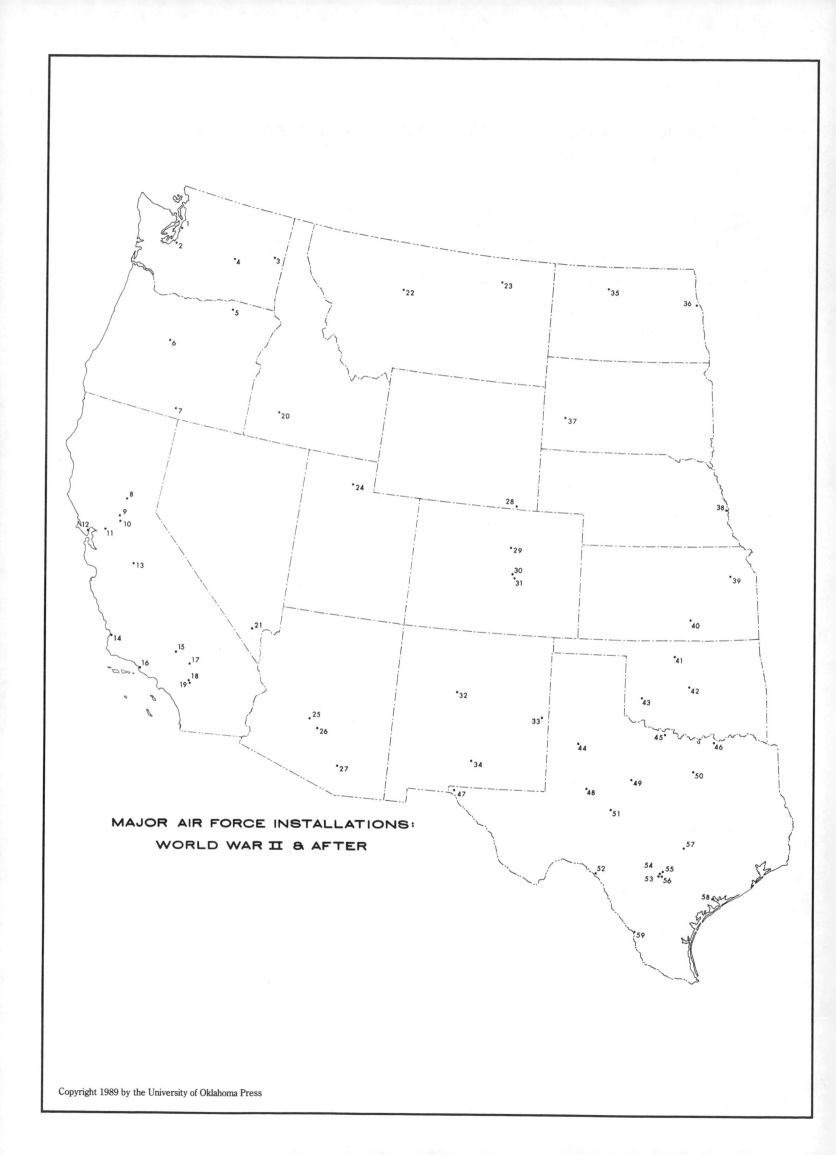

MAJOR AIR FORCE INSTALLATIONS:
WORLD WAR II & AFTER

75. MAJOR AIR FORCE INSTALLATIONS: WORLD WAR II AND AFTER

NEAR THE END OF 1943, Army Air Force (AAF) installations in the United States reached a peak figure of 345 main bases, 116 subbases, 322 auxiliary fields, 12 air depots, 68 specialized depots, and 480 bombing and gunnery ranges. In addition, the AAF often used naval installations for periods of time. Since 1943, as the need for training facilities lessened, this number has declined sharply, especially after the conclusion of World War II. The American West has a disproportionately large number of these installations because Texas and California, especially, had been early leaders in the development of aviation, with some of the first fields around San Antonio and at March,

near Riverside. Second, both California and Texas, as well as other parts of the West, had weather conditions which seldom curtailed flying. The West also had wide-open spaces that could be converted to flying fields or gunnery ranges at a relatively low cost. The great expanse made it possible to disperse airfields to lessen the possibility of a disaster in case of attack. The Pacific Coast states were preferred for AAF sites for purposes of continental defense in case of a Japanese surprise attack.

Following are the most important Air Force bases and other installations in the West:

Washington
1. Paine Air Force Base (AFB) (inactive)
2. McChord AFB
3. Fairchild AFB
4. Larson AFB (inactive)

Oregon
5. Pendleton AFB (inactive)
6. Redmond AFB (inactive)
7. Kingsley Field

California
8. Beale AFB
9. McClellan AFB (Sacramento Air Material Area Headquarters)
10. Mather AFB
11. Travis AFB (XXII Air Force Headquarters)
12. Hamilton AFB (Western Air Force Reserve Region Headquarters)
13. Castle AFB
14. Vandenburg AFB
15. Edwards AFB
16. Oxnard AFB (inactive)
17. George AFB
18. Norton AFB
19. March AFB (XV Air Force Headquarters)

Idaho
20. Mountain Home AFB

Nevada
21. Nellis AFB

Montana
22. Malmstrom AFB
23. Glasgow AFB

Utah
24. Hill AFB (Ogden Air Material Area Headquarters)

Arizona
25. Luke AFB
26. Williams AFB
27. Davis-Montana AFB

Wyoming
28. Francis E. Warren AFB

Colorado
29. Lowry AFB
30. Colorado Springs (U.S. Air Force Academy)
31. Peterson AFB

New Mexico
32. Kirtland AFB
33. Cannon AFB
34. Holloman AFB

North Dakota
35. Minot AFB
36. Grand Forks AFB

South Dakota
37. Ellsworth AFB

Nebraska
38. Offutt AFB (Strategic Air Command Headquarters)

Kansas
39. Forbes AFB
40. McConnell AFB

Oklahoma
41. Vance AFB
42. Tinker AFB (Oklahoma City Air Material Area Headquarters)
43. Atlus AFB

Texas
44. Reese AFB
45. Sheppard AFB
46. Perrin AFB
47. Biggs AFB (inactive)
48. Webb AFB
49. Dyess AFB
50. Carswell AFB
51. Goodfellow AFB (Air Force Security Service Headquarters)
52. Laughlin AFB
53. Lackland AFB
54. Kelly AFB
55. Randolph AFB (Air Training Command Headquarters)
56. Brooks AFB
57. Bergstrom AFB (XII Air Force Headquarters)
58. Ellington AFB (Central Air Force Reserve Region Headquarters)
59. Laredo AFB (inactive)

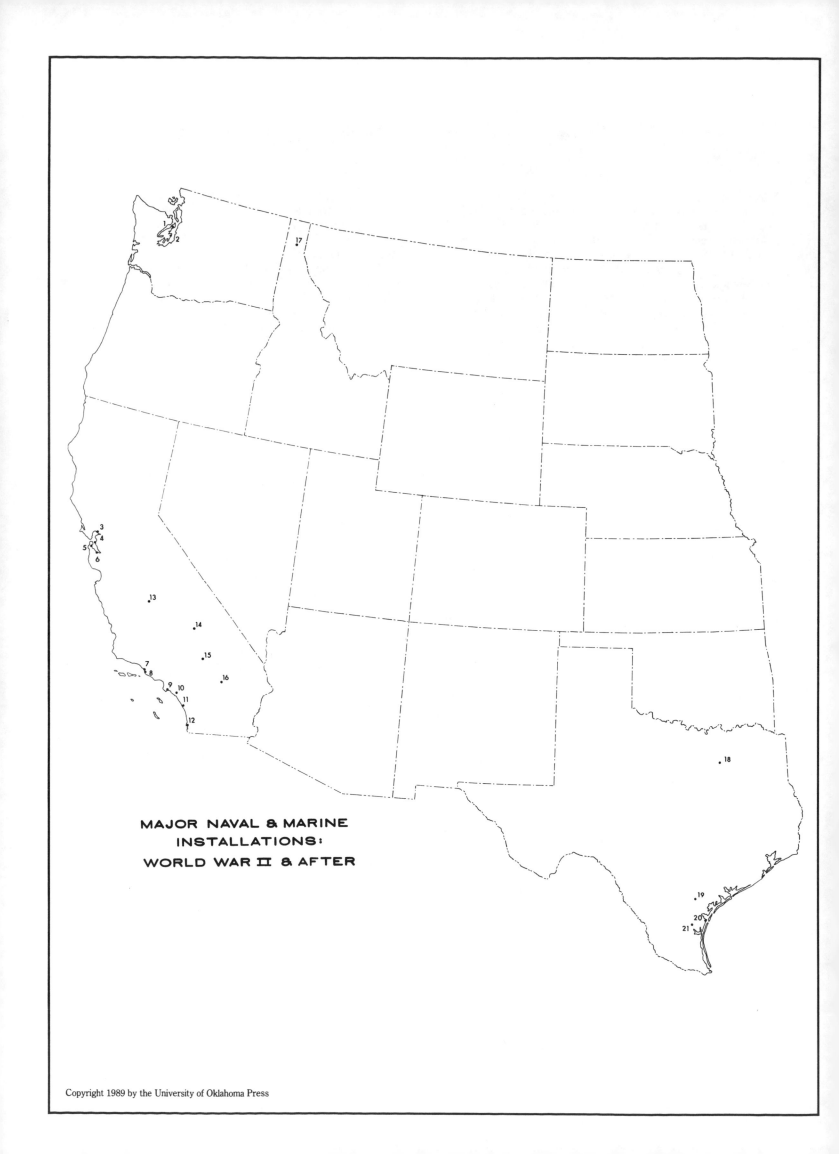

MAJOR NAVAL & MARINE
INSTALLATIONS:
WORLD WAR II & AFTER

76. MAJOR NAVAL AND MARINE INSTALLATIONS: WORLD WAR II AND AFTER

UNLIKE THE U.S. ARMY, the navy did not figure prominently in the early history of the American West. Not until the Spanish-American War resulted in our involvement in the Philippines and the acquisition of Hawaii was there a significant naval presence on the Pacific Coast, mainly at Seattle, the San Francisco Bay area, and San Diego. In the 1930s there was some expansion of facilities, but it was World War II and the importance of the Pacific theater which prompted the Bureau of Yards and Docks to build hundreds of installation in the three Pacific Coast states and in Texas; however, many naval facilities were also scattered throughout the West. For example, one of the most important new naval training stations was Farragut at Lake Pend Oreille in Idaho. Since 1945 many navy and Marine installations have been deactivated, but as the map indicates, the navy is very much present in the American West.

The modern navy reflects the advanced technology of the twentieth century and thus needs a vast industrial and administrative plant to operate its ships and airplanes and to train its manpower. They included numerous shipyard facilities, a bewildering array of Coast Guard stations, ordinance and supply depots, naval and Marine training centers, naval and Marine aviation bases, along with hospitals and receiving centers.

Washington
1. Pacific Bremerton (Polaris Missile facility)
2. Puget Sound Bremerton (shipyard, naval support and supply center)

California
3. Mare Island (shipyard)
4. Treasure Island (command school and station)
5. Hunter's Point (shipyard)
6. Moffett Field (air station)
7. Port Hueneme (Construction Battalion center)
8. Point Mugu (Pacific Missile Test Center and air station)
9. Long Beach (shipyard, air station, and supply center)
10. Twenty-nine Palms (Marine Corps base)
11. El Toro (Marine Corps air station)
12. Camp Pendleton (Marine Corps base)
13. San Diego (air station, antisubmarine fleet supply, and training center)
    Barstow (Marine Corps supply center)
    China Lake (naval weapons center)
    Lemoore (naval air station)

Idaho
Lake Pend Oreille (Farragut Naval Training Station)

Texas
14. Dallas (air station)
15. Beeville (Chase Field air station)
16. Corpus Christi (air station)
17. Kingsville (air station)

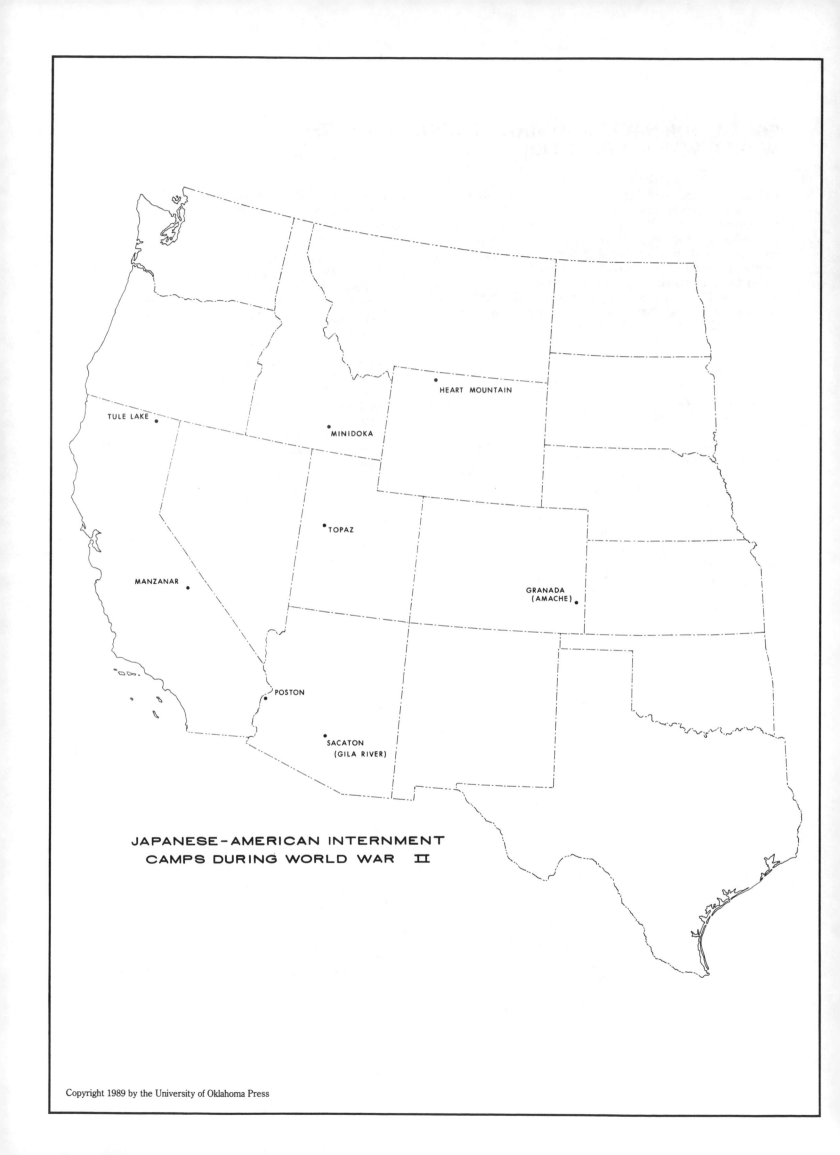

JAPANESE-AMERICAN INTERNMENT
CAMPS DURING WORLD WAR II

HEART MOUNTAIN

TULE LAKE

MINIDOKA

TOPAZ

MANZANAR

GRANADA
(AMACHE)

POSTON

SACATON
(GILA RIVER)

77. JAPANESE-AMERICAN INTERNMENT CAMPS DURING WORLD WAR II

IN TIME OF WAR it has been accepted that belligerent nations have the right to intern or deport enemy aliens who may constitute a threat to domestic order. Immediately after the attack on Pearl Harbor, about six thousand Japanese-born (*issei*) residing in the United States were apprehended by federal authorities. West Coast Japanese were upset by this action, but most understood the reasons for it. In fact, when a leading member of the *issei* community in Redwood City, California, was arrested, his son said he realized it was the "proper procedure" when war broke out. In Japan, resident Americans were detained or subjected to house arrest after December 7. In England, large numbers of German nationals, many of whom had fled from Hitler, were placed in prison camps when war began and held until it could be proven they were not security risks.

In the United States, on the other hand, an action was taken that had no precedent under international law and was a clear violation of domestic law; it was, in fact, "the worst single violation of the civil rights of American citizens in our history." This action was the mass internment of some 112,000 Japanese-Americans in ten camps; eight in the American West, as depicted on the map, and two more, Camps Rohwer and Jerome, in Arkansas. President Roosevelt's Executive Order 9066, issued in March, 1942, authorized the military to move any persons it chose from areas which might become combat zones. This was interpreted to mean the West Coast, and those removed were of Japanese ancestry. The reasons for the action were deeply rooted in popular resentment toward the Japanese; bitterness over the sneak attack on Pearl Harbor; mass hysteria over the shelling of an oil field at Goleta, California, in February, 1942, which many saw as the prelude to an enemy invasion; and military necessity. This last reason is the one most frequently cited for the measure, but as there were almost triple the number of such citizens in the Hawaiian Islands, which were really threatened by the Japanese, such an excuse to imprison American citizens without legal recourse was absolutely ridiculous. Perhaps the saddest part of the whole affair was that virtually all public figures joined with the press in supporting this violation of constitutional liberties.

The final evacuation order did not allow adequate time for these unfortunate people to sell their property. Accordingly, the evacuees incurred huge losses as they wound up their affairs and disposed of their homes, land, businesses, and personal property. They could only take with them what they could personally carry. The amount of loss they suffered has never been determined, but the figure may be as high as $500 million. For example, one family received fifteen cents on the dollar for a large farm they were forced to sell. Those 75,000 evacuees who were American citizens received $38 million by act of Congress in 1948, and in 1967 the United States Supreme Court awarded $10 million for those whose savings had been confiscated.

Most Japanese accepted their dismal fate and went off to the internment camps, which were usually isolated and in areas that could only charitably be designated as forlorn. Initially they were housed in wooden barracks through which the wind blew sand into the interior. Deprived of privacy, often subsisting on poor rations, and suffering the stigma of being incarcerated behind barbed wire, the Japanese-Americans usually improved the camps as they waited for the end of the war.

The irony of the internment was that the army's 442nd Regimental Combat Team, made up mostly of Japanese-Americans, won more medals than any other unit of its size. Less well known but of equal importance was the contribution of some six thousand Japanese-Americans servicemen in the Pacific theater. They were indispensable in intelligence work because of their knowledge of the Japanese language. At the war's end, despite the injustice that had been done them, only eighteen hundred Japanese who held dual citizenship elected to return to Japan.

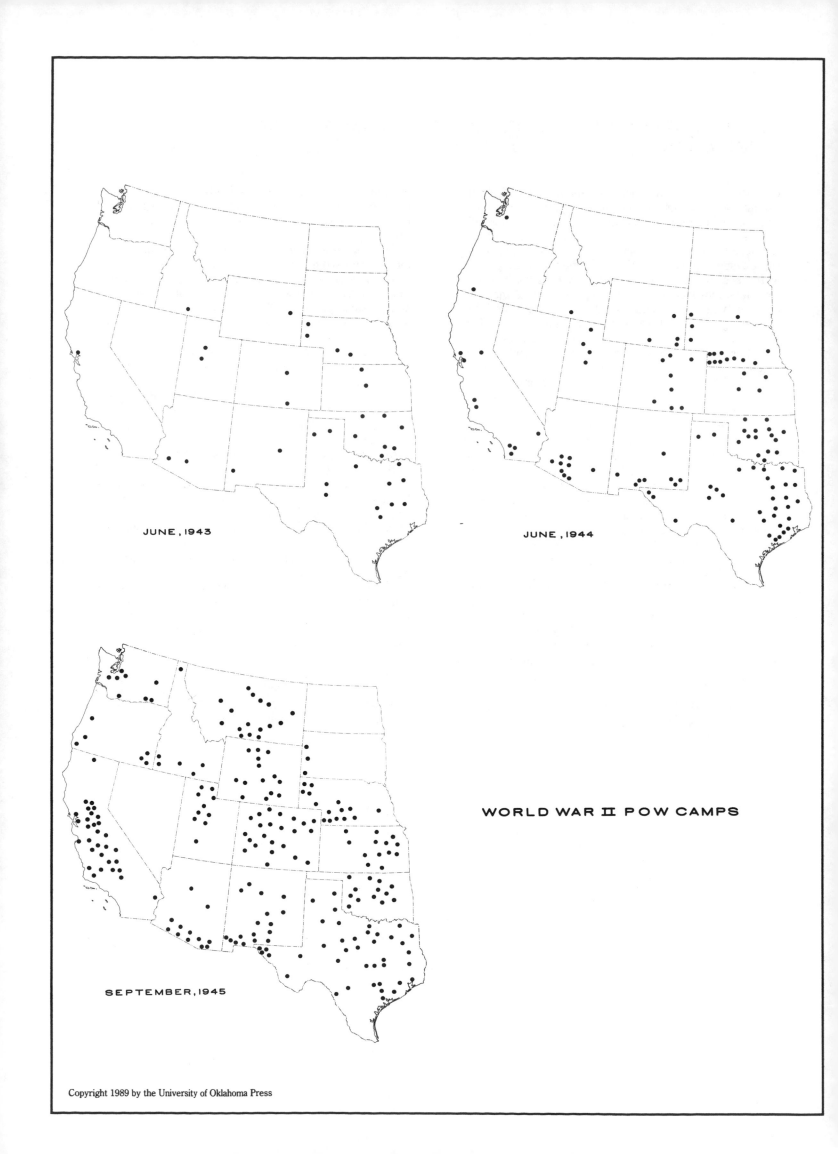

JUNE, 1943

JUNE, 1944

WORLD WAR II POW CAMPS

SEPTEMBER, 1945

78. WORLD WAR II POW CAMPS

DURING WORLD WAR II, 371,683 Germans, 51,156 Italians, and 5,413 Japanese prisoners of war (POWs) were interned in the United States. Their numbers grew rapidly with the success of Allied armies in North Africa and Italy in 1943. As late as June, 1943, there were only 36 base (permanent) and branch (temporary) camps in the American West. One year later this number was 113, and by September, 1945, there were 227. Although the nation had little experience in handling such large numbers of prisoners of war, the operation must be judged a success, as only 1,800 POWs attempted to escape; of them 1,048 were free for only one day or less, and only 31 escapees achieved freedom for two weeks or more.

More importantly, frequent inspection of the camps by an international team found few important complaints; Germans protested that they were fed too few potatoes and too much meat; the Italians complained that they received too little pasta. The diet fed the POWs, according to the Geneva Convention, had to be the same as that fed American troops. But such complaints were easily handled, and changes were made to satisfy national dietary customs. Most POWs looked back on their period of detention with nostalgia. A German prisoner once even offered this advice: "If there is another war, get on the side that America ain't, then get captured by the Americans— you'll have it made."

Security was a major consideration in locating prisoner of war camps. They could not be located near heavily populated areas nor close to shipyards, aircraft plants, or similar vital war installations. Less populated places would be easier to guard, so they were preferred. Therefore, the South and the West attracted a large share of these installations.

The War Department had made extensive plans to build the necessary camps, but in actual practice improvisation was the rule instead. Fairgrounds, armories, schools, hotels, and even the famed Santa Anita racetrack were used as holding areas for newly arrived POWs. Civilian Conservation Corps camps became the sites of the first bases; usually located in rural areas, they were built as barracks and could be easily modified to house POWs. More importantly, by 1943 they were empty and thus available. The labor of the POWs was used to get them ready to house the detainees. However, about three-fifths of the base camps were located on army installations. One reason why the military did not build new POW camps was because surplus troop housing would soon become available. In fact, as American soldiers completed training and began going overseas in large numbers, prisoners of war began entering the country to take the housing they were leaving. In some cases the new arrivals simply took over an abandoned facility. More often, the POWs moved into an empty portion of an existing army camp and provided a needed labor supply. Others did agricultural work and were sometimes moved into small temporary camps to be closer to their work. Some even worked for individual farmers. The number in individual camps ranged from 150 to 7,000, with the average about 2,500.

APPENDIX

SPANISH-MEXICAN LAND GRANTS—LOWER RIO GRANDE VALLEY, WEST OF THE NUECES RIVER, TEXAS

General Land Office File No., San Patricio	Grantee	Name of Ranch or *Porción* No.	Acreage
1-341	Salinas, José Luis	"San Antonio de Baluarte"	22,140
1-306	Cuellar, José Antonio	"Palo Blanquito"	8,856
1-307	Vela, Luis	"Agostadero del Sordo"	25,229.14
1-308	Farias, Francisco	"Santa Cruz"	17,713
1-309	Garza, Apolinario	"Las Preseñas"	11,626
1-311	Cordente, Francisco	"Agostadero de la Santa Cruz de Concepción"	22,140
1-312	García, Nicolas & Bruno	"Las Animas"	66,426
1-313	Vela, Salvador	*Porción* 90	6,247.95
1-314	Vela, Rafael	*Porción* 26	6,018
1-315	Vela, Ventura	*Porción* 84	5,737.18
1-316	Vela, Nicolás	*Porción* 82	5,756.89
1-317	Vela, Pedro	*Porción* 34	6,079.28
1-319	Sánchez, Ysabel María	*Porción* 21	6,366.24
1-320	Guerra, María Josefa	*Porción* 19	6,525.66
1-321	Ramírez, José Cristobal	*Porción* 18	6,159
1-322	López, Santiago	*Porción* 92	4,428.38
1-323	Sais, Rafael Garza	"Palitos Blancos"	13,472
1-324	Benavides, Pedro	*Porción* 30	7,413
1-325	Gutiérrez, Joseph	*Porción* 20	6,061.57
1-326	Treviño, Marcel	*Porción* 33	6,109.68
1-327	Benavides, Josefa	*Porción* 91	5,791.44
1-328	Quintanilla, Ramón	*Porción* 95	5,668.33
1-330	Cuellar, Joaquín	*Porción* 35	6,100.54
1-331	García, Diego	*Porción* 78	5,756.89
1-332	Peña, Joaquín	*Porción* 22	6,691.36
1-333	Zapata, Nicolás	*Porción* 77	6,080.77
1-334	Martínez, María Marcela	*Porción* 83	5,770.18
1-335	Farias, Manuel	"Paso Ancho de Arriba"	11,070
1-336	Longoria, Antonio	"Las Sauces"	17,712
1-337	Garza, Juan José de la	*Porción* 89	5,779
1-338	Longoria, Pedro	*Porción* 94	4,649.80
1-339	Ramírez, José Miguel	"Agua Nueva de Arriba"	35,427.20
1-340	Rivas, Luciano	"Paso Ancho de Abajo"	11,070
1-342	Sais, Vicente	"La Sal Colorada"	17,889
1-343	Rosa, Antonio de la	*Porción* 85	5,756.89
1-344	Garza, José Salvador de la	*Porción* 88	5,756.89
1-345	Lugo (Lago), Pedro	*Porción* 74	6,740
1-346	Ramírez, Antonio	*Porción* 67	6,399.01
1-348	Garza, Agustín de la	*Porción* 73	4,513
1-349	Gutiérrez, Juana Josefa	*Porción* 72	4,605.51
1-350	Peña, Jacinto de la	*Porción* 25	6,876.39

General Land Office File No., San Patricio	Grantee	Name of Ranch or *Porción* No.	Acreage
1-351	Peña, Mateo	*Porción* 32	6,111.77
1-352	Garza, Francisco de la	*Porción* 71	4,572
1-353	Juárez, Manuel	*Porción* 31	6,336
1-354	Serna, Juan (Joseph) Benavides	*Porción* 23	6,245.79
1-355	Benavides, Ysidro	*Porción* 24	7,259
1-356	Garza, Andrés de la	"Las Comitas"	13,285
1-357	García, Cristobal	*Porción* 76	6,244.02
1-358	Ynojosa, Diego	*Porción* 68	6,399.54
1-359	Longoria, Matias	*Porción* 93	7,971
1-361	Tabares, José	*Porción* 27	6,444.18
1-362	Gonzales, Isabel	*Porción* 28	5,984
1-363	Sánchez, Antonio	*Porción* 69	6,399
1-364	Salinas, Rafael García	"La Mesteña y Gonzalena"	22,140
1-365	García, Ysidro	"Las Mesteñas"	22,142
1-366	García, Rafael	"La Mesteña"	22,142
1-367	Sánchez, Guadalupe	"La Rucia"	22,140
1-368	Zarate, Gil	"La Blanca"	22,140
1-369	Zarate de Bayarena, Pilar	"La Alameda"	13,132
1-370	Salinas, Joaquin	*Porción* 70	5,756.89
1-371	Salinas, Juan	*Porción* 71	5,756.89
1-372	Sáens, Juan Ángel	*Porción* 72	5,756.89
1-373	Ramirez, Juan Manuel	"Agua Nueva de Abajo"	44,284
1-374	Falcón, José Antonio de la Garza	*Porción* 80	11,427.45
1-375	Herrera, Vicente López de	"El Diezmero"	18,039
1-377	López, Marcelino	"Las Preseñas"	16,149.60
1-378	Garcia, Bernardo	"El Infiernillo"	21,471.53
1-379	Ynojosa, Ramón de	"El Rincón de Corpus Christi"	81,407.38
1-380	Cabazos, José Antonio	"Santa Petronilla"	28,437.60
1-381	Farias, Policarpo	"San Antonio del Alamo"	4,428.40
1-382	Falcón, Blas María	"El Chiltipín" and "San Francisco"	26,605.36
1-384	Treviño, Andrés	"Las Comitas"	20,509.11
1-386	García, Matias	"Palo Alto"	30,998.80
1-388	Gonzales, Ramón	*Porción* 70	4,601.51
1-391	Cisneros, Juan	*Porción* 79	6,115.81
1-396	Ynojosa, José de	*Porción* 105	6,200.44
1-398	Rivas, Ygnacio	"La Blanca"	9,508
1-404	Garza, Ramón	"El Paisano"	11,070
1-405	Moreno, Juan	"San Juan"	4,428.4

General Land Office File No., San Patricio	Grantee	Name of Ranch or *Porción* No.	Acreage
1-411	Treviño, José Ygnacio de	"San Martín"	27,289.5
1-414	Ynojosa, Vital	"La Anima Sola"	20,009
1-415	Moreno, Santos	"La Trinidad"	17,157
1-416	Ynojosa, Vicente de	"Las Anacuas"	16,026
1-418	García, Rafael	"Santa Isabel"	32,355
1-419	Sánchez, Eugenio	*Porción* 42	5,314
1-420	Rodríguez, Eugenio Rodrigo	*Porción* 41	5,314
1-422	García, José María	"La Vaca"	22,142
1-423	Flores, Julian & Ventura	"San Diego"	39,680
1-424	Salinas, José Rafael García	"San Leandro"	17,712
1-425	Ramírez, Antonio	"Las Jaboncillos"	25,860
1-427	Barrera, Manuel	"La Tinoja de Lara"	25,684
1-432	Garza, José Salvador de la	"Espiritu Santo"	284,418
1-433	Treviño, Juan José	"Agostadero del Gato"	23,067.78
1-434	Leál, Benigno	"Santa Ana"	9,883.16
1-439	García, Santos	"El Charco de Palo Blanco"	22,142
1-440	Ynojosa, José Marcelo	"Palo Blanco"	61,992
1-441	Ynojosa, Diego	"San Rafael de los Encinos"	42,072
1-442	Peña, Antonio	"Palo Blanco"	18,939
1-443	Peña, Francisco	"Palo Blanco"	7,217
1-444	Peña, Ygnacio	"Los Magueyes de Palo Blanco"	16,004
1-445	Canales, José María	"El Socorro"	8,856.80
1-446	Flores, Santos	"Agua Poquita"	26,745
1-447	Ramírez, José Miguel Antonio and María Rita López	*Porción* 76	6,049.1
1-448	Benavides, Juan	*Porción* 77	6,049.17
1-450	Ramírez, Rafael	"San Pedro del Charco Redondo"	22,142
1-451	Ramírez, Rafael	"Santa Rosalía"	22,584.84
1-453	Falcón, (Juan) José de la Garza	*Porción* 81	5,756.89
1-454	Garza, Francisco de la	*Porción* 78	6,049.17
1-455	Gonzales, Florencio	*Porción* 75	6,049.17
1-456	Sáens, Gerónimo	*Porción* 74	6,049.17
1-457	Sáens, Miguel	*Porción* 73	6,049.17
1-458	Ochoa, José Antonio	*Porción* 29	3,616
1-459	Rivas, Ygnacio & heirs of Maximo Villareal	"San Rafael"	13,873

General Land Office File No., San Patricio	Grantee	Name of Ranch or *Porción* No.	Acreage
1-461	Arispe, Mariano	"Las Lajas"	3,883.47
1-462	Falcón, Joaquín de la Garza	*Porción* 104	6,197.08
1-465	Garza y Soza, Manuel de la	"El Potrero de Buena Vista"	30,217.71
1-470	Fuente, Andrés (F.) de la	"Puentecitas"	17,713.60
1-471	García, Rafael	"Agua Dulce"	26,131
1-472	García, Onofre	"El Grullo"	17,713.60
1-473	Flores, Juan	"Agostadero del Javali"	17,712
1-474	Villarreal, Juan Flores	*Porción* 87	4,650
1-475	Villarreal, Juan B.	*Porción* 75	6,297.15
1-476	Salinas, Antonio Canales	"La Sacatosa"	8,856.80
1-477	Rodríguez, Francisco Xavier	*Porción* 86	5,756.89
1-480	García, Joseph Salvador	*Porción* 109	6,288.30
1-481	Garza, Santiago de la	*Porción* 110	6,199.73
1-482	Guajardo, José Antonio	*Porción* 111	6,198.50
1-491	Gutiérrez, Miguel	"Santa Gertrudis"	11,683
1-500	Cuéllar, Joaquín	*Porción* 36	6,021
1-501	Cuéllar, Bartolomé	*Porción* 37	7,233
1-502	Cuéllar, José	"La Huerta"	2,756
1-503	Garza, Leonardo Longoria de la	"El Rincón del Grullo"	28,640
1-505	Díaz, José Miguel	*Porción* 35	5,314
1-508	Garza, José Lorenzo, José Domingo, & José Julián	"Santa Gertrudis"	78,228
1-511	Montemayor, Juan José de la Garza and sons José Manuel, Perfecto, & Augustín	"Casa Blanca"	70,848
1-514	Ramírez, Rafael	"Rincón de Penascal"	39,390
1-517	Fuentes, Valentín de las	"San Casimiro"	17,713.60
1-520	Treviño, Gabriel	"Rincón de la Boveda"	28,784.60
1-521	Gonzáles, Margarita	*Porción* 103	6,218.26
1-528	Gonzáles, Victoriano	"Las Cuevitas"	17,412
1-529	García, Dolores	*Porción* 44 & 45	10,628
1-531	García, Andrés	"San Andrés"	23,043
1-534	Mindiola, Juan	"Rincón de Santa Gertrudis"	15,499.4

APPENDIX *xiv.*

General Land Office File No., San Patricio	Grantee	Name of Ranch or *Porción* No.	Acreage
	(assignee, Richard King)		
1-535	Guerra, Juan José	"El Tule or Charco Redondo"	22,538
1-536	Guerra, Ysidora (Ysidro)	"Palo Blanco"	17,713.6
1-537	Falcón, Juan José Manuel de la Garza	"San Francisco"	20,721
1-538	Gutiérrez, Antonio	"El Pasadizo"	13,243.26
1-539	Gonzáles, José Antonio	"La Huerta"	23,781.39
1-540	Jaen (Xaen), Benito López de	"San Antonio de Agua Dulce"	9,343.08
1-541	Herrera, José Vicente López de	"El Diezmero"	18,525.35
1-542	Elizonda, Dionisio	"El Señor de la Carrera"	10,078
1-545	Garza, Pedro de la	"Santa Rosa de Arriba"	28,784.60
1-547	Garza, Juan Nepomuceno de la	"Los Finados"	51,484
1-548	Gómez, Irineo	"Las Barrosas"	24,660
1-549	Villarreal, Ygnacio	"Rincón de Mirasoles"	23,837.5
1-550	Balli (Cabazos), Juan Antonio	"El Paístle"	25,790
1-552	Peña, Ygnacio de la	"Los Olmos de Loma Blanca"	44,284
1-553	Peña, Ynacio de la	"Los Olmos"	22,140
1-554	Galán, Joaquín	"Balconcitos"	139,482
1-554½	Vela, Xavier	"San Antonio Viejo"	17,713.60
1-555	Garza, Teodoro	"El Alazán"	18,532
1-556	García, Antonio	"El Tule"	10,839
1-557	Chapa, Francisco Guerra	"Los Olmos"	22,142
1-558	Gonzáles, José	"Las Pintas"	18,795.6
1-561	Ramírez, Cristóbal	*Porción* 17	5,896.39
1-562	Gutiérrez, Bartolomé	*Porción* 16	5,570.78
1-563	Gutiérrez, Ysidro	"Los Ojuelos"	8,856.80
1-564	Pereda, Andrés Bautista	"Charca de la India"	17,713.60
1-565	Gutiérrez, José Clemente	*Porción* 15	6,123.56
1-566	Gutiérrez, Bernardo or Bernave	*Porción* 14	7,576.61
1-567	Gutiérrez, Antonio Martínez	"Blas María"	8,856.80
1-568	Dávila, Eduardo	"San Antonio de Miraflores"	22,453.34
1-569	Ynojosa, Simón de	"Las Noriacitas"	22,142
1-570	Pereda, José Manuel	"Cerrito Blanco"	17,713.60

General Land Office File No., San Patricio	Grantee	Name of Ranch or *Porción* No.	Acreage
1-574	Farias, Maximo	"Las Preseñas de Arriba"	8,856.80
1-575	García, José Antonio Morales & Apolinario Morales García	"San Antonito"	27,812
1-576	Montalba, Francisco	"Las Viboritas, Santa Rita y Loma del Sordo"	17,713.60
1-577	Silva, Antonio	"La Noría de Santo Domingo"	22,140
1-578	Ysaguirre, Antonio	"Santo Domingo de Arriba"	18,018
1-579	Garza, Dionisio	"Santo Domingo de Abajo"	17,889
1-581	Rey, José Pérez, José María Pérez Rey & Manuel García	"Rincón de los Laureles"	100,848
1-612	Guerra, Ramón Cabazos	"Santa Quintería"	22,140
1-623	Chapa, José María de	"La Encantada"	22,400
1-624	Chapa, Severano	"El Enciño del Pozo"	17,713.60
1-634	Vela, Gregorio	"Santa Teresa"	8,856
1-638	Laredo, City of	*Porciones* 47, 48, 49, 50 & 51	26,570
1-639	Zapata, Antonio	"Villa"	22,142
1-640	Vela, Trinidad	"Santa María de los Angeles de Abajo" or "El Mesquite"	22,142
1-641	Cuéllar, Santiago Vela	"El Peyote"	17,713.60
1-642	Peña, Felipe de la	"Las Animas" or "Alberca de Abajo"	22,140
1-643	Cuéllar, Josefa	"Las Cabeceras de los Angeles"	8,856
1-644	Fuentes, Valentín de las	"Alberca de Arriba"	22,142
1-645	Arispe, Mariano	"Santa María de los Angeles"	22,140
1-646	Peña, Rafael de la	"Las Moritas"	22,140
1-650	Laredo, City of	"Egidos de Laredo"	8,393.30
1-652	Martínez, Estevan	"La Noría de Tío Ayala"	18,756.87
1-653	Rivas, Ygnacio	"San Rafael"	8,856
1-654	Díaz, Juan Garza	"Vargas"	17,712
1-655	García, Pedro	"El Perdido"	17,712
1-656	Flores, José María	"Laguna Larga"	8,856
1-657	Gutiérrez, Ygnacio	"Los Mogotes"	8,856.80
1-658	García, Antonio	"El Rendado"	22,140
1-661	Domingues, Máximo	"Agostadero de los Toritos"	8,856
1-677	Mindiola, Pablo	*Porción* 59	5,314
1-678	Bocanegra, Nicolás	*Porción* 58	7,749.70
1-679	Manguilla, Ramón	*Porción* 59	4,720.50
1-680	Elizondo, Antonio	"El Lucero"	13,358
1-683	Cabazos, Narciso	*Porción* 71	5,314

APPENDIX *xvi*.

General Land Office File No., San Patricio	Grantee	Name of Ranch or *Porción* No.	Acreage
1-684	Cerda, José de la	*Porción* 61	4,860.99
1-685	Camacho, Gregorio	*Porción* 68	5,133
1-686	Guajardo, Francisco	*Porción* 62	4,833.54
1-687	Fonseca, Domingo	*Porción* 67	5,004
1-688	Gutiérrez, Antonio	*Porción* 63	4,835.12
1-689	Hinojosa, José Felix	*Porción* 66	5,031
1-690	Quiroga, Yldefonso	*Porción* 60	5,930.57
1-691	Hinojosa, Juan or Juan José	*Porción* 69	12,799
1-692	Velasco, Antonio	*Porción* 70	6,330
1-693	Villarreal, Juan Antonio	*Porción* 64	4,911.68
1-694	Ríos, María Ujarda de los	*Porción* 65	5,003.32
1-695	Balli, José María	*Porción* 72	5,904
1-697	Balli, Rosa María Hinojosa de	"La Feria"	53,140.80
1-712	Vega, Juan	*Porción* 38	6,647
1-713	Villarreal, (Joseph) Antonio	*Porción* 39	4,718
1-714	Zamora, Nicolas (J. A. Castañeda)	*Porción* 40	4,705
1-715	Treviño, Bartolomé (heirs, Bartolomé & Ygnacio Treviño)	*Porción* 97	6,198
1-716	Treviño, Ygnacio (heirs of)	*Porción* 96	4,434.7
1-717	Treviño, Ygnacio (heirs of)	*Porción* 98	5,987
1-718	Treviño, Ygnacio (heirs of)	*Porción* 99	5,774
1-719	Treviño, Ygnacio (heirs of)	*Porción* 100	4,318.5
1-720	Cantú, Joseph Antonio	*Porción* 55	4,785
1-721	Manguilla, Gabriel	*Porción* 56	4,818.58
1-722	Luna, María de	*Porción* 57	7,291.42
1-723	Balli Ynojosa de, Juan José	"Llano Grande"	127,625
1-724	Farias, Julián	"San Román"	22,602.47
1-725	Cabazos, Lino	"La Blanca"	24,060
1-726	Borrego, José Vásquez	"Hacienda de Dolores"	276,350
1-728	Chapa, Joaquín	*Porción* 58	5,733.87
1-729	Vela, Lázaro	*Porción* 57	5,570.90
1-730	Garza, Manuel	*Porción* 58	5,314
1-731	Cano, Antonio Miguel	*Porción* 44	5,134.85

General Land Office File No., San Patricio	Grantee	Name of Ranch or *Porción* No.	Acreage
1-732	Villarreal, Anastacio	*Porción* 43	4,793.38
1-733	Zamora, Dionisio	*Porción* 42	4,716.76
1-734	Villarreal, Pedro	"San Pedro de Carricitos"	12,730.59
1-735	Canales, José Cayetano	*Porción* 38	6,034.17
1-736	Cuéllar, Miguel	*Porción* 1	6,066
1-736	Cuéllar, Miguel	*Porción* 2	6,969
1-737	Fernandez, Bartolomé & Eugenio	"Concepción de Carricitos"	57,569.20
1-738	Balli, Juan José	"San Salvador del Tule" also known as "Las Cardenas" or "El Sal del Rey"	315,341
1-739	Ynojosa, Vicente de	"Las Mesteñas, Pititas y La Abra"	146,670.75
1-740	Cantú, Francisco	*Porción* 80	5,599.76
1-741	Flores, Lázaro	*Porción* 76	5,536
1-742	Flores, Nicolás	*Porción* 75	5,536
1-743	Martínez, Manuel	*Porción* 74	6,695.71
1-744	Ramírez, Dionisio	*Porción* 78	5,535.48
1-745	Ramírez, Yldefonso	*Porción* 79	5,536
1-746	Zamora, Javier	*Porción* 41	4,726.43
1-747	Santos, Antonio de los	*Porción* 73	5,701.54
1-748	Zamora, Nicolás	*Porción* 48	7,077
1-749	Reynosa	"Town of Reynosa" or "Los Egidos de Reynosa"	10,124.65
1-750	Chapa, José Manuel & Luciano	"La Encantada"	39,855.60
1-751	Bocanegra, Salvador	*Porción* 51	5,057.87
1-752	Cano, Miguel	*Porción* 45	6,178.74
1-753	Flores, Segundo	"Los Guajes"	13,322.20
1-754	Garza, José Francisco de la	*Porciones* 52 & 53	6,257.17
1-755	Leál, Juan	*Porción* 55	5,783.60
1-756	Ysaguirre, Juan de León	*Porción* 56	5,757
1-757	Salinas, Nicolasa	"Las Magueyes"	12,260.42
1-758	Tijerina, José Matias	*Porción* 46	6,244.51
1-759	Zamora, José Antonio	*Porción* 50	5,314
1-760	Zamora, Toribio	*Porción* 49	5,314
1-761	Ponce, Joaquín Ysidro	*Porción* 47	6,713.57
1-762	Flores, Pedro	*Porción* 77	5,535.48
1-763	Bartolo, (Peña) María	*Porción* 61	3,949.96
1-764	Cabazos, José Narciso	"San Juan de Carricitos"	601,657
1-765	Cruz de Peña, José	*Porción* 64	1,291.23
1-766	Farias, Alexandro	"San José"	17,713.60
1-766	Farias, Blas	*Porción* 60	5,639.20

APPENDIX *xviii.*

General Land Office File No., San Patricio	Grantee	Name of Ranch or *Porción* No.	Acreage
1-767	García, Joaquín	*Porción* 62	2,656
1-768	García, Juan de Dios	*Porción* 59	5,739.18
1-769	García, Antonio	*Porción* 65	1,592.23
1-770	Guerra, Francisco	*Porción* 66	4,299.88
1-771	Gutiérrez, Ygnacio	*Porción* 63	1,699.47
1-772	Benavides, Jesús	"El Pedernál"	9,809
1-773	Cuéllar, Santiago	*Porción* 4	6,615
1-774	García, Francisco	*Porción* 3	7,366
1-775	Ramírez, José Luis	*Porción* 5	6,695.14
1-776	Gutiérrez, José Clemente	*Porción* 41	6,489.5
1-777	Vidaurri, Juan Antonio	*Porciones* 39 & 40	10,370
1-778	Gómez, Manuel	"Santa Anita"	95,202
1-780	Laredo, City of	*Porciones* 52 & 55	10,628
1-781	Garza, José María de la	*Porción* 57	5,314
1-782	Moreno, José Francisco Córdova	*Porción* 30	5,535.5
1-783	Treviño, José Dionisio	*Porción* 53	5,314
1-784	Villarreal, Juan Bautista	*Porción* 29	5,570.93
1-785	Herrera, Joaquín López de	"El Diezmero"	18,640.70
1-786	Morales, José Antonio	"El Venadito"	22,648.52
1-787	Chapa, José Bartolo	*Porción* 37	5,314
1-788	Nasario, José Antonio	*Porción* 39	5,528.81
1-789	Salinas, Laureano	*Porción* 36	5,314
1-790	Sánchez, Tadeo	*Porción* 38	5,681.97
1-791	Treviño, Blas	*Porción* 46	5,314
1-792	Flores, Ygnacio	"Agostadero del Panal"	9,854.40
1-793	Pérez, Miguel	*Porción* 106	6,343.21
1-794	Solís, Juan José	*Porción* 107	6,184
1-795	Villarreal, Francisco Antonio	*Porción* 108	6,199.39
1-796	Ynojosa, Vicente de	"El Rincón del Alazán"	29,374.95
1-797	Farias, Gregorio	"El Diezmero"	17,704.79
1-798	García, Andrés	"El Tanque"	17,713.60
1-799	García, Anastacio	"Charco Redondo"	22,140
1-800	Garza, Alvino de la, & Domingo de la Garza	"La Parra"	66,426
1-802	Herrera, Mariano López de	"El Diezmero"	20,602.56
1-803	Lascano, Miguel Alegría de	*Porción* 6	9,803.11
1-804	León, José Antonio Leál de	"San Antonio del Encinál"	27,878.1

General Land Office File No., San Patricio	Grantee	Name of Ranch or *Porción* No.	Acreage
1-806	Ramirez, Manuel	"La Laguna de los Venados"	8,856.8
1-807	Sais, Juan José	"Los Retaches"	13,285.20
1-808	Salinas, Xavier	"San Pedro de las Motas"	22,140
1-809	Salinas, Leonardo	"La Barreta"	22,140
1-811	Vargas, Leonardo	"Guadalupe del Encinál"	13,285.20
1-814	Ynojosa, Miguel	"El Palmito" or "San Pedro de las Motas"	22,140
1-831	Balli, José Francisco	"La Barreta"	124,297
1-832	Treviño, José	*Porción* 31	5,535.5

General Land Office File Bexar

	Grantee	Name of Ranch or *Porción* No.	Acreage
1-1237	Rivas, Antonio	"The Rivas Grant"	125,834
1-1251	Lombrano, Juan Francisco	"Las Isletas"	32,556
1-1346	García, José Manuel	*Porción* 11	9,286
1-1394	Días, Blas María	"Las Islitas" *Porciones* 6, 7, 8 & 9	21,256
1-1395	García, Joaquín	*Porción* 19	5,310
1-1396	García, Dolores	*Porción* 16	5,310
1-1397	Sánchez, María Jésus	*Porción* 22	5,314
1-1398	García, Bautista	*Porción* 20	5,310
1-1399	García, Leonardo	*Porción* 21	5,310
1-1448	Guajardo, José	*Porción* 14	5,314
1-1453	García, Juan Francisco	*Porción* 25	5,318
1-1472	Días, José Antonio	*Porción* 34	5,314.06
1-1485	Benavides, Basilio	*Porción* 54	5,314
1-1486	Sánchez, Tomás	*Porción* 10	5,313.6
1-1487	Sánchez, Tomás	*Porción* 11	5,313.60
1-1488	Sánchez, Leonardo	*Porción* 53	5,316.4
1-1491	García, José Miguel	*Porción* 13	5,314
1-1492	Gonzales, Antonio	"Santo Tomás"	53,136
1-1493	Treviño, José Antonio	"Paraje de Abiones" or *Porción* 56	5,316.56
1-1494	Laredo, City of	*Porciones* 1, 2, 3, & 4	21,256
1-1529	García, Dolores	*Porción* 17	5,314
1-1530	Sánchez, María Gertrudis	*Porción* 27	5,570.93
1-1532	Garza, José Cayetano de la	*Porción* 43	5,314
1-1534	Sánchez, Augustín	*Porción* 26	5,314
1-1535	García, José Prudencio	*Porción* 15	5,314
1-1536	Bustamante, José de	*Porción* 18	8,527
1-1543	Rodríguez, Toribio	*Porción* 24	5,314
1-1544	Sánchez, Leonardo	*Porción* 23	5,314

APPENDIX *xx*.

General Land Office File No., San Patricio	Grantee	Name of Ranch or *Porción* No.	Acreage
1-1601	Martínez, Eugenio	*Porción* 28	5,570.93
1-1678	Treviño, Antonio	*Porción* 32	5,535.5
1-1781	Guerra, Antonio		13,953.22
1-1784	Gonzales, Manuel	*Porción* 5	5,314

Grants confirmed but without a file number in land office records

	Balli, Nicolás & Juan	"Padre Island"	50,925.80
	Bustamante, Pedro	"Las Comitas"	22,142
	Ochoa, Ermenegildo	*Porción* 54	5,314
	Sánchez, Santiago	*Porción* 12	5,314
	Villarreal, Enrique	"Rincón del Oso"	42,840

The above information is based on Virginia H. Taylor, *Index to Spanish and Mexican Land Grants* (Austin, 1976) and is also in accord with *Guide to Spanish and Mexican Land Grants in South Texas* (Austin, 1988). Some grants have the same land office file number and some have the same *porción* number.

References

1. Relief

Atwood, Wallace W. *Physiographic Provinces of the United States* (Boston, 1940).

Fenneman, Nevin M. *Physiography of the Western United States* (New York, 1931).

Hunt, Charles B. "Physiography of the United States." In *The Reader's Encyclopedia of the American West*, 912–34. Ed. Howard R. Lamar (New York, 1977).

Loomis, Frederic B. *Physiography of the United States* (Garden City, N.Y., 1937).

Raisz, Erwin. *Landforms of the United States* (Map, Boston, Mass., 1957 edition).

Watson, J. Wreford. *North America: Its Countries and Regions* (New York, 1967).

2. Geomorphic Provinces

Atwood. *Physiographic Provinces.*

Fenneman. *Physiography of Western United States.*

Hunt. "Physiography of the United States."

Loomis. *Physiography of the United States.*

U.S. Geological Survey (USGS). *The National Atlas of the United States of America* (Washington, D.C., 1970).

Webb, Walter Prescott. *The Great Plains* (Boston, 1931).

3. Mean Annual Rainfall

U.S. Department of Commerce, Environmental Science Services Administration. *Climatic Maps of the United States,* 1966.

USGS. *National Atlas.*

Visher, Stephen Sargent. *Climatic Atlas of the United States* (Cambridge, Mass., 1954).

Ward, Robert DeCourcy. *The Climates of the United States* (Boston, 1925).

4. Daily Average Temperature—January

U.S. Department of Commerce. *Climatic Maps of the United States, 1966.*

U.S. Department of Commerce, Environmental Data Service. *Weather Atlas of the United States* (Detroit, 1968).

U.S. Department of Commerce, National Oceanic and Atmospheric Administration. *Climates of the States* (Port Washington, N.Y., 1974). Vol. II.

Visher. *Climatic Atlas of the United States.*

Ward. *Climates of the United States.*

5. Daily Average Temperature—July

Same as Map 4.

6. Barriers to the West

Allen, John Logan. *Passage Through the Garden* (Urbana, Ill., 1975).

Austin, Mary. *The Land of Little Rain* (Boston, 1903).

Cline, Gloria Griffen. *Exploring the Great Basin* (Norman, Okla., 1963).

Dodge, Richard Irving. *The Plains of the Great West* (New York, 1959).

Lavender, David. *Westward Vision: The Story of the Oregon Trail* (New York, 1963).

McGinnies, William G. "What is a Desert?" *Desert Plants,* Vol. 6, no. 4: 182–88.

Powell, John Wesley. *The Lands of the Arid Region of the United States* (Cambridge, Mass., 1962).

Smith, Henry Nash. *Virgin Land* (New York, 1957).

Stewart, George R. *The California Trail* (New York, 1962).

Webb. *The Great Plains.*

7. Major Forest Types

Eliot, Willard Ayres. *Forest Trees of the Pacific Coast* (New York, 1948).

Farb, Peter. *The Forest* (New York, 1961).

Greeley, William B. *Forests and Men* (Garden City, N.Y., 1951).

Haden-Guest, Stephen, et al. *A World Geography of Forest Resources* (New York, 1956).

McCormick, Jack. *The Living Forest* (New York, 1959).

McMinn, Howard E., and Evelyn Maino. *An Illustrated Manual of Pacific Coast Trees* (Berkeley, Calif., 1959).

Peattie, Donald Culross. *A Natural History of Western Trees* (Boston, 1953).

Preston, Richard J., Jr. *Rocky Mountain Trees* (New York, 1968).

8. Native Tribal Areas

Beck, Warren A., and Ynez D. Haase. *Historical Atlas of California* (Norman, Okla., 1974).

Kroeber, Alfred. *Cultural and Natural Areas of Native North America* (Berkeley, Calif., 1947).

Lowie, Robert H. *Indians of the Plains* (New York, 1963).

National Geographic Society. *Indians of North America.* Map (Washington, D.C., 1972).

Wissler, Clark. *Indians of the United States* (New York, 1967).

9. Dispersion of the Horse

Dobie, J. Frank. *The Mustangs* (Boston, 1934).

Ewers, John C. "The Horse in Blackfoot Indian Culture, with Comparative Material from Other Western Tribes." In *Smithsonian Institution Bureau of American Ethnology Bulletin No. 159* (Washington, D.C., 1955).

Haines, Francis. "Horses for Western Indians," *American West,* Vol. 3, no. 2 (Spring, 1966): 5–15, 92.

———. *The Plains Indians* (New York, 1976).

Roe, Frank Gilbert. *The Indian and the Horse* (Norman, Okla., 1955).

Worcester, D. E. "Spanish Horses Among the Plains Tribes," *Pacific Historical Review,* Vol. 19 (1944): 409–17.

———. "The Spread of Spanish Horses in the Southwest," *New Mexico Historical Review,* Vol. 19 (1944): 225–32.

Wyman, Walker D. *The Wild Horses of the West* (Caldwell, Idaho, 1946).

10. The Buffalo Herds

Barnett, Le Roy. "Ghastly Harvest: Montana's Trade in Buffalo Bones," *Montana: The Magazine of Western History,* Vol. 25 (Summer, 1975): 2–13.

Barsness, Larry. *Heads, Hides, and Horns: The Compleat Buffalo Book* (Fort Worth, 1985).

Dary, David A. *The Buffalo Book* (Chicago, 1974).

Dodge, Richard Irving. *The Hunting Grounds of the Great West* (London, 1877).

———. *Plains of the Great West.*

Gard, Wayne. *The Great Buffalo Hunt* (New York, 1959).

Haines, Francis. *The Buffalo* (New York, 1959).

Hornaday, William T. "The Extermination of the American Bison, with a Sketch of Its Discovery and Life History." In *Reprint of the U.S. National Museum Under the Direction of the Smithsonian Institution,* Part II, Section III, 369–548 (Washington, D.C., 1889).

McDonald, Jerry N. *North American Bison: Their Classification and Evolution* (Berkeley, Calif., 1981).

McHugh, Tom. *The Time of the Buffalo* (New York, 1972).

O'Connor, Jack, and George G. Goodwin. *The Big Game Animals of North America* (New York, 1961).

Sandoz, Mari. *The Buffalo Hunters: A Story of the Hide Men* (New York, 1954).

Webb. *The Great Plains.*

11. Native Fauna I

Allen. *Passage Through the Garden.*

Chapman, Joseph A., and George A. Feldhamer (eds.). *Wild Mammals of North America* (Baltimore, 1982).

Ingles, Lloyd G. *Mammals of the Pacific States* (Stanford, Calif., 1965).

Jones, J. Knox, Jr.; David M. Armstrong; Robert S. Hoffmann; and Clyde Jones. *Mammals of the Northern Great Plains* (Lincoln, Nebr., 1983).

McCullough, Dale R. *The Tule Elk: Its History, Behavior, and Ecology.* University of California Publications in Zoology, Vol. 88 (Berkeley, Calif., 1971).

Murie, Olaus J. *The Elk in North America* (Washington, D.C., 1951).

O'Connor and Goodwin. *Big Game Animals.*

Rue, Leonard Lee, III. *Pictorial Guide to the Mammals of North America* (New York, 1967).

———. "Elk," *American Hunter,* January, 1982, pp. 31–34.

———. "Mule Deer," *American Hunter,* October, 1980, pp. 36–37.

———. "Pronghorn," *American Hunter,* April, 1980, pp. 44–45.

———. "Whitetail Deer," *American Hunter,* June, 1980, pp. 50–51.

Savage, Arthur and Candace Savage. *Wild Mammals of Northwest America* (Baltimore, 1981).

Taylor, Walter P. (ed.). *The Deer of North America* (Washington, D.C., 1956).

Webb. *The Great Plains.*

12. Native Fauna II

Chapman, Joseph A., and George A. Feldhamer. *Wild Mammals of North America.* (New York, 1959). Vol. 2.

Hall, E. Raymond, and Keith R. Kelson. *The Mammals of North America.*

O'Connor and Goodwin. *Big Game Animals of North America.*

Rue, Leonard Lee, III. "Grizzly Bear," *American Hunter,* February, 1980, pp. 44–45.

Webb. *Great Plains.*

13. Fur-Bearing Mammals

Armstrong, David M. *Distribution of Mammals in Colorado.* Monograph of the Museum of Natural History, The University of Kansas, No. 3 (Lawrence, Kans., 1972).

Burt, William Henry, and Richard Philip Grossenheider. *The Field Guide to the Mammals: Giving Field Marks of All Species Found North of the Mexican Boundary* (Boston, 1961).

Chapman and Feldhamer. *Wild Mammals of North America.*

Deems, Eugene F., Jr., and Duane Pursley (eds.). *North American Furbearers: Their Management, Research and Harvest Status in 1976* (College Park, Md., 1978).

Grinnell, Joseph; Joseph S. Dixon; and Jean M. Linsdale. *Furbearing Mammals of California* (Berkeley, Calif., 1937). 2 vols.

Hall, E. Raymond. *Mammals of Nevada* (Berkeley, Calif., 1946).

Hall and Kelson. *Mammals of North America.* Vol. 2.

Miller, Daniel J. *The Sea Otter, Enhydra Lutris: Its Life History, Taxonomic Status, and Some Ecological Relationships.* California Marine Resources Leaflet No. 7 (Long Beach, Calif., 1974).

Odgen, Adele. *The California Sea Otter Trade, 1784–1848.* University of California Publications in History, Vol. 26 (Berkeley, Calif., 1941).

Savage and Savage. *Wild Mammals of Northwest America.*

14. Extinct and Rare Birds

Allen, Robert Porter. *On the Trail of Vanishing Birds* (New York, 1957).

———. *The Whooping Crane.* National Audubon Society Research Report No. 3 (New York, 1952).

Darlington, David. *In Condor Country* (Boston, 1987).

Greenway, James C., Jr. *Extinct and Vanishing Birds of the World.* Special Publication of the American Committee for International Wild Life Protection, No. 13. (New York, 1958).

Jasper, Theodore. *Studer's Popular Ornithology: The Birds of North America* (New York, 1881; reprint, 1977).

Koford, Carl B. *The California Condor* (New York, 1966).

———. *The California Condor.* National Audubon Society Research Report No. 4 (New York, 1953).

McNulty, Faith. *The Whooping Crane* (New York, 1966).

Schorger, A. W. *The Passenger Pigeon: Its Natural History and Extinction* (Madison, Wis., 1955).

Smith, Richard Jay, and Robert Easton. *California Condor* (Charlotte, N.Car., 1964).

15. Explorations, 1500–1599

Bancroft, Hubert Howe. *History of the North Mexican States and Texas* (San Francisco, 1889). 2 vols.

Bannon, John Francis. *The Spanish Borderlands Frontier, 1513–1821* (New York, 1970).

Beck and Haase. *Historical Atlas of California.*

———. *Historical Atlas of New Mexico* (Norman, Okla., 1969).

Bolton, Herbert Eugene. *Rim of Christendom: A Biography of Eusebio Francisco Kino* (New York, 1960).

———. *Coronado, Knight of Pueblos and Plains* (Albuquerque, N.Mex., 1949).

———, and Thomas Maitland Marshall. *The Colonization of North America, 1492–1783* (New York, 1920).

Hague, Harlan. *The Road to California: The Search for a Southern Overland Route, 1540–1848* (Glendale, Calif., 1978).

Hammond, George Peter, and Agapito Rey (eds.). *The Rediscovery of New Mexico, 1580–1594: The Explorations of Chamuscado, Espejo, Castaño de Sosa, Morlete, and Leyva de Bonilla and Humaña* (Albuquerque, N.Mex., 1966).

Thomas, Alfred Barnaby. "Spanish Expeditions into Colorado," *Colorado Magazine,* Vol. 1, no. 7 (November, 1924): 289–300.

USGS. *National Atlas.*

Williams, D. W. "Route of Cabeza de Vaca in Texas," *Texas Historical Association Quarterly,* Vol. 3 (1899–1900): 54–64.

16. Explorations, 1600–1699

Bancroft. *North Mexican States and Texas.* Vol. I.

Bannon. *Spanish Borderlands Frontier.*

Beck and Haase. *Historical Atlas of California.*

———. *Historical Atlas of New Mexico.*

Bolton. *Rim of Christendom.*

———. *Spanish Explorations in the Southwest, 1542–1706* (New York, 1916).

——— and Marshall. *Colonization of North America.*

Carter, Hodding. *Doomed Road of Empire: The Spanish Trail of Conquest* (New York, 1963).

Morfi, Fray Juan Agustín de. *The History of Texas, 1673–1779.* Tr. Carlos Eduardo Castañeda (Albuquerque, N.Mex., 1935). 2 vols.

Pool, William C. *A Historical Atlas of Texas* (Austin, Tex., 1975).

USGS. *National Atlas.*

Walker, Henry P., and Don Bufkin. *Historical Atlas of Arizona* (Norman, Okla., 1979).

17. Explorations, 1700–1771

Bancroft, Hubert H. *A History of Arizona and New Mexico, 1530–1888* (San Francisco, 1889).

———. *North Mexican States and Texas.* Vol. I.

Bannon. *Spanish Borderlands Frontier.*

Bolton. *Spanish Explorations.*

——— and Marshall. *Colonization of North America.*

Carter. *Doomed Road of Empire.*

Fehrenbach, T. R. *Lone Star* (New York, 1968).

John, Elizabeth A. H. *Storms Brewed in Other Men's Worlds: The Confrontation of Indians, Spanish, and French in the Southwest, 1540–1795* (College Station, Tex., 1975).

Pool. *Historical Atlas of Texas.*

Robinson, Elwyn B. *History of North Dakota* (Lincoln, Nebr., 1966).

Weddle, Robert S. *San Juan Bautista: Gateway to Spanish Texas* (Austin, Tex., 1968).

18. Northern Frontier of New Spain, 1776–1780

Bancroft, *North Mexican States and Texas.* Vol. I.

Fireman, Janet R. *The Spanish Royal Corps of Engineers in the Western Borderlands: Instrument of Burton Reform, 1765 to 1815* (Glendale, Calif., 1977).

Kinnaird, Lawrence (ed.). *The Frontiers of New Spain; Nicolás de la Fora's Description, 1766–1768* (Berkeley, Calif., 1958).

Krocber. *Cultural and Natural Areas.*

Sonnischen, C. L. *The Mescalero Apaches* (Norman, Okla., 1958).

Thomas, Alfred Barnaby (ed.). *Forgotten Frontiers: A Study of the Spanish Indian Policy of Don Juan Bautista de Anza, Governor of New Mexico, 1777–1787* (Norman, Okla., 1941).

———. *Teodoro de Croix and the Northern Frontier of New Spain, 1776–1783* (Norman, Okla., 1941).

Weber, David J. (ed.). *New Spain's Far Northern Frontier: Essays on Spain in the American West, 1540–1821* (Albuquerque, N.Mex., 1979).

Wheat, Carl I. *Mapping the TransMississippi West, 1540–1861,* vol. I, *The Spanish Entrada to the Louisiana Purchase, 1540–1804* (San Francisco, 1959).

19. Explorations, 1772–1799

Bolton, Herbert Eugene. *Pageant in the Wilderness: The Story of The Escalante Expedition in the Interior Basin, 1776* (Salt Lake City, 1950).

———. *Outpost of Empire: The Story of the Founding of San Francisco* (New York, 1939).

———. *Kino's Historical Memoir of Pimería Alta* (Berkeley, Calif., 1948).

———. *Rim of Christendom.*

———. *Texas in the Middle Eighteenth Century* (Austin, Tex., 1970).

Burpee, Lawrence J. "La Vérendrye, Pathfinder of the West," *Annals of Wyoming,* Vol. 17 (1945): 107–11.

Folmer, Henri. "The Mallet Expedition of 1739 Through Nebraska, Kansas, and Colorado to Santa Fe," *Colorado Magazine,* Vol. 16, no. 5 (September, 1939): 161–73.

Garces, Fr. Francisco. *A Record of Travels in Arizona and California, 1775–1776.* Ed. Jon Galvin (San Francisco, 1967).

Hammond, George Peter. "The Zuñiga Journal, Tucson to Santa Fe: The Opening of a Spanish Trade Route, 1788–1795," *New Mexico Historical Review,* Vol. 6, no. 1 (January, 1930): 3–23.

Hill, Joseph J. "Spanish and Mexican Exploration and Trade Northwest from New Mexico into the Great Basin, 1765–1853," *Utah Historical Quarterly,* Vol. 3, no. 1 (January, 1930).

Josephy, Alvin M., Jr. "David Thompson." In *The Mountain Men and the Fur Trade of the Far West,* 59–71. Ed. Leroy R. Hafen (Glendale, Calif., 1966).

Nelson, Al B. "Campaigning in the Big Bend of the Rio Grande in 1787," *Southwestern Historical Quarterly,* Vol. 34, no. 3 (January, 1936): 200–27.

Robinson, Doane. "Additional Verendrye Material," *Mississippi Valley Historical Review,* Vol. 3, no. 3 (December, 1916): 368–99.

Sauer, Carl O. "A Spanish Expedition into Arizona Apacheria," *Arizona Historical Review,* Vol. 6, no. 1 (1935): 3–13.

Smith, G. Hubert. *The Explorations of the Verendryes in the Northern Plains, 1738–1743.* Ed. W. Raymond Wood (Lincoln, Nebr., 1980).

Thomas. *Forgotten Frontiers.*

———. *The Chiricahua Apache, 1695–1876.* Mescalero-Chiricahua Land Claims Project Contract Research No. 290-154 (Albuquerque, N.Mex., 1959).

———. *The Mescalero Apache, 1653–1874.* Mescalero-Chiricahua Land Claims Project Contract Research No. 290-154 (Albuquerque, N.Mex., 1954).

Treutlein, Theodore E. "Fages as Explorer, 1769–1772," *California Historical Quarterly,* Vol. 51, no. 4 (Winter, 1972): 338–56.

20. Spanish-Mexican Land Grants

Army Map Service. *Douglas, Arizona–New Mexico.* 1:250,000. (Washington, D.C., 1959; limited revision, 1967).

———. *Nogales, Arizona.* 1:250,000. (1956; limited revision, 1962).

Beck and Haase. *Historical Atlas of California.*

———. *Historical Atlas of New Mexico.*

Bowden, J. J. *Spanish and Mexican Land Grants in the Chihuahuan Acquisition* (El Paso, Tex., 1971).

Carr, Ralph. "Private Land Claims in Colorado," *Colorado Magazine,* Vol. 25, no. 1 (January, 1948): 10–30.

Cook, Charles A. "The Hunter Claim: A Colossal Land Scheme in the Papagueria," *Arizona and the West,* Vol. 15, no. 3 (Autumn, 1973): 213–44.

Cookridge, E. H. *The Baron of Arizona* (New York, 1967).

Hofen, Le Roy R. "Mexican Land Grants in Colorado," *Colorado Magazine,* Vol. 4, no. 3 (May, 1927): 81–93.

Mattison, Ray H. "Early Spanish and Mexican Settlements in Arizona," *New Mexico Historical Review,* Vol. 21, no. 4 (October, 1946): 273–327.

Miller, Thomas Lloyd. *The Public Lands of Texas, 1519–1970* (Norman, Okla., 1972).

Powell, Donald M. *The Peralta Grant* (Norman, Okla., 1960).

Stallcup, Evan S. "The Hunter Claim," *Arizona Historical Review,* Vol. 4, no. 1 (April, 1931): 23–28.

Van Ness, John R., and Christine M. (eds.). *Spanish and Mexican Land Grants in New Mexico and Colorado* (Santa Fe, N.Mex., 1980).

Westphall, Victor. *Mercedes Reales: Hispanic Land Grants of the Upper Rio Grande Region* (Albuquerque, N.Mex., 1983).

Williams, R. Hal. "George W. Julian and Land Reform in New Mexico." In *Public Land Policies,* 71–84. Ed. Paul W. Gates (New York, 1979).

21. Empresario Grants, 1833

Bancroft. *North Mexican States and Texas.* Vol. II.

Estep, Raymond. "The First Panhandle Land Grant," *Chronicles of Oklahoma,* Vol. 36 (1958–59): 358–70.

Fehrenbach. *Lone Star.*

Frantz, Joe B. "Empresario System." In Lamar, *Reader's Encyclopedia of the American West,* 349.

Mattison. "Early Spanish and Mexican Settlements in Arizona."

Pool, William C. *A Historical Atlas of Texas.* (Austin, 1975). The Texas State Historical Association. *Contours of Discovery: Printed Maps Delineating the Texas and Southwestern Chapters in the Cartographic History of North America, 1534–1930* (University of Texas, Austin, 1981).

22. Spanish-Mexican Land Grants, Lower Rio Grande Valley, West of Nueces River, Texas

Dobkins, Betty Eakle. *The Spanish Element in Texas Water Law* (Austin, 1959).

Fehrenbach. *Lone Star.*

Guide to Spanish and Mexican Land Grants in South Texas (Austin, Tex., 1988).

Maps in General Land Office (Austin, Texas).

Brooks County, July, 1912.
Cameron County, n.d.
Duval County, n.d.
Hidalgo County, April, 1913.
Jim Hogg County, April, 1913.
Nueces County, September, 1913.
San Patricio, November, 1896.
Starr County, n.d.
Willacy County, n.d.
Zapata County, n.d.
Lang, Aldon Socrates. *Financial History of the Public Lands in Texas.* Baylor Bulletin, Vol. 35, no. 3 (Waco, Tex., 1932).
McKitrick, Reuben. *The Public Land System of Texas, 1832–1910.* Bulletin of the University of Wisconsin No. 905 (Madison, Wis., 1905).
Taylor, Virginia H. *Index to Spanish and Mexican Land Grants* (Austin, Tex., 1976).
———. *The Spanish Archives of the General Land Office of Texas* (Austin, Tex., 1955).
Von Bluecher, Felix A. *Map of San Patricio District.* Copied from a map compiled by Felix A. Von Bluecher, former district surveyor of Nueces District, General Land Office, June 24, 1870, Austin, Texas.
Wooten, Dudley G. *A Comprehensive History of Texas 1685 to 1897* (Austin and Dallas, 1898). Vol. II.

23. Spanish-Mexican Land Grants, Eagle Pass–Del Rio, Texas

Bowden, J. J. *Spanish and Mexican Land Grants in the Chihuahuan Acquisition* (El Paso, Tex., 1971).
Dobkins. *Spanish Element in Texas Water Law.*
Foscue, Edwin J. "Historical Geography of the Lower Rio Grande Valley of Texas," *Texas Geographical Magazine,* Vol. 3, no. 1 (Spring, 1939): 1–12.
Graf, Le Roy P. "Colonizing Projects in Texas South of the Nueces, 1820–1845," *Southwestern Historical Quarterly,* Vol. 50, no. 4 (April, 1947): 431–48.
Meyer, Michael C. *Water in the Hispanic Southwest: A Social and Legal History, 1550–1850* (Tucson, Ariz., 1984).
Scott, Elton M. *Texas Geography* (Oklahoma City, 1953).
Webb, Walter Prescott (ed.). *The Handbook of Texas.* (Austin, 1952). 2 vols.

24. Explorations 1800–1810

Barry, J. Neilson. "John Colter's Map of 1814," *Wyoming Annals,* Vol. 10, no. 3 (July, 1938): 100–16.
Beck and Haase. *Historical Atlas of California.*
———. *Historical Atlas of New Mexico.*
Chittenden, Hiram Martin. *The American Fur Trade of the Far West.* (New York, 1902). 3 vols.
Cline. *Exploring the Great Basin.*
Coues, Elliott (ed.). *The Expeditions of Zebulon Montgomery*

Pike to the Headwaters of the Mississippi River through Louisiana Territory, and in New Spain, During the Years 1805–6–7 (Minneapolis, 1965). 2 vols.
Gregg, Josiah. *Commerce of the Prairies* (Norman, Okla., 1954).
DeVoto, Bernard (ed.). *The Journals of Lewis and Clark* (Boston, 1953).
Ferris, Robert G. (ed.). *Lewis and Clark* (Washington, D.C., 1975).
Goetzmann, William H. *Exploration and Empire* (New York, 1967).
Hafen, Leroy R. (ed.). *The Mountain Men and the Fur Trade of the Far West* (Glendale, Calif., 1965).
Harris, Burton. *John Colter: His Years in the Rockies* (New York, 1952).
Meinig, D. W. *The Great Columbia Plain* (Seattle, 1968).
Moulton, Gary E. (ed.). *Atlas of the Lewis and Clark Expedition* (Lincoln, Nebr., 1983).
USGS. *National Atlas.*
Wheat. *Mapping the TransMississippi West.* Vol. II.

25. Explorations 1810–1820

Chittenden. *American Fur Trade.*
Goetzmann, William H. *Army Explorations in the American West, 1803–1863* (New Haven, Conn., 1959).
———. *Exploration and Empire.*
Johansen, Dorothy O., and Charles M. Gates. *Empire of the Columbia* (New York, 1967).
Phillips, Paul Chrisler. *The Fur Trade* (Norman, Okla., 1961). 2 vols.
USGS. *National Atlas.*
Weber, David J. *The Taos Trappers* (Norman, Okla., 1971).

26. Fur Trapper Rendezvous (Mountain Fairs)

Cleland, Robert Glass. *This Reckless Breed of Men: The Trappers and Fur Traders of the Southwest* (New York, 1950).
DeVoto, Bernard. *Across the Wide Missouri* (Boston, 1947, 1964).
Gowans, Fred R. *Rocky Mountain Rendezvous* (Provo, Utah, 1976).
Hafen. *Mountain Men and the Fur Trade.*
Russell, Carl P. "Wilderness Rendezvous Period of the American Fur Trade," *Oregon Historical Quarterly,* Vol. 42, no. 1 (March, 1941): 1–47.
Smith, Alson J. *Men Against the Mountains* (New York, 1965).
Wishart, David J. *The Fur Trade of the American West, 1807–1840: A Geographical Synthesis* (Lincoln, Nebr., 1979).

27. Explorations of Peter S. Ogden

Binns, Archie. *Peter Skene Ogden: Fur Trader* (Portland, Ore., 1967).
Cleland. *This Reckless Breed of Men.*
Cline. *Exploring the Great Basin.*

———. *Peter Skene Ogden and the Hudson's Bay Company* (Norman, Okla., 1974).

Dodds, Gordon, B. "Peter Skene Ogden." In Lamar, Reader's *Encyclopedia of the American West*, 858–59.

Goetzmann. *Exploration and Empire*.

Hafen. *Mountain Men and the Fur Trade*, 213–38.

Wheat. *Mapping the TransMississippi West*. Vol. II.

28. Expeditions of Jedediah S. Smith

Brooks, George (ed.). *The Southwest Expedition of Jedediah S. Smith* (Glendale, Calif., 1977), 259.

Carter, Harvey L. "Jedediah Smith." In Hafen, *Mountain Men and the Fur Trade*. Vol. VIII, 331–48.

Cline. *Exploring the Great Basin*.

Morgan Dale L. *Jedediah Smith and the Opening of the West* (New York, 1953).

———, and Carl I. Wheat. *Jedediah Smith and His Maps of the American West* (San Francisco, 1954).

Riddle, Kenyon. *Records and Maps of the Old Santa Fe Trail* (Raton, N.Mex., 1949).

Smith, Alson J. *Men Against the Mountains: Jedediah Smith and the Southwest Expedition of 1826–1829* (New York, 1965).

Woodbury, A. M. "The Route of Jedediah S. Smith in 1826 from the Great Salt Lake to the Colorado River," *Utah Historical Quarterly*, Vol. 4, no. 2 (April, 1931): 35–48.

29. First Commerce Trails

Beck and Haase. *Historical Atlas of California*.

Gregg. *Commerce of the Prairies*.

Hafen, Leroy R., and Ann W. Hafen. *Old Spanish Trail, Santa Fe to Los Angeles* (Glendale, Calif., 1954).

Haley, J. Evetts. "The Comanchero Trade," *Southwestern Historical Quarterly*, Vol. 38, no. 3 (January, 1935): 157–76.

———. *The XIT Ranch of Texas and Early Days on the Llano Estacado* (Norman, Okla., 1967).

Hill, Joseph J. "Spanish and Mexican Exploration and Trade Northeast from New Mexico into the Great Basin, 1763–1853," *Utah Historical Quarterly*, Vol. 3 (1930): 3–23.

Moorhead, Max L. *New Mexico's Royal Road* (Norman, Okla., 1958).

Riddle. *Records and Maps of the Old Santa Fe Trail*.

Vest, Deed L. "The Chihuahua Road," *Texana*, Vol. 5 (1967): 1–10.

30. Texas Cattle Trails

Billington, Ray Allen, and Martin Ridge. *Westward Expansion: A History of the American Frontier* (New York, 1982).

Gard, Wayne. "Retracing the Chisholm Trail," *Southwestern Historical Quarterly*, Vol. 60 (1956): 54–68.

———. "The Role of the Cattle Trails," *Nebraska History*, Vol. 29 (1958): 287–301.

Haley, J. Evetts. *Charles Goodnight, Cowman and Plainsman* (Norman, Okla., 1949).

———. *XIT Ranch of Texas*.

Jordan, Terry G. *Trails to Texas: Southern Roots of Western Cattle Ranching* (Lincoln, Nebr., 1981).

Love, Clara M. "History of the Cattle Industry in the Southwest," *Southwestern Historical Quarterly*, Vols. 19, 20 (April, July, 1916).

Osgood, Ernest S. *Day of the Cattlemen* (Minneapolis, 1954).

Stout, Joe A. "Cattle Industry." In *Reader's Encyclopedia of the American West*, 174–82.

Tennant, H. S. "The Texas Cattle Trails," *Chronicles of Oklahoma*, Vol. 13 (1936): 84–122.

31. The Great Sheep Trails, 1870–1900

Herrington, George Squires (ed.). "Levancia Bent's Diary of a Sheep Drive, Evanston, Wyoming, to Kearney, Nebraska, 1882," *Annals of Wyoming*, Vol. 24, no. 1 (1952): 24–51.

Hollen, W. Eugene. "Sheep Ranching." In Lamar, *Reader's Encyclopedia of the American West*, 1103–1104.

Towne, Charles Wayland, and Edward Norris Wentworth. *Shepherd's Empire* (Norman, Okla., 1945).

Wentworth, Edward Norris. *America's Sheep Trails* (Ames, Iowa, 1948).

——— (ed.). "Trailing Sheep from California to Idaho in 1865: The Journal of Gorham Gates Kimball," *Agricultural History*, Vol. 28 (1954): 49–83.

32. Oregon-California Trail

Boyack, Mrs. A. R. "Oregon Trail Trek No. Eight, Lander Road," *Annals of Wyoming*, Vol. 31 (1959): 73–93.

Carley, Maurine. "Emigrant Trail Trek No. Nine," *Annals of Wyoming*, Vol. 31 (1959): 213–26.

———. "Emigrant Trail Trek No. 10," *Annals of Wyoming*, Vol. 32 (1960): 103–23, 219–38.

———. "Oregon Trail Trek No. Four," *Annals of Wyoming*, Vol. 29 (1957): 67–85.

———. "Oregon Trail Trek No. Five," *Annals of Wyoming*, Vol. 29 (1957): 177–94.

———. "Oregon Trail Trek No. Six," *Annals of Wyoming*, Vol. 30 (1958): 37–62.

———. "Oregon Trail Trek No. Seven," *Annals of Wyoming*, Vol. 30 (1958): 193–213.

Cramer, Howard Ross. "The Range and Hudspeth's Cutoff, Southeastern Idaho," *Rangeman Journal*, October, 1976, pp. 156–59.

Harstad, Peter T. "The Lander Trail," *Idaho Yesterdays*, Vol. 12, no. 3 (Fall, 1968): 14–28.

Hastings, Lansford W. *The Emigrant's Guide to Oregon and California* (Princeton, N.J., 1932).

Kelly, Charles. "The Hastings Cutoff," *Utah Historical Quarterly*, Vol. 3, no. 3 (July, 1930): 67–82.

Miller, David. "The Donner Road Through the Great Salt

Lake Desert," *Pacific Historical Review,* Vol. 27, no. 1 (1958):39–44.

Paden, Irene D. *The Wake of the Prairie Schooner* (New York, 1943).

Stewart. *California Trail.*

33. Overland Tragedies

Caughey, John Walton. "Southwest from Salt Lake in 1849," *Pacific Historical Review,* Vol. 6 (1937):143–81.

Kelly. "Hastings Cutoff."

Manly, William Lewis. *Death Valley in '49* (Los Angeles, 1949).

———. *The Jayhawkers' Oath and Other Sketches* (Los Angeles, 1949).

McGlashan, C. F. *History of the Donner Party: A Tragedy of the Sierra* (Stanford, Calif., 1947).

Miller. "Donner Road."

Nusbaumer, Louis. *Valley of Salt, Memories of Wine: A Journal of Death Valley, 1849.* Ed. George Koenig. (Berkeley, Calif., 1967).

Outland, Charles F. *Man-Made Disaster: The Story of St. Francis Dam* (Glendale, Calif., 1977).

Serven, James Edsall. "The Ill-Fated '49er Wagon Train," *Historical Society of Southern California Quarterly,* Vol. 42, no. 1 (March, 1960):29–50.

Stewart, George R. *Ordeal by Hunger: The Story of the Donner Party* (New York, 1936).

Wheat, Carl I. "The Forty-Niners in Death Valley (A Tentative Census)," *Historical Society of Southern California,* Vol. 21, no. 4 (December, 1939):102–17.

———. "Trailing the Forty-Niners Through Death Valley," *Sierra Club Bulletin,* Vol. 24, no. 3 (June, 1939):74–108.

34. Overland Mail and Connecting Lines

Austerman, Wayne R. *Sharps Rifles and Spanish Mules: The San Antonio–El Paso Mail, 1851–1881* (College Station, Texas, 1985.

Banning, William, and George H. Banning. *Six Horses* (New York, 1930).

Conkling, Roscoe P., and Margaret B. Conkling. *The Butterfield Overland Mail, 1857–1869* (Glendale, Calif., 1947). 3 vols.

Hafen, Le Roy R. *The Overland Mail, 1849–1868* (Cleveland, 1926).

Winther, Oscar Osborn. *Express and Stagecoach Days in California* (Stanford, Calif., 1936).

———. *The Transportation Frontier, 1865–1900* (New York, 1964).

———. *Via Western Express and Stagecoach* (Stanford, Calif., 1945).

35. Pony Express Routes

Bradley, Glenn D. *The Story of the Pony Express* (Chicago, 1913).

Bloss, Roy S. *Pony Express—The Great Gamble* (Berkeley, Calif., 1959).

Chapman, Arthur. *The Pony Express* (New York, 1932).

Gray, John S. "The Northern Overland Pony Express," *Montana,* Vol. 16, no. 4 (October, 1966):58–73.

Hafen. *Overland Mail.*

Hanson, Robert A. "Notes on the Trail of the Pony Express" (mimeo. copy, Berkeley, Calif., n.d.). Also map, *The Trail of the Pony Express, San Francisco, Calif., to St. Joseph, Mo., April 1860 to Nov. 1861* (scale 1″ = 30 miles).

Howard, Robert West. *Hoofbeats of Destiny: The Story of the Pony Express* (New York, 1960).

Smith, Waddell F. (ed.). *The Story of the Pony Express* (San Rafael, Calif., 1964).

Visscher, William Lightfoot. *The Pony Express* (Chicago, 1908).

36. Explorations of John C. Frémont

Egan, Ferol. *Fremont, Explorer for a Restless Nation* (New York, 1977).

Frémont, John C. *Reprint of the Exploring Expedition to the Rocky Mountains in the Year 1842 and to Oregon and North California in the Years 1843–44* (Washington, 1845).

———. *The Expeditions of John Charles Frémont,* Vol. I, *Travels from 1838 to 1844.* Ed. Donald Jackson and Mary Lee Spence (Urbana, Ill., 1970).

———. *The Expeditions of John Charles Frémont, Map Portofolio.* Ed. Donald Jackson and Mary Lee Spence, (Urbana, Ill., 1970).

Hafen and Hafen. *Old Spanish Trail.*

Jackson, W. Turrentine. *Wagon Roads West* (New Haven, Conn., 1965).

37. U.S. Military Forts, 1819–1895

Brandes, T. Donald. *Military Posts of Colorado* (Fort Collins, Colo., 1973).

Brandes, Ray. "A Guide to the History of the U.S. Army Installations in Arizona," *Arizona and the West,* Vol. 1 (1959):42–65.

Frazer, Robert W. *Forts of the West* (Norman, Okla., 1965).

Heitman, Francis B. *Historical Register and Dictionary of the United States Army, from its Organization, September 29, 1789–March 3, 1903* (Washington, D.C., 1903). 2 vols.

Hart, Herbert M. *Old Forts of the Far West* (Seattle, 1965).

———. *Pioneer Forts of the West* (Seattle, 1968).

———. *Tour Guide to Old Western Forts* (Fort Collins, Colo., 1980).

Koury, Michael J. *Military Posts of Montana* (Bellevue, Nebr., 1970).

Mattison, Ray H. "The Army Post on the Northern Plains, 1865–1885," *Nebraska History,* Vol. 35, no. 1 (March, 1954):17–44.

Outline Description of U.S. Military Posts and Stations in the Year 1871 (Washington, D.C., 1872).

Prucha, Francis Paul. *A Guide to the Military Posts of the United States, 1789–1895* (Madison, Wis., 1964).

Whiting, J. S., and Richard J. Whiting. *Forts of the State of California* (Seattle, 1960).

38. Federal Wagon Roads, 1849–1869

Goetzmann. *Army Exploration.*

Haywood, C. Robert. *Trails South: The Wagon-Road Economy in the Dodge City–Panhandle Region* (Norman, Okla., 1986).

Jackson, W. Turrentine. "The Army Engineers as Road Surveyors and Builders in Kansas and Nebraska, 1854–1858," *Kansas Historical Quarterly*, Vol. 17 (1949): 37–59.

———. *Wagon Roads West.*

Winther. *Transportation Frontier.*

39. The Mormon Empire

Arrington, Leonard J. *Great Basin Kingdom: An Economic History of the Latter-Day Saints* (Cambridge, Mass., 1958).

Bufkin, Donald. "The Lost County of Pah-Ute," *Arizoniana*, Vol. 1, no. 1 (1960): 1–11.

Comeaux, Malcolm L. *Arizona: A Geography* (Boulder, Colo., 1981).

Edwards, Elbert B. "Early Mormon Settlements in Southern Nevada," *Nevada Historical Society Quarterly*, Vol. 7 (1965): 27–43.

Larson, Gustave O. *Outline History of Utah and the Mormons* (Salt Lake City, 1958).

———. *The Americanization of Utah* (San Marino, Calif., 1971).

McClintock, James H. *Mormon Settlement in Arizona* (Phoenix, Ariz., 1931).

Morgan, Dale L. "The State of Deseret," *Utah Historical Quarterly*. Vol. 8, nos. 2–4 (April, July, October, 1940): 67–239.

Neff, Andrew Love. *History of Utah, 1847–1869* (Salt Lake City, 1940).

Peterson, Charles S. *Take Up Your Mission: Mormon Colonizing Along the Little Colorado River, 1870–1900* (Tucson, Ariz., 1973).

Wagoner, Jay J. *Arizona Territory, 1863–1912: A Political History* (Tucson, Ariz., 1970).

40. Territorial Expansion I

Bancroft, Hubert H. *History of Arizona and New Mexico, 1530–1888* (Albuquerque, N.Mex., 1962).

Beck and Haase. *Historical Atlas of New Mexico.*

Beck, Warren A. *New Mexico: A History of Four Centuries* (Norman, Okla., 1962).

Colton, Ray C. *The Civil War in the Western Territories* (Norman, Okla., 1959).

Gibson, Arrell Morgan. *Oklahoma: A History of Five Centuries* (Norman, Okla., 1981).

Morris, John W., and Edwin C. McReynolds. *Historical Atlas of Oklahoma* (Norman, Okla., 1965).

Pool. *Historical Atlas of Texas.*

Shepherd, William R. *Historical Atlas* (Pikesville, Md., 1956). 8th ed.

Wesley, Edgar B. *Our United States: Its History in Maps* (Chicago, 1956).

Van Zandt, Franklin K. "Boundaries of the United States and the Several States." In *U.S. Geological Survey Bulletin 1212* (Washington, D.C., 1966).

41. Territorial Expansion II

Same as Map 40.

42. Territorial Expansion III

Same as Map 40.

43. European Settlement

Bancroft. *History of Arizona and New Mexico.*

Beck and Haase. *Historical Atlas of California.*

Brown, Ralph H. *Historical Geography of the United States* (New York, 1948).

Davis, James E. *Frontier America, 1800–1840* (Glendale, Calif., 1977).

Fehrenbach. *Lone Star.*

Fite, Gilbert C. *The Farmer's Frontier, 1865–1900* (New York, 1966).

Sale, Randall D., and Edwin D. Karn. *American Expansion: A Book of Maps* (Homewood, Ill., 1962).

44. The Mexican War, 1846–1848

Bauer, K. Jack. *The Mexican War: 1846–48* (New York, 1974).

Beck. *New Mexico.*

Beck and Haase. *Historical Atlas of California.*

———. *Historical Atlas of New Mexico.*

Esposito, Vincent J. *The West Point Atlas of American Wars* (New York, 1959). Vol. 1, 1689–1900.

Smith, Justin H. *The War with Mexico* (Gloucester, Mass., 1919, 1963). 2 vols.

Weems, John Edward. *To Conquer a Peace: The War Between the United States and Mexico* (College Station, Tex., 1987).

45. Battles of the Civil War

Alberts, Don E. "The Battle of Peralta," *New Mexico Historical Review*, Vol. 58, no. 4 (October, 1983): 369–79.

Beck. *New Mexico.*

Beck and Haase. *Historical Atlas of New Mexico.*

Colton, Ray C. *The Civil War in the Western Territories* (Norman, Okla., 1959).

Fehrenbach, T. R. *Lone Star: A History of Texas and the Texans* (New York, 1968).

Gibson, Arrell Morgan. *Oklahoma: A History of Five Centuries* (Norman, Okla., 1981).

Long, E. B. *The Civil War Day by Day* (New York, 1971).

Morris and McReynolds. *Historical Atlas of Oklahoma.*

U.S. Department of War. *The War of the Rebellion: A Compilation of the Official Records of the Union and Confederate Armies* (Washington, D.C., 1880–1901). Series I, various vols., including the atlas.

46. *Battles Between Indian Forces and the U.S. Army*

Billington and Ridge. *Westward Expansion.*

Dunn, J. P. *Massacres of the Mountain: A History of the Indian Wars of the Far West* (New York, 1886; reprint, 1969).

Leckie, William H. *The Military Conquest of the South Plains* (Norman, Okla., 1963).

Marshall, S. L. A. *Crimsoned Prairie: The Wars Between the United States and the Plains Indians During the Winning of the West* (New York, 1972).

Utley, Robert M. *Frontier Regulars: The United States Army and the Indian, 1866–1891* (New York, 1973).

———, and Wilcomb E. Washburn. *The American Heritage History of the Indian Wars* (New York, 1977).

47. *Cheyenne and Nez Percé Evasion Treks*

Allred, B. W. "Massacre of the Dull Knife Band." In *Great Western Indian Fights*, 295–306 (Lincoln, Nebr., 1960).

Beal, Merrill D. *"I Will Fight No More Forever": Chief Joseph and the Nez Percé War* (Seattle, 1963).

Brown, Mark H. *The Flight of the Nez Percé* (New York, 1967).

Chalmers, Harvey. *The Last Stand of the Nez Percé: Destruction of a People* (New York, 1962).

Grinnell, George Bird. *The Fighting Cheyennes* (Norman, Okla., 1955).

Haines, Francis. *The Nez Percé* (Norman, Okla., 1955).

Sandoz, Mari. *Cheyenne Autumn* (New York, 1953).

Utley. *Frontier Regulars.*

Wright, Peter M. "The Pursuit of Dull Knife from Fort Reno in 1878–1879," *Chronicles of Oklahoma*, Vol. 46, no. 2 (Summer, 1968): 141–54.

48. *Battle of the Little Big Horn*

Ambrose, Stephen E. *Crazy Horse and Custer: The Parallel Lives of Two American Warriors* (New York, 1986).

Connell, Evan S. *Son of the Morning Star: Custer and the Little Big Horn* (New York, 1985).

Godfrey, Edward S. *American History Illustrated*, Vol. 19, nos. 8–9 (December 1984, January 1985): 18–21, 44–49; 30–45.

Graham, W. A. *The Story of the Little Big Horn: Custer's Last Fight* (New York, 1959).

Hammer, Kenneth (ed.). *Custer in '76: Walter Camp's Notes on the Custer Fight* (Provo, Utah, 1976).

Lavender, David. *The American Heritage History of the Great West* (New York, 1965).

Miller, David Humphreys. *Custer's Fall* (New York, 1963).

Monaghan, Jay. *"Custer": The Life of General George Armstrong Custer* (Boston, 1959).

Parks, Michael W. "Echoes from the Custer Battlefield," *American History Illustrated*, Vol. 19, no. 8 (December 1984): 7, 10–17.

Rosenberg, Bruce. *Custer and the Epic of Defeat* (Harrisburg, Penn., 1974).

Sandoz, Mari. *The Battle of the Little Big Horn* (New York, 1966).

———. *Crazy Horse: The Strange Man of the Oglalas* (New York, 1942).

Scott, Douglas D., and Richard A. Fox, Jr. *Archeological Insights into The Custer Battle* (Norman, Okla., 1987).

Utley, Robert M. "The Battle of the Little Big Horn." In *Great Western Fights.*

———. *Custer and the Great Controversy: The Origin and Development of a Legend* (Los Angeles, 1962).

U.S. Geological Survey. *Crow Agency Quadrangle.* 1 : 24,000.

———. *Custer Battlefield.* 1″ = 2,000′ (1891).

Van de Water, Frederic F. *Glory-Hunter: A Life of General Custer* (New York, 1963).

Vestal, Stanley. *Sitting Bull, Champion of the Sioux* (Norman, Okla., 1957).

Wellman, Paul I. *Death on the Prairie.* Indian Wars of the West, Vol. I. (New York, 1963).

49. *Ghost Dance Religion*

Lowie, Robert H. *Indians of the Plains* (New York, 1963).

Marshall. *Crimsoned Prairie.*

Miller, David Humphrey. *Ghost Dance* (New York, 1959).

Mooney, James. *The Ghost-Dance Religion and the Sioux Outbreak of 1890* (Chicago, 1895).

Olson, James C. *Red Cloud and the Sioux Problem* (Lincoln, Nebr., 1965).

Utley, Robert M. *The Last Days of the Sioux Nation* (New Haven, 1963).

Vestal, Stanley. *New Sources of Indian History, 1850–1891: The Ghost Dance–The Prairie Sioux* (Norman, Okla., 1934).

———. *Sitting Bull, Champion of the Sioux* (Norman, Okla., 1956).

Wissler, Clark. *Indians of the United States* (New York, 1967).

50. *Tragedy at Wounded Knee, December 29, 1890*

Andrist, Ralph K. *The Long Death: The Last of the Plains Indians* (New York, 1964).

Metcalf, George. "Tragedy at Wounded Knee." In *Great Western Indian Fights.*

Marshall. *Crimsoned Prairie.*

Mooney. *Ghost Dance Religion*

U.S. Geological Survey. *Manderson and Wounded Knee.* 7½″ quadrangle maps (1967).

Utley. *Frontier Regulars.*

———. *Last Days of the Sioux Nation.*

51. Indian Lands

Chamberlin, J. E. *The Harrowing of Eden: White Attitudes Toward Native Americans* (New York, 1975).

Clawson, Marion. *The Land System of the United States* (Lincoln, Nebr., 1968).

Harris, Marshall. *Origins of the Land Tenure Systems in the United States* (Ames, Iowa: 1953).

Hill, Edward E. *The Office of Indian Affairs, 1824–1880: Historical Sketches* (New York, 1974).

Josephy, Alvin M., Jr. (ed.). *The American Heritage Book of Indians* (New York, 1961).

Kickingbird, Kirke, and Karen Ducheneaux. *One Hundred Million Acres* (New York, 1973).

Kinney, Jay P. *A Continent Lost—A Civilization Won: Indian Land Tenure in America* (Baltimore, 1937).

Sutton, Imre. *Indian Land Tenure: Bibliographical Essay and a Guide to the Literature* (New York, 1975).

Vecsey, Christopher, and Robert W. Venables (eds.). *American Indian Environments: Ecological Issues in Native American History* (Syracuse, N.Y., 1980).

52. Indian Judicial Land Areas

Hilliard, Sam B. "Indian Land Cessions," *Annals of the Association of American Geographers,* Vol. 62, no. 2 (June, 1972), map supplement.

———. "Land Cessions West of the Mississippi," *Journal of the West,* Vol. 3, no. 3 (July, 1971).

Kickingbird and Ducheneaux. *One Hundred Million Acres.*

Sutton. *Indian Land Tenure.*

Sutton, Imre (ed.). *Irredeemable America: The Indian's Estate and Land Claims* (Albuquerque, N.Mex., 1985).

U.S. Indian Claims Commission. *Final Report* (Washington, D.C., 1978). With map of *Indian Land Acres Judicially Established,* 1978.

53. Principal Meridians and Base Lines Governing Public Land Surveys

Billington and Ridge. *Westward Expansion: A History of the American Frontier.*

Carstensen, Vernon (ed.). *The Public Lands: Studies in the History of the Public Domain* (Madison, Wis., 1963).

Manual of Instructions for the Survey of the Public Lands of the United States, 1947 (Washington, D.C., 1947).

54. Gold and Silver Bonanzas

Billington and Ridge. *Westward Expansion.*

Caughey. John W. *Gold in the Cornerstone* (Berkeley, Calif., 1948).

Greever, William S. *The Bonanza West: The Story of the Western Mining Rushes* (Norman, Okla., 1963).

Lewis, Marvin (ed.). *The Mining Frontier* (Norman, Okla., 1967).

Paul, Rodman Wilson. *Mining Frontiers in the Far West, 1848–1880* (New York, 1963).

Paxon, F. L. *The Last American Frontier* (New York, 1924).

Wallace, Robert. *The Miners* (Alexandria, Va., 1976).

Young, Otis E., Jr. *Western Mining: An Informal Account of Precious-Metals Prospecting, Placering, Lode Mining, and Milling on the American Frontier from Spanish Times to 1893* (Norman, Okla., 1970).

55. Stagecoach Routes

Austerman. *Sharps Rifles and Spanish Mules.*

Bliss, Edward. "Denver to Salt Lake By Overland Stage," *Colorado Magazine,* Vol. 8, no. 5 (September, 1931): 190–97.

Briggs, Harold E. "Early Freight and Stage Lines in Dakota," *North Dakota Historical Quarterly,* Vol. 3, no. 4 (July, 1929): 229–61.

Danker, Donald F. "The Influence of Transportation upon Nebraska Territory," *Nebraska History,* Vol. 47, no. 2 (June, 1966): 187–208.

"Dodge City, Camp Supply, Fort Elliott Stage Line." Manuscript in Kansas Historical Society, Topeka.

Frederick, J. V. *Ben Holladay, The Stagecoach King* (Glendale, Calif., 1940).

Gendler, Carol. "Territorial Omaha as a Staging and Freighting Center," *Nebraska History,* Vol. 49, no. 2 (Summer 1968): 103–20.

Hafen, Leroy R. "Early Mail Service to Colorado," *Colorado Magazine,* Vol. 2, no. 1 (January, 1925): 23–32.

Hoffman, H. Wilbur. *Sagas of Old Western Travel and Transport* (San Diego, Calif., 1980).

Jackson, W. Turrentine. *Wells Fargo in Colorado Territory.* Colorado Historical Society Monograph Series, No. 1. (Denver, 1982).

———. "Wells Fargo & Co.: Into the Inland Empire and Idaho Territory," *Idaho Yesterdays,* Vol. 25, no. 4 (Winter, 1982): 2–19.

———. "Wells Fargo & Co. in Idaho Territory: Old and New Routes, 1865," *Idaho Yesterdays,* Vol. 26, no. 1 (Spring, 1982): 2–23.

———. "Wells Fargo & Co. in Idaho Territory: to the 'Grand Consolidation' of 1866," *Idaho Yesterdays,* Vol. 26, no. 2 (Summer, 1982): 9–19.

———. "Wells Fargo & Co. in Idaho Territory: The Railroads and the Demise of Staging," *Idaho Yesterdays,* Vol. 26, no. 4 (Winter, 1983): 9–17.

———. *Wells Fargo Stagecoaching in Montana Territory* (Helena, Mont., 1979).

———. "Wells Fargo Staging over the Sierra," *California Historical Society Quarterly,* Vol. 49, no. 2 (June, 1970): 99–133.

Jones, Larry R. "Staging to the South Boise Mines," *Idaho Yesterdays,* Vol. 29, no. 2 (Summer, 1985).

Mantor, Lyle E. "Stage Coach & Freighter Days at Fort Kearny," *Nebraska History,* Vol. 29, no. 4 (December, 1948): 324–38.

McIntosh, Clarence F. "The Chico and Red Bluff Route: State Lines from Southern Idaho to the Sacramento Valley, 1865–1867," *Idaho Yesterdays,* Vol. 6, no. 3 (Fall, 1962): 12–19.

Root, George A. "Notes Gathered by Mr. Root on Various Stage Lines of Kansas." Manuscript in Kansas Historical Society, Topeka.

Sanford, Albert B. "Mountain Staging in Colorado," *Colorado Magazine,* Vol. 9, no. 2 (March, 1932): 66–74.

Scott, Harvey, W. *History of the Oregon Country* (Cambridge, Mass., 1924). Vol. III.

Taylor, Morris F. "The Barlow and Sanderson Stage Lines in Colorado, 1872–1884," *Colorado Magazine,* Vol. 50, no. 2 (Spring, 1973): 142–62.

Thonhoff, Robert H. *San Antonio Stage Lines, 1847–1881* (El Paso, Tex., 1971).

Winther, Oscar Osburn. "California Stage Company in Oregon," *Oregon Historical Quarterly,* Vol. 35, no. 2 (June, 1934): 131–38.

———. "Inland Transportation and Communication in Washington, 1844–1859," *Pacific Northwest Quarterly,* Vol. 30, no. 4 (October, 1939): 371–86.

———. *The Old Oregon Country: A History of Frontier Trade, Transportation and Travel* (Bloomington, Ind., 1950).

———. *The Transportation Frontier: Trans-Mississippi West, 1865–1890* (New York, 1964).

———. *Via Western Express and Stagecoach* (Stanford, Calif., 1945).

56. Railroads I: Union Pacific

Athearn, Robert G. *Union Pacific Country* (New York, 1971).

Martin, Albro. "Union Pacific Railroad." In Lamar, *Reader's Encyclopedia of the American West,* 1204–1206.

Riegel, Robert Edgar. *The Story of The Western Railroads* (Lincoln, Nebr., 1926).

Union Pacific Railroad. *Map of the United States* (1971).

Yost, Nellie Snyder. "The Union Pacific." In *Trails of the Iron Horse,* 19–34. Ed. Don Russell (Garden City, N.Y., 1975).

For a more complete bibliography the reader should see Don L. Hofsommer (ed.). *Railroads in the West* (Manhattan, Kans., 1978).

57. Railroads II: Atchison, Topeka & Santa Fe

Atchison, Topeka and Santa Fe. Map (Santa Fe, N.Mex., 1969).

Bryant, Keith L., Jr. *History of the Atchison, Topeka and Santa Fe Railway* (New York, 1974).

Duke, Donald. "The Old Santa Fe Trail Becomes a Steel Highway." In Russell, *Trails of the Iron Horse,* 177–93.

Duke, Donald, and Stan Kistler. *Santa Fe: Steel Rails Through California* (San Marino, Calif., 1963).

Marshall, James. *Santa Fe: The Railroad That Built an Empire* (New York, 1945).

Martin, Albro. "Atchison, Topeka and Santa Fe Railroad." In Lamar, *Reader's Encyclopedia of the American West,* 61–62.

Waters, Lawrence L. *Steel Trails to Santa Fe* (Lawrence, Kans., 1950).

Wilkins, Thurman. *Thomas Moran, Artist of the Mountains* (Norman, Okla., 1966).

58. Railroads III: Southern Pacific

Ballard, Todhunter. "Building the Impossible." In Russell, *Trails of the Iron Horse,* 46–62.

Daggett, Stuart. *Chapters on the History of the Southern Pacific* (New York, 1922; reprint, 1966).

Hofsommer, Don, *The Southern Pacific, 1901–1985* (College Station, Tex.: 1986).

Martin, Albro. "Southern Pacific Railroads." In Lamar, *Reader's Encyclopedia of the American West,* 1131–32.

Southern Pacific Railroad. *Southern Pacific Cotton Belt.* Map (1970).

Wheeler, Keith. *The Railroaders.* (New York, 1973).

Wilson, Neill C., and Frank J. Taylor. *Southern Pacific: The Roaring Story of a Fighting Railroad* (New York, 1952).

59. Railroads IV: Burlington Northern

Burlington Northern Railroad. *Burlington Northern.* Map of the United States (1971).

Clinch, Thomas A. "The Northern Pacific Railroad and Montana's Mineral Lands," *Pacific Historical Review,* Vol. 34 (1965): 323–35.

Hall, Edith Thompson. "Everywhere West: The Burlington." In Russell, *Trails of the Iron Horse,* 35–45.

Lewis, Sol H. "A History of the Railroads in Washington," *Washington Historical Quarterly,* Vol. 3 (1912): 186–97.

Martin, Albro. "Burlington Northern Railroad." In Lamar, *Reader's Encyclopedia of the American West,* 139–41.

Overton, Richard C. *Burlington Route: A History of the Burlington Lines* (New York, 1965).

———. *Burlington West: A Colonization History of the Burlington Railroad* (Cambridge, Mass., 1941).

Smalley, Eugene Virgil. *History of the Northern Pacific Railroad* (New York, 1883; reprint, 1975).

Stevens, John F. "Great Northern Railway," *Washington Historical Quarterly,* Vol. 20 (1929): 111–13.

Turner, William O. "Across the Top: Building the Northern Roads." In Russell, *Trails of the Iron Horse,* 90–112.

60. Railroads V: Denver & Rio Grande Western and Western Pacific

Athearn, Robert G. *Rebel of the Rockies: A History of the Denver and Rio Grande Western Railroad* (New Haven, Conn., 1962).

Borneman, Walter R. "The Race for the Gunnison Country: Bold Rivalry of Mountain Railroads to Conquer Colorado

Rockies," *American West,* Vol. 21, no. 1 (January–February, 1984): 70–77.

DeNevi, Don. *The Western Pacific* (Seattle, 1978).

Frazee, Steve. "The Baby Road." In Russell, *Trails of the Iron Horse,* 113–31.

Martin, Albro. "Denver and Rio Grande Western Railroads." In Lamar, *Reader's Encyclopedia of the American West,* 298–99.

61. States and Their Capitals

Beck and Haase. *Historical Atlas of California.*

Lamar, Howard Roberts. *Dakota Territory, 1861–1889* (New Haven, Conn., 1956).

Malone, Michael P., and Richard B. Roeder. *Montana: A History of Two Centuries* (Seattle, 1976).

Ostrander, Gilman M. *Nevada: The Great Rotten Borough 1859–1964* (New York, 1966).

Peirce, Neal R. *The Mountain States of America* (New York, 1972).

Webb, Walter Prescott. "The American West: Perpetual Mirage," *Harper's,* Vol. 214 (May 1957): 25–31.

62. Counties

Arizona Legislature, SB 1267 (1983).

Arizona Republic (Phoenix), November 4, 1982.

Duncombe, Herbert Sydney. *County Government in America* (Washington, D.C., 1966).

Thomas, Benjamin E. "The Historical Geography of Idaho Counties," *Idaho Historical Quarterly,* Vol. 50 (1949): 186–204.

USGS. *National Atlas.*

Wager, Paul. *County Government Across the Nation* (Chapel Hill, N.Car., 1950).

63. Agricultural Regions

Brown, Ralph H. *Historical Geography of the United States* (New York, 1948).

U.S. Department of Agriculture. *Crops in Peace and War: Yearbook of Agriculture, 1950–1951* (81st Cong., 2d sess., House Doc. 691).

Fite, Gilbert C. *The Farmer's Frontier, 1865–1900* (New York, 1966).

Hargreaves, Mary Wilma M. *Dry Farming in the Northern Great Plains* (Cambridge, Mass., 1957).

Shannon, Fred A. *The Farmer's Last Frontier* (New York, 1966).

Shideler, James H. (ed.). *Agriculture in the Development of the Far West* (Washington, D.C., 1975).

Watson. *North America.*

64. Field Crops I

Bryant. *History of the Atchison, Topeka and Santa Fe Railway.*

U.S. Department of Agriculture. *Crops in Peace and War.*

Fite. *Farmer's Frontier.*

Hardeman, Nicolas P. *Shucks, Shocks, and Hominy Blocks:*

Corn as a Way of Life in Pioneer America (Baton Rouge, La., 1981).

Hargreaves. *Dry Farming.*

Jelinek, Lawrence J. *Harvest Empire: A History of California Agriculture* (San Francisco, 1979).

Shideler. *Agriculture.*

65. Field Crops II

Beck and Haase. *Historical Atlas of California.*

U.S. Department of Agriculture, *Crops in Peace and War.*

Fite. *Farmer's Frontier.*

Highsmith, Richard M., and Jon M. Leverenz. *Atlas of the Pacific Northwest: Resources and Development* (Corvallis, Ore., 1968).

Jelinek. *Harvest Empire.*

Shideler. *Agriculture.*

66. Fruits and Nuts

Beck and Haase. *Historical Atlas of California.*

U.S. Department of Agriculture. *Crops in Peace and War.*

Cullinan, F. P. "Plums." In *United States Department of Agriculture Yearbook* (Washington, D.C., 1937), 702–23.

Fite. *Farmer's Frontier.*

Highsmith and Leverenz. *Atlas of the Pacific Northwest.*

Jelinek. *Harvest Empire.*

Paterson, J. H. *North America: A Geography of Canada and the United States* (New York, 1975).

67. Livestock and Poultry

Clemen, Rudolf Alexander. *The American Livestock and Meat Industry* (New York, 1923).

Fletcher, Robert H. *Free Grass to Fences: The Montana Cattle Range Story* (New York, 1960).

Gressley, Gene M. *Bankers and Cattlemen* (New York, 1966).

Marsden, Stanley J., and J. Holmes Martin. *Turkey Management* (Danville, Ill., 1939).

Schlebecker, John T. *Cattle Raising on the Plains, 1900–1961* (Lincoln, Nebr., 1963).

Smith, Page, and Charles Daniel. *The Chicken Book* (Boston, 1975).

Towne, Charles Wayland, and Edward Norris Wentworth. *Shepherd's Empire* (Norman, Okla., 1946).

Walsh, Margaret. *The Rise of the Midwestern Meat Packing Industry* (Lexington, Ky., 1982).

Wood, Charles L. *The Kansas Beef Industry* (Lawrence, Kans., 1980).

68. Major Mineral Lodes

Same as Map 54.

69. Petroleum Fuels

Landes, Kenneth K. *Petroleum Geology of the United States* (New York, 1970).

Rister, Carl Coke. *Oil: Titan of the Southwest* (Norman, Okla., 1949).

Terra Graphics. *Oil and Gas Production of the United States.* Map (Denver, 1977).

Williamson, Harold F., and Arnold R. Daum. *The American Petroleum Industry* (Evanston, Ill., 1959). 2 vols.

70. Catastrophic Natural Events

Beck and Haase. *Historical Atlas of California.*

Hoyt, William G., and Walter B. Langbein. *Floods* (Princeton, 1955).

Iacopi, Robert. *Earthquake Country* (Menlo Park, Calif., 1971).

Salt Lake Tribune. *Spirit of Survival: Utah Floods, 1983* (Indianapolis, 1983).

USGS. *National Atlas.*

U.S. National Oceanic and Atmospheric Administration. *Some Devastating North Atlantic Hurricanes of the 20th Century* (Washington, D.C., 1977).

Ward. *Climates of the United States.*

Walker, Bryce. *Earthquake* (Chicago, 1982).

Whittow, John. *Disasters: The Anatomy of Environmental Hazards* (Athens, Ga., 1979).

71. The Great Salt Lake, Utah

Angler, Natalie. "Preserving the Great Salt Lake," *Time,* August 13, 1984, p. 86.

Greer, Deon C., et al. *Atlas of Utah* (Provo, Utah, 1981).

Miller, David E. "The Great Salt Lake." In *The Valley of the Great Salt Lake* (Salt Lake City, 1967).

Morgan, Dale L. *The Great Salt Lake* (Indianapolis, 1947).

Salt Lake Tribune. *Spirit of Survival.*

72. Mount St. Helens, Washington, May 18, 1980

Alpern, Avid M., and Pamela Abramson. "The Convulsion of St. Helens," *Newsweek,* Vol. 95 (June 2, 1980): 22–31.

Alpha, Tau Rho; James G. Moore; James M. Morley; and David R. Jones. "Physiographic Diagrams of Mount St. Helens, Washington, Showing Changes in Its Summit Crater, Summer, 1980," *USGS Miscellaneous Field Studies, Map MF-1279* (Reston, Va., 1981).

Farmer, Judith; Julie Harris, and Richard Carson. *Mt. St. Helens Volcanic Weather Book* (Portland, Ore., 1980).

Findley, Rowe. "Mount St. Helens Aftermath," *National Geographic,* Vol. 160, no. 6 (December, 1981): 710–33.

———. "St. Helens with a Death Wish," *National Geographic,* Vol. 159, no. 1 (January, 1981): 3–33.

"God I Want to Live!" *Time,* Vol. 115 (June 2, 1980): 26–35.

Harnly, Caroline D., and David A. Tyckoson. *Mount St. Helens: An Annotated Bibliography* (Metuchen, N.J., 1984).

Kelso, Linda. *Mount St. Helens Volcano* (Beaverton, Ore., 1980).

Lipman, Peter W., and Donal R. Ullineaux (eds.). *The 1980*

Eruptions of Mount St. Helens, Washington (Washington, D.C., 1981).

Mark Hurd Aerial Surveys. *Mount St. Helens* (Minneapolis, n.d.).

National Aeronautics and Space Administration. *Mount St. Helens Eruptions of 1980: Atmospheric Effects and Potential Climatic Impact* (Washington, D.C., 1982).

Pardo, Richard. "Rehabilitating St. Helen's" *American Forests,* November, 1980, pp. 30–63.

Robert, Rich. "Mt. St. Helens: Destruction Defies Imagination," *Los Angeles Times,* July 15, 1983, part III, pp. 18, 20.

Sedell, James R.; Jerry F. Franklin; and Frederick J. Swanson. "Out of the Ash," *American Forests,* October, 1980, pp. 26–68.

U.S. Forest Service. *Mount St. Helens.* Information Pamphlet (Washington, D.C., 1980), 299–331.

Williams, Chuck. *Mount St. Helens: A Changing Landscape* (Portland, Ore., 1980).

73. Federal Lands

Carstensen, Vernon (ed.). *The Public Lands: Studies in the History of the Public Domain* (Madison, Wis., 1962).

Clawson, Marion. *Uncle Sam's Acres* (New York, 1951).

Clawson, Marion, and Burnell Held. *The Federal Lands: Their Use and Management* (Lincoln, Nebr., 1957).

Endicott, William. "Sagebrush Revolt Is On. Federal Land is the Prize," *Los Angeles Times* (August 5, 1979).

Francis, John G., and Richard Ganzel (ed.). *Western Public Lands: The Management of Natural Resources in a Time of Declining Federalism* (Totowa, N.J., 1984).

Gates, Paul Wallace (ed.). *Public Land Policies: Management and Disposal* (New York, 1979).

Nash, Roderick. *Wilderness and the American Mind* (New Haven, Conn., 1982).

New Mexico State Land Office. *Land Resources of New Mexico Report* (Santa Fe, 1959).

Robbins, Roy M. *Our Landed Heritage: The Public Domain, 1776–1970* (Lincoln, Nebr., 1976).

Sutton, Imre. "Indian Land Rights and the Sagebrush Rebellion," *Geographical Review,* Vol. 72, no. 3 (July, 1982): 357–59.

USGS. "Federal Lands," *National Atlas.*

Willwerth, James. "Stalagmites and Stunning Vistas: Great Basin is Nevada's Majestic New National Park," *Time* (August 24, 1987), p. 46.

Wyant, William K. *Westward in Eden: The Public Lands and the Conservation Movement* (Berkeley, Calif., 1982).

74. Major Army Installations: World War II and After

Defense Mapping Agency Topographic Center. *Map: Major Army, Navy and Air Force Installations in the United States.* (February, 1974).

Fine, Lenore, and Jesse A. Remington. *The Corps of En-*

gineers: Construction in the United States (Washington, D.C., 1972).

Scanlon, Tom (ed.). *Army Times: Guide to Army Posts* (Harrisburg, Penn., 1963).

75. Major Air Force Installations: World War II and After

Craven, Weley Frank, and James Lea Cate. *The Army Air Forces in World War II: Men and Planes* (Chicago, 1955). Vol. VI.

Defense Mapping Agency Topographic Center. *Map: Major Army, Navy and Air Force Installations.*

"U.S. Army and Navy Directory of Airfields," February 1, 1944 (Air Force Museum, Dayton, Ohio).

76. Major Naval and Marine Installations: World War II and After

"Locations of Naval Shore Establishments as of 15 February, 1944," Navy Department, Bureau of Yards and Docks.

Defense Mapping Agency Topographic Center. *Map: Major Army, Navy and Air Force Installations.*

Various maps showing Marine, Navy, and Coast Guard installations in Bureau of Yards and Docks, Port Hueneme Naval Center.

U.S. Department of the Navy, Bureau of Yards and Docks. *Building the Navy's Bases in World War II.* (Washington, D.C., 1947). 2 vols.

77. Japanese-American Internment Camps During World War II

Beck, Warren A., and David A. Williams. *California: A History of the Golden State* (Garden City, N.Y.: 1972).

U.S. Senate, Committee on Naval Affairs. *Report on the Subcommittee on Japanese War Relocation Centers to the Committee on Naval Affairs, May 7, 1943* (Washington, D.C., 1943).

Daniels, Roger. *Concentration Camps USA: Japanese-Americans and World War II* (New York, 1971).

Girdner, Audrie, and Anne Loftis. *The Great Betrayal: The Evacuation of the Japanese-Americans During World War II* (New York, 1969).

Kitano, Harry H. L. *Japanese-Americans: The Evolution of a Subculture* (New York, 1969).

78. World War II POW Camps

Byrd, Martha H. "Captured by the Americans," *American History Illustrated,* February, 1977, pp. 24–35.

Krammer, Arnold. *Nazi Prisoners of War in America* (New York, 1979).

Mason, John Brown. "German Prisoners of War in the United States," *American Journal of International Law,* April, 1945, pp. 198–215.

Mazuan, George T., and Nancy Walker. "Restricted Areas: German Prisoner-of-War Camps in Western New York, 1944–1946," *New York History,* January, 1978.

Pluth, Edward J. "The Administration and Operation of German Prisoners of War Camps in the United States During World War II," Ph.D. dis., Ball State University, 1970.

INDEX

Numbers in this index refer to map numbers; there are no page numbers. *Italic* numbers mean that the item will be found on the map.

Abilene (Kans.): 30, *30, 31*
Absarok Mountains: 1
Acoma (N. Mex.): *15, 16*
Adams-Onís Treaty: 40
Agostadero, de: 23
Aguayo, Marqués de: 17, *17*
Alarcón, Martin de: 17, *17*
Albuquerque (N. Mex.): *30, 38*
Aleut Indians: 24
Alexis, Grand Duke: 10
Allande, Pedro de: 19, *19*
Anza, Juan Bautista de: 19, *19*
Apache Indians: 8, *8,* 18, 46
Apples: 66, *66*
Arapaho Indians: 8, *9,* 46
Arikara Indians: 8, *8*
Arkansas River: 40
Arkansas Territory: 40
Army, U.S.: 46, *46*
Army of the West: 44, *44*
Ash forests: *7*
Ashley, William H.: 26, 28, *28*
Assiniboin Indians: *8*
Astor, John Jacob: 25
Astoria (Oreg.): 25, *25, 38*
Atlantic & Pacific Railroad: 57
Atomic Energy Commission: 73, *73*
Austin, Moses: 21
Austin, Stephen F.: 20, *21*
Austin (Tex.): *30,* 38
Ayala, Manuel de: 19, *19*

Bakersfield (Calif.): *31*
Balli, Juan José: 22
Balli, Nicholas: 22
Bancroft, Hubert H.: 61
Banning Line: *34*
Banning, Phineas: 34
Bannock Indians: 8, *8,* 46
Barley: 64, *64*
Baron of Arizona: 20
Barrett, Col. Theodore H.: 45
Base lines: 53, *53*
Basin and range provinces: 1, 2, *2*
Basques: 31
Baylor, Col. John R.: 41, *41,* 45
Beales, Dr. John Charles: 21
Bear Lake: 26, *26*
Bearpaw Mountains: 1, 47, *47*
Bears, grizzly: 12, *12*
Beaver (Utah): *39*
Beavers: 13, *13,* 24
Becknell, William: 29
Bell, Capt. John R.: 25, *25*
Benson (Ariz.): 39
Benteen, Capt. Frederick W.: 48, *48*
Benton, Jessie: 36
Benton, Senator Thomas Hart: 36
Bent's Fort (Colo.): 34, *34,* 36, *36,* 38, *38*

Bidwell, John: 6
Big Hole (Mont.): 47, *47*
Big Horn Mountains: 1
Billington, Ray Allen: 68
Birch, James E.: 34, 55
Bisbee (Ariz.): 39
Bismarck, (N. Dak.): *10*
Black Canyon: 1
Blackfoot Indians: 8, *9*
Black Hills: 1, 17, 48, 54
Bodega Bay: 7
Boise (Idaho): *31, 34*
Bonilla, Francisco Leyva de: 15
Borica, Diego de: 19, *19*
Bosque, Fernando del: 16, *16*
Bosque Redondo: 29, *29*
Bozeman Trail: *38*
Brazito, Battle of: 44, *44*
Bridgeport (Nebr.): *34*
Bridger Pass: 1
Brownsville (Tex.): 45, *45*
Buenaventura River: 36
Buena Vista, Battle of: 44, *44*
Buenavista (Mex.): 18, *18*
Buena Vista Lake: 24
Buffalo: 9, 10, *10*
Bureau of Land Management: 73, *73*
Burlington Route: 59, *59*
Burnet, David G.: 21, *21*
Bustíllo y Zevallos, Juan de: 17, *17*
Butterfield Overland Mail: 34, *34*

Caballeria: 23
Cabazos, Jose Narciso: 22
Cabrillo, Juan Rodriguez: 15, *15*
Caddo Indians: *8*
Cahuenga (Calif.): 44, *44*
Cajon Pass: 39
Calahorra y Saenz, Father José de: 17, *17*
Caldwell (Kans.): 30, *30*
California: *41,* 43, *61*
California Column: 45
California Line: 34, *34*
California Trail: 33, *39*
Camargo: *17*
Camas Meadow: 46, 47, *47*
Cameron, John: 21, *21*
Camp Funston at Fort Riley: 74
Camp Lewis (Wash.): 74
Camp Supply (Okla.): 47, *47*
Camp Travis at Fort Sam Houston: 74
Canby, Col. E. R. S.: 45
Canizares, José: 19, *19*
Cañon del Rescate: 29, *29*
Canton (China): 25
Canyon Creek: 47, *47*
Carleton, Gen. James Henry: 45
Carson, Christopher "Kit": 36
Carson City (Nev.): *34, 35*

Carson Valley (Nev.): 39
Casa Grande (Ariz.): *16*
Cascade Mountains: 2, *2*
Cascade Range: 1
Casper (Wyo.); *34, 35*
Castillo, Captain Diego del: 16
Cattle: 67, *67*
Caughey, John Walton: 68
Cavelier, Robert, Sieur de la Salle: 16, *16*
Caving Banks: 45, *45*
Cazorla, Luis: 19, *19*
Cedar City (Utah): 39, *39*
Central Lowland: 2, *2*
Central Overland Line: 34, *34*
Central Overland Pony Express: *35*
Central Pacific: 56
Central Valley: 63
Cermenho, Sebastian Rodríguez: 15, *15*
Chamuscado, Captain Francisco Sanchez: 15, *15*
Chaparral: 7, *7*
Cherokee Indians: 45, *51*
Cherokee Trail: *34*
Cheyenne Indians: 8, *9,* 46
Chickasaw Indians: 45
Chickens: 67, *67*
Chief Joseph: 47
Chihuahua (Mex.): 18, *18,* 29, *29,* 44, *44*
Chihuahuan Desert: 6
Chihuahuan Road: 29, *29*
Chinese: 58
Chino Rancho: 44, *44*
Chinook Winds: 4
Chisholm, Jesse: 30
Chisholm Trail: 30, *30*
Choctaw Indians: 45
Chustenahlah: 45, *45*
Cibola, Seven Cities of: 15, *15*
Cicuyé (N. Mex.): 15, *15*
Civilian Conservation Corps: 78
Clark, William: 11, 24
Clearwater (Idaho): 47, *47*
Coahuiltec Indians: 8, *8*
Coastal Plain: *2*
Cochetopa Pass: 1, 36
Cody, William F.: 10
Colonia Dublán: 39
Colonia Juarez: 39
Colorado: 42, *42,* 54
Colorado River: 1
Colter, John: 24, *24*
Columbia Basin: 25
Columbia Plateaus: 1, 2, *2,* 63
Columbia River: 1, 8
Comanche Indians: 8, *9,* 18, 46
Comancheros: 29
Commerce Trails: 29, *29*
Compromise of 1850: 41, *41*

Comstock Lode: 54
Cooke, Jay: 59
Cooke, Capt. Philip St. George: 38, 44, *44*
Condors: 14, *14*
Confederate Territory of Arizona: 41, *41*, 45
Continental Divide: 1, 27, 32
Convention of 1818: 40
Cordero, Antonio: 19, *19*
Corn: 63, 64, *64*
Coronado, Francisco Vásquez de: 15, *15*
Cotton: 65, *65*
Cottonwood: *7*
Cottonwood Creek: 47, *47*
Council Bluffs (Iowa): 25, *25*, 39
Counties: 62, *62*
Court of Private Land Claims: 21
Cow Island: 47, *47*
Coyotes: 12
Craven, Avery: 61
Creek Indians: 45
Crespe, José Antonio: 21
Crocker, Charles: 58
Croix, Teodoro de: 18, *18*
Crook, Gen. George: 48
Crow Indians: *8, 9*, 46, *49, 51, 52*
Custer, Col. George Armstrong: 10, 48
Cyclonic storms: 5

Dakota Territory: 51
Dallas (Tex.): *30*, 38, *38*
Death Valley: 5, *33*
Deer, black-tailed: 11, *11*
Deer, mule: 11, *11*
Deer, white-tailed: 11, *11*
Deer Lodge: *27*
d'Eglise, Jacques: 19, *19*
Delano, Columbus: 10
Del Norte: *17, 19*
Del Rio: 23, *23*
Denver (Colo.): *10, 30, 34*
Denver & Rio Grande Railroad: 57, 60, *60*
Deschutes River: 36
Deseret, State of: 39
DeWitt, Green: 21, *21*
Diamond City (Mont.): *35*
Dickson, Joseph: 24, *24*
Dimmit County: 23, *23*
Dodge, Grenville M.: 56
Dodge City (Kans.): *30, 30, 31, 34*
Dominguez Rancho: 44, *44*
Doniphan, Col. Alexander William: 44, *44*
Donner, George: 33
Donner, Jacob: 33
Donner Lake: 33, *33*
Donner Party: 33, *33*
Donner Pass: 36
Dove Creek: 45, *45*
Drake, Sir Francis: 15, *15*
Drouillard, George: 24, *24*
Drum Creek: 45, *45*
Dull Knife, Chief: 47, *47*
Durant, Will: 70

Eagle Pass: 23, *23*
Earthquakes: 70, *70*
Edwards Plateau: 63
Eggs: 67
El Camino Real: 29, *29*
El Embrudo (N. Mex.): 44, *44*
Elk, Nelson: *11*
Elk, Roosevelt: 11, *11*
Elk, Tule: 11, *11*
Ellsworth (Kans.): 30, *30*
Elm forests: *7*
El Pasaje (Mex.): 18, *18*
El Paso (Tex.): 16, *17*, 18, *18, 19, 34*
Empresario Grants: *20*, 21, *21*
Escalante, Fray Silvestre Vélez de: 19, *19*, 29
Escandón, Colonel José de: 22
Eugene (Oreg.): *34*
Executive Order 9066: 77
Exeter, Richard: 21, *21*

Fages, Pedro: 17, *17*
Farming, dry: 63
Ferrelo, Bartolomé: 15, *15*
Filisola, General Vicente: 21, *21*
Flathead House: 27, *27*
Flathead Indians: *8, 9*
Floods: 70, *70*
Fort Abercrombie: 35, *35*
Fort Abraham Lincoln: 48
Fort Bellingham: *38*
Fort Benton: *35, 38*, 38
Fort Berthold: 35
Fort Boise: *32*, 36, *36*
Fort Bonneville: *26*
Fort Bridger: *32, 32*, 33, *33*, 34, 35, *35*, 38, *39*, 39
Fort Buford: *35*
Fort Churchill: *35*
Fort Collins: *31*
Fort Ellis: *38*, 48
Fort Esperanza: 45, *45*
Fort Fetterman: *38*, 48
Fort Hall: 32, *32, 33*, 34, *36, 38, 39*, 39
Fort Hawley: *35*, 35
Fort Henry: *24*, 24
Fort Howie: 35
Fort Kearny: *32*, 32, 34, *35*, 35
Fort Keogh: *47*, 47
Fort Laramie: *32*, 32, 33, 34, 35, 36, 38, 39, *39*, 51
Fort Leavenworth: *38*
Fort Lyon: *34*
Fort Mandan: *19*
Fort Manuel: 24, *24*
Fort Nez Percés: 27, *27*
Fort Peck: *35*
Fort Pierre: *38*
Fort Randall: *38*
Fort Ransom: *35*
Fort Reno: *38*
Fort Riley: 74
Fort Robinson: 47, *47*

Fort Ruby (Nev.): 37
Fort St. Louis: 16, *16*
Fort St. Vrain: 36
Fort Sedgewick: *38*
Fort C. F. Smith: *38*
Fort Smith: 34, *34, 38*, 38
Fort Stevenson: 35
Fort Stockton: *38*
Fort Sumner: 30, *30*
Fort Thompson: *38*
Fort Totten: *35*
Fort Uintah: 36, *36*
Fort Union: 45
Fort Vancouver: 27, 28, *32, 36*
Fort Worth: 10, 30, *30*
Fort Yuma: 37, *37*
Forsyth, Col. James W.: 50
Freeman, Thomas: 24
Frémont, Capt. John C.: *36*, 44, *44*
Fremont Peak: 36
Fresno County (Calif.): 63
Front Range: 1

Gadsden Purchase: 21, 41, *41*
Gaignard, J.: 19, *19*
Gali, Francisco: 15, *15*
Galveston (Tex.): 70
Galveston Bay and Texas Land Company: 21
Gard, Wayne: 10
Gas, natural: 69, *69*
Gavilan Peak: 36
General Land Office: 20
Geneva Convention: 78
Ghost Dance: 49, *49*
Gibbon, Col. John: 48
Gibbons Pass: 27
Gila Mountains: *2*
Gila River: 1, 41
Gillespie, Lt. Archibald: 36
Glass, Anthony: 24, *24*
Glorieta Pass: 44, 45, *45*
Goat, Rocky Mountain: 12, *12*
Goetzmann, William: 38
Gold: 54, *54*
Goleta (Calif.): 77
Goodnight, Charles: 30
Goodnight Trail: 30, *30*
Gould, George: 60
Gould, Jay: 56
Grand Canyon: 1
Grants Pass (Oreg.): *38*
Grapefruit: 66
Grapes: 66, *66*
Grasshoppers: 70
Great American Desert: 2, 6, 25, 51
Great Basin: 1, 8, 19
Great Basin Desert: *6*
Great Central Valley: 1, 23
Great Falls (Mont.): *31*
Great Northern: 59
Great Plains: 1, 2, *2*, 6, *6*, 8, *8*, 11, 46, 63
Great Salt Desert: 1, *33*

Great Salt Lake: 1, 33, 36, 71
Great Salt Lake Rendezvous: *26*
Greeley (Colo.): *34*
Green River: 26, *26*, 36
Greer County: 41, *41*
Gros Ventre Indians: *8*
Guadalupe Hidalgo, Treaty of: 22, 41, 44
Gulf Coast (of Texas): 69
Gulf of Mexico: 3, 40
Gulf Plain: 1
Gunnison River: 1, 36
Gwin, Senator William: 35

Hafen, Leroy: 29
Hailstorms: 70
Ham's Fork: *26*
Hancock, Forest: 24, *24*
Hardeman, Nicolas: 64
Hardwood forests: *7*
Harriman, Edward H.: 58
Harvey Houses: 57
Hastings Cutoff: 32, *32*, 33
Helena (Mont.): *31*, *34*, 35, *35*
Henry's Fork: *26*
Hidatsa Indians: 8, *8*
Hill, James J.: 59
Hogs: 67, *67*
Holbrook (Ariz.): 39, *39*
Holladay, Ben: 34
Holliday, Cyrus K.: 57
Hollister, W. W.: 31
Hopi Indians: 8, *8*, *16*, 51, 52
Hopkins, Mark: 58
Hornaday, William T.: 10
Horse Creek: *26*
Horses: *99*
Houston (Tex.): *30*
Howard, Gen. Oliver O.: 47
Hudson's Bay Company: 27, 28
Humaña, Antonio Gutierrez de: 15, *15*
Humboldt River: 6, 27, 33
Hunt, Jefferson: 33
Hunt, Wilson Price: 25
Hunter Claim: 20, *20*
Huntington, Collis P.: 58
Hurricanes: 70, *70*
Hurtado, Juan Páez: 17, *17*

Imperial Valley: 1, 63
Inca Indians: 8
Independence (Mo.): *28*, *29*, 32, *32*, 33, *33*, 34
Indian battles: 46, *46*
Indian Claims Commission, U.S.: 52
Indian Judicial Land Areas: 52
Indian Territory: 42, *42*, 45
Indianola (Tex.): *34*
Intermontane Plateau: 1
Iowa Territory: 40, *40*
Issei: 77

"Jackass Line": 34
"Jackson Mail": 55
Jackson, David: 28
Janos: 18, *18*, *19*
Japanese-Americans, 442nd Regimental Combat Team: 77
Jefferson, President Thomas: 40
Jemez (N. Mex.): *15*, 16, *16*
Johnson, Hiram: 58
Johnson Ranch: 33, *33*
Joutel, Henri: 16, *16*
Judah, Theodore D.: 58
Judith Mountains: 1
Julesberg (Colo.): *34*, 35
Jumanos: 16

Kalapuyai Indians: 8
Kansas City (Kansas, Missouri): *10*, *30*, 34, *34*
Kansas Pacific: 56
Karankawa Indians: 8
Kearny, Gen. Stephen Watts: 44, *44*
Kern, Edward: 36
Kiddie, Arthur W.: 60
Kimball, Major Gorham Gates: 31
Kinney County (Tex.): *23*
Kino, Father Eusebio Francisco: 16, *16*, 17, *17*
Kiowa Indians: 8, 9, 46
Klamath Indians: *8*
Klamath Lake: 36
Klamath River: 36
Kullyspell House: *24*
Kuskov, Ivan Aleksandrovich: 24, *24*

La Cañada (N. Mex.): 44, *44*
La Cienga (N. Mex.): 44, *44*
La Cuesta (N. Mex.): 44, *44*
La Harpe, Benard de: 17, *17*
La Junta (Colo.): 57
Lake Bonneville: 71
Lake Pend Oreille (Idaho): 76
La Laguna: 29, *29*
LaLande, Jean Baptiste: 24, *24*
Lambert, Clement: 36
Lander Cutoff: 32, *32*
Land grants: 20, 22, *22*, 23
Lands, federal: 73, *73*
La Paz: 62, *62*
Laredo (Tex.): *17*
Larios, Father Juan: 16
Laroque, Antoine: 24, *24*
Latter-day Saints, Church of Jesus Christ of the (Mormons): 39
Las Cruces (N. Mex.): *34*, 38
Las Tecoyas (Texas): 29, *29*
Lead: 68, *68*
Lee's Ferry (Ariz.): 39, *39*
Lemhi Pass: 27
Lemons: 66
León, Alonso de: 16, *16*
León, Martín de: 21, *21*

Lesser prairie chicken: 14, *14*
Lewis, Meriwether: 11, 24
Lewis and Clark Expedition: 6, 24, *24*
Limantour, José Y.: 20
Little Big Horn River: 48, *48*
Littlefield (Ariz.): *39*
Little Wolf, Chief: 47
Lisa, Manuel: 24, *24*
Livingston, Robert R.: 40
Llano Estacado: 5, 16
Locust Grove: 45, *45*
Long, Maj. Stephen H.: 25, *25*
Longhorns: 30
Lopez, Father Nicolas: 16, *16*
Los Angeles (Calif.): 29, *29*, 30, 33, *34*, 36, *38*, 43
Los Angeles County: 62, *62*
Lost Chokecherry Creek: 47, *47*
Louisiana Purchase: 24, 40, *40*
Luna, Antonio José: 31
Luna (N. Mex.): *39*
Lusk (Wyo.): *30*

McCoy, Joseph G.: 30
McGloin, James: 21, *21*
McKinzie, Donald: 25, *25*
McLanahan, Joseph: 24, *24*
McMullen, John: 21, *21*
Majors, Alexander: 34
Mallet, Paul: 17, *17*
Mandan Indians: 8, *8*, 9, 24
Manilla Galleon: 15, *15*
Manuel's Fort (Mont.): 25, *25*
Marcy, Capt. Randolph B.: 6, 38
Martin, Capt. Hernando: 16, *16*
Martin, Robert: 20
Martinez, Capt. Francisco: 19, *19*
Marysville (Calif.): *34*
Mason Valley: 49, *49*
Matamoros (Mex.): 44, *44*
Maverick County: 23, *23*
Maxwell, Lucien: 36
Maya Indians: 8
Medina, Roque de: 19, *19*
Mendoza, Juan Dominguez de: 16, *16*
Merced River: 24
Meridians, principal: 53, *53*
Mesa (Ariz.): *39*
Mexican Cession: 56
Mézières, Athanase de: 19, *19*
Middle Rocky Mountains: *2*
Miles, Col. Nelson: 47
Miles City (Mont.): *30*, *31*
Mine Creek: 45, *45*
Miniconjou Sioux Indians: 50
Minnesota Territory: 41, *41*
Missoula (Mont.): *10*
Missouri Pacific Railroad: 30
Missouri River: 1
Moab (Utah): *39*

Modoc Indians: *8*, 46, *53*
Moffat Tunnel: 60, *60*
Mojave (Calif.): *31*
Mojave Desert: *6*, 28
Monroe, President James B.: 51
Montana: *42*, 42, 43, 61, *61*
Montana Trail: *30*
Monterey (Calif.): *19, 28, 34*
Monterrey (Mex.): 44, *44*
Moqui (Ariz.): 15, *15*
Mora (N. Mex.): 44, *44*
Moraga, Gabriel: 24, *24*
Moran, Thomas: 57
Morgan, Dale: 71
Mormon Battalion: 33, 38
Mormon Colonies in Mexico: 39
Mormon Corridor: 33, 39, *39*
Mormons (Latter-day Saints): 32
Mormon Station: *39*
Mormon Trail: 39, *39*
Mother lode: *54*
Mountain Meadows Massacre: 39, *39*
Mountainmen: 26
Mount Lassen: 72, *72*
Mount Misery: 33, *33*
Mullen Road: 38
Mussel Slough (Calif.): 58
Muskrats: 13, *13*

Natchitoches: 19
Natividad (Calif.): 44, *44*
Navajo Indians: *8*, 8, 9, *51*, 52
Nebraska: 42, *42*, 61, *61*
New Mexico: *42*, 43, *61, 62*
Nez Percé Indians: *8, 8, 9*, 46, 47, *47, 51, 52*
Nez Percé War: 47
Nicollet, Joseph: 36
Niza, Fray Marcos de: 15, *15*
"No Man's Land": *42, 42*
Northern Overland Express: *35*
Northern Pacific: 59
Northern Rocky Mountains: *2*
North Pacific Slope: 3
Northwest Ordinance of 1785: 53
Northwest Passage: 15
Northwest Territory: 51
Nueces (Civil War battle): 45, *45*
Nueces River: 23, *23*, 44

O'Cain, Joseph: 24, *24*
O'Conor, Hugo: 18
"Octopus": 58
Ogden, Peter S.: 27, *27*
Ogden (Utah): *10*
Oil: 69, *69*
Okanagon Indians: 8, *8*
Oklahoma City (Okla.) *30*
Old San Antonio Road: 23
Old Spanish Trail: 29, *29, 33, 33,* 36
Omaha Indians: 8
Omaha (Nebr.): *10, 38,* 56, *56*

"Omnibus Bill": 42
Oñate, Juan de: 9, 15, *15, 16,* 16
Oranges: 66
Oregon City (Oreg.): *32*
Oregon Short Line Railroad: 56
Oregon Territory: 41, *41,* 56
Oregon Trail: 28, 36, 38
Ortega, José Francisco: 17, *17*
Orobio Bazterra, Joaquin de: 17, *17*
Osage Indians: 8, *8,* 45, *51,* 56
Osgood, Ernest S.: 30
Otero, Miguel A.: 31
Otters, sea: 13, *13*
Otters, river: 13, *13*
Ovedista (Tex.): *17*

Pacific Coast Ranges: 1, 2, *2*
Pacific Fur Company: 25
Pacific Northwest: 3
Pacific Railroad Act of 1862: 56
Padre Island (Tex.): 22
Paiute Indians: *8, 8,* 46, 49, *52*
Palmer, Gen. William Jackson: 60
Palmito Ranch, Battle of: 45, *45*
Palo Alto, Battle of: 44, *44*
Panama: 34
Papago Indians: 8, *8, 51, 52*
Park Range: 1
Parowan (Utah); 36, *36,* 39, *39*
Parrilla, Colonel Diego Ortiz: 17, *17*
Passenger pigeon: 14, *14*
Pawnee Indians: 8, 46, *51, 52*
Paxon. Frederic Logan: 54
Peanuts: 64, *64*
Pearl Harbor: 77
Pecans: 66, *66*
Pecos (N. Mex.): *16*
Pecos River: 15, 30
Peralta: 45, *45*
Peralta Claim: 20, *20*
Permian Basin: 69
Petaluma (Calif.): 67
Picacho Pass: 45, *45*
Piegan Indians: *8*
Pierre's Hole: 26, *26*
Pike, Lt. Zebulon M.: 24, *24*
Pike's Peak: 54
Pike's Peak Express Company: 34, *34*
Pilar: 18, *18*
Pilot Peak: *32*
Pima Indians: 8, *8, 52*
Piñeda, Alonso Alvarez: 15, *15*
Pine Ridge Agency (Sioux Reservation): 47, *47*
Pine Ridge Reservation: 50, *51*
Piñon-juniper: *7*
Placerville (Calif.): *38*
Platte River: 25, 36
Plums: 66, *66*
Poinsett, Joel R.: 36

Polk, President James K.: 34, 44
Pomerene (Ariz.): *39*
Ponderosa pine: 7
Pony express: 35, *35*
Popo Agie: *26*
Porciones: 22, *22,* 23
Portland (Oreg.): *34*
Port Lavaca: 29, *29*
Potatoes, Irish: 65, *65*
Portola, Gaspar de: 17, *17*
Powder River: 26
Powers, James: 21, *21*
POW camps: 78, *78*
Prairie fires: 70
Presidios: 18, *18,* 43
Preuss, Charles: 36
Price, Col. Sterling: 44
Promontory (Utah): 58
Pronghorns: 11, *11*
Pueblo (Colo.): *30, 34, 36,* 57, *60*
Pueblo Indians: 8, *8, 9,* 46
Pueblo Revolt of 1680: 9
Puget-Willamette Lowlands: *2*
Puget Sound: 59
Punished Woman's Fork: 47, *47*

Quantrill, William: 45, *45*

Rábago y Terán, Pedro de: 17, *17*
Raton Pass: 57, 60
Rawlins (Wyo.): *34*
Reavis, James Addison: 20
Red Bluff (Calif.): 31, *31, 34*
Redding (Calif.): *34*
Red River: 40
Redwoods: 7
Relief: 1, *1*
Rendezvous (fur trappers'): 26, *26*
Reno (Nev.): *31*
Reno, Major Marcus A.: 48, *48*
Resaca de la Palma, Battle of: 44, *44*
Revolt of the Pueblo Indians: 16
Rice: 65, *65*
Ridge, Martin: 68
Riego, de: 23
Rinconada Pass: 44
Ring of Fire: 72
Rio de Los Angeles, Battle of: 44, *44*
Rio de San Gabriel, Battle of: 44, *44*
Rio Grande: 1, 17
Rivera, Juan María: 17, *17*
Rocky Mountains: *6*
Rocky Mountain Provinces: 2
Rodríguez, Fray Agustín: 15
Royal Regulations of 1772: 18
Rubí, Marqués de: 18, *18*
Russell, William H.: 35

Sabine Pass: 45, *45*
Sacajawea: 24
Sacramento (Calif.): *32, 34,* 35, *35*

Sacramento River: 1
Sagebrush Revolt: 73
Saint David (Ariz.): 39, *39*
St. Denis, Louis Juchereau de: 17, *17*
St. George (Utah): *39*
Saint Joseph (Mo.): 34, *34*, 35, *35*
Saint Louis (Mo.): 19, 24, 26
Salas, Father Juan de: 16, *16*
Salem (Oreg.): *34*, *38*
Salinas Valley: 44
Salish House: *24*
Saltillo (Mex.): 44, *44*
Salt Lake: 27
Salt Lake City (Utah): *31*, 32, *32*, 33, *33*, 34, *34*, *35*, *38*, *39*
Salt Lake Valley: 39
Salton Sea: 1
Salt River: 1
San Antonio (Tex.): *17*, *18*, *19*, 19, 24, 29, *29*, *30*, *34*, 34, *38*, 43, 44, *44*, 55, *55*
San Bernardino (Calif.): *31*
San Bernardino County: 62, *62*
San Bernardino Ranch: 39
San Buenaventura (Mex.): 18, *18*
San Diego (Calif.): *19*, 28, *30*, 34, *34*, *38*
San Fernando Mission: *33*
San Francisco (Calif.): *30*, *34*
San Gabriel (Calif.): 24, *24*, 28, *28*
Sangre de Cristo Range: 1, 36
San Joaquin River: 1
San Joaquin Valley: 28, 36
San Jose (Calif.): 24, *24*, 28, *34*, 43
San Juan Bautista: 17, *18*, *19*, 23, 24
San Juan de Carricitos: 22
San Luis Obispo (Calif.): *34*
San Pascual, Battle of: 44, *44*
San Saba: 18
Santa Anita: 78
Santa Barbara (Calif.): *34*
Santa Cruz County: 7, *62*
Santa Fe (N. Mex.): 9, *9*, *15*, 16, *16*, 17, *17*, 18, *18*, 19, *19*, 24, *24*, 25, *25*, 29, *29*, *30*, *31*, *34*, *38*, 45, 55, *55*, *61*
Santa Fe Trail: 29, *29*, 32
Sappa Creek: 47, *47*
Sarracino, José Rafael: 25, *25*
Sawatch Range: 1
Scott, Gen Winfield: 44, *44*
Scottsburg (Oreg.): *38*
Seattle (Wash.): *38*
Sedalia (Mo.): 30
Seminole Indians: 45, *51*
Sequoyah: 42
Shasta City (Calif.): 32, *32*
Shawnee Trail: *30*
Sheep: 67, *67*
Sheep, bighorn: 12, *12*
Sheridan, Gen. Philip: 10
Sherman, Gen. William T.: 46
Shoshoni Indians: 8, *8*, *9*, *52*

Sibley, Gen. Henry H.: 45
Sierra Nevada: *6*
Sierra Nevada Mountains: 2, *2*
Silver: 54, *54*
Sioux City (Iowa): *38*
Sioux Indians: 8, *8*, 46, *52*
Sitio de ganado mayor: 23
Sitio de ganado menor: 23
Sitting Bull, Chief: 49
Smith, Jedediah: 28, *28*
Smith, Capt. O. K.: 33
Snake River: 1, 25
Snake River Valley: 3
Soda Springs (Idaho): 32, *32*
Sonoran Desert: *6*
Sosa, Gaspar Castaño de: 15
Soto, Hernando de: 15
Southern Pacific: 58, *58*
Southern Rocky Mountains: 2, *2*
South Pass: 1, 6, 26, 28, 32, *32*, *34*, *35*, 36, *38*, *38*
Sparks, Capt. Richard: 24
Spokane House: 24, *24*
Stagecoach: 55, *55*
Staked Plains (Llano Estacado): 1, 63
Stanford, Leland: 58
Stansbury, Capt. Howard: 71
Stevens, John: 59
Stewart, William Drummond: 10
Stockton (Calif.): *32*
Strobridge, James Harvey: 58
Stuart, Robert: 25
Sublette, William: 28
Sublette Cutoff: 32, *32*
Suerte: 23
Sugar beets: 65, *65*

Talbot, Theodore: 36
Talbot-Kern Party: *36*
Talleyrand, Charles de: 40
Tamaulipas (Mex.): 22
Taovayas (Tex.): 17, *17*
Taos (N. Mex.): *15*, 16, *16*, *17*, 29, 31, 36, *36*, *38*
Tavibo: 49
Taylor, Gen. Zachary: 44, *44*
Techachapi Pass: 24, 36
Tejon Pass: 24
Tempe (Ariz.): *39*
Temporal, de: 23
Tenino Indians: *8*
Terry, Gen. Alfred H.: 48
Teton Sioux Indians: 48
Texas: 40, *42*, 43, *61*
Texas Gulf Coast: 1, 3
Texas Panhandle: 5, 63
Thatcher: *39*
The Dalles (Oreg.): 8, *32*, *34*
Thompson, David: 19, *19*, 24, *24*
Tiguex: 15
Timber: 7, *7*

Tisne, Charles Claude du: 17, *17*
Tombstone (Ariz.): 39
Tonkawa Indians: *8*
Tonty, Henri de: 16, *16*
Topeka (Kans.): *30*
Tornadoes: 70, *70*
Tres Alamos: 21, *21*
Trinidad (Colo.): *30*, 34
Truckee Lake: 33
Truckee River: 32
Tuacana (Tex.): *17*
Tuba City (Ariz.): 39, *39*
Tubac (Ariz.): *18*, *19*, 19
Tucson (Ariz.): *18*, 19, *19*, *30*, 34
Turkeys: 67, *67*
Turkey Springs: 47, *47*
Turner, Frederick Jackson: 70

Ugalde, Juan de: 19, *19*
Umpqua River: 28, *28*
Uncompahgre River: 36
Union Pacific: 56, *56*
Urdaneta, Andres de: 15, *15*
Urribarri, Juan de: 17, *17*
Utah: 39, *61*
Utah Lake: 36
Ute Indians: 8, *8*, *9*, 46, *49*, *52*

Vaca, Cabeza de: 15, *15*
Valverde: 45, *45*
Varennes, Pierre Gaultier de Sieur de La Vé-rendrye: 17, *17*
Vargas, Diego de: *16*
Vehlein, Joseph: 21, *21*
Veniard, Étienne, Sieur de Bourgmont: 17, *17*
Ventura (Calif.): *34*
Vera Cruz: 44
Vial, Pedro: 19, *19*
Vildosola, Captain José Antonio: 19, *19*
Villard, Henry: 59
Villasur, Pedro de: 17, *17*
Virginia City (Mont.) 31, *38*
Virginia City (Nev.): *34*, *54*, 54
Vizcaíno, Sebastián: 16, *16*
Volcanoes: 72, *72*

Waco (Tex.): *30*
Walker, Joseph R.: 36
Walker Lake: 36
Walker Pass: 33
Walker River: 32
Walla Walla (Wash.): *31*, 38, *38*
Walnuts: 66, *66*
War Department: 78
Wasatch Mountains: 1
Washington Territory: 41, *41*
Webb, Walter Prescott: 11, 12, 61
Weber River: *26*
Weir, Capt. Thomas B.: 48, *41*
Weller, Senator John B.: 34, 38
Wells, Fargo & Co.: 34

Wentworth, Edward Norris: 31
Western Pacific: 60
Western Trail: 30, *31*
Westport: 36, *36*
Wheat: 64, *64*
Wheat, spring: 63, *63*
Wheat, winter: 63, *63*
White Bird creek: 47, *47*
Whooping Crane: 14, *14*
Wichita (Kans.): *15*, 30, *30*, 31, *31*
Wilkinson, Lt. N. G.: 24, *24*
Williams, Ezekiel: 25, *25*
William's Ranch: 33
Wilson, Stephen Julian: 21
Wilson-Exeter Grant: 21, *21*

Wind River Mountains: 1
Wind River Range: 36
Wolf, gray: 12, *12*
Woodward (Okla.): 70
Wooton, Richard L.: 60
Wounded Knee: 49, *49*, 50, *50*
Wovoka: 49
Wyoming Basin: 1, 2, *2*, 6

Yakima Indians: *8, 9, 51, 52*
Yanktoni Indians: *8*
Yavapai Indians: *8, 51, 52*
Ybarbo, Gil: 19, *19*
Yellowstone Park: 47
Yerba Buena: *27, 36*

Yreka (Calif.): 32, *32, 34*
Young, Brigham: 36, 39
Yuma (Ariz.): *34*
Yuma Indians: 8, *8*
Yuma uprising: 18

Zalvidea, Father José María de: 24, *24*
Zavala, Lorenzo de: 21, *21*
Zavala County: *23*
Zinc: 68
Zuñi (N. Mex.): *16*, 19
Zuñi Indians: 8, *8, 51, 52*
Zuñiga, José de: 19, *19*